S0-BNF-663

THE
ASIAN AMERICAN
ENCYCLOPEDIA

THE
ASIAN AMERICAN
ENCYCLOPEDIA

Volume 1

A. Magazine – Chinese in mining

Editor
FRANKLIN NG

Managing Editor
JOHN D. WILSON

Marshall Cavendish
New York • London • Toronto

LIBRARY
COLBY-SAWYER COLLEGE
NEW LONDON, NH 03257

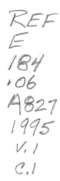

REF
E
184
.06
A827
1995
V. 1
C. 1

3091584 3

Published By
Marshall Cavendish Corporation
2415 Jerusalem Avenue
P.O. Box 587
North Bellmore, New York 11710
United States of America

Copyright © 1995, by Marshall Cavendish Corporation

All rights in this book are reserved. No part of this work may be used or reproduced in any manner whatsoever or transmitted in any form or by any means, electronic or mechanical, including photocopy, recording, or any information storage and retrieval system, without written permission from the copyright owner except in the case of brief quotations embodied in critical articles and reviews. For information address the publisher.

∞ The paper in these volumes conforms to the American National Standard for Permanence of Paper for Printed Library Materials, Z39.48-1984.

Library of Congress Cataloging-in-Publication Data

The Asian American encyclopedia / editor, Franklin Ng.
    p. cm.
  Includes bibliographical references and index.
  Contents: v. 1. A. magazine—Chinese in mining.
  1. Asian Americans—Encyclopedias. I. Ng, Franklin, 1947-   .
E184.O6A827 1995
973′ .0495′003—dc20   94-33003
ISBN 1-85435-677-1 (set).   CIP
ISBN 1-85435-678-X (vol. 1).

First Printing

PRINTED IN THE UNITED STATES OF AMERICA

Contents

Publisher's Note

Asian Americans are the fastest-growing ethnic minority in the United States. *The Asian American Encyclopedia* is the first large-scale reference work encompassing the histories and cultures of this diverse community.

In the preface to her book *Asian American Panethnicity* (1992), Yen Le Espiritu observes that "Asian Americans are a complex and changing population: far from homogeneous, we are a multicultural, multilingual people who hold different worldviews and divergent modes of interpretation. Thus, although this book tells the story of the construction of pan-Asian ethnicity, it is not about obscuring our differences, but rather about taking seriously the heterogeneities among our ranks." The same can be said of *The Asian American Encyclopedia*. While acknowledging commonalities—particularly the struggle against prejudice and discrimination—the encyclopedia will also enable readers to understand the ways in which each Asian American group's experience is unique.

The six volumes of the encyclopedia include a total of more than 2,000 entries and more than 1,100 illustrations. Arranged alphabetically (by word rather than by letter) and ranging in length from brief definitions of terms to 4,000-word essays, the entries cover the full spectrum of the Asian American experience.

Biographical sketches document the achievements of Asian Americans in the arts, education and scholarship, government and politics, science and technology, sports, and other fields. Historical articles recount significant events, including key court cases. Because the shifts and countershifts in U.S. immigration policy have profoundly affected the development of the various Asian American communities, the encyclopedia includes many entries on this topic.

Community studies, including demographic profiles based on 1990 census data, provide overviews of each of the six largest groups: Chinese Americans, Filipino Americans, Japanese Americans, Asian Indian Americans, Korean Americans, and Vietnamese Americans. Smaller groups are covered as well: Hmong Americans, Pacific Islander Americans, and many others.

The emphasis of the encyclopedia, as its title indicates, is firmly on the experience of Asian immigrants and the communities which they and their descendants have created in the United States. To understand the Asian American experience, however, it is necessary to have access to basic information about the history, language, and culture of Asian Americans' diverse countries of origin. Thus, the encyclopedia includes entries that provide this essential background.

Charts, tables, and graphs and more than fifty maps complement the text. Back matter consists of a detailed chronology; lists of organizations, museums, research centers and libraries, Asian American Studies programs, and newspapers, newsletters, magazines, and journals; a filmography; a subject list; and a general index.

In the subject list, entries appear under both population and subject headings. For example, all of the articles that focus on Korean Americans are listed under the heading Korean Americans and the Korean Diaspora (which also lists articles on Koreans in China, Koreans in Japan, and Koreans in Mexico). All of the articles focusing on artists and the arts are listed under Arts, Entertainment, and Media. Many entries are listed under multiple subject headings. The general index, which includes cross-references, helps further with the location of specific events, people, places, and organizations discussed in the text.

Many people contributed to the creation of this encyclopedia. The editors worked with a panel of consultants (identified at the beginning of each volume) to establish a well-balanced list of contents. The entries were written by scholars representing a wide variety of academic and cultural backgrounds. All of the writers who contributed are listed at the beginning of volume 1; cumulatively their work attests the substantial achievements and the great promise of Asian American Studies. Copyediting, research, photo acquisition, and production played essential roles. Librarians and archivists also provided invaluable help. The efforts of all are greatly appreciated.

Usage Notes

Transliteration and Treatment of Names. In transliterating Asian names and terms, several sometimes incompatible criteria must be taken into account, including consistency, scholarly practice, and customary usage. In many Asian countries, in contrast to the Western convention, the surname of an individual precedes the personal name (for example, Mao Zedong). When rendering the names of individuals whose lives and work were exclusively or primarily in an Asian context (as opposed to an Asian American context), the encyclopedia follows the Asian convention. On the other hand, for individuals such as Kyutaro Abiko, a significant figure in the early Japanese American community, the Western convention is followed.

In general, Chinese names and terms are given in the *pinyin* transliteration, which has replaced Wade-Giles as the most widely used system of Chinese romanization. There are some exceptions to this rule, in accordance with customary usage (for example, Chiang Kai-shek; Sun Yat-sen; Canton). Moreover, names and terms from the early Chinese American community, which was almost exclusively Cantonese, are transliterated on the basis of Cantonese pronunciation, following the form in which they appeared in their original context. Names of later Chinese immigrants, such as Chang-Lin Tien, Chancellor of the University of California, Berkeley, are given in the form which the individuals themselves have chosen. A similar balance between consistency and flexibility has governed transliteration and treatment of names from other Asian languages.

Scholarly transliterations of many Asian languages employ diacritics. Please note that, following popular usage, all diacritics have been omitted from these volumes.

Census Data. Figures from the 1990 census relating to Asian Americans will vary slightly depending on the source. The encyclopedia's statistical profiles of each Asian American group are based primarily on the U.S. Bureau of the Census publication *Asians and Pacific Islanders in the United States* (1993), which provides extensive data for a sample of Asians and Pacific Islanders from the 1990 census. Totals for national groups (e.g., Japanese Americans) and for Asian Americans as a whole from this source differ slightly from those in the bureau's *General Population Characteristics* reports, which are based on 100 percent of the census. In general, though not across the board, the numbers in the Asian and Pacific Islander document are smaller.

Introduction

Asian Americans and American Society

In recent years, Asian Americans have become an increasingly visible group in American society. Adding to the population of Asians born in the United States, changes in immigration policy have played a great part in swelling the numbers of Asian immigrants to these shores. In addition, the end of the Vietnam War triggered a mass exodus of refugees who sought political asylum and economic opportunity. As a result, Asian Americans are now recognized as the fastest growing group in the United States.

The diversity of these new arrivals has dramatically altered the traditional face of Asian America. Among the Chinese, for example, Cantonese is no longer the only major Chinese dialect spoken. Depending upon the neighborhood, one may hear other dialects spoken by those from mainland China, Fujian, or Taiwan. In the Filipino population, Tagalog is spoken among the newer immigrants as contrasted with the Ilocano spoken by the earlier arrivals who worked in the fields of Hawaii and California. Korean, Japanese, Thai, Vietnamese, Lao, Hmong, and Mon-Khmer are only some of the many languages to be found in Asian American communities. Moreover, Asians in the United States may be monolingual, bilingual, trilingual, or even multilingual. Thus, some Chinese-Vietnamese may speak English, French, Vietnamese, and several dialects of Chinese.

The changing character of the Asian American population due to the influx of immigrants and refugees has led to shifts in the rankings of different groups. Thus, Japanese Americans, who were the largest Asian American group for several decades, have been displaced by other populations. In the 1990 census, Chinese Americans constituted the largest Asian American group, with Filipino Americans rising to second place. Japanese Americans ranked third. Other groups that are growing rapidly in numbers are Asian Indians, Koreans, and Vietnamese. At the same time, there are interesting regional variations. Filipinos are the most numerous among the Asian Americans in California, but the Japanese remain the largest Asian American group in Hawaii.

These demographic changes have reshaped many neighborhoods and cities. Whereas Chinese Americans and Japanese Americans were once concentrated in Chinatowns or Little Tokyos, today many of them are living in suburbs, away from the traditional downtowns of large cities. On the other hand, many Taiwanese have elected to reside in newer geographical areas such as Monterey Park, California, and Flushing-Queens, New York. But Asian American communities today include more than just the Chinese and Japanese. In California, Vietnamese have concentrated in Westminster and Orange County, while Cambodians live in large numbers in Stockton and Long Beach. In the same state, Filipinos favor Daly City and National City, while the greatest concentration of Hmong in the United States is found in Fresno. In the Midwest, states such as Minnesota and Wisconsin have likewise witnessed the growth of sizable communities of Hmong and other Southeast Asian refugees.

The dramatic growth of the Asian American population is also transforming American society on several different levels. For example, it has obvious economic implications. First, Asian Americans constitute a burgeoning consumer population, and many businesses are keen on marketing goods and services to them. Second, many Asian Americans are human capital in the sense that they bring special skills and knowledge into the United States. Their language skills and ability are enhancing the competitiveness of the United States in the world arena. From the individual entrepreneur to the computer professional, Asian Americans are showing that they can help to open new markets and foster trans-Pacific trade. In a way, they are helping to internationalize the United States and link it to the global economy.

On another level, Asian Americans are changing the cultural landscape in the United States. The flavors and colors of Asian foods are becoming familiar to other Americans. Chinese food has joined Mexican and Italian food among the most popular ethnic cuisines in the United States. But besides Chinese food, the general public is learning to appreciate Japanese, Vietnamese, Thai, Filipino, and Asian Indian cuisines. Supermarkets now routinely display Asian fruits, vegetables, herbs, and foods such as lemon grass, tofu, or Asian Indian curries. In restaurants and homes, karaoke machines allow people to sing along with popular melodies and songs. Gardeners and homeowners appreciate Asian ornamental design and landscape architecture; bonsai plants and koi ponds grace many parks and yards.

Other examples of change in the cultural landscape

include Asian religions and the arts. As Asian Americans practice a variety of different religions and philosophies, American society is learning about other worldviews. Adding to the better known Zen and Pure Land sects of Buddhism, Southeast Asian Americans are introducing Theravada Buddhism while Tibetans are acquainting others with Tantric Buddhism. Annual celebrations in honor of Nobel Prize-winner Martin Luther King, Jr., are accompanied by discussions of Mohandas K. Gandhi and his philosophy of nonviolence. Asian Americans are also viewing Asian movies, programs, and concerts, whether at theaters or by videotapes, satellite dishes, and cable television. Asian cultural festivals are helping people to cross cultural borders and boundaries. Thus, the public is becoming more familiar with Vietnamese lion dances, Japanese *taiko* drum performances, and Filipino *tinikling* variations.

Still another instance of change in the cultural landscape is in the area of scholarship. That many Asian Americans emphasize success in education is well known. Newspapers and magazines are replete with stories about Asian American students being chosen as Westinghouse scholars, scoring high on Scholastic Aptitude Tests, and winning admission to prestigious universities. But the noticeable presence of a growing Asian American population has had a much broader impact. First, it has led to growing recognition that more emphasis should be placed on Asian and Pacific Studies. As a result, school districts and universities are reevaluating their courses of study to achieve a more inclusive, less Eurocentric orientation. Moreover, the Educational Testing Service in Princeton, New Jersey, has started offering tests for advanced placement and college credit in Chinese, Japanese, and other Asian languages. Second, the large numbers of Asian Americans in colleges and universities has led to new developments in the professional study of Asia and the United States. In the past, scholars focusing on Asia and the United States routinely neglected the study of Asian Americans and their experiences. This is no longer the case. Many professional and cultural organizations and publications now devote significant attention to Asian Americans.

Asian American writers, artists, and performers can claim a role in enriching the cultural landscape in the United States. Writers such as Maxine Hong Kingston, Hisaye Yamamoto, Amy Tan, Frank Chin, Bharati Mukherjee, and Bienvenido Santos have redefined the scope of American literature. Poets such as Cathy Song, Marilyn Chin, Jeff Tagami, Wing Tek Lum, and Garrett Kaoru Hongo have shared their keen insights into the textures of Asian American life. Filmmakers such as Arthur Dong, Christine Choy, Loni Ding, and Steven Okazaki have portrayed in poignant fashion the complex issues and experiences within the Asian American community. Performers such as the musical groups Hiroshima, the actors in the East-West Players, and the drummers in the San Jose Taiko convey different ways to look at a distinctive Asian American sensibility. Collectively, they foster an awareness that Asian Americans are an integral part of the rich multicultural mosaic that is the United States. In myriad ways, they are participating in the cross-fertilization of ideas and the hybridization of behavior that gives American culture its distinctive vitality and dynamism.

The greater prominence of Asian Americans in American society can be symbolically linked to the expansion of Asian/Pacific American Heritage Week to Asian/Pacific Heritage Month. An observance that was first initiated by President Jimmy Carter, it was initially only one week long. Its purpose was to cast light on the contributions and key issues pertaining to Asian and Pacific Islander Americans. But as the population grew, the event was extended to a month in duration. The use of the term "Asian American" or "Asian Pacific American" reflects the effort, beginning in the 1960's and 1970's, to forge a single panethnic Asian American identity among the different Asian populations in the United States. While conflicts and tensions have sometimes occurred, successes have also been achieved. Whether such a culturally constructed identity can maintain its viability or utility is a question that only the future can determine. Regardless of the outcome, however, Asian Americans seem destined to play an increasingly visible role in shaping the makeup of American society.

The History of Asians in the United States

The history of Asians in the United States has been one of ethnic succession. Due to forces in the global political economy and localized considerations of push and pull factors, Asians have ventured away from their homelands to neighboring countries in Asia and eastward across the Pacific to America. Their history in the United States can be divided into two periods—that of the era before World War II and that after World War II.

In the period before World War II, the Chinese were the first group of Asians to emigrate to the United States in large numbers. During the nineteenth century, internal factors such as conflict with foreign powers, rebellions, population increase, and interethnic conflict led some Chinese to consider migration to other lands. Beckoning opportunities for employment in Hawaii and the West Coast of the continental United States, as well as the discovery of gold in California in 1848, were other considerations that drew them across the Pacific.

The Qing empire, established by the Manchu conquerors of China in 1644 and lasting until 1911, had long confined much of Sino-Western trade to the single port of Canton in Guangdong province. From this lengthy legacy of commerce with the outside, the residents of this southeastern coastal area were more familiar with the United States than were Chinese of other regions. As a result, during the nineteenth century, most Chinese immigrants to the United States came from Canton and various districts adjoining it. The Taishan subdialect, a variant of the Cantonese dialect of Chinese, was dominant among early Chinese immigrants to the continental United States. In Hawaii, on the other hand, the Zhongshan subdialect was dominant. Its wide usage reflected the many immigrants from the Zhongshan (earlier known as Xiangshan) area, also in Guangdong province and close to Canton, who had immigrated to the Polynesian kingdom.

As they arrived in Hawaii and the mainland United States, the Chinese became an important labor force in the regional economies. In Hawaii, they worked on rice, sugar, pineapple, and coffee plantations. On the West Coast, they mined for gold, helped build railroads, established factories, fished from the sea, reclaimed land, and toiled in agriculture. In both regions, the Chinese also entered other occupations and started businesses.

The presence of the Chinese eventually was challenged by an anti-Chinese movement aimed at exclusion. Nativists, labor leaders, unions, and other opponents saw the Chinese as an inferior people and viewed them as competitors for jobs. Various actions were taken to drive away the Chinese, including mob violence, school segregation, and local and state statutes and ordinances. While all these measures harassed and obstructed the efforts of the Chinese to make a living, the most troublesome was the Chinese Exclusion Act of 1882. While originally passed as a temporary measure, its provisions were extended and finally made permanent so that Chinese immigrants would be virtually excluded from the United States until 1943.

Nonetheless, the dynamic young economy of the United States still required large pools of labor for agriculture. In a cycle of ethnic succession, Japanese, Koreans, Filipinos, and Asian Indians were recruited to work on the West Coast and in Hawaii. Like the Chinese, these immigrants came from specific regions in their home countries. While their labor contributed greatly to the development of the American economy, their presence was also resented. The Barred Zone Act of 1917 severely restricted Asian Indian immigration. Similarly, the Immigration Act of 1924 curtailed Japanese and Korean immigration. Finally, the Tydings-McDuffie Act of 1934, while providing for independence for the Philippines in ten years, limited Filipino immigration to the United States—previously unrestricted—to a quota of fifty persons per year.

Despite the differences in terms of entry to and exclusion from the United States, there were some commonalities among the different groups of Asians. First, Asians played an essential and vital role in the development of agriculture in the West. Their exclusion only meant that others such as Mexicans would be required to replace them. Second, all of the Asians were subjected to varying degrees of prejudice and discrimination. Whether it was confinement at the Angel Island immigration station off San Francisco, antimiscegenation statutes, Alien Land Laws, or denial of citizenship and naturalization for the first generation, Asians sensed that they were not wanted.

Regardless of the circumstances that drew them to the United States, Asians attempted to adapt to their new environment. They created a range of ethnic organizations to serve their community needs—locality associations, fraternal organizations, language schools, burial societies, musical groups, churches and temples, guilds, and newspapers. At the same time, many were intensely interested in the fate of their homelands, and the politics in their communities reflected this concern. Thus, there were Chinese revolutionaries and reformers, Koreans advocating independence from Japan, and Asian Indians in the Ghadr movement who sought independence from Britain.

As a second generation appeared, questions about cultural identity surfaced. The degree of assimilation, the relationship to the ancestral homeland, the desirability of conversion to Christianity, and the necessity of learning the parental language were among the recurring issues. The responses to these questions might be variously framed by geographical setting, cultural isolation, class status, and personal temperament. But irrespective of their outlook on these matters, the second generation was different in one crucial aspect. Born in this country, they possessed U.S. citizenship that was denied to their Chinese, Japanese, Korean, Filipino, and Asian Indian parents.

Historians often say that World War II changed the world as most people knew it. Certainly it led to independence from colonialism for many peoples and to a Cold War rivalry between the United States and the Soviet Union. At the same time, it introduced incremental improvements to the status of some Asians in the United States. As a result of the Immigration Act of 1943 and the Luce-Celler Bill of 1946, Chinese, Filipinos, and Asian Indians were granted immigration quotas and the right of naturalization for the first generation. The McCarran-Walter Act of 1952 extended the same rights to Japanese and Koreans. In addition, other legislation allowed war brides and displaced persons from Asia to immigrate to the United States.

During World War II, however, the United States also incarcerated more than 120,000 Japanese in ten camps (officially designated as "relocation centers") scattered throughout the country. These Japanese, both aliens and citizens alike, had for the most part been removed from the West Coast states of California, Oregon, Washington, and Arizona. President Franklin Roosevelt had signed Executive Order 9066 on February 19, 1942, which authorized their removal. The commonly voiced justification for the action was "military necessity" to secure the West Coast. Yet the more than 150,000 Japanese in Hawaii, the site of the Japanese attack on Pearl Harbor, did not have to undergo a similar evacuation. Despite the incarceration, Japanese Americans from Hawaii and the camps enlisted in the 442nd Regimental Combat Team, the 100th Infantry Battalion, and the Military Intelligence Service. Fighting and serving with distinction in both Europe and Asia, they proved their heroism and patriotism. In 1988, the U.S. Congress and President Ronald Reagan issued an official apology and offered reparations to the former internees.

In 1959, Hawaii became the fiftieth state in the union. As a result, it elected the first Asian American and Chinese American, Hiram Fong, to serve in the Senate. Soon thereafter, Hawaii also elected Daniel Inouye to be the first Japanese American to serve in the House and later the Senate, while George Ariyoshi became the first Asian American to serve as the governor of a state.

The Immigration and Nationality Act of 1965 ended the national-origins quota system that had been in place since 1924 and opened the door to significant increases in Asian immigration. Larger numbers were permitted for family reunification and to make amends for a long history of restriction and exclusion. With these more liberalized provisions, greater numbers of Asians entered the United States. The close of the Vietnam War in Southeast Asia also led to a sizable influx of refugees from Vietnam, Laos, and Cambodia. These significant political and demographic developments accelerated changes in the Asian American community and also attracted notice from the larger society.

Asian American Studies

The 1960's and 1970's were a turbulent era in American history. The Civil Rights movement, the Vietnam War, the appearance of a counterculture, and the banding of interethnic coalitions resulted in heightened political activism and increased minority consciousness. Because of these catalysts, Asian Americans became much more sensitive and concerned about their status and identity in American society.

Student activists participating in the Third World strikes in 1968-1969 at San Francisco State College and the University of California, Berkeley, had demanded the establishment of ethnic studies classes. Courses about Asian Americans and Asian American Studies programs generally focused on several concerns. One objective was to address topics pertaining to civil rights and minority empowerment. As a result, there was a heavy emphasis on political participation and an identification with progressive causes. Another primary goal was the formulation of a curriculum and educational materials that centered on Asian Americans. This emphasis required the development of courses, publications, and research programs.

The initial phase for Asian American Studies was one marked by a struggle for acceptance as a legitimate academic field. While activists pressed for the establishment of Asian American Studies courses, programs, or departments, universities and colleges were slow to see the need for these changes. Administration and faculty in traditional academic disciplines felt that existing courses could adequately treat Asian American subjects. Moreover, the introduction of separate Asian American Studies programs and departments entailed faculty and administrative costs. Not unexpectedly, then, in the first twenty years of the field there were relatively few Asian American Studies programs and departments, and they were confined mostly to California.

For many years, the most prominent Asian American Studies programs and departments were those housed at the University of California, Berkeley, and the University of California, Los Angeles. The faculty, staff, and students at the two institutions maintained the visibility of Asian American Studies in academe and the community. In addition, they published articles, working papers, monographs, anthologies, journals, and bibliographies to lend weight to the idea that Asian American Studies was a legitimate area of study and research. In this endeavor, they also cooperated with writers, poets, artists, local historians, and community activists.

But in the 1990's, circumstances have changed. The remarkable growth of the Asian American population in many states has strengthened demands for the funding of Asian American Studies programs and departments. School districts, human service professions, the media, and other sectors in society are desirous of learning more about the Asian Americans in their communities. At the same time, Asian Americans are interested in finding out more about their history and their present status in American society. Community events and celebrations, such as an Asian American heritage week or month, also encourage a desire to be more informed about the Asian American experience. And the United States as a whole is now recognized to be a multicultural society with its many ethnic and racial groups charting its future direction.

All of these factors have enhanced the prospect for Asian American Studies. Many colleges and universities now offer courses in the subject. In addition, Asian American Studies programs and departments are being started outside of California. Undergraduate and graduate degrees in Asian American Studies are offered at several institutions. Students are interested in pursuing graduate work and eventually teaching or doing research in the area. Many journals and periodicals now focus on Asian American subjects, and several major university presses, including Temple University, the University of California, Stanford University, the University of Hawaii, the University of Washington, and the University of Illinois, regularly publish books in Asian American Studies.

But with expansion has also come growing pains and tensions. The establishment of the Association for Asian American Studies indicated that professionalization was beginning to occur. The presentation of awards and the burgeoning of journals indicate a degree of maturity in the field. But many difficult issues remain. Scholars must wrestle with the choice to affiliate with a traditional discipline or with Asian American Studies—or with both. Related to this is the organizational matter or creating separate programs and autonomous departments, or offering joint appointments in a traditional department and an Asian American Studies program. Moreover, as a new generation of scholars surfaces in Asian American Studies, there is less consensus that the field entails commitment to community activism as well as scholarship. Some argue that both community and scholarship are badly served by this linkage. Others question the existence of an "Asian American community" or "Chinese American community," terms that suggest a monolithic group with a single viewpoint. In fact, some complain that scholars, publications, and research in Asian American Studies have tended to neglect immigrant and refugee groups that have arrived since World War II. On the other hand, dissent and differences of opinion may be healthy for the field. New questions are being asked and innovative research is being initiated.

Furthermore, the field of Asian American Studies is moving into new directions that may augur well for the future. One development is the recognition that Asian Studies and Asian American Studies can cooperate. During the formative phase of Asian American Studies, Asian American activists were preoccupied with identity issues and an emphasis on being born in America. As a result, they tended to disaffiliate themselves from scholars who read Asian languages. Today, there is a recognition that Asia and Asian Americans have intricate relationships that are worth acknowledging and exploring. Asian language materials both abroad and at home need to be utilized more. A second development is the budding partnership with museums and historical societies. Public history, interpretation, and exhibitions are viewed as important concerns that deserve closer attention. Scholars and students are delving into social and cultural history, cultural studies, art history, and popular culture to expand the scope of Asian American Studies. Cross-disciplinary cooperation with American Studies, religious studies, and other disciplines may also be helpful.

At the same time, Asian American Studies continues to be closely linked with educational issues. As textbooks and curricula in schools and universities are revised or developed, information about Asian Americans needs to be widely disseminated. Study of the history and experiences of Asian Americans, as well as their outlooks and beliefs, can help to promote harmony and understanding. It highlights the contributions of Asians to American society and fosters a deeper appreciation for the richness and complexity of U.S. history. Asian American studies can thus help to realize the founding ideals and the enduring promise of American society.

Franklin Ng

Editor

Franklin Ng
California State University, Fresno

Consulting Editors

Elaine Kim
University of California, Berkeley

Him Mark Lai
California State University, San Francisco

Don T. Nakanishi
University of California, Los Angeles

Franklin S. Odo
University of Hawaii, Manoa

Jane Singh
University of California, Berkeley

Contributors

Ruth F. Adaniya
Leeward Community College

Jaideep Singh Alag
University of California, Berkeley

Allan Beekman
Heritage Press of Pacific

Shobha Bhatia
Independent Scholar

Tej K. Bhatia
Syracuse University

Stephen T. Boggs
University of Hawaii at Manoa

Malcolm B. Campbell
Bowling Green State University

Patricia Shehan Campbell
University of Washington

Ethan Casey
The Bangkok Post

Amy Catlin
University of California, Los Angeles

Marn J. Cha
California State University, Fresno

Tsze H. Chan
University of Maryland, College Park

Aloysius Chang
Washington State University

Maria Hsia Chang
University of Nevada, Reno

Toy Len Chang
Independent Scholar

Marian Chatterjee
Independent Scholar

Pranab Chatterjee
Case Western Reserve University

Mao Chen
Union College

Min Chen
*American Graduate School of
    International Management*

Karleen C. Chinen
The Hawaii Herald

Alice Chin-Myers
Simon's Rock of Bard College

Yong-ho Choe
University of Hawaii at Manoa

Key Ray Chong
*Soka University, Hachioji
Japan*

Michaelyn Chou
University of Hawaii at Manoa

Peggy Myo-Young Choy
University of Wisconsin, Madison

Renny Christopher
University of California, Santa Cruz

C. L. Chua
California State University, Fresno

Richard Y. Chuang
Northern State University

Sue Fawn Chung
University of Nevada, Las Vegas

Edwin Clausen
Pacific Lutheran University

John W. Connor
California State University, Sacramento

John F. Copper
Rhodes College

P. Scott Corbett
Nebraska Wesleyan University

Enrique de la Cruz
University of California, Los Angeles

Eric Crystal
University of California, Berkeley

Peng Deng
High Point University

Margaret B. Denning
Slippery Rock University

Charles Desnoyers
LaSalle University

Howard DeWitt
Ohlone College

Chitra Banerjee Divakaruni
Foothill College

Hien Duc Do
San Jose State University

Lorraine Dong
San Francisco State University

Dana Dunn
University of Texas at Arlington

David G. Egler
Western Illinois University

Daniel Emerick
Florida State University

Robert Y. Eng
University of Redlands

Augusto Espiritu
University of California, Los Angeles

Carol C. Fan
University of Hawaii at Manoa

Michael S. Findlay
California State University, Chico

Dianna Fitisemanu
Columbia University

Enya P. Flores-Meiser
Ball State University

Colleen Fong
California State University, Hayward

Rowena Fong
University of Hawaii at Manoa

Timothy Fong
University of California, Davis

Anne Frank
University of California, Irvine Library

Stephan Fugita
Santa Clara University

Inoke F. Funaki
Brigham Young University, Hawaii

Robert W. Gardner
Independent Scholar

Leonard H. D. Gordon
Purdue University

Donald L. Guimary
San Jose State University

Surendra Gupta
Pittsburg State University

Michael Haas
University of Hawaii at Manoa

David Hall
Brigham Young University, Hawaii

Patricia Wong Hall
Arizona Asian American Association

Arthur Hansen
California State University, Fullerton

Farhat Haq
Monmouth College

Ann M. Harrington
Loyola University of Chicago

Charles Hayford
Independent Scholar

Ceferina Gayo Hess
Lander University

Fred W. Hicks III
*Coastal Carolina College of the
    University of South Carolina*

Kenneth M. Holland
Memphis State University

Ellen Rhoads Holmes
Independent Scholar

Lowell D. Holmes
Wichita State University

Alice Y. Hom
University of California, Los Angeles

Harry K. Honda
Pacific Citizen

Florence M. Hongo
*Japanese American Curriculum
    Project, Inc.*

George J. Hoynacki
Merrimack College

Yunsheng Huang
University of Virginia

James Huffman
Wittenberg University

Eric Hyer
Brigham Young University

Tracy Irons
Independent Scholar

George P. Jan
University of Toledo

Karen A. Joe
University of Hawaii at Manoa

Linda L. Johnson
Concordia College

Byung I. Jung
University of Central Oklahoma

Karina Kahananui
Brigham Young University, Hawaii

B. Winston Kahn
Arizona State University

Lo Hyun-yi Kang
University of California, Santa Cruz

Randy Barbara Kaplan
Association for Asian Performance

Melinda Tria Kerkvliet
University of Hawaii at Manoa

Charles Keyes
University of Washington

E. Jane Keyes
Independent Writer/Researcher

Peter Kiang
University of Massachusetts at Boston

H. C. Kim
Western Washington University

Glen Kitayama
University of California, Los Angeles

P. Christiaan Klieger
Bishop Museum

Alan Koch
California State University, Fullerton

Stephen W. Kohl
University of Oregon

D. W. Y. Kwok
University of Hawaii at Manoa

Bruce La Brack
University of the Pacific

Him Mark Lai
Chinese Historical Society of America

Harry Lamley
University of Hawaii at Manoa

Michael A. Launius
Central Washington University

Bonnie Lee
Independent Scholar

Jae-Bong Lee
University of Hawaii at Manoa

Peter C. Y. Leung
University of California, Davis

Marjorie H. Li
*Rutgers, The State University of
    New Jersey*

Peter Li
*Rutgers, The State University of
    New Jersey*

Ivan Light
University of California, Los Angeles

Patricia Lin
California State Polytechnic University, Pomona

Huping Ling
Northeast Missouri State University

Chang-Hwai Wang Liu
University of Hawaii at Manoa

Lee Liu
Stephen F. Austin State University

Ann Hsu Lo
Tallahassee Community College

Winston W. Lo
Florida State University

James W. Loewen
Independent Scholar

Roger D. Long
Eastern Michigan University

Scott Lowe
University of North Dakota

Theodore M. Ludwig
Valparaiso University

Wing Tek Lum
Independent Scholar

L. Eve Armentrout Ma
Independent Scholar

Sheng-mei Ma
James Madison University

Robert McClenaghan
Independent Scholar

Brucetta McKenzie
Brigham Young University, Hawaii

Sarita Rai MacLeod
University of Hawaii at Manoa

Paul D. Mageli
Independent Scholar

Therese Mahoney
University of California, Los Angeles

Lee A. Makela
Cleveland State University

Deborah Malone
Buddhist Churches of America

Chalvadurai Manogaran
University of Wisconsin—Parkside

John Marney
Oakland University

Amy Iwasaki Mass
Whittier College

James A. Matisoff
University of California, Berkeley

Machiko Matsui
Southern Methodist University

William Matta
University of Guam

Sucheta Mazumdar
Duke University

Laura Miller
Philadelphia College of Textiles & Science

Pyong Gap Min
Queens College of the City University of New York

William M. Modrow
Florida State University

Noreen Mokuau
University of Hawaii at Manoa

Catherine T. Motoyama
College of San Mateo

James S. Moy
University of Wisconsin, Madison

John E. Myers
Simon's Rock of Bard College

Cynthia Nakashima
University of California, Berkeley

Dorri Nautu
Brigham Young University, Hawaii

David J. Nemeth
University of Toledo

Wing Chung Ng
University of British Columbia Canada

Hal Robert Nicholas
Florida State University

Jonathan Y. Okamura
University of Hawaii at Manoa

James Okutsu
San Francisco State University

Loretta Pang
Kapiolani Community College University of Hawaii at Manoa

Haein Park
Independent Scholar

Wayne Patterson
St. Norbert College

Paul Pedersen
Syracuse University

George Anthony Peffer
Prestonsburg Community College

Robert C. Petersen
Middle Tennessee State University

Chanh C. Phan
San Jose State University

Donald L. Platt
University of Guam

Vincent Kelly Pollard
University of Hawaii at Manoa

Michael John Polley
Columbia College

Arthur Pontynen
University of Wisconsin—Oshkosh

Wei Chi Poon
University of California, Berkeley

Elliot Einzig Porter
Independent Scholar

John Powell
Erie Behrend College Pennsylvania State University,

Padma Rangaswamy
University of Illinois at Chicago

N. Madhusudana Rao
Bridgewater State College

Christopher A. Reichl
University of Hawaii at Hilo

Thomas D. Reins
California State University, Fullerton

Linda A. Revilla
University of Washington

Edward J. M. Rhoads
University of Texas at Austin

Michael Robinson
University of Southern California

Rodney J. Ross
Harrisburg Area Community College

Roshni Rustomji-Kerns
Sonoma State University

Wendy Sacket
Independent Scholar

Chaman L. Sahni
Boise State University

Sunil K. Sahu
DePauw University

Steffi San Buenaventura
University of California, Los Angeles

E. San Juan, Jr.
University of Connecticut

Anne Schiller
Ithaca College

Asit K. Sen
Texas Southern University

Richard A. K. Shankar
Stonehill College

Chenliang Sheng
Northern Kentucky University

Narasingha P. Sil
Western Oregon State College

Jane Singh
University of California, Berkeley

Tanya Gay Smith
University of California, Berkeley

Alvin Y. So
University of Hawaii at Manoa

Chunghee Sarah Soh
San Francisco State University

Paul R. Spickard
Brigham Young University, Hawaii

James Stanlaw
Illinois State

Carol Stepanchuk
*Folk Art International Resources
for Education*

David L. Sterling
University of Cincinnati

Bruce M. Sullivan
Northern Arizona University

Betty Lee Sung
*City College of the City University
of New York*

Kumiko Takahara
University of Colorado

Jane S. Takahashi
*University of California, Los Angeles
Japanese American National Museum*

Eileen H. Tamura
University of Hawaii at Manoa

George J. Tanabe, Jr.
University of Hawaii at Manoa

Izumi Taniguchi
California State University, Fresno

Alison Taufer
California State University, Los Angeles

Shiree Teng
University of California, Berkeley

Graham Thurgood
California State University, Fresno

Liang Tien
University of Washington

Qui-Phiet Tran
Schreiner College

Shih-shan H. Tsai
University of Arkansas

Daniel C. Tsang
University of California, Irvine

Taitetsu Unno
Smith College

Jiu-Hwa Lo Upshur
Eastern Michigan University

Hari Vishwanadha
Santa Monica College

Indu Vohra
DePauw University

William R. Wallace III
Brigham Young University, Hawaii

George C. Y. Wang
George Washington University

Qun Wang
University of Wisconsin—River Falls

Youqin Wang
Stanford University

Tony Waters
University of California, Davis

William Wei
University of Colorado

Andrew N. Weintraub
University of California, Berkeley

John K. Whitmore
University of Michigan

Bruce M. Wilson
St. Mary's College of Maryland

John Wilson
Independent Scholar

Richard L. Wilson
*University of Tennessee at
Chattanooga*

Lora Wolfe
Independent Scholar

Diane Yen-Mei Wong
Independent Scholar

Hoover Wong
Fuller Theological Seminary

K. Scott Wong
Williams College

Nechelle Wong
*California State University,
Los Angeles*

Philip Wong
Independent Scholar

Sau-ling Cynthia Wong
University of California, Berkeley

Shawn Woodyard
Independent Scholar

Debbie Hippolite Wright
Brigham Young University, Hawaii

Fatima Wu
Loyola Marymount University

Victor Cunrui Xiong
Western Michigan University

David T. Yamada
Monterey Peninsula College

Alexander Y. Yamato
San Jose State University

Richard Yasko
University of Wisconsin—Whitewater

Xiao-huang Yin
Occidental College

In-Jin Yoon
*University of California, Santa
Barbara*

Won Z. Yoon
Siena College

Renqiu Yu
*State University of New York
at Purchase*

Judy Yung
*University of California,
Santa Cruz*

Yuehua Zhang
Independent Scholar

Helen Zia
Independent Scholar

Judy Van Zile
University of Hawaii

THE
ASIAN AMERICAN
ENCYCLOPEDIA

A

A. Magazine: General-interest Asian American magazine. Debuting in 1991, *A. Magazine* has been described by its publisher, Phoebe Eng, as "a *Life* magazine for Asians," aimed primarily at upscale readers between eighteen and forty. In feature stories, profiles, and regular departments the magazine covers a wide range of topics: business, politics, fashion, the arts, anti-Asian violence, and discrimination.

ABC: Abbreviation for "American-born Chinese," used by CHINESE AMERICANS to refer to people of Chinese descent born in the United States.

Abe, Tokunosuke (1885, Iwate Prefecture, Japan—Jan. 3, 1941, San Diego, Calif.): Commercial fisherman. An Issei descendant of an old samurai family, Abe arrived in Seattle, Washington, in 1900. He later moved to Los Angeles, where he studied business at Woodbury College. From about 1920 until 1931, he worked for the MK Fishing Company, which under Abe was eventually reorganized into the Southern Commercial Company. The business prospered, becoming within five years the largest privately managed fishing fleet in Southern California.

For many years, however, Abe and other Issei commercial fishermen in California had been forced to contend with anti-Japanese state legislation enacted to drive them out of business. This legislation stipulated that only U.S. citizens were eligible to receive commercial fishing licenses. Federal statute, however, made all Issei ineligible for naturalization. In the early 1930's the state's attorney general began prosecuting Abe for fishing without a license, as mandated by the California fish and game code. Abe then filed a lawsuit to challenge the rule. In *Abe v. Fish and Game Commission* (1935), the state supreme court agreed that the code violated the equal protection clause of the federal constitution's Fourteenth Amendment. A few years later, after a major battle, Abe helped overturn an assembly bill introduced by future Los Angeles mayor Sam Yorty. The bill's provisions were such that many Japanese commercial fishermen would have found themselves out of work.

Abiko, Kyutaro (June 23, 1865, Suibara, Kita-Kambara-Gun, Japan—May 31, 1936, San Francisco,

Through his influential newspaper, the Nichibei Shimbun, *Abiko urged Japanese immigrants to plant roots in America through land ownership and starting families.* (Japanese American National Museum)

Calif.): Labor contractor, banker, and publisher. Abiko was one of the most important Issei leaders. He sought to fight the ANTI-JAPANESE MOVEMENT by addressing the ignorance of Japanese Americans. He arrived in San Francisco at the age of twenty. Unlike other Issei, Abiko planned to settle in America. He came to America with the idea of being a student and a laborer. He went to grammar school and completed Boys High School. He developed the skills to read, write, and speak English.

Abiko was the editor and publisher of the San Francisco Japanese newspaper NICHIBEI SHIMBUN (*Japanese American News*), which he founded in 1899. He wrote editorials urging Japanese immigrants to commit themselves to living in the United States permanently rather than planning to return to Japan. By 1910 the

Nichibei Shimbun had become the most influential Japanese newspaper in the United States, with a distribution on the West Coast and in many inland states where Japanese were farmers. Starting in 1925 Abiko added an English section to the newspaper for the Nisei, who were born and raised in the United States and many of whom did not read Japanese.

Abiko was concerned about the anti-Japanese movement, which supported the exclusion of Japanese immigrants to the United States and sought to deny basic rights to Japanese Americans. He believed that one way to counter the criticism of Japanese immigrants as SOJOURNERS was for the Japanese to become permanent settlers through the ownership of land. In addition he believed that Japanese immigrants should establish families and thus supported the PICTURE-BRIDE arrangement, by means of which the Issei were able to marry without returning to Japan.

Abiko formed the American Land and Produce Company, which purchased 3,200 acres of land located near Livingston, California, in 1906. He recruited primarily Issei Christians to settle on the tracts of land, called the YAMATO COLONY. He was also a banker, utilizing his bank, the Japanese American Bank, to make loans to those Japanese willing to settle at the Yamato Colony, although the bank had closed by 1910. In 1919, with a European American, Abiko purchased additional land in the area for Japanese settlers, forming the Cortez Colony. Acutely aware of the conflict and prejudice with which Japanese immigrants were confronted in California, Abiko believed that Japanese immigrants should not compete with white store owners.

Abiko was also one of the founders of the Japanese American Industrial Corporation of San Francisco in 1902. The corporation acted as an intermediary between businesses looking to hire Japanese laborers. The laborers were placed in jobs such as mining coal in Wyoming, farming sugar beets in Utah and Idaho, and working on the railroads in Nevada and Wyoming.

Abiko, Yasuo (1910—1988): Newspaper editor. Abiko was the son of Kyutaro ABIKO, editor of the *NICHIBEI SHIMBUN*. By the advent of World War II, Yasuo had risen to become English-section editor of that publication. After the war, he helped keep the newspaper going, often producing it by himself when necessary.

Abuba, Ernest (b. Aug. 25, 1947, Honolulu, Hawaii): Actor and director. A leading Asian American actor

since the 1960's, he received the 1983 Best Actor Obie Award for his performance in R. A. SHIOMI's *Yellow Fever* (pr. 1982). As senior artist with New York City's PAN ASIAN REPERTORY THEATRE, Abuba directed and performed in numerous productions, and was instrumental in nurturing new Asian American playwrights. His musical drama *Cambodia Agonistes*, the first American play to address the Kampuchean genocide, premiered at the Pan Asian Repertory Theatre in 1992.

Acheson v. Murakami (1949): Federal court case handed down by the U.S. Ninth Circuit Court of Appeals, reinstating U.S. citizenship to a Japanese American renunciant. During World War II, more than fifty-seven hundred Japanese Americans renounced their American citizenship while under internment; the bulk of these declarations came from the relocation camp at TULE LAKE, up near the California-Oregon border. Miye Mae Murakami, evacuated to Tule Lake in 1944, claimed to have renounced her citizenship out of fear for her safety and because she did not want to be separated from her husband, who wanted to return to Japan. The court found that flawed governmental policies and cruel treatment at the camp created an atmosphere of undue influence, coercion, and duress. As such, Murakami's renunciation was not free and voluntary, as required by law; any such act was therefore null and void. Her citizenship was restored.

ACLU. *See* **American Civil Liberties Union**

Acupuncture and moxibustion: Two separate but related systems of medical treatment devised by the Chinese many centuries ago and still practiced in many parts of the world. Chinese American practitioners have popularized these systems in the United States. Acupuncture involves the stimulation of designated points on the skin's surface by means of the insertion of very fine needles. Moxibustion is the application of heat to the body by the burning of small cones of dry leaves on designated points, many of them the same ones used in acupuncture. Modern Chinese surgeons, using acupuncture as anesthesia, have operated on patients who remained fully awake throughout the procedure but felt no pain. Acupuncture and moxibustion are occasionally combined to treat various diseases and as anesthesia. The physiological basis for these forms of therapy has never been fully explained.

Acupuncture is based on the meridian theory, in which *qi*, or "vital energy," is believed to travel through precise meridians, or pathways within the hu-

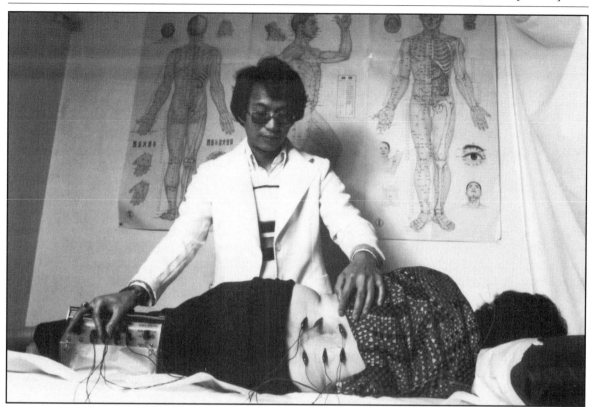

Although of ancient origin, acupuncture remains a popular form of medical treatment among the Chinese. (Asian American Studies Library, University of California at Berkeley)

man body. These meridians connect the bodily organs to one another and the interior of the body to the exterior. To an acupuncturist, illnesses are a matter of "imbalance": They result when the *qi* flowing through the body is somehow interrupted and thrown out of balance, adversely affecting the body's normal and healthy operation. Treatment therefore consists of inserting the needles at specified points along these meridians in order to stimulate or mute vital energy and thereby prevent, control, or cure disease. For this reason, practitioners do not think only in terms of specific diseases, each with its own particular etiology, when diagnosing patients. All told, there are twelve meridians and about 365 points throughout the body, not counting those that pertain to the modern auricular, or ear, systems of acupuncture.

As early as the Stone Age, the Chinese discovered that heating certain points on the body improved blood circulation and relieved pain, such as that caused by rheumatism. The term "moxibustion" is taken from the name of the plant that this method has traditionally used, *Artemisia moxa*, the leaves of which have first been dried to a tinder. The classical method is to shape the tinder into a cone, apply it to the skin, and allow it to burn. It is economical and can be self-administered. The heat penetrates the skin effectively, and the stimulus, if properly applied to raise a small blister, is relatively long-lasting.

In modern practice, various herbs may be used in place of *moxa*. Moreover, modern methods dictate that merely warming (as opposed to blistering, the ancient practice) the portion to be stimulated is enough. For example, the crushed, dried herb is typically wrapped in special paper and, when lit, is either held above the skin or placed directly atop the skin but removed before overheating can occur. Moxibustion has been used to relieve congestion, tone the skin, and treat respiratory disorders.

Adams, Ansel [Easton] (Feb. 20, 1902, San Francisco, Calif.—Apr. 22, 1984, Carmel, Calif.): Photographer and environmentalist who helped to document the experience of Japanese American internment during World War II. Adams made his first visit to Yosemite National Park in 1916, and from that trip he dated his interest in both conservation and photography. Indeed, the two interests fed one another throughout his career. His photographs document his development as an artist and the development of his commitment to conservation of the environment. Adams was a particularly avid supporter of the national park system.

Adams' interest in the artistic potential of photography was clear from the publication of his first portfolio, *Parmelian Prints of the High Sierras*, in 1927. Adams had his first one-man exhibit at the Sierra Club in San Francisco in 1928 and went on to exhibit at the Smithsonian Institution in Washington, D.C., New York's Museum of Modern Art, the Metropolitan Museum of Art, also in New York, and many other prestigious venues. His work was influenced by that of photographers such as Paul Strand, Edward Weston, and Imogen Cunningham; and he had fruitful associations with Alfred Stieglitz and Georgia O'Keeffe. Adams helped to establish photography as an art form in its own right. He developed a process of exposure and development that he called the "Zone System," and late in his life he worked with the Polaroid Corpo-

ration to explore the artistic potential of its products.

Adams' commitment to photography as an art form was sustained by a willingness to undertake commercial assignments. Among them was a project for the U.S. Department of the Interior, for which he spent 1941 and 1942 photographing national parks and monuments. He resumed the project, which had been interrupted by World War II, in 1946 with the help of a Guggenheim Foundation Fellowship; it was the first of three he was to receive. Adams became interested in the plight of Japanese Americans interned by the U.S. government, and in 1943 he began to photograph the MANZANAR relocation center. This resulted in a photo-essay published in 1944 as *Born Free and Equal: Photographs of the Loyal Japanese Americans at Manzanar Relocation Center, Inyo County, California.* The book was Adams' chief political statement outside the area of nature conservation.

Adams produced thirty or more books: collections

Determined that Japanese Americans forcibly evacuated to the relocation centers not be forgotten, Ansel Adams spent 1943 documenting life inside the Manzanar compound, shown here. (National Japanese American Historical Society)

of photographs such as *Yosemite Valley* in 1959, volumes in his *Basic Photo* series of 1948 with a technical emphasis, and monographs such as his *Ansel Adams* in 1972. He was elected a fellow of the American Academy of Arts and Sciences in 1966, and in 1980 President Jimmy Carter presented him with the Presidential Medal of Freedom. Following his death in 1984, Adams' work to protect the environment was recognized by creation of the Ansel Adams Wilderness Area near Yosemite National Park, and in 1985 a peak near the southeast edge of the park was named Mt. Ansel Adams.

Adi Granth: Sacred canon of SIKHISM. It is also referred to as *Granth, Guru Granth Sahib,* or *Granth Sahib*. Sikhs regard the *Adi Granth* as the visible embodiment of the Eternal Guru or Absolute Truth. The compilation of the *Adi Granth* began under Guru Angad, the second guru of the Sikh religion, who collected hymns composed by Guru NANAK (1469-1539), the founder of Sikhism, and by earlier teachers of devotional religion. In 1706, under Guru GOBIND SINGH, the *Adi Granth* took its final form.

The *Adi Granth* contains a unique array of devotional hymns that reflect the highest wisdom of humankind and a spirit of tolerance that all devout Sikhs must accept and that none may dispute. Its focus is on the Nam, or "divine name," a shortened reference to the absolute being and nature of the Akal Purakh, or God as the Timeless One, Creator, Benefactor, Overseer, and all-pervading presence in the universe. Its Eternal Truth can be effectively heard only by meditating upon its immanent presence within the innermost depths of one's heart and soul.

The *Adi Granth* is, therefore, held in great reverence by all members of the Sikh community who consider Truth and God as synonymous terms. It symbolizes all that is sacred and establishes all people as equal in the eyes of God and human beings alike. To this sacred text all veneration is due. Recitation from it in a Sikh *gurdwara*, or temple, continues as long as the temple remains open. Before it devout Sikhs bow with folded hands and sit in its presence listening to the message of Guru Nanak and his four successors.

After 1604, the *Adi Granth* was installed by the Guru Arjun in the Golden Temple at Amritsar, the most sacred and distinctive Sikh historic *gurdwara*. The tenets of the *Adi Granth*, recorded in the Punjabi Gurumukhi script, have played a cohesive role in the history of the Sikh community, where their sanctity is affirmed by even the most secular of Sikhs as the foundation of

Sikh tradition and community. After 1706 and the end of the guruship of Gobind Singh (the tenth and last human guru of the Sikh religion), complete and final authority was taken from human representation and vested in the *Adi Granth*, or *Guru Granth Sahib*, alone.

Adobo: Filipino food featuring pork or pork fat cooked with other ingredients, including chicken, vinegar, garlic, and pepper. Originally a Mediterranean dish, it is representative of the amalgamation of Spanish and indigenous influences in Filipino cuisine.

Aduja, Peter Aquino (b. Oct. 19, 1920, Vigan, Ilocos Sur, the Philippines): Politician and business executive. Aduja emigrated to Hawaii with his family in 1927 and graduated from high school in Hilo before attending the University of Hawaii. He graduated with a B.A. degree in 1944, the same year he became a naturalized citizen. After graduation, Aduja joined the army and served in the 1ST FILIPINO INFANTRY REGIMENT from 1944 to 1946. After World War II ended, Aduja entered law school at Boston University and graduated with his J. D. degree in 1951. He returned to Hawaii, where he passed the bar examination in 1953 and went into private practice in Hilo. After running as a Democratic candidate for a seat in the Territorial Legislature in 1954, Aduja became the first Filipino American to be elected to the Hawaiian legislature prior to statehood. Although he was defeated for reelection, Aduja was appointed to serve as deputy attorney general by Governor Samuel W. King from 1957 through 1960. He then accepted an appointment as a judge in the state's district court and served from 1960 until 1962. In 1966, Aduja ran successfully as a candidate for a seat in the state legislature to represent the district of Windward on Oahu. He was reelected to this office for two additional terms and served as a delegate to the state's constitutional convention in 1968. During his legislative terms, Aduja became a licensed real estate broker in Honolulu and served as president of Aduja Corporation and Travel-Air International.

AFL. *See* **American Federation of Labor**

Agricultural Workers Organizing Committee (AWOC): Founded in 1959 by Larry ITLIONG's Filipino Farm Labor Union to work for higher wages, better working conditions, and union recognition from California growers. The AWOC was an AMERICAN FEDERATION OF LABOR-Congress of Industrial Organizations (AFL-CIO) sponsored union providing Fili-

The increase in the number of Filipinos working the fields of central California by the 1950's made unionization not merely attractive but also inevitable. (Library of Congress)

pino farm workers legitimacy in the fields.

The attempt by Filipino and other ethnic farm workers to unionize the California fields was resisted by agribusiness interests successfully until the 1960's. From the onset of the Great Depression, the Associated Farmers of California and other agribusiness pressure groups prevented large-scale unionization, but two successful strikes by the FILIPINO LABOR UNION in Salinas in 1934 and 1936 made ethnic unionization a viable alternative.

Early Years of AWOC Organization. By the mid-1950's, building on these earlier successes, ITLIONG began organizing Filipino vegetable and grape workers. He recognized that there was no chance of union success without AFL-CIO support, so he convinced union officials to consider a broad-based mainstream farm union.

Itliong then united a number of different groups under the Filipino Farm Labor Union and made over-

tures to all farm workers. Ethnic unity and working for a common prosperity made Itliong's message an attractive one. Soon he became friendly with César Chavez's fledgling Chicano union, the National Farm Workers Association, and they developed common goals. Then Itliong approached the AFL-CIO for a union charter for all farm workers.

Norman Smith of the AFL-CIO called a meeting of the Filipino Farm Labor Union, and he and Itliong founded the AWOC. Under Smith's leadership, Itliong was hired as a paid organizer, and in June, 1960, the new union was granted a charter.

The AWOC waged a lengthy campaign for better wages and better working conditions. For half a decade Itliong quietly built the union and encouraged Chavez's 800-member union to join Filipinos in the movement to force grape growers around Delano to unionize.

The Delano Grape Strike. In the San Joaquin Valley,

Filipino farm workers had been abused by local growers for thirty years. On September 5, 1965, when the AWOC called a strike against thirty-three grape growers near Delano in northern Kern County, Filipinos were prepared for a bitter and lengthy strike. The average wage for grape pickers was $1.20 an hour, but the *bracero* brought in from Mexico received $1.40. When Filipino, Euro-American, and Mexican American workers demanded a raise, growers refused.

ITLIONG led the AWOC out on strike, and Chavez's group considered joining the picket line. By September 8 the AWOC struck four Delano vineyards, ordering all local workers to leave the fields, thereby crippling the grape harvest. A bitter, often violent seven-month strike ensued. The Filipino-Mexican American labor unions boycotted Safeway stores and built up a great deal of public sympathy. The arrogant attitude of the Gallo Winery engendered resentment, and the public pronouncement by winery officials that the unionists were radicals had a hollow ring in the 1960's.

The support of the AFL-CIO helped Itliong and Chavez as they set up picket lines around key ranches to discourage strikebreakers from crossing into the fields. When two Filipino picket captains climbed onto the roof of a car and used loudspeakers to keep strikebreakers away from the Delano fields, they demonstrated the unity of ethnic workers.

During the Delano strike, Filipino labor leaders were so vocal that the Kern County Sheriff's Department assigned ten extra patrol units to the area. The fear of violence prompted Judge Leonard Ginsburg of Visalia to issue a restraining order setting a limit of five pickets at any one location. The picketers cooperated until they were beaten by angry Euro-American mobs. Despite grower repression, Itliong announced to a throng of newspaper reporters that the walkout had stalled production at sixty farms.

Sporadic violence continued as the growers brought in Spanish-speaking strikebreakers. This convinced Chavez to bring all the members of his union out of the fields.

On September 16, 1965, Mexican Independence Day, the National Farm Workers Association voted to support the AWOC strike. As almost three thousand Filipino and Mexican American farm workers left the fields, Delano's grape harvest was on the verge of spoiling. On September 24, Itliong announced that 95 percent of all grape pickers were on strike.

The ethnic labor unions disagreed, however, on strike tactics. Soon the Delano labor dispute became

two strikes, with Itliong's and Chavez's organizations jockeying for a leadership role. There was a tenuous cooperation between Itliong and Chavez, and this lack of unity hurt the movement.

Finally, after seven months, Schenley Industries, owner of California's largest vineyards, recognized the National Farm Workers Association as the sole field labor bargaining agent. Itliong then wisely united the AWOC with Chavez's union. The AWOC had a large treasury, and this allowed Itliong a voice in Chavez's stronger union.

In August, 1966, the two unions merged as the United Farm Workers Organizing Committee and became the bargaining agent for workers employed by the Di Giorgio Corporation, another gigantic Kern County vineyard.

The UNITED FARM WORKERS ORGANIZING COM-

AWOC cofounder Larry Itliong was instrumental in securing better pay and working conditions for Filipinos farmworkers in California. (Filipino American National Historical Society)

MITTEE secured an AFL-CIO charter on August 22, 1966, and this marked a major turning point in California agricultural labor relations. Filipinos and Chicanos worked together to secure better wages and working conditions. Still, many growers refused to recognize the committee. Filipinos broke ranks with Chavez and urged Itliong to organize a new pressure group.

Impact of AWOC. In 1969 the Filipino-American Political Association was organized and held its first annual convention in Delano, where Itliong was elected president. Chavez was the featured speaker, and the convention emphasized the need for ethnic labor unity. A tenuous cooperation developed between Filipinos and Chicanos, and the Filipino Community Hall on Greenwood Street in Delano was the scene of many meetings to work for better working conditions.

Although AWOC was defunct, its purpose lived on as Filipinos continued to improve field pay and conditions. Two major growers, Bianco Vineyards and Bruno Dispoto, finally signed union contracts on May 21, 1970. This was four and a half years after the initial Delano strike and more than a decade after Itliong had founded the AWOC.

On June 26, 1970, the conflict between the Filipino and Chicano unions and local growers ended when all 26 of Delano's grape growers signed union contracts. Much of the success of this agreement was attributable to the Filipino-led AWOC. As a result, Itliong remains one of the most unsung, albeit important, labor leaders in California ethnic history.—*Howard A. DeWitt*

SUGGESTED READINGS: • Chan, Sucheng. *Asian Americans: An Interpretive History.* Boston: Twayne, 1991. • Crouchett, Lorraine Jacobs. *Filipinos in California: From the Days of the Galleons to the Present.* El Cerrito, Calif.: Downey Place Publishing House, 1982. • DeWitt, Howard A. *Anti-Filipino Movements in California: A History, Bibliography and Study Guide.* San Francisco: R and E Research Associates, 1976. • DeWitt, Howard A. *Images of Ethnic and Radical Violence in California Politics, 1917-1930: A Survey.* San Francisco: R and E Research Associates, 1975. • DeWitt, Howard A. *Violence in the Fields: Filipino Farm Labor Unionization During the Great Depression.* Saratoga, Calif.: Century Twenty One Publishing, 1980. • Melendy, H. Brett. *Asians in America: Filipinos, Koreans and East Indians.* Boston: Twayne, 1977.

Aguinaldo, Emilio (Mar. 22, 1869, Kawit, Cavite Province, Philippines—Feb. 6, 1964, Manila, Republic of the Philippines): Revolutionary, soldier, and politician. He was the first among prominent Filipino revolutionaries and a predecessor of Asian nationalists who struggled to overcome Western colonial rule.

As a Chinese-mestizo youth of the *principalía*, or elite, Aguinaldo lived in Kawit and attended Catholic school. Skilled in the use of swords and firearms, he trimmed his hair short, and, once he became renowned, young males in the Philippines copied his haircut.

Aguinaldo was a *gobernadorcillo*, or petty governor, when in 1895 he joined the revolutionary Katipunan, or "Highest and Most Honorable Society of Sons of the Country." The following year, he directed attacks against Spanish troops at both Kawit, where he gained sudden fame, and Binakayan, in the initial phase of the revolution to end Spain's domination and win independence. Elected leader of the resistance, he wrested control of the Katipunan, having its founder Andrés Bonifacio arrested and executed. Superior Spanish forces, however, chased him out of Cavite and into mountainous Biak-na-Bato, where Aguinaldo negotiated terms with the Spaniards for his exile to Hong Kong in 1897.

Once war broke out between Spain and the United States, Aguinaldo returned to the Philippines on the American ship *McCulloch.* Believing that Commodore George Dewey had promised him aid in the struggle against the Spaniards, he declared the independence of the Philippines on June 12, 1898, and established the republic's capital at Malolos. After American forces occupied Manila, however, fighting started the next year between Filipinos and Americans outside the city. The ensuing PHILIPPINE-AMERICAN WAR (1899-1902) saw Aguinaldo switch from conventional to guerrilla tactics as the revolutionaries suffered repeated defeats. Hampered by defections and quarreling within the leadership, he fled to northeastern Luzon's Palanan, where he was decoyed by a fake letter and apprehended by General Frederick Funston's command. Soon after, Aguinaldo pledged his loyalty to the United States.

In 1930, Aguinaldo married for a second time after the death of his first wife, Hilaria, with whom he had six children. An advocate of immediate independence, he supported the TYDINGS-MCDUFFIE ACT OF 1934. Aguinaldo ran for the presidency of the Commonwealth of the Philippines the following year (1935) but lost to Manuel QUEZON. Accused of collaboration with Japan during World War II (1939-1945), he was exonerated and, before his death, helped veterans and advised presidents in his homeland.

Aguinaldo's valiant efforts to free his native country from both Spanish and American rule made him a Philippine national hero. (Library of Congress)

Philip Ahn, a familiar face among American audiences as one of the busiest working actors in Hollywood until his death in 1978. (Korea Times)

Ahn, Philip (Mar. 29, 1911, Los Angeles, Calif.— Feb. 28, 1978, Los Angeles, Calif.): Actor. Eldest son of Korean political activist AHN CHANG-HO, he appeared in more than three hundred Hollywood films beginning in the mid-1930's, including *The Good Earth* (1937) and *Love Is a Many Splendored Thing* (1955). He is also remembered for his role on the television show *KUNG FU* (1972-1975). Ahn was the first Asian American actor to be honored with a star on the Hollywood Walk of Fame.

Ahn Chang-ho (Nov. 9, 1878, Pyongan, Korea— Mar. 10, 1938, Korea): Political activist. Educated at an American missionary school in Seoul, Ahn came to the United States in 1899 to continue his studies. After his graduation he returned to Korea, where he taught at a Presbyterian school and then founded a school of his own. Married in 1902, he and his wife came to San Francisco, where a small community of Korean immi-

grants was forming. In 1903, Ahn founded the CHINMOK-HOE (Friendship Society), the first Korean American social organization; in 1905, he founded the KONGNIP HYOP-HOE (Mutual Assistance Society), the first Korean American political organization.

In 1907, two years after Japan had established a protectorate in Korea, Ahn returned to his homeland to work for the cause of Korean sovereignty, but he was forced to flee. Back in San Francisco, he founded the HUNGSA-DAN (Corps for the Advancement of Individuals), a Korean nationalist cultural organization, in 1913. Just as, decades later, Aleksandr Solzhenitsyn was to argue that rebuilding Russia after decades of Communism would require repentance and spiritual renewal on a national scale, so Ahn believed that Korean independence required national regeneration.

Japan had annexed Korea in 1910. Dedicated to Korean independence, Ahn returned to Korea yet again, leaving his wife and children in the United States. In China he served as the Korean provisional government's interior and labor secretary and as acting prime minister. Charged with anti-Japanese activities, he was arrested by the Japanese police in Korea in 1935. Imprisoned and tortured, he died in 1938 shortly after his release.

On both sides of the Pacific, Ahn Chang-ho worked tirelessly to advance the cause of Korean national sovereignty. (University of Southern California East Asian Library)

Ai (Florence Anthony; b. Oct. 21, 1947, Albany, Texas): Poet. In a May, 1978 article in *Ms.* magazine, "One Being ½ Japanese, ⅛ Choctaw, ¼ Black, and ¹⁄₁₆ Irish" (¹⁄₁₆ remains unaccounted for), Ai has described her complex ancestry. Her father, who was not married to her mother and whom she never met, was "Japanese with some ethnic ties to the Philippines." She grew up in Albany, Texas, Las Vegas, and San Francisco, where she was generally classified by others as black. At the University of Arizona, she majored in Oriental Studies ("Ai," the name she adopted, means "love" in Japanese). She writes that she "learned well the lesson most multiracial people must learn in order to live with the fact of not belonging: there is no identity for me 'out there.'"

Ai's first book of poems, *Cruelty* (1973), was acclaimed for its vivid images of life among the rural poor. Her second collection, *Killing Floor* (1979), won the Lamont Prize of the American Academy of Poets. Her subsequent volumes include *Sin* (1986), which won an American Book Award from the Before Columbus Foundation, *Fate* (1991), and *Greed* (1993). Many of her poems are dramatic monologues, some in the imagined voices of public figures (e.g., George Armstrong Custer, James Dean, Alfred Hitchcock, John and Robert Kennedy, Mary Jo Kopechne), some in the voices of nameless people. Many of the poems depict violence and cruelty, often in a way that deconstructs American myths.

Ai has been the recipient of numerous fellowships and grants, including a Guggenheim Fellowship, a Radcliffe Fellowship, and two fellowships from the National Endowment for the Arts.

Aion: Radical Asian American magazine which grew out of the SAN FRANCISCO STATE COLLEGE STRIKE of 1968; it lasted only two issues, both of which appeared in 1970. In his book *The Asian American Movement* (1993), William WEI describes *Aion* as "the first Asian American magazine."

Aiso, John (Dec. 14, 1909, Burbank, Calif.—Dec. 29, 1987, Los Angeles, Calif.): Military officer and state court justice. Aiso was a trailblazer among Japanese Americans. His parents were Japanese immigrants. From the very beginning Aiso demonstrated his ambitiousness as he became the first Japanese American to be elected student body president of Le Conte Junior High School. Unfortunately, he never had the chance to serve: Parents demanded either that Aiso be removed or that the principal resign. Still, Aiso was not

discouraged. At Hollywood High School he distinguished himself as captain of the debating team and led it to the Southern California championship in 1926. In the same year he was graduated as the valedictorian of his class and was the first Japanese American elected to the prestigious Ephebian society.

After graduation, Aiso studied for a year at Sijo Gakuen in Tokyo and then resumed his education at Brown University, where he was graduated cum laude in 1931. Harvard Law School was next, and following graduation in 1934, Aiso studied Japanese law at Chuo

Following military service in World War II, John Aiso became a well-respected California state justice. (AP/Wide World Photos)

University in 1936 and 1937. The following three years were spent working for a British-American tobacco company in the Japanese puppet state of Manchukuo. In 1940, as war between Japan and the United States was near, Aiso returned to the United States to be treated for hepatitis.

Aiso's life was forever changed following his return to the United States. In December of 1940 he was informed that at age thirty-one he was to be drafted into the Army for military service. In April of the following year, he reported for service in a unit that repaired trucks. Fortunately for both the Army and Aiso, he showed no aptitude for the assignment and was later transferred to the intelligence section of the Fourth Army to study at the planned JAPANESE-LANGUAGE SCHOOL. Because the Army recognized Aiso's abilities in Japanese, he was made the head instructor of the MILITARY INTELLIGENCE SERVICE LANGUAGE SCHOOL (MISLS) when it opened in San Francisco in November of 1941. Approximately six thousand students (including forty-five hundred Nisei) were graduated from the MISLS under the guidance of Aiso. Many were later assigned intelligence duty in the Pacific war, where they worked as interpreters and deciphered Japanese codes. At the end of the war, Aiso left the MISLS to work with the allied occupation forces in Japan. In 1945 he retired from the Army with the rank of lieutenant colonel, the highest rank given to a Japanese American during World War II.

Aiso's accomplishments continued after the war. Upon returning to Los Angeles, he resumed his private law practice until he was appointed a commissioner of the Los Angeles Superior Court in 1952. The following year Aiso was appointed a judge of the Los Angeles Municipal Court, making him the first Japanese American ever to achieve that status. In 1958 he was elevated to the Los Angeles Superior Court and later accepted an appointment to the California Court of Appeals in 1968. Aiso retired in 1972 and joined the firm of O'Melveny and Myers as special counsel. A mild stroke in February of 1984 forced Aiso to retire from the firm. Three years later, on December 29, 1987, he was killed by a thief at a gasoline station in the Crenshaw area of Los Angeles. He was seventy-eight years old.

Aizu-wakamatsu: City in Fukushima Prefecture, Honshu, Japan, from which a group of Japanese emigrated to California in 1869. The immigrants were compelled to leave Japan because they supported Tokugawa shoguns during the Meiji revolution in 1868. Recruited by John Henry Schnell, the immigrants started the six-hundred-acre WAKAMATSU TEA AND SILK FARM COLONY (1869-1871).

Akaka, Daniel Kahikina (b. Sept. 11, 1924, Honolulu, Territory of Hawaii): U.S. senator. He earned bachelor's and master's degrees in education from the University of Hawaii and served as a high school teacher and principal. A Democrat, he was elected to the 95th Congress to represent the Second District of Hawaii in the U.S. House of Representatives on Nov. 2, 1976. While serving his seventh consecutive term in Congress he was appointed, effective May 16, 1990, to

Daniel Akaka was the first native Hawaiian ever elected to the U.S. Senate. (Asian Week)

fill the vacant U.S. Senate seat of the late senator Spark MATSUNAGA, who had died a month earlier. Senator Akaka, the first Native Hawaiian to serve in the Senate, was then elected in November of 1990 to serve a full Senate term.

Akaka faced one of his greatest political challenges in the fall of 1990, when he was challenged by a popular U.S. representative from Honolulu, moderate Republican Patricia SAIKI, in a special election to determine who would ultimately assume the vacant Senate seat. Saiki, the choice of many retired Caucasian former mainlanders and by the 1990's the only Republican ever elected to the House from Hawaii, was expected to attract many Hawaiians of Japanese American ancestry. She also won the support of the National Organization for Women (NOW)—although the Hawaii NOW branch endorsed Akaka—and was thus nationally considered the Republican Party's best hope to win a Democratic-held Senate seat in the 1990 elections.

The 1990 Akaka-Saiki contest also garnered national headlines as perhaps the least-negative Senate race run during a time when negative campaigning had brought politics and politicians into widespread disfavor. Rather than smearing each other, the candidates (both former schoolteachers) chose to emphasize the positive achievements reflected in their own political records. A staunch defender of Hawaiian sugar and textile interests, Akaka was ultimately carried to victory by his popularity among Native Hawaiians and the working class.

Akali movement: Indian term that refers to the Sikh secessionist movement, Sikh freedom fighters, and the dominant Sikh political party. Literally meaning a "worshipper of the Timeless One," Akali has been used since the late seventeenth century to refer to a militant movement to preserve Sikh identity through religious, military, and political struggle. Appearing first during the reign of the tenth guru, GOBIND SINGH, Akali militant freedom fighters were dubbed *nihangs* (Persian for "crocodiles") by the Mughals for their suicidal tactics and distinctive blue uniforms. (Even today some Akalis continue to don a blue tunic and turban and brandish a sword.) They adhered rigidly to Khalsa precepts, rejected Hindu rites completely, and considered themselves as self-appointed guardians of the Sikh faith. Retaining considerable prominence and

respect from foe and ally alike throughout the eighteenth century, their numbers dwindled considerably during the nineteenth. A few Akalis that survived were neglected as harmless cranks.

The term again resumed renewed prominence between 1921 and 1925, when a Sikh movement agitated to reform the corrupt management of the Golden Temple in Amritsar, the holy city of Sikhism. The British colonial government had been using *gurdwaras*, or Sikh temples, to monitor Sikh activity and steer the Sikhs away from nationalist politics. The *gurdwara* reform movement appeared as a semimilitary corps of volunteers, the Akalis, to oppose the British government and the *mahants*, or hereditary caretakers, of the *gurdwaras*, who were considered lackeys of the British overlords. The four-year struggle against the British for control of the *gurdwaras* terminated in the passage of the Sikh Gurdwaras Act of 1925. It placed the management of all *gurdwaras* under an elected body of Sikhs called the Shiromani Gurdwara Prabandhak Committee.

After 1925 the Akalis continued their agitation by

A young Asian Indian boy marches in a Sikh Independence Day parade in New York City. (Richard B. Levine)

demanding an independent Punjabi-speaking Sikh-majority state, a goal realized in 1966, when the province of PUNJAB was divided into the two new states of Punjab (the Sikh-majority state) and Haryana (in which Hindi speakers predominated). The major Sikh political party, Shiromani Akali Dal, then resurrected in the 1970's an old dream first advocated after partition in 1947, that of a separate Sikh homeland, KHAL-ISTAN, with autonomy and sovereignty granted to the Sikhs, and defense, communications, and foreign affairs to be administered by India. Since the mid-1980's the Akali Dal has given renewed impetus to this dream with continued conflict and agitation against the central government of India. (See GOLDEN TEMPLE INCIDENT.)

Akiyoshi, Toshiko (b. Dec. 12, 1929, Ryoyo, Manchuria, China): Composer and jazz pianist. The youngest daughter born to a Japanese industrialist living in Manchuria, Akiyoshi began studying classical piano at the age of six. She and her family moved back to Japan in 1946 in the wake of growing civil unrest surrounding the incipient communist revolution. Akiyoshi found employment on a U.S. Army base in Tokyo as a pianist with a dance band and began to study American jazz in earnest, listening to popular records and transcribing the solos she heard.

After founding her own quartet in 1951 and working with saxophonist Sadao Watanabe, Akiyoshi caught the attention of visiting jazz pianist Oscar Peterson, who invited her to record with him and encouraged her to study music in the United States. She studied at the Berklee School of Music in Boston from 1956 to 1959 and began performing with various jazz ensembles in New York during the late 1950's and early 1960's. After forming a short-lived big band in 1967, Akiyoshi met and married jazz flutist and saxophonist Lew Tabackin. Moving to Los Angeles in 1972, the couple formed their own big band with Akiyoshi as pianist, composer, and arranger and showcasing Tabackin as featured soloist. The Toshiko Akiyoshi/Lew Tabackin Big Band received critical acclaim and numerous *Down Beat* awards for its work during the 1970's and 1980's. During this period, Akiyoshi began to incorporate more Asian musical themes and instrumental parts in her jazz compositions.

In 1985, the group was disbanded and Toshiko Akiyoshi's New York Jazz Orchestra was formed as its replacement. Capping her thirty-five-year career as the world's foremost woman jazz composer, Akiyoshi and her orchestra released an album of live music from a concert held at Carnegie Hall in 1991.

Alabama and Chattanooga Railroad: Shortly after the American Civil War, brothers John C. and Daniel L. Stanton entered a joint venture aimed at connecting Chattanooga, Tennessee, with Meridian, Mississippi. In August, 1870, about 960 Chinese laborers arrived in Alabama by railroad from California. The company chose to contract Chinese laborers because of their reputation for being a more compliant workforce than recently freed African Americans. A few years later the project went bankrupt, and most of the Chinese stayed on in the region, many to work on plantations in Louisiana.

Chinese immigrant laborers were vital to building the railroads of the American frontier. (Asian American Studies Library, University of California at Berkeley)

Alien Land Law of 1913 (Webb-Heney Bill): State statute barring all "aliens ineligible to citizenship" (or corporations with more than 50 percent ineligible alien ownership) from the legal right to own agricultural land in California. The law (directed against Japanese immigrant farmers) further limited land leasing contracts in the state to three years' duration. The statute was approved by both houses of the state legislature by overwhelming margins and was signed into law by Governor Hiram Johnson (a staunch nativist, who had long championed anti-Japanese views). California voters did not repeal the ALIEN LAND LAWS until 1956.

Although applicable only within California, the legislation was opposed from the outset by U.S. president Woodrow Wilson, who pointed out that such a ban would run counter at the national level to treaty rights granted Japanese immigrants in 1911 (opponents argued the treaty did not refer specifically to agricultural land). The Japanese government also indicated a willingness, as an alternative, to stop permitting "PICTURE

BRIDES" to join their Japanese immigrant husbands in the United States. Yet even an unprecedented effort to discourage passage, made by sending Secretary of State William Jennings Bryan to meet in executive session with members of the California legislature, failed to dissuade supporters of the bill.

The immediate impact of this legislation proved minimal. Enforcement of the law was left to local authorities, many of whom looked the other way—especially during World War I, when foodstuffs were needed for the war effort. Most immigrants merely renegotiated their leases in light of the new three-year limitation. Others established corporate entities with majority ownership residing in the hands of (white) American citizens. Those with children (U.S. citizens by birth) transferred land property ownership to them, acting as legal guardians on their behalf.

The racist discrimination apparent in the original legislation, however, did not go unnoticed within the Japanese immigrant community. As a result many were further discouraged about their chances of ever being accepted into American society, even if only as resident aliens. Moreover, anti-Japanese activists redoubled their efforts when it became clear that the 1913 law had not had the desired effect. Ultimately they were successful in winning passage of the much more restrictive ALIEN LAND LAW OF 1920.

Alien Land Law of 1920: State statute resulting from a legal initiative undertaken by the citizens of California to deny agricultural land rights to Japanese "aliens ineligible to citizenship." The law, passed by a three-to-one majority vote in a statewide election, forbade land transfer by sale or lease to any noncitizen, either as an individual or as a partner in a corporate entity. It disallowed as well the establishment of guardianships by noncitizens in land tenure situations.

The Japanese immigrant community had been accused of violating an existing state statute in effect since 1913. In fact the new law sought to deal with such "abuses" by curtailing Japanese agricultural competition throughout California. Although the total percentage of land in Japanese hands had decreased as a part of the expanding acreage brought under cultivation since 1913, by 1919 fully 10 percent of California's agricultural output still came from Japanese-controlled acreage.

Following approval of the new law, Japanese Associations in the United States challenged the reformulation in court, contending that the measure contravened the "equal protection of the law" provisions of the Fourteenth Amendment and the "deprivation of rights" clauses in the CIVIL RIGHTS ACT OF 1870. In November, 1923, however, the U.S. Supreme Court, in a series of four related decisions, found the provisions of the new law constitutional, enacted under "state rights" privileges in the absence of any limiting treaty obligations to the contrary.

Passage of the California initiative had been preceded by a similar law in Arizona (1917) and was followed by measures enacted in Louisiana and Washington (1921), New Mexico (1922), Idaho, Montana, and Oregon (1923), and Kansas (1925). Measures were enacted in Wyoming, Arkansas, and Utah (1943) to discourage Japanese settlement following the dissolution of World War II RELOCATION CENTERS within their borders.

As a result of the tightening of the law, many Japanese immigrant landowners were reduced once again to laborer status; those who were able to remain independent farmers were often able to do so only by circumvention of the established legal code, leading to a feeling for many of being forced outside the law. Though some considered emigration from the United States to Mexico, Manchuria, or Brazil, most eventually remained in the United States despite the personal discouragement derived from their increasingly circumscribed place in American society as "aliens ineligible to citizenship."

California voters repealed all ALIEN LAND LAWS in 1956.

Alien Land Laws: Beginning in the second decade of the twentieth century, fifteen states enacted legislation to prevent Japanese immigrants from owning farmland. A majority of early Japanese immigrants were involved in agriculture, and some were notably successful. Most were tenant farmers rather than landowners, however, and only a very small percentage of agricultural land in California and the West was owned by Japanese. Nevertheless, the ANTI-JAPANESE MOVEMENT was able to exploit resentment caused by the modest success of hardworking Issei farmers.

Since it would not have been constitutional to target the Japanese specifically, the euphemistic term, "aliens ineligible to citizenship," was substituted instead. The phrase had been created by the federal government to categorize Asian immigrants, who had the unfortunate distinction of being the only group of aliens in American history that could not become naturalized citizens. As a result of the phrasing, legislation prompted by anti-Japanese sentiments affected all Asian immigrants.

California's Role. California was in the forefront of anti-Japanese activities, and legislation passed there had an impact throughout the United States. Attempts to pass an alien land bill in California began in 1907. Republican presidents Theodore Roosevelt and William Howard Taft, however, exercised pressure on California's Republican-controlled legislature, and these first attempts were unsuccessful.

The situation changed with the election of President Woodrow Wilson, a Democrat, in 1912. After a number of alien land bills were introduced into the 1913 session of the California legislature, Wilson sent Secretary of State William Jennings Bryan to Sacramento, hoping to head off such legislation, which could threaten U.S. relations with Japan. Wilson, however, lacked the leverage of his Republican predecessors.

Under the Alien Land Law enacted in May, 1913 (also known as the Webb-Heney Bill), immigrants who were eligible for citizenship held the same rights to land ownership as the native born. Aliens not eligible for citizenship and corporations in which the majority of the stock was owned by ineligible aliens had to comply with the land ownership provisions of any treaty existing between the countries involved. The U.S.-Japan Treaty of 1911 made no mention of any right of Japanese aliens to own land. The treaty did allow for land leasing for business or residential purposes, so a clause in the land law allowed for agricultural land leasing for three years. Another provision involved escheat and authorized the state to gain control of any land determined to be in violation of the law.

The initial effect of the 1913 law was not as significant as its supporters had hoped, as resourceful Japanese American farmers found many ways in which to circumvent it. As a result, the ANTI-JAPANESE MOVEMENT successfully campaigned for passage of a more severely restrictive law. The ALIEN LAND LAW OF 1920, passed by California voters in a statewide election by a three-to-one margin, prohibited transfer of land to noncitizens by sale or lease. The provision against leasing land to noncitizens was clearly aimed at Japanese Americans. The 1920 law also closed an important loophole in the 1913 law by preventing Issei parents from acting as the guardians of property held in the names of their underage American-born children. The 1920 law also established new criminal penalties for those aliens caught attempting to circumvent the 1913 law. If it was determined that an Asian immigrant provided the funds to purchase real estate in the name of another person, it was presumed that the sale

was done intentionally to get around the Alien Land Law. The purchase would be void and the land would belong to the state.

In an amendment passed in 1923, California legislated out sharecropping contracts with "aliens ineligible to citizenship." It also established the escheat as of the date of the land purchase instead of the date of the court judgment to prevent the Japanese from selling their property in the meantime. Likewise, a 1927 amendment required the expenses of proving citizenship in a land ownership dispute to be the responsibility of the individual involved and not the state.

Despite the punitive provisions of the Alien Land Laws, evasions were largely ignored. Between 1912 and 1946, only seventy-six escheat proceedings were filed in California under the Alien Land Laws, of which seventy-three were against Japanese, two against Chinese, and one against an Asian Indian.

In addition to California, other states enacting alien land laws included Arizona (1917); Washington, Texas, Louisiana (1921); New Mexico (1922); Oregon, Idaho, Montana (1923); Kansas (1925); Missouri (1939); Utah, Arkansas, Nebraska (1943); and Minnesota (1945).

Constitutionality. Eleven major cases involved Alien Land Laws, of which six were U.S. Supreme Court decisions. The constitutionality of the California Alien Land Laws was upheld in PORTERFIELD V. WEBB (1923); however, the landmark case is TERRACE V. THOMPSON (1923), which upheld the constitutionality of Washington's law.

Frank Terrace and his wife, both of whom were American citizens, were prevented under state law from leasing their farmland to a Japanese alien. The Court held that land ownership was a privilege and not a right so a state had a valid interest in controlling who could own and use land in a state. In addition, the classification by Congress of who was eligible for citizenship provided a reasonable standard for the state to use to determine who could enjoy the privilege of land ownership. Finally, the Court found that the U.S.-Japan Treaty of 1911 did not provide Japanese immigrants with the right to own or to lease farmland.

After World War II. Near the end of World War II, it was determined that the 1923 and 1927 amendments to the 1920 California law were invalid due to a procedural violation. Laws approved by voter initiative, as was the case with the 1920 law, could only be amended by another ballot proposition. A proposition to validate the two amendments was put to the voters in the 1946 election but was defeated.

Painting of Woodrow Wilson. Unwilling to compromise treaty rights granted to Japanese immigrants in 1911, he unsuccessfully opposed the bill. (White House Historical Society)

Next, in O*YAMA V. CALIFORNIA* (1948), the 1920 law itself was found unconstitutional. In this case, Issei parents had purchased farmland in the name of their American-born son, who was a minor at the time of purchase. Under the 1920 law, putting the land in the son's name was automatically presumed to be an intentional circumventing of the law. The court declared that because of the presumption clause, the son was being discriminated against solely due to his parent's nationality. It violated the equal protection clause of the Fourteenth Amendment.

In F*UJII SEI V. STATE OF CALIFORNIA* (1952), the California Supreme Court found the ALIEN LAND LAW OF 1913 unconstitutional. Fujii Sei, a Japanese alien, deliberately decided to challenge the legality of the California law after the *Oyama* verdict by purchasing farmland in his own name. Finally, in 1956, California voters repealed all Alien Land Laws.—*James Okutsu*

SUGGESTED READINGS: • Chuman, Frank F. *The Bamboo People: The Law and Japanese-Americans.* Del Mar, Calif.: Publisher's Inc., 1976. • Fukuda, Moritoshi. *Legal Problems of Japanese-Americans.* Tokyo: Keio Tsushin, 1980. • Ichihashi, Yamato. *Japanese in the United States.* Stanford, Calif.: Stanford University Press, 1932. Reprint. New York: Arno Press, 1969. • Ichioka, Yuji. *The Issei: The World of the First Generation of Japanese Immigrants, 1885-1924.* New York: Free Press, 1988. • Konvitz, Milton R. *The Alien and the Asiatic in American Law.* Ithaca, N.Y.: Cornell University Press, 1946. • McGovney, Dudley. "The Anti-Japanese Land Laws of California and Ten Other States." California Law Review 35 (1947): 7-54.

Aliens ineligible to citizenship: Statutory language used to deny the naturalization rights of Asian Americans. The NATURALIZATION ACT OF 1790 stated that only "free white" persons could become naturalized citizens of the United States. Federal laws of the post-Civil War period extended the right of naturalization to individuals of African descent. By using the racially neutral phrase "aliens ineligible to citizenship," fra-

For decades American naturalization laws prevented Japanese and other Asian immigrant families from securing U.S. citizenship. (City of Sacramento Archives)

mers of anti-Asian legislation masked their intent to target Asians. Under this guise, laws were passed denying Asian immigrants the right to own and lease land, the right to testify in court for or against white persons, and the right to immigrate to America. Naturalization status was challenged unsuccessfully by immigrants in the U.S. Supreme Court cases Ozawa v. United States (1922) and United States v. Bhagat Singh Thind (1923).

Allen, Horace Newton (Apr. 23, 1858, Delaware, Ohio—Dec. 11, 1932, Toledo, Ohio): Physician, missionary, and political appointee. Allen entered Korea in 1884 to serve as a physician to the American embassy in Seoul. He secured the gratitude and special favor of the Korean royal family after saving the life of one of the royal children. With King Kojong's approval, Allen established a hospital in Seoul in 1885. Unlike other missionaries whose primary focus was on preaching and direct conversion, Allen attempted to gain the confidence and friendship of the Korean people through education and medical assistance as a means to gain their conversion to Christianity.

Allen's continuing disagreements with fellow missionaries led him to resign from the Presbyterian Mission in 1887 and return to the United States, where he worked as a foreign secretary with the Korean embassy in Washington, D.C. Interested in the possibility of securing a diplomatic appointment from the U.S. government, Allen resigned his secretarial post and resumed his missionary work in Korea. In 1890, with the assistance of Ohio governor George Nash, who had personal and political ties to the McKinley Administration, he was appointed to serve as secretary for the U.S. embassy in Seoul. During his seven years in this post, Allen lobbied the Korean government on behalf of American entrepreneurs seeking franchises and business concessions—including rights to operate Korean gold mines—in Korea.

In 1897, Allen was appointed to serve as the U.S. minister to Korea. During his tenure, Allen visited Hawaii and spoke with representatives of the Hawaiian Sugar Planters' Association (HSPA) who were eager to import workers from Korea. Concealing his connection with the HSPA, Allen proposed the plan to the Korean emperor and secured his approval. Allen then contacted David W. Deshler, Nash's stepson, to serve as an intermediary between the HSPA and the newly established Korean emigration bureau. Some seven thousand Koreans emigrated to Hawaii between December, 1902, and May, 1905. Although Allen re-

ceived little direct benefit from this enterprise, he was able to repay his political debt to Nash by extending the emigration franchise to his stepson.

Aloha aina: Rural Hawaiians in the nineteenth century regarded the land and sea as the providers of everything necessary to sustain life and therefore felt toward them the same *aloha* (love) reserved for the *ohana* (extended family grouping). During the last two decades of the nineteenth century, when Hawaii's government was being taken over by the Americans, *aloha aina* came to symbolize loyalty to Hawaii. In the 1970's the movement to protect the island of Kahoolawe from continued bombing by the U.S. Navy was carried out in the name of traditional values, summed up as *aloha aina*.

Because *aloha* entails giving and sharing, *aloha* for the *aina* requires giving or returning something to the land by caring for it (*malama*), by beautifying it and using it properly. The particular land of one's birth provided a strong, positive sense of identity to rural Hawaiians because the ohana worked, lived, and stayed on the land, and the spirits of the beloved dead were believed to return to the land, leading some to speak of *aina* as a *piko* (umbilical cord), or link with previous generations. For urban Hawaiians, cut off from the *aina* and frequently dispossessed of land holdings, *aloha aina* reasserted their identity by claiming Hawaii as the land of their birth and their link to the past.

While some have claimed that *aloha aina* is a symbol "reinvented" by urban Hawaiians to further political goals, the attitudes upon which it is based clearly existed long before its use as a political symbol in the late 1900's, and probably prior to 1900 as well. After Hawaii became a U.S. state in 1959, and particularly after 1970, the concept came into greater use as tourism and development increasingly threatened the Hawaiian lifestyle. Various movements to protest the misuse of Hawaiian lands, the most determined and enduring of which was the movement to protect Kahoolawe, began almost simultaneously in both rural and urban areas. Since then, the concept has accompanied a deeper awareness and further interpretation of many aspects of Hawaiian tradition.

Amae: Japanese term that means to presume upon another's kindness. Positively defined, it reflects the individual's need to be loved and cherished by others. In a social context, if parents thought a child's misbehavior involved the need to be loved, they would not necessarily respond with anger. By contrast, if parents

The concept of amae *is a distinctive feature of Japanese and Japanese American culture, whether applied to the context of family relationships or that of personal relationships among friends.* (City of Sacramento Archives)

believed the behavior involved some other factor, they might spank the child. Some scholars have discussed *amae* in conjunction with another concept, *enryo* (exercise of restraint in personal relationships), in analyzing distinctive features of Japanese and Japanese American culture; see for example Harry H. L. KITANO, *Japanese Americans: The Evolution of a Subculture* (1969).

Amendment of 1884: Amendment to the 1882 CHINESE EXCLUSION ACT, which represented the first-ever attempt by the United States to single out a group on a racial basis and which suspended immigration of Chinese laborers for a period of ten years (extended by subsequent legislation). The amendment broadened the act by restricting immigration of "hucksters, peddlers, or those engaged in taking, drying, or otherwise preserving shell or other fish for home consumption or exportation."

Amerasia Bookstore and Gallery: Retail outlet established in Los Angeles in 1971 to serve the needs of the ASIAN AMERICAN MOVEMENT. The store houses a collection of Asian/Pacific American books and other materials and provides a forum for the public display and performance of works by Asian artists and artisans. Located in downtown Los Angeles, it began as a community enterprise and featured Asian American cultural, political, and literary publications unavailable in mainstream or corporate-owned bookstores. Despite financial difficulties since its inception, it moved from its original hole-in-the-wall location to the Little Tokyo Mall.

Amerasia Journal: Self-described "national interdisciplinary journal of scholarship, criticism, and literature on Asian and Pacific Americans," founded in 1971. Lowell Chun-Hoon, a Yale University senior from Hawaii, edited the first issue, which was published in March, 1971, by the Yale University Asian American Students Association. The journal then moved to the ASIAN AMERICAN STUDIES CENTER at the University of California, Los Angeles, where it continues to be published.

The journal's second editor, Megumi Dick Osumi, focused on civil-rights issues. Its third editor, Carolyn Yee, coedited an issue with Osumi on literature. Chun-Hoon, Osumi, and Yee later became lawyers. Russell LEONG, a poet who became editor in 1977, broadened the journal's perspective, emphasizing new areas of research, such as sexualities, and addressing the concerns of the Filipino, Pacific Islander, Korean, Vietnamese, Hmong, and other communities while continuing to encourage new studies of Chinese and Japanese Americans, the focus of most of the research in the field prior to the 1980's. The journal has played a significant part in the creation of a new field, ASIAN AMERICAN STUDIES, maintaining its links to its constituent communities while establishing its place in the academic world.

The journal's own index of its first thirteen volumes, compiled by Yen Le ESPIRITU, reflected its scope: The fifteen broad subject categories were Asian Americans and Asia, Asian American Studies, Culture, Education, Ethic Identity/Assimilation, Labor, Legal Issues, Legislation and Exclusion, New Immigrants and Refugees, Regional and Demographic Studies, Women, World War II and Japanese Americans, Literature and Criticism, Author/Books Reviewed, and Bibliographies.

Amerasia Journal was the first refereed, interdisciplinary publication in Asian American Studies. With its annual bibliographies, compiled in succession by Gary Y. OKIHIRO, John M. Liu, and Glenn OMATSU, it is an indispensable source for scholarly research, creative work, and activist essays, reflecting both the shared concerns and the diversity of Asian Pacific Americans.

Amerasian Homecoming Act of 1987: Act passed by the U.S. Congress allowing any eligible Amerasian (offspring of an American father and an Asian mother) in Vietnam to immigrate to the United States within a specific time period. By the end of 1993, more than 75,000 Amerasians and accompanying family members had arrived in the United States under this bill.

The act's stated purpose is to facilitate the departure from Vietnam and the arrival to the United States of any Vietnamese Amerasian born after January 1, 1962, and before January 1, 1977—in other words, those conceived during the involvement in Vietnam during the Vietnam War—as an immigrant eligible to receive U.S. government refugee benefits.

In its original form, the act allowed each Amerasian to bring only one branch of his or her family—for example, either his/her mother, stepfather, and unmarried half-siblings or his/her spouse and children. The total number of Amerasians and family members provided for in the original act was thirty thousand, and the original deadline for departure from Vietnam was March, 1990.

Soon after the act passed and Amerasians began to apply for immigration, it became clear that those who had sponsored the law had greatly underestimated the number of Amerasians in Vietnam, and that the original deadline for departure would be impossible to meet. Also, as Amerasians and their family members arrived in the United States and interacted with social service agencies, service providers called attention to the fact that most Amerasians were not "children" anymore and, in fact, many had children of their own. These providers suggested that forcing Amerasians to choose only some of the members of their immediate families to accompany them was a threat to their adjustment and to their mental health.

Eventually, two amendments to the act were passed: The first amendment extended the deadline to 1991; the second amendment (the Foreign Operations Bill, signed by President George Bush in November, 1990) extended the deadline indefinitely until all Amerasians who wish to immigrate to the United States have done so. The Foreign Operations Bill also allows Amerasians to bring all of their immediate family members, and those Amerasians who immigrated before the amendment was passed can retroactively bring over their family members who were left behind.

The passage and enactment of the Amerasian Homecoming Act has been important for many reasons. For one thing, it was the first cooperative effort between the United States and Vietnam since the United States severed diplomatic relations with Vietnam in 1975. The act is also significant in that it facilitated the first large-scale immigration of "abandoned" Amerasians and their family members to the United States (as opposed to Amerasians accompanying their American parents back to the United States, such as with the immigration of Asian "war brides," their Amerasian children, and their American military husbands).

While the act is seen by most as a progressive law, it does have flaws. The most frequent and long-standing criticism is that it "came too late," as most Amerasians were already in their late teens and early twenties by the time it was enacted. A second criticism is that it focused narrowly on the expedient emigration of Amerasians from Vietnam, with little regard given to the issues and costs of resettlement. A federal agency (the

Office of Refugee Resettlement, Department of Health and Human Services) has been in charge of providing funding for Amerasian resettlement, but some critics feel that a fiscal allocation for resettlement should have been written into the original act.

Finally, the act has been criticized for its vulnerability to misuse and exploitation by men and women who pose as family members of Amerasians as a means to immigrate to the United States.

American-born Chinese. *See* **ABC**

American-Born Confused Deshis (ABCDs): Term used half-humorously by South Asian Americans for members of the first generation born in the United States, who are sometimes perceived as being caught between the demands of their ancestral culture and the radically different assumptions of American society.

American Citizens for Justice (ACJ): Pan-Asian advocacy and civil rights organization founded in Detroit, Michigan, by Asian Americans to advance the grassroots movement known as "Justice for Vincent Chin." CHIN, a twenty-seven-year-old Chinese American, was severely beaten by two white men on June 19, 1982. According to eyewitnesses, Chin's killers were auto workers who thought he was Japanese and blamed him for their economic woes. After a state criminal court set Chin's killers free with probation and a fine, concerned Asian Americans in Detroit formed the ACJ and, supported by Asian Americans nationally, mobilized to demand a retrial. The organization staged rallies and protests locally, raised money for Chin's defense, and initiated a letter-writing campaign to U.S. Justice Department officials. Various other pan-Asian associations sprang up in major American cities and, guided by the ACJ, launched similar campaigns for justice. Through it all, the ACJ stressed repeatedly that what happened to Chin affected Asian Americans everywhere and that it was therefore vital for all of them to back the pan-Asian coalition and present a united front.

Eventually, the ACJ was able to persuade the Justice Department to prosecute both defendants under federal civil rights statutes. A U.S. district court convicted one of the defendants, only to be overturned on appeal. Following a Justice Department-ordered retrial, that defendant was acquitted of all charges.

American Civil Liberties Union (ACLU): Political and legal reform organization, established in 1920, that seeks to protect and defend the Constitution's Bill of Rights. Its goal is to ensure the individual rights and liberties within a democratic society of majority rule. Headquartered in New York, with fifty local and regional affiliates, the union consists of two related entities. The ACLU handles virtually all legislative lobbying; the ACLU Foundation handles legal work and conducts public education about fundamental rights.

The West Coast affiliates have been most active in cases and issues particularly affecting the Asian Pacific American community. During world War II the Northern California affiliate represented Fred T. KOREMATSU, who had refused to obey federal orders forcibly relocating Americans of Japanese descent into INTERNMENT CAMPS. That challenge, *Korematsu v. United States* (1942), headed by attorney and ACLU director Ernest Besig, failed.

The Northern California affiliate, in 1989, also joined in efforts to challenge a federal law that prohibited noncitizens from piloting fishing boats and thus threatened the livelihood of Vietnamese fishermen. Congress passed a bill the next year giving permanent residents the right to fish off the coast.

On a national level the group has been active in many areas affecting immigrants. In 1984 and 1985 its major immigration fight centered around opposition to the Simpson-Mazzoli immigration bill, which sought to impose employer sanctions against anyone who hired undocumented workers. Those provisions, argued the group, would add to the discriminatory impact on those—such as Asians and Latinos—who might be mistaken as an "illegal."

Nationally the ACLU opposed the "English Only" movement that would have placed restrictions on foreign language signs and limited use of other languages in the workplace. In 1984 it also challenged the U.S. attorney's decision to investigate people requesting bilingual election ballots; the organization argued that this act of intimidation could discourage people from voting. In 1992 the group worked successfully to persuade Congress to reauthorize the Voting Rights Act and to expand bilingual ballots.

Though its first cases focused on the right of laborers to organize unions and the right of dissenters to express antiwar opinions, the group is best known nationally for its zealous defense of the First Amendment right of free speech.

American Federation of Labor (AFL): A federation or formal coalition of various craft or trade union organizations in the United States, founded in 1886.

The AFL, which continues to function in the United States, is a large master organization of a wide variety of specific craft unions. Unlike its companion organization, the Congress of Industrial Organizations (CIO), which unionizes workers across an industry without regard to skill, the AFL unionizes only specific skilled and unskilled trades, such as carpenters, plumbers, and electricians. For this reason the AFL has always been regarded as the more "conservative" since it resembles the older traditions of "guilds" of artisans. Under the direction of its founder, Samuel Gompers, the AFL succeeded where the earlier union organization, The KNIGHTS OF LABOR, failed. The AFL preceded, and opposed, the later attempts to form large unions of working persons without regard to skill such as the International Workers of the World (IWW) and the CIO.

As was true of all nineteenth century labor organi-

Under Samuel Gompers, head of the American Federation of Labor, the push for unionization in America took a great leap forward. (AP/Wide World Photos)

zations, the AFL strenuously opposed allowing Chinese laborers to immigrate to the United States, believing that they would displace white workers and—because they were willing to work for lower wages—bring down the standard of living for all workers. More than one hundred years later, in the 1990's, the same arguments are being used to call for new restrictions on immigration.

In the intervening century, American unions rose to the peak of their influence and then, beginning in the 1970's, entered a period of decline. During this same period, following passage of the IMMIGRATION AND NATIONALITY ACT OF 1965, immigration—particularly from Asia—has skyrocketed. Many of these immigrants are nonunion workers. As a result, organized labor and Asian American labor activists are beginning to find common ground. In his article "Organizing Asian Pacific American Workers in the AFL-CIO: New Opportunities," in *AMERASIA JOURNAL* 18, no. 1 (1992): 141-148, Alex HING observes that "Unions are beginning to see that their very survival depends on a struggle against the 'third worldization' of minority community economies—and organizing the unorganized."

In the unions, as in other sectors of American life, Asian Americans are an increasingly significant presence. Hing cites a 1992 AFL-CIO survey which estimates that there are more than 200,000 Asian Pacific American union members. At last, as Hing writes, "The doors of the AFL-CIO have been pushed open to Asian Pacific Americans." (See ASIAN PACIFIC AMERICAN LABOR ALLIANCE.)

American Friends Service Committee (AFSC): Quaker social service agency. It provided financial aid for college to young Japanese Americans during the internment period of World War II. Through the AFSC program, approximately 4,300 individuals were allowed to leave the relocation camps and enter colleges and universities.

American Institute in Taiwan (AIT): The de facto embassy of the United States in Taiwan (officially the Republic of China, or ROC). The U.S. government severed formal diplomatic relations with the ROC and established them with the People's Republic of China on January 1, 1979. A few weeks later the United States founded the nongovernmental AIT in order to maintain unofficial relations with Taiwan. (See COORDINATION COUNCIL FOR NORTH AMERICAN AFFAIRS.)

Congress enacted the Taiwan Relations Act on April

10, 1979. The act authorizes the "continuation of commercial, cultural, and other relations between the people of the United States and the people on Taiwan." It stipulates that these unofficial relations will be carried out by the AIT, which was established on January 16, 1979. The AIT is a nonprofit organization funded by the U.S. government under the supervision of Congress. Its main office is in Washington, D.C. The Washington office serves as the channel of communication between the United States and Taiwan through the Coordination Council for North American Affairs (CCNAA), the unofficial embassy of Taiwan in the United States.

AIT offices have been established in Taipei and Kaohsiung, Taiwan's two major cities. These offices provide economic, trade, cultural, and tourist information about the United States. The AIT provides program guidance and administrative support to carry out activities on behalf of U.S. government agencies in Taiwan and administers a Chinese-language school in Taipei for the U.S. Department of State. The AIT also functions as a consulate and issues visas to people traveling to the United States for business or tourism.

American Loyalty League (ALL): Civil rights organization founded in Fresno, California, in 1923; its purpose was to provide a medium through which Americans of Japanese ancestry could more effectively participate in the mainstream of American society. The ALL was the predecessor of the JAPANESE AMERICAN CITIZENS LEAGUE (JACL), the only organization of its kind with a national network.

The name American Loyalty League was first applied to a San Francisco group organized in 1919 by several Americans of Japanese ancestry who were among the first Japanese born in the United States. Because of the many humiliating and painful experiences that these people endured as a result of political, economic, and social discrimination in the United States, they formed this group in an effort to educate the greater society that they were upstanding, loyal American citizens. The group, however, met only a few times and lapsed into inactivity.

In 1922, Thomas T. YATABE, one of the leaders of the San Francisco group, moved his dental practice to Fresno. Soon after his move, Yatabe was asked to attend a meeting in San Francisco to help revive the ALL. At that meeting, most of the Nisei delegates were teenagers inexperienced in organization, so no significant action was taken except to agree to meet again in early 1923.

At the 1923 meeting, delegates from nine or ten areas in California were present, and they agreed to organize ALL chapters in their respective regions. Although several chapters were formed, all except the Fresno one faded away for various reasons. The Fresno chapter, under the strong leadership of Yatabe, its first president, took advantage of every opportunity to be involved in the larger Fresno community and remained a viable organization. Yatabe helped to lay the groundwork for the formation of JACL, and when that was accomplished in 1930, the Fresno chapter became the ALL chapter of the JACL.

American Samoa: Eastern portion of the Samoa Island archipelago in the southwest Pacific Ocean. A territorial possession of the United States since 1900 (1904 for the Manua island group), it consists of the islands of Tutuila, Aunuu; the Manua islands of Ofu, Olosega, and Tau; and two distant atolls, Swains Island and Rose Island. In 1990 the territory's seventy-seven square miles of land contained a population of about 46,770, about 90 percent of which is Samoan. Caucasians (primarily Americans), other Polynesians, and Asians make up the remaining 10 percent.

The islands are volcanic in origin with limited level land area along the shore, rising steeply inland (except on the atolls). The climate is tropical, with average daily temperatures in the 80 degree Fahrenheit range and high rates of rainfall—as much as two hundred inches a year in Pago Pago harbor. This climate produces lush vegetation, flowering plants and trees, and Samoan dietary staples such as bananas, papaya, coconut, taro, and breadfruit. Villages are typically located near the shoreline.

From 1900 to 1951 the U.S. Navy administered American Samoa, with naval officers serving as governors. In 1951 the territory was placed under the jurisdiction of the U.S. Department of the Interior, with governors (Americans) appointed by the U.S president. Since 1977 American Samoans have elected their own governors. There is an elected legislature, and a nonvoting delegate in the U.S. Congress.

The main port is Pago Pago, located in Pago Pago Harbor, perhaps the best naturally protected harbor in the South Pacific. Within the bay area are the government center, retail stores, extensive dock facilities, and two tuna canneries, all of which are significant elements in the local economy. Wage-based employment has become standard in American Samoa, with very few modern Samoans relying on the traditional mode of subsistence—agriculture.

Samoan fire-walker relaxing between performances at the Polynesian Cultural Center on the Hawaiian island of Oahu. (Brigham Young University, Hawaii)

As U.S. nationals, American Samoans have free access to the United States. Since the 1950's, migration to Hawaii and the mainland United States by those seeking better education and economic opportunities or to join family members has been increasingly significant. Consequently large Samoan communities are found in Hawaii and in major metropolitan areas on the West Coast of the United States.

Americanization movement: Many-faceted effort to bring immigrants fully into the mainstream of American society. Beginning in the 1890's, reaching a peak during World War I, and ending as a movement around 1920, Americanization more broadly conceived has remained an ongoing theme in American life.

In his classic study *Strangers in the Land: Patterns of American Nativism, 1860-1925* (1955), John Higham describes the Americanization movement as "a conscious drive to hasten the assimilative process, to heat and stir the melting pot." As Higham observes, from the outset the movement contained contradictory impulses. On the one hand, it sprang from a growing consciousness of the miserable conditions in which many immigrants were forced to live and the exploitation to which they were routinely subjected. From this direction it was a reformist social welfare movement. On the other hand, the campaign for Americanization reflected fears that high levels of immigration might fragment American society; the proposed solution was to "Americanize" immigrants in a systematic fashion.

A Unique Process. In its strict sense, to Americanize simply means to naturalize as a citizen of the United States. The broader meaning of the term is to make American in character, manners, methods, or ideals. It is closely associated with such terms as Americanism and un-American (anything inconsistent with the institutions and ideals of the United States).

To become American does not essentially mean to acquire a particular language, dress, set of eating habits, or religion but to accept the abstract principles on which the United States political system is based. These doctrines are found in the country's founding documents: the Declaration of Independence, the Constitution, and the Bill of Rights. The primary elements of the creed are the beliefs that all human beings are created equal, that they are endowed with natural rights, including life, liberty, and the pursuit of happiness, that the purpose of government is to secure these rights, and that governments can only rule with the consent of the governed. The United States is unique in having a political credo, a national "I believe," adherence to which is the main qualification for citizenship. Thus citizens of the United States do not pledge allegiance to a homeland, or particular place, but to a republic, which promises liberty and justice for all.

The Americanization crusade, then, was primarily an educational program, carried out through adult extension courses, lectures and public meetings, pamphlets, and other media, as well as through pressure on the public school system. The core of the curriculum was the English language, American history, and American government, knowledge of which subjects was necessary for naturalization, but which was also intended to create a unified populace.

Wartime Hysteria. From its origins, as noted above, there was a dark undercurrent to the Americanization movement. Patriotic societies, Higham writes, "preached a loyalty that consisted essentially of submission. . . . The main object of such self-constituted champions of America was to combat the danger of

Particularly in the early decades of the twentieth century, Asian immigrants in the United States were targeted for assimilation into American life and culture. (Library of Congress)

immigrant radicalism or discontent; their chief motive, fear." Moreover, in seeking to make immigrants "100 percent Americanized," these civic crusaders sent the message—implicitly or explicitly—that being American meant giving up the cultural traditions of the homeland.

During World War I, this explosive combination of fear and cultural arrogance made Americanization a watchword, a truly national campaign. In Higham's words, the Americanizers "opened a frontal assault on foreign influence in American life. They set about to stampede immigrants into citizenship, into adoption of the English language, and into an unquestioning reverence for existing American institutions."

The Red Scare of 1919-1920 sustained the Americanization crusade after the war, but with the end of that false alarm and the beginning of an economic slump, the movement lost its impetus and much of its financial support. Many of the issues involved in the crusade, however, were still current in the 1990's, when immigration became the subject of sustained national debate for the first time in decades. For example, fears that multicultural education might lead to the "balkanization" of American society echo the concerns of the Americanizers in the first decades of the twentieth century. Indeed, while the Americanization movement petered out after 1920, Americanization more broadly understood—in the context, say, of assimilation—continues to draw on conflicting impulses in American society.

Asian Americans and Americanization. During the heyday of the Americanization movement, many nativists regarded Asian immigrants as too foreign to become fully assimilated Americans, and thus outside the scope of their campaign. Moreover, discriminatory legislation denied Asian immigrants the right to naturalize. At the same time, however, there was a growing population of Chinese Americans, Japanese Americans, and, in smaller numbers, other Asian Americans who had been born in the United States and thus were American citizens.

In the case of Asian Americans, then, the contradictions built into the Americanization movement were even more starkly apparent. In her pioneering book *Americanization, Acculturation, and Ethnic Identity: The Nisei Generation in Hawaii* (1994), Eileen Tamura shows how these contradictions played out in Hawaii, where—in contrast to the mainland—the movement was strong throughout the 1920's and continued up to World War II.

All Nisei who were born before 1924, and some who were born after that year, had dual citizenship; they were citizens both of Japan and of the United States. Thus, in addition to the usual pressures of Americanization, the Nisei had to deal with the question of whether to expatriate (that is, renounce their Japanese citizenship). In the case of Nisei born after 1924, Issei parents had to decide whether to register their children's birth at the Japanese consulate, Japanese citizenship no longer being automatic.

Such questions were distinctive to the Japanese American community of that time, yet they are relevant to the experience of Asian Americans as a whole. How, for example, do Vietnamese Americans born in the United States, the children of refugees in the aftermath of the Vietnam War, relate to their homeland in the 1990's, and how is that issue connected to their "Americanization"? By the same token, Tamura's larger discussion of the Nisei's desire to become fully American while retaining their ethnic identity is powerfully relevant to the concerns of a new generation of Asian immigrants and their children.—*Kenneth Holland and John Wilson*

SUGGESTED READINGS: • Berkson, Issac B. *Theories of Americanization: A Critical Study, with Special Reference to the Jewish Group.* 1920. Reprint. New York: Arno Press, 1969. • Hartmann, Edward George. *The Movement to Americanize the Immigrant.* 1948. Reprint. New York: AMS Press, 1967. • Higham, John. *Strangers in the Land: Patterns of American Nativism, 1860-1925.* New Brunswick, N.J.: Rutgers University Press, 1955. • Tamura, Eileen H. *Americanization, Acculturation, and Ethnic Identity: The Nisei Generation in Hawaii.* Urbana: University of Illinois Press, 1994.

Americans of Japanese ancestry (AJA): Term adopted by Japanese Americans in Hawaii during World War II, primarily as a means of defining themselves as true Americans. As the loyalty of Japanese Americans was being called into question, a number of islanders began to feel that terms such as "NISEI" and "Japanese American" implied that they were un-American or less than fully American. "Americans of Japanese ancestry," a widely accepted alternative, was used by Hawaii Nisei troops serving in the U.S. military during the war. Since then the popularity of the term has declined somewhat.

Amerika mura: Japanese phrase describing villages in Japan whose inhabitants included mostly those who had spent some time in America. Many of these towns

Numerous Japanese villages have benefited from money that villagers' children have earned in America and sent home. (Japan Air Lines)

were modernized with money sent back from villagers' children who had gone to live and work overseas.

Amidism: Worship by the Pure Land devotional sect of Buddha Amida, also known as Buddha Amitabha. The term "Amidism" was coined by Westerners and is based on the name "Amida," which originated as the coalescence of two Sanskrit terms for Buddha Amida: Amitayus (Immeasurable Life) and Amitabha (Immeasurable Light).

Amidism originated in India in the first century B.C.E., spread throughout China and Korea around the fourth century, and was brought by the ninth century to Japan, where it subsequently culminated in the Pure Land sects of Jodo and Jodo Shinshu (Shin Buddhism).

In contrast to monastic forms of Buddhism, such as Zen, the Pure Land tradition focuses on the salvific activities of Amida, the Buddha of Immeasurable Life and Immeasurable Light, whose Primal Vow, fulfilled timeless eons ago, ensures the salvation of all beings. The Primal Vow is especially directed to those who were excluded from traditional Buddhism (peasants and merchants, fishermen and hunters, unfrocked monks and nuns, and women of all classes), which was primarily monastic.

The compassionate working of Buddha Amida is concretely manifested in the Japanese invocation formula *namu Amida Butsu* (also called *nembutsu*). *Nembutsu* means "name that calls me," to awaken to the fundamental reality of life. Thus, the calling of *namu*

Buddhist monks. (Hazel Hankin)

An image of Buddha. (Library of Congress)

Amida Butsu comes from the source of Life and Light, and the human response in the saying of *namu Amida Butsu* enables a person to return to that selfsame source.

In ordinary language, this means that a person becomes truly human not by asserting his or her ego but by awakening to fundamental reality, so that the centripetal force of egocentric impulses is transformed into a centrifugal power of compassion.

Unlike most forms of Buddhism, which stress precepts, meditation, spiritual discipline, and merit accumulation, the Pure Land tradition is based solely on the compassionate working of Immeasurable Life and Immeasurable Light, actively engaging each person through nembutsu.

Amirthanayagam, Indran (b. Nov. 17, 1960, Colombo, Ceylon, now Sri Lanka): Poet and diplomat. Amirthanayagam's first book of poems, The Elephants of Reckoning (1993), was widely acclaimed. His poems are rooted in his experience, in Colombo and Jaffna, Sri Lanka, in London, Honolulu, and New York. The recipient of a 1993 New York Foundation for the Arts fellowship in poetry, he has a B.A. from Haverford College and an M.A. from Columbia University's Graduate School of Journalism. He has taught at the New School for Social Research in Manhattan. Amirthanayagam is now a diplomat with the U.S. Information Agency.

Amritsar: Holy city of the Sikh religion, located in the PUNJAB in northwestern India, some thirty miles from the Pakistani border. A commercial and manufacturing hub, particularly in textiles, Amritsar is also the production center of agricultural goods throughout the Punjab region.

Amritsar's religious significance, however, far outweighs any economic importance. Its name comes from Amrita Saras (the pool of immortality), which was built by the fourth Sikh guru, or teacher, Ram Das, in 1577. In the center of this square pool is located the Harimandir, or Golden Temple, which serves as the chief shrine of the Sikh faith. The temple is enclosed with a copper dome covered with gold foil.

Amritsar's Golden Temple was the depository for the holy book of the Sikh faith, the ADI GRANTH. Sikhs believe that the *Adi Granth* is the source of all truth and law, and thus through its scriptures the believer can obtain wisdom and peace. Sikhs also believe that by immersing oneself in the holy pool, one will be cleansed of sin, for the pool is filled with sacred waters.

The history of Amritsar over the past one hundred years reflects the turmoil in India. In 1919, it was the site of a massacre, by British-led troops, of four hundred Indian men, women, and children in the Jallianwala Bagh, an enclosed public garden, where the crowd had gathered to celebrate a religious festival. The British use of force had been in reaction to earlier Indian political agitation against repressive acts of the British government.

With the partition of British India in 1947 and the granting of independence to India and Pakistan, Amritsar was once more the scene of widespread violence and carnage. Master Tara Singh, the leader of the more militant Sikhs, attempted to establish a separate Sikh nation. This Sikh minority continued to seek independence through its political party, the Akali Dal. (See AKALI MOVEMENT.)

In 1984, a radical Sikh leader, Jarnail Singh Bhindranwale, and his followers seized control of the Golden Temple and fortified the Akal Takht, the chief center of religious authority for the Sikhs. They refused to leave the temple until the government granted the Sikhs an independent state. When the army moved in to suppress the uprising, a massacre resulted, and the temple's library of Sikh scriptures was desecrated. (See GOLDEN TEMPLE INCIDENT.) The incident and its aftermath galvanized support for the separatists. In the 1990's Amritsar remains a focal point for Sikh aspirations for an independent homeland.

Amur River Society. *See* **Kokuryukai**

Ancestor worship: Ancient Chinese practice of performing ritual services to deceased ancestors. This ancestral cult is still widely practiced among older generations of Chinese Americans in the United States. Although physically the family ancestors have expired, their spirits, which are believed after the person's death to be invested with power, continue to live. Yet these deified ancestral spirits depend on their kin for sacrifices, while the living descendants pray to heaven for blessings, prosperity, and good harvests through their ancestors.

Early records of the ancestral cult can be found in *Shih Ching (Book of Songs)* and *Shu-ching (Book of Documents)*, both edited and compiled by China's famous philosopher Confucius. Although Confucius was not interested in the dead, he included ancestral rites in his theories of *li* (rites), which was the foundation of basic social decorum.

The actual practices of ancestor worship can be explained in three main rituals: the funeral, the mourn-

The practice of ancestor worship involves three primary rituals, one of which is the funeral ceremony. Here mourners attend a traditional Chinese burial service in 1891 for a man named High Lee. (Library of Congress)

The ancient Chinese rite of ancestor worship can be traced to the ideas of Confucius. This twelfth century print depicts him playing a lute beneath a plum tree. (Library of Congress)

ing period, and the continuous sacrifices to the deceased. The richer the family, the more elaborate the funeral becomes. The eldest son and the eldest grandchild are the key performers of the ritual, while the rest of the household are also required to wear a special mourning garb. After the burial, a tablet bearing the name of the deceased is brought home and placed at the family altar next to other ancestral tablets. The burial site is always decided by a FENG SHUI man (a geomancer) for the prosperity of the descendants.

A mourning period for the dead is three years if the deceased is the head of the household or the ruler of the country. In the first year, the eldest son of the deceased lives in a cottage built next to the grave, sleeping on hay, eating coarse rice to survive, and wailing daily. A year later, he may eat fruits and vegetables. The mourner is allowed to go back to his career and other duties only after the mourning period has ended.

Continuous sacrifices to the deceased by one's relatives assure the family of blessings. At the cemetery or in front of the family altar, the whole family will gather together on special days and "talk" to the ancestral spirits, paying their respects.

Andersen, Patrick W. (b. Dec. 29, 1952, Long Beach, Calif.): Editor. As managing editor of *ASIAN WEEK*, a community-based newspaper in San Francisco, California, from 1982 to 1991, he capitalized on political, business, and artistic developments to bring Asian American news to mainstream America. A graduate of San Francisco State University, he authored early stories about homosexuals and AIDS in the Asian American community.

Angel Island Asian American Theatre Company (AIAATC): First professional Asian American theater company in the midwestern United States, established in Chicago in 1989. Led by founding president Christina Adachi, the company began producing works by David Henry HWANG (*FOB*, 1989), Gary Iwamoto (*Who Killed the Dragon Lady?*, 1990), and Dwight Okita (*The Salad Bowl Dance*, 1993). The AIAATC was also instrumental in focusing public attention on inequitable casting practices at the Goodman Theatre when that company neglected to utilize Asian American talent in its 1992 production of Bertolt Brecht's *Good Person of Setzuan*. As a result of these efforts, more Asian American actors were able to secure professional employment in the Chicago area.

Angel Island immigration station: From 1910 to 1940 immigrants seeking to enter the United States were processed in an immigration station established on Angel Island in San Francisco Bay. Since San Francisco was the principal port of entry for arrivals from the Far East, most Chinese immigrants to America during the period were detained and processed at Angel Island to determine their eligibility for entry under the CHINESE EXCLUSION ACTS. In addition to Chinese immigrants, whose experience at Angel Island has been most thoroughly documented, immigrants from other countries in Asia also came through this station.

Chinese Exclusion. During the exclusion era the majority of Chinese applying for entry claimed the right based on exempt class status, derivative citizenship status, or American birth. Usually Chinese immigrants did not have independent evidence and documentation to corroborate their claims. Thus the evidence was often confined to testimony offered by the applicant and his or her witnesses. For this reason immigration officials subjected Chinese arrivals to in-

Immigrant arrivals at Angel Island. (National Archives)

tensive detailed interrogations in order to ascertain the validity of this evidence by cross-examination and comparison of testimony on every matter that might reasonably tend to show whether or not the claim was valid. Under these guidelines the board of inquiry had great latitude in pursuing the interrogations. Over the years one of the persistent complaints of the Chinese concerned questions that went into minute details and apparently had no relevance to the objectives of the board.

During the late nineteenth and early twentieth centuries, Chinese arrivals at San Francisco were detained in a shed at the PACIFIC MAIL STEAMSHIP COMPANY wharf until immigration inspectors could rule on their admissibility. Up to four hundred or five hundred people could be crammed into the unsafe and unsanitary facility. Chinatown leaders addressed numerous complaints to U.S. officials, and in 1903 the Immigration Commissioner-General recommended that a new immigration station be constructed on Angel Island.

History of the Immigration Station. The new station opened in 1910. The government soon found that the facility was located too far from San Francisco to be convenient and that operating costs were high. The structures were fire hazards and were unsanitary. Nevertheless, the station continued to be used as a deten-

LIBRARY
COLBY-SAWYER COLLEGE
NEW LONDON, NH 03257

Japanese picture brides arriving at Angel Island. (National Archives)

tion facility for immigrants, mostly Chinese. During World War I it was also used to intern enemy aliens, and before 1925 it was also a temporary detention center for federal prisoners. The immigration facility was finally moved to San Francisco after a fire in 1940, but the detention and interrogation were not discontinued until the 1950's. Meanwhile the U.S. Army used the barracks to house Japanese prisoners of war during World War II.

Detention. When a ship arrived, passengers whose documents were deemed valid by immigration inspectors would be allowed to land immediately or within a few days. The rest, including most of the Chinese, were ferried to the Angel Island immigration station to await hearings and rulings on their applications for entry.

The immigrants were first given medical examinations. Because of poor health conditions in rural China, some immigrants were afflicted with parasitic diseases. The U.S. government classified certain of these ailments as dangerously contagious and loathsome and sought to use them as grounds for denial of admission. At one time or another the list included trachoma, hookworm and filariasis, and liver fluke. It was only after the Chinese made numerous protests that the authorities allowed some cases to stay for medical treatment.

After the examination the Chinese stayed in guarded, locked dormitories to await hearings. Men and women lived in separate communal rooms, each equipped with rows of single bunks arranged in two or three tiers. Typically there were two hundred to three hundred male and thirty to fifty female detainees at any one time.

A large percentage were new arrivals. Others might be returning residents whose documents were suspect. There might also be some whose entry had been denied and were awaiting decisions on their appeals or orders for their departure. Mixed among these were Chinese who had been arrested and sentenced to be deported, as well as transients traveling between China and neighboring countries such as Mexico and Cuba.

To forestall the passing of information to help the applicant at his or her hearing, no inmate could receive outside visitors before the case had been finalized. The authorities also opened and scrutinized mail to and from detainees as well as inspected and searched gift packages for coaching messages.

Angel Island Liberty Association. Male detainees organized an Angel Island Liberty Association around 1922. If the immigrants had complaints or requests, the association was the channel for negotiating with the authorities. The organization sometimes organized activities to ease the boredom of the confinement. It also was a link in a communications chain connecting the detainees to the Chinese community.

Chinese kitchen help on Angel Island, visiting San Francisco Chinatown on their days off, would pick up and smuggle coaching messages into the station. These were then transmitted through various subterfuges into the hands of the association's officers, who then passed them on to the addressees.

The Hearing. Sometime after a new immigrant's arrival, he or she would be summoned to a hearing to determine eligibility for entry. During the early years the waiting period between arrival and hearing could be months, but by the mid-1920's it averaged two or three weeks.

The hearing usually lasted two to three days. If the testimony of the witnesses largely corroborated that of the applicant, the immigration officials usually recommended admittance. If an unfavorable decision was handed down, then the applicant's family had the choice of allowing him or her to be deported or of appealing to higher authorities in Washington, D.C., or to the courts. Some immigrants had to languish under detention on Angel Island for as long as two years before final decisions were rendered on their appeals.

Poems on the Walls. The confinement was frustrating to many detainees. Some vented their frustrations by writing or carving Chinese poems on the walls as they awaited the immigration officers' rulings, results of appeals, or orders for their deportation. This was the inspiration for much of the poetry that covered the walls of the detention quarters at one time.

These poems, which were usually undated and anonymous, were written mostly before the 1930's. Running through many works were feelings of disillusionment, resentment, and bitterness at the immigrants' treatment. Other poems expressed the immigrants' worries about families they had left behind in China and also about their own uncertain future.

After a state park ranger, Alexander Weiss, rediscovered the poems in 1970, Asian Americans launched a lobbying effort to save and preserve the abandoned detention barracks, which were scheduled to be razed. Their efforts led the California legislature to appropriate $250,000 in 1976 for restoration work.—*Him Mark Lai*

SUGGESTED READINGS: • D'Emilio, Frances. "The Secret Hell of Angel Island: The Golden Gate Lost Its Lustre When Sweet Hopes Turned Sour." *American West* 21 (May/June, 1984): 44-51. • Lai, Him Mark. "Island of Immortals: Chinese Immigrants and the Angel Island Immigration Station." *California History* 57 (Spring, 1978): 88-103. • Lai, Him Mark, Genny Lim, and Judy Yung. *Island: Poetry and History of Chinese Immigrants on Angel Island, 1910-1940.* 1980. Reprint. Seattle: University of Washington Press, 1991. • Yu, Connie Young: "Rediscovered Voices: Chinese Immigrants and Angel Island." *Amerasia Journal* 4, no. 2 (1977): 123-139. • Yung, Judy. " 'A Bowlful of Tears': Chinese Women Immigrants on Angel Island." *Frontiers* 2, no. 2 (1977): 52-55.

Angell's Treaty (1880): Agreement that gave the United States the right to regulate or suspend, but not to exclude absolutely, the immigration of Chinese laborers to the United States. China in return obtained American assurances that Chinese living in the United States would receive protection for themselves and their property and would be allowed to travel in and out of the country freely. Representing the U.S. government in the negotiations was American jurist and historian James B. Angell. Ratification of the treaty meant that the free and open Chinese immigration stipulated by the BURLINGAME TREATY of 1868 was at an end.

Angkor Wat: Largest religious building in the world, located in the plain of Siem Reap in Cambodia. Built in the twelfth century under the reign of Khmer king Suryavarman II, it is the greatest single work of architecture in Southeast Asia.

Anglo-Japanese Alliance (1902): In the event of war with Russia, England and Japan formed an alliance that recognized England's interests in China and Japan's interests in Korea. While acknowledging Japan's growing determination to take over the Korean peninsula, this treaty had the effect of promoting the HAWAIIAN SUGAR PLANTERS' ASSOCIATION's (HSPA) Korean immigration project by influencing the U.S. government to support actively Korea's independence and to monitor Japan's expanding influence.

Animism: Belief or religion that attributes conscious life to nature as a whole or to inanimate objects. Such beliefs are widespread among most of the world's tribal or indigenous cultures.

Annexation Club: Lobby formed in Honolulu in 1892 by Lorrin Thurston and Henry E. Cooper in order to persuade the U.S. government to annex the Hawaiian Islands. Thurston himself visited Washington, D.C., to propose such a move. There he found an administration open to the idea. Returning to the islands, Thurston began organizing plans for annexation, such as staging a coup d'etat and influencing the state legislature. In 1893 most club members became part of the COMMITTEE OF SAFETY, which later that year overthrew the government of Queen LILIUOKALANI and established a provisional government.

Anti-Asian violence: Any physical force, harassment, intimidation, or threat of violence directed against people of Asian descent that is motivated on account of race, ancestry, or national origin is considered to be anti-Asian violence. This phrase was adopted in the 1980's when Asian American groups linked harassment and assault of Asians to racism and prejudice.

History. Anti-Asian violence is a contemporary concept, but there is nothing new about the phenomenon. Such bias-motivated assaults against Asian immigrants began with their arrival in North America. Discriminatory government laws and policies often accompanied and sanctioned such violence. Regardless of whether a single Asian ethnic group is targeted, all Asian Americans are affected because of the tendency to view Asians as one group.

During the anti-Chinese movement of the nineteenth century, the U.S. labor movement directed its anger over unemployment against immigrant Chinese laborers; lynch mobs beat and killed Chinese, burning and razing entire communities.

Other Asian nationalities immigrating to the United States met similar hostility. Filipino farmworkers faced frequent assault and violence during the Great Depression as white working-class resentment led to beatings, riots, and gunfire.

As Japan advanced its war machine, Japanese American farmers encountered a virulent "YELLOW PERIL" hysteria propagated through the media, which portrayed Japanese Americans as agents and spies. The images were so effective that in 1942 more than 110,000 Japanese Americans and aliens living on the American West Coast were rounded up, forced to abandon their homes, and incarcerated in remote RELOCATION CENTERS for the duration of World War II—simply because of their ancestry. By the war's end, the total number of Japanese interned in these camps at some point would surpass 120,000.

After the war in Vietnam, Southeast Asian immigrants, mostly refugees and former U.S. allies, endured constant attacks and assaults near their homes and schools. Vietnamese fishers living on the Texas coast were targets of Ku Klux Klan and other assailants. Sometimes entire communities of new immigrants were forced from their homes, as were several Hmong families in Philadelphia in the mid-1980's. The 1991 Persian Gulf War and its anti-Arab, anti-Muslim images resulted in violent attacks against South Asians, many of whom are Muslim.

During the 1980's, Korean shopkeepers, who have often established their businesses in poor, low-rent

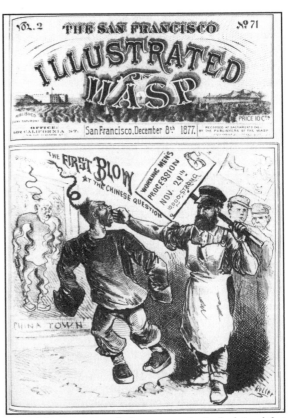

White laborers, many of whom were unionized, claimed that the Chinese were taking jobs from them. (Asian American Studies Library, University of California at Berkeley)

A Korean shopkeeper surveys the rubble of his southwest Los Angeles store the morning after it was burned by rioters in the wake of the acquittal. (AP/Wide World Photos)

areas, became the focal point of racial tension with other people of color, particularly African Americans. Highly visible boycotts of Korean stores have taken place in many major cities. Korean businesses were especially targeted in the LOS ANGELES RIOTS OF 1992 after four white police officers were acquitted in the beating of Rodney King; revenge for the killing of Latasha Harlins, a fifteen-year-old African American girl, by a Korean shopkeeper was often cited as a contributing cause for the targeting of Koreans during the riots.

With the upsurge of far-right white supremacist activity in the 1980's and 1990's, Asian immigrants have been blamed for domestic problems ranging from real estate valuation to deforestation. "English-only" movements of this period have also contributed to anti-Asian, anti-immigrant violence.

Causes of Anti-Asian Prejudice. Prejudice associated with anti-Asian violence is rooted in racism, xenophobia, and anti-immigrant attitudes that frequently have been part of U.S. attitudes toward "darker" people. Asian immigrants have been targets of anti-immigrant prejudice especially during periods of economic recession.

Patriotism and the use of racist stereotypes to dehumanize Asian "enemies" were also factors in the years following World War II and the wars in Korea and Vietnam. ANTI-JAPANESE prejudice was aroused during the decline of the U.S. manufacturing sector in the 1980's, when images of a Japanese "economic invasion" were often cited by business leaders, politicians, and the news media.

The MODEL MINORITY myth, which falsely depicts Asians as successful overachievers in contrast to other people of color and low-income groups, has added to the resentment against Asian Americans.

Violence against Asian women is rooted in prejudice based on both race and gender, factors that in turn give rise to specific stereotypes of Asian women as docile and exotic. Homophobia can also fuel anti-Asian sentiment when Asian lesbians and gays are the subjects of bias-motivated crimes.

Some Contemporary Incidents. Anti-Asian violence is much more common than one might conclude from routine news coverage. A report released in April, 1994, by the NATIONAL ASIAN PACIFIC AMERICAN LEGAL CONSORTIUM (NAPALC) documented the high incidence of hate crimes against Asians. The report found that thirty Asian Americans died in 1993 as a result of racially motivated assaults (a figure which includes cases in which anti-Asian bias was suspected but not proved). While such instances are the most terrible expressions of anti-Asian violence, it is important to remember that for every extreme case there are many lesser acts of violence and intimidation, the majority of them unreported, which nonetheless take a toll. The following list is representative of anti-Asian violence in the 1980's and 1990's, not comprehensive.

• June 19, 1982, Detroit, Michigan. Chinese American Vincent CHIN is beaten to death by two white autoworkers.

• January 30, 1985, Chapel Hill, North Carolina. Eight-year-old Chinese orphan Jean Har-Kew Fewel is found raped and murdered, hanging from a tree, one month after *Hustler* magazine published several pornographic photos depicting Asian women in various deathlike poses, including hanging from trees.

• September 15, 1987, Lowell, Massachusetts. Thirteen-year-old Cambodian American Vandy Phorng drowns after being struck in the face and thrown into a canal by an eleven-year-old white boy; the attack was preceded by racist name-calling.

• September 27, 1987, Jersey City, New Jersey. During a period of harassment by a group known as the "Dotbusters," whose avowed purpose was to rid the area of "Hindus," South Asian Navroze Mody is killed by a group of Latino teenagers.

• January 17, 1989, Stockton, California. Five Southeast Asian children die after a white man fires a machine gun at a large group of students in their STOCKTON SCHOOLYARD playground.

• July 29, 1989, Raleigh, North Carolina. Chinese American Jim Ming Hai Loo is killed by two white men.

Family and friends of Vincent Chin gather at his grave in 1992 on the tenth anniversary of his death. (Jim West)

At the funeral for six-year-old Thuy Tran, one of the victims of the Stockton schoolyard shootings, family members watch as the priest gives the blessing before interment. (AP/Wide World Photos)

• August 9, 1990, Houston, Texas. Vietnamese American high-school student Hung Truong is beaten to death by two white-power skinheads.

• October 26, 1991, Dallas, Texas. Gay Vietnamese American Thanh Nguyen and his lover are robbed and beaten by three men, then shot to death in a combined anti-Asian and gay-bashing incident.

• August 15, 1992, Coral Springs, Florida. Nineteen-year-old Luyen Phan Nguyen, a student at the University of Miami, is beaten to death at a party by a group of young men who shout racial slurs during the incident.

• August 14, 1993, Fall River, Massachusetts. Two Cambodian American men, Sam Nang Nhem and Sophy Soeng, are attacked by a group of white men yelling racial slurs; Soeng survives the beating, but Nhem dies of his injuries two days later.

• October 2, 1993, Sacramento, California. The office of the JAPANESE AMERICAN CITIZENS LEAGUE (JACL) is firebombed by a white supremacist group; three days later, the home of Asian American city councilman Jimmy Yee is bombed.

Responses to Anti-Asian Violence. As the NAPALC's 1994 report confirmed, law enforcement's response to anti-Asian violence has typically been weak, with police and prosecutors often unwilling to consider the possibility of bias-motivation in crimes committed against Asian Americans. Failure of the news media to recognize and cover such incidents has contributed to the lack of awareness. Too often, perpetrators of anti-Asian violence receive sentences that are not commensurate with their crimes; even more frequently, they are not even brought to trial.

In the Asian American community, this issue has been a rallying cry. The 1982 killing of CHIN and the resulting national campaign for justice led to the first federal civil rights prosecution involving an Asian American. It was the first time that racism against Asian Americans was raised as a national issue, with many diverse Asian American groups united in coalition. The case is documented in the film *Who Killed Vincent Chin?* (1988), by Christine CHOY and Renee TAJIMA.

Numerous Asian American organizations in the United States have taken up the issue of anti-Asian violence. In 1987 a coalition dedicated to this issue, the National Network Against Anti-Asian Violence, was formed; it is composed of local and national

Hate Crimes in the U.S. and Selected Cities, 1983-1991

Anti-Asian Hate Crimes, Selected Cities (% of all hate crimes)

Philadelphia, 1988: 20%

Los Angeles, 1980-1989: 15%

Boston, 1983-1987: 23%

New York City, 1988: 4%

Motivations for Hate Crimes Reported in U.S., 1991

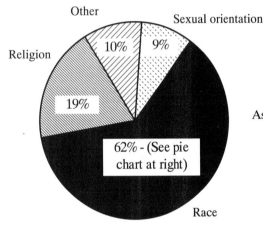

Race-Related Crimes by Ethnic Group

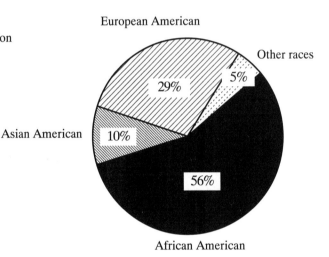

Sources: Susan B. Gall and Timothy L. Gall, eds. *Statistical Record of Asian Americans.* Detroit: Gale Research, Inc., 1993. U.S. Commission on Civil Rights, *Civil Rights Issues Facing Asian Americans in the 1990's,* 1992. *Note:* Data are from reports on hate crimes by police departments and human relations commissions.

groups such as the JACL and the ORGANIZATION OF CHINESE AMERICANS (OCA). Since its founding in 1993, the NAPALC has played an active role in monitoring anti-Asian violence and official responses to it. Yet resources to counter the increasingly widespread problem of anti-Asian violence are limited, and Asian American communities are often reluctant to confront racism or anti-Asian hate crimes that also involve sexual assault or gay bashing. Raising the visibility and understanding of such issues is one of the major challenges facing Asian Americans.—*Helen Zia*

SUGGESTED READINGS: • Conference on Anti-Asian Violence. *Break the Silence: A Conference on Anti-Asian Violence.* San Francisco: Break the Silence Coalition, 1986. • U.S. Commission on Civil Rights. *Civil Rights Issues Facing Asian Americans in the 1990s: A Report of the United States Commission on Civil Rights.* Washington, D.C.: Government Printing Office, 1992. • U.S. Commission on Civil Rights. *Recent Activities Against Citizens and Residents of Asian Descent.* Washington, D.C.: Government Printing Office, 1986. • *Who Killed Vincent Chin?* Filmmakers Library. 1988. Film/video. • Yun, Grace, ed. *A Look Beyond the Model Minority Image: Critical Issues in Asian America.* New York: Minority Rights Group, 1989.

Anti-Chinese movement: The anti-Chinese movement was a widespread reaction against the presence of the Chinese in the United States during the nineteenth century. Beginning in the 1850's, when they first arrived in large numbers, Chinese immigrants encountered prejudice and discrimination that were sometimes manifested in violence. Not until the 1870's, however, did they have to contend with sustained, organized opposition at local, state, and national levels. Ultimately, the anti-Chinese movement produced legislation that severely restricted Chinese immigration from the 1880's to the 1940's. The Chinese were the first group to be denied entry into the United States on the basis of ancestry or nationality.

Causes. The development of the anti-Chinese movement can be attributed to several factors. First, some Americans harbored unfavorable attitudes toward the Chinese and their civilization. They regarded China as a backward, decaying society characterized by poverty, superstition, corruption, and filth. They believed that immigrants from such an empire were not desirable and could not be assimilated into American society.

Second, the American West—where most nineteenth century Chinese immigrants settled—was a frontier region, lacking the legal and educational institutions long established in the eastern United States.

These conditions created an environment in which violence was common and widely accepted.

A third factor was the perception that the Chinese immigrants were depressing wages for white workers or depriving them of jobs. Samuel GOMPERS, the president of the AMERICAN FEDERATION OF LABOR, co-authored a pamphlet entitled *Some Reasons for Chinese Exclusion: Meat Versus Rice, American Manhood Against Coolieism—Which Shall Survive?* (1909). Gompers advocated exclusion of the Chinese from the United States, and he refused to permit them to join any chapter affiliated with his union. Other labor leaders and workers, along with their political allies, shared similar sentiments. These economic fears combined with prejudice and xenophobia to form an explosive mix. West Coast labor leaders seized upon the anti-Chinese theme as a catalyst to help them build a strong unionist movement.

A fourth cause was economic change in the West. The region was experiencing a dramatic transformation of the mining and transportation industries. Surface mining was exhausted, and it was increasingly

Anti-Chinese alarmists fueled widespread perceptions that cheap Chinese labor left few available prospects for white males in America. (Asian American Studies Library, University of California at Berkeley)

Both the Democratic and the Republican parties advocated Chinese exclusion from America during the latter half of the 1800's. (Asian American Studies Library, University of California at Berkeley)

difficult for individual prospectors to eke out a living. Individual mining was giving way to corporate mining throughout the West. At the same time, the completion of the transcontinental railroad (1869) connected the East and the West and led to the economic integration of the two regions. Eastern merchants, blessed with greater capital and economies of scale in production, began to compete directly with their Western counterparts. The railroad also brought laborers and immigrants from the Atlantic seaboard to compete for jobs. As prices and wages fell as a result of these changes, miners and laborers in the West sought scapegoats, and the Chinese became a convenient target.

Local, State, and Federal Actions. Fueled by prejudice, competition, and economic change, an extensive anti-Chinese movement emerged in the United States. It took the form of laws and statutes, immigration restrictions, and violent incidents. The legal measures alone were remarkably varied and detailed. The case of the city of San Francisco—the center of the early Chinese American community—illustrates the point.

In the 1870's, San Francisco passed a series of discriminatory ordinances designed to harass its Chinese population. The CUBIC AIR ORDINANCE, for example, required lodging houses to provide at least five hundred cubic feet of air space for each tenant. Most of the early Chinese immigrants were bachelors or men whose families had remained in China; they saved money by living in crowded quarters. This ordinance was clearly aimed at them. Refusing to pay the fine for failing to comply with the ordinance, many Chinese were jailed—so many that the jail itself violated the law. This prompted the Board of Supervisors to pass a QUEUE ORDINANCE, which specified that male prisoners must have their hair cut to within one inch of their scalp. This was a severe punishment that could jeopardize the immigrants' return to China, since a Chinese man without his queue (a kind of braid) was considered to be a rebel against the ruling Manchu Dynasty.

These local ordinances reflected strong anti-Chinese attitudes throughout California, the state in which Chinese immigrants were most numerous. (In 1870, 80 percent of the Chinese in the United States were living in California.) Exploiting this hostility toward the Chinese, Denis KEARNEY, a colorful sandlot orator, organized the WORKINGMEN'S PARTY OF CALIFORNIA in San Francisco in 1870 and molded it into a powerful political force. Although the Republican and Democratic parties in California already endorsed anti-Chinese positions, Kearney captured the public's attention by coining the slogan "The Chinese Must Go!" The Workingmen's Party grew quickly, with branches in Oakland, Sacramento, and Los Angeles.

In 1879, when California organized a convention to revise its state constitution, the Workingmen's Party was able to influence the outcome. Article Nineteen of the Second California Constitution dealt with the "Chinese or Mongolian" issue. Section Three of this article stated that no corporation formed in California should employ Chinese, under penalty of a fine, imprisonment, or both. Section Four said that Chinese were not to be employed by any unit of the state, county, or municipal government, except as punishment for a crime.

At the same time, politicians and pressure groups in California attempted to prohibit further Chinese immigration. As early as 1858, California had passed a measure forbidding Chinese from entering the state. Such measures, however, had been dismissed as unconstitutional, with the courts ruling that immigration policy was a matter reserved for the federal government. As a result, the arena shifted from state legislatures to the U.S. Congress. Throughout the 1870's, congressmen and senators from California and other Western states pressed for exclusionary legislation against the Chinese.

Exclusion. These efforts led to the passage of the CHINESE EXCLUSION ACT OF 1882, which stipulated that Chinese laborers would be denied entry into the United States for ten years. Certain groups of Chinese, such as educators, students, and businesspeople, could still be admitted. Subsequent legislation, however, steadily tightened the restrictions, culminating in the IMMIGRATION ACT OF 1924, which made the ban on Chinese immigration virtually complete.

The passage of the Chinese Exclusion Act did not curb hostility and prejudice against the Chinese. In 1885, an ANTI-CHINESE RIOT in ROCK SPRINGS, Wyoming, left twenty-eight Chinese dead and fifteen wounded, and compulsory deportations took place in Seattle and Tacoma, Washington, and Portland, Oregon, during 1885 and 1886. Anti-Chinese attitudes also took the form of school segregation in San Francisco and Mississippi, antimiscegenation laws, and discriminatory quarantine practices at the ANGEL ISLAND IMMIGRATION STATION.

The Chinese were not passive victims. They lodged protests and even hired lawyers to engage in court challenges. Although there were some victories, their efforts often were to no avail. Many Chinese Americans were relegated to marginal status in the period before World War II, living in the shadow of exclusion and discrimination. Not until China and the United States became allies against Japan would exclusion be ended, in 1943.—*Franklin Ng*

SUGGESTED READINGS: • Miller, Stuart C. *The Unwelcome Immigrant: The American Image of the Chinese, 1752-1882.* Berkeley: University of California Press, 1969. • Sandmeyer, Elmer C. *The Anti-Chinese Movement in California.* Urbana: University of Illinois Press, 1939. • Saxton, Alexander. *The Indispensable*

Enemy: Labor and the Anti-Chinese Movement in California. Berkeley: University of California Press, 1971. • Wu, Cheng-Tsu, ed. *"Chink!": A Documentary History of Anti-Chinese Prejudice in America.* New York: World, 1972.

Anti-Chinese riots: Anti-Chinese riots, violence, protests, and expulsions periodically occurred in California and the Western United States during the ANTI-CHINESE MOVEMENT of the late nineteenth century. The movement and its accompanying violence began among white miners in California during the 1850's, spread to white laborers and others in San Francisco in the 1860's, and eventually reached throughout the Western states.

The first major wave of anti-Chinese violence broke out in California during a mining depression in the late 1850's. Hurt by the depression and resentful of competition from Chinese miners, white miners rioted and attempted expulsion of the Chinese from more than a dozen small mining communities such as Sacramento

Artist's rendering of an outbreak of anti-Chinese mob violence in Denver, Colorado. (Library of Congress)

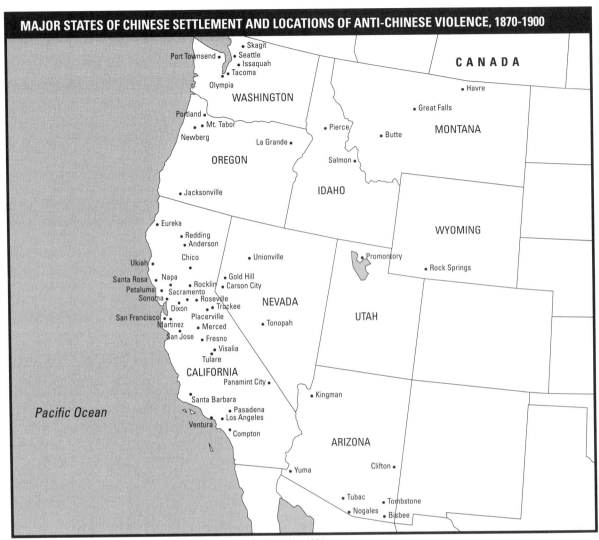

MAJOR STATES OF CHINESE SETTLEMENT AND LOCATIONS OF ANTI-CHINESE VIOLENCE, 1870-1900

Source: John Wilson, *Chinese Americans.* Vero Beach, Fla.: Rourke, 1991

Bar, Coyote Flat, and Rock Creek.

The next wave of anti-Chinese violence hit California during the depression of the late 1870's. Riots, robberies, murders, and expulsions rocked the countryside between 1876 and 1880, while San Francisco, with its swelling population of unemployed white laborers, exploded with anti-Chinese riots in the summer of 1877. Bands of white youths roamed San Francisco, robbing and beating Chinese, stoning incoming immigrants, and burning buildings. In addition to the violence, inflammatory rhetoric condemned the Chinese presence and demanded expulsion. In response, the U.S. Congress curtailed Chinese immigration with the passage of the CHINESE EXCLUSION ACT OF 1882, the first of a series of discriminatory acts culminating in the IMMIGRATION ACT OF 1924.

Despite the passage of immigration restrictions, however, another wave of anti-Chinese violence hit in 1885. It was triggered by the brutal expulsion of the Chinese from Rock Springs, Wyoming, where twenty-eight Chinese were killed and fifteen were wounded. (See ROCK SPRINGS RIOT.) The violence spread rapidly throughout California and the Pacific Northwest, resulting in riots, protests, and expulsions in Seattle, Tacoma, and several smaller communities. As before, deep-seated anti-Chinese sentiment, coupled with an economic downturn, contributed to this 1885 outbreak.

Finally, during the depression of 1893, an outbreak of anti-Chinese riots and violence struck fruit-growing areas in California, where unemployed whites agitated for the jobs of the Chinese migrant farmworkers. By 1900, with the shift of Chinese immigrants from rural areas and small towns to urban centers and significant economic and demographic changes in California and the West, the waves of mass violence receded, although Chinese Americans continued to be the victims of discrimination and sporadic acts of violence.

Anticommunism among refugees: Much of the twentieth century's refugee flight has been away from newly established communist governments. This has been particularly true in the case of refugees from China, Eastern Europe, Cuba, and the Indochinese countries of Vietnam, Laos, and Cambodia. All these refugees were fleeing the incarceration, persecution, and social upheavals that followed communist revolutions in those countries. Large numbers of refugees fleeing communism in Cuba and Indochina have been resettled in the United States.

Since the refugees from Indochina were fleeing successful communist revolutions, anticommunism inevitably has played an important role in their political perspective. The refugees blame communists for causing them to abandon their homes in the first place.

While most refugees are firmly anticommunist in their views, however, this does not mean that they form more than a loose political coalition relative to this or any other issue. This is because the ways that communist revolutions developed in Laos, Cambodia, and Vietnam were different. As a result, the groups singled out for persecution varied from country to country. How this happened in each of the three Indochinese countries is summarized below.

Vietnam. In 1975, the United States evacuated more than one hundred thousand Vietnamese from Saigon (HO CHI MINH CITY). These refugees had, by and large, close ties to the fallen South Vietnamese government and were, as a result, firmly anticommunist in their views. These people were "anticipatory refugees," meaning that they left as the communist government took power, anticipating that their positions in the old government put them at risk of persecution. Relative to later waves of Vietnamese refugees, the anticipatory refugees of 1975 were better educated, were more likely to be ethnic Vietnamese, and were more sophisticated in their political views; they also often had strong connections in the American and South Vietnamese governments.

Beginning in 1978, a second wave of Vietnamese refugees left their country. These were the BOAT PEOPLE who had decided to stay in Vietnam after 1975 despite the threat presented by the new communist government. Some of these refugees had peasant ori-

gins, and others were ethnic Chinese shop owners from urban areas. Individuals from neither group necessarily had close relationships to the defeated South Vietnamese government. As a result, unlike those of the anticipatory refugees, their anticommunist views were often shaped by firsthand experience with communist authorities. One experience often cited by refugees is the corruption of communist officials, who had to be bribed in order to facilitate escape. In the case of ethnic Chinese, anticommunist attitudes were often shaped by the seizure (nationalization) of businesses, relocation to rural "New Economic Zones" where conditions were hard, and requirements that Chinese citizenship be renounced.

The anticommunism of none of the Vietnamese groups has been channeled into active anticommunist military resistance movements to the extent of the Hmong from Laos or the Cambodian resistance groups established along the Thai-Cambodian border. This is probably in part because of the absence of a land border from

Among the more eminent Vietnamese evacuees was Nguyen Cao Ky, former South Vietnamese premier. He eventually settled in the fishing village of Dulac, Louisiana, where he operated a shrimp-processing plant. (AP/Wide World Photos)

which to establish camps and not because of an absence of anticommunist fevor. Vietnamese American groups in the United States have actively organized groups to assist fleeing refugees with political and humanitarian support.

Laos. Two major ethnic groups from Laos have become refugees: the ethnic Lao and the Hmong. Each refugee group had a different relationship relative to the victorious communists and their communist Vietnamese allies. As a result, while individuals from each refugee group were anticommunist, their view were shaped by different experiences.

The ethnic Lao are the largest ethnic group in Laos and have traditionally controlled the government, whether communist or not. After the fall of Laos in 1975, the ethnic Lao who had worked for the old rightist government stayed in Laos in the hope that an amicable agreement could be reached with the victors. Notably, this was different than either the Vietnamese or the Hmong experience. Despite this trust, however, deportations to internal "reeducation camps" of many

former rightist government members began in about 1977. The result was that large numbers of ethnic Lao fled to Thailand in 1978-1982.

Typically, these ethnic Lao refugees focus their anticommunism on the cruelties they suffered or feared in the reeducation camps. Sometimes they blame not only the communist Lao for the harshness of conditions but also the occupying Vietnamese army, which had been allied with the communist victors.

The Hmong relationship to the communist victors was different from that of the ethnic Lao. The Hmong forces allied with the defeated rightist government did not seek accommodation with the new government in 1975. Rather, a large group of anticipatory refugees associated with the Hmong general VANG PAO retreated into Thailand. Another portion of this Hmong group remained in Laos. This group was attacked by communist forces during the late 1970's, and defeats resulted in the flight of more Hmong to Thailand during the 1970's and 1980's. In referring to their anticommunist beliefs, Hmong often refer to these attacks.

A Laotian refugee sharpens his English skills at a learning center in Merced, California. (L. Gubb/UNHCR)

General Vang Pao in a photograph from 1972. (AP/Wide World Photos)

Anticommunism among Hmong refugees is, as a result, also focused on formal groups of fighters, some of which are funded from Hmong in the United States. The best known of these groups include the Chao Fa (sky soldiers), who operated along the Thai-Lao border in the 1980's. The Neo Hom (United Lao National Liberation Front) was a Hmong agency founded in the United States by General Vang Pao to collect money in support of resistance activities. It is not clear, though, how much support this group was able to provide to soldiers fighting in Laos.

Cambodia. Cambodia was occupied first by the communist Khmer Rouge government (1975-1978) and subsequently by the Vietnamese-backed communist government of Hun Sen. The result was a refugee flight from Cambodia during the chaos caused by the change in governments in 1979 and the reestablishment of the communist Khmer Rouge as a major force on the Thai-Cambodian border. As a result, anticommunist efforts among Khmer refugees has focused on two separate communist governments.

Unifying anticommunist feelings among Cambo-

dian refugees are two resistance groups that, during the 1980's, were found on the Thai-Cambodian border. One has been headed by Prince Nordom Sihanouk, a member of the Cambodian royal family who was premier from 1953 to 1970. The second group was loyal to Son Sann, a man who had been a cabinet minister for Prince Sihanouk before splitting with him in the 1960's. Both leaders established their groups with the support of the Thai and Western governments that wanted to support an alternative to the communist groups. Notably, though, these groups were not founded on a specific anticommunist ideology, but one of Khmer nationalism. This was particularly true for the group associated with Prince Sihanouk, who, himself, had briefly formed an alliance of convenience with the Khmer Rouge in the 1970's.

Until the late 1980's, though, less support for these groups was found among Cambodian refugees than for the communist Khmer Rouge. Indeed, outside Thailand, including in the United States, Cambodian refugee response to anticommunism has been much less organized than in the case of Laos or Vietnam.

Nevertheless, in the case of Prince Sihanouk, heading this nationalist group has proved to be an effective strategy. As a result, in 1991 he was appointed the interim leader of Cambodia in the government sponsored by the United Nations.—*Tony Waters*

Suggested Readings: • Garrett, W. E. "Thailand: Refuge from Terror." *National Geographic Magazine* 157 (May, 1980): 633-642. • Hammond, Ruth E. "Sad Suspicions of a Refugee Rip-off: The Hmong Are Paying to Free Laos—but What's Happening to the Money (Contributions to the Neo Hom)?" *The Washington Post*, April 16, 1991, p. B1. • Hitchcox, Linda. "Why They Had to Leave." In *Vietnamese Refugees in Southeast Asian Camps.* Oxford, England: St. Antony's College, 1990. • Pedraza-Bailey, Silvia. "The Function of Political Migration." In *Political and Economic Migrants in America: Cubans and Mexicans.* Austin: University of Texas Press, 1985. • Shawcross, William. *The Quality of Mercy: Cambodia, Holocaust, and Modern Conscience.* New York: Simon & Schuster, 1984.

Anti-Filipino violence: Racially motivated riots and assaults directed against Filipino agricultural laborers. They occurred in the late 1920's and early 1930's, especially in Northern California but also in Washington, Oregon, and Florida.

The primary cause of these race riots was the antagonism toward Filipino farmworkers, who were accused of displacing white labor and lowering wages and working conditions. This violence was also part of a larger political movement to exclude Filipinos from further immigration to the United States, led by organized labor and conservative groups in California. Exclusion proponents maintained, largely for racist reasons, that Filipinos represented unfair competition to white labor and were socially undesirable and unassimilable.

The first anti-Filipino riot occurred in EXETER, California, on October 24, 1929, when about three hundred white men stoned a labor camp of some fifty Filipinos and drove out more than two hundred of them from the area. This violence was attributed to the hostility engendered among white laborers who had been displaced by Filipinos in the harvesting of grapes and figs.

Another factor in the attacks on Filipinos in California was resentment of their relationships with white women. On January 19, 1930, in WATSONVILLE, a four-day riot began when some one hundred fifty white youths assaulted the Filipino patrons of a dance hall that a Filipino social club had leased to hold taxi dances. The youths were apparently angered that white women had been hired as the dance partners of the club members. On the fourth day, the violence escalated into destruction of the dwellings of Filipinos and attacks on them by a mob of five hundred to seven hundred white rioters, which resulted in the death of a Filipino farmworker. Several comparatively minor fights between Filipinos and whites in San Jose and San Francisco immediately followed the Watsonville riot. Then on January 28, 1930, a Filipino clubhouse in Stockton was bombed, although none of the sleeping occupants was seriously hurt.

Anti-Japanese Laundry League: White-supremacist organization formed around 1905. Composed mainly of white laborers who harbored resentment about Japanese immigrant competition in the laundry business, the group formed in San Francisco and supported the ASIATIC EXCLUSION LEAGUE, which called for a denial of citizenship, immigration, and economic and civil rights to Japanese Americans. In one instance, the organization collected money from white laundry drivers and owners to promote a boycott of Japanese laundries.

Anti-Japanese movement: The anti-Japanese movement was a continuation of the anti-Asian prejudice and discrimination first directed against the Chinese in the United States. Japanese immigrants arrived in small numbers in the 1890's, and it was not until the 1900's that organized opposition formed against them. A wide range of organizations and groups formed coalitions to agitate for laws restricting the rights of Japanese immigrants and their children at the local, state, and federal levels. The movement was successful in influencing the passage of anti-Japanese legislation beginning in the 1900's, peaking in the 1920's with the exclusion of Japanese immigrants from the United States in 1924.

Causes. The development of the anti-Japanese movement was the result of a number of factors. First, Americans held prejudicial attitudes toward the Japanese. The anti-Japanese movement first started in San Francisco, the base for the ANTI-CHINESE MOVEMENT. While there were isolated anti-Japanese activities in the 1890's and early 1900's on the West Coast, beginning in 1905 influential newspapers, labor leaders, and politicians took active leadership in the anti-Japanese movement. As early as May 7, 1900, in the first mass protest in California, such politicians as James D. PHELAN, the mayor of San Francisco, argued that the Japanese and the Chinese made inferior citizens and could not assimilate as Americans.

In 1905 the *San Francisco Chronicle* publicized the RUSSO-JAPANESE WAR, declaring that the Japanese were "no more assimilable than the Chinese" and that they threatened to displace white workers by working for lower wages. Beginning on December 20, 1906, the HEARST newspaper the *San Francisco Examiner* initiated an anti-Japanese stance that would span four decades. The *Examiner* adapted the Chinese stereotypes of invasion and added a new concept, that the Japanese coming into the United States were not immigrants but an advance army in disguise. For the next ten years Americans believed that a war was about to break out between the United States and Japan despite a lack of supporting evidence. Writers such as H. G. Wells and Homer LEA, legislators such as Richmond Pearson Hobson and James D. Phelan, and V. S. McCLATCHY, publisher of *The Sacramento Bee*, wrote much-publicized books and articles that warned against a "YELLOW PERIL" and an imminent invasion of the United States by Japan.

A second factor was the perception that the Japanese were unfair economic competitors. From the 1890's to the 1900's the Japanese filled a need for migrant laborers, but they were quickly disliked as they organized to raise the wages of farmworkers. Japanese immigrants began to purchase and lease land. The real issue be-

Using his newspaper, the widely circulated San Francisco Examiner, *as his mouthpiece, publisher William Randolph Hearst stoked the fires of anti-Japanese hysteria and lobbied for exclusion.* (AP/Wide World Photos)

came one of whether or not the Japanese could become farmers in their own right.

The third factor was political. Politicians, regardless of party lines, supported the anti-Japanese movement. Among political activists who were opposed to the immigration of the Japanese were California governors Hiram W. Johnson and William D. Stephens, who were progressive Republicans; Chester Harvey Rowell, a progressive; the Socialist Jack LONDON; and James D. Phelan, a progressive Democrat. In California, from 1906 to 1914, state Republicans had to mute support for the anti-Japanese movement because of pressure from the Republican federal administration and concern that anti-Japanese agitation would harm treaty relationships between Japan and the United States.

Local, State, and Federal Actions. Japanese immigrants were denied the right to become naturalized citizens. Naturalization rights were not available to all immigrants. The first NATURALIZATION ACT was passed in 1790, specifying that only free white persons were eligible to become citizens. African Americans became citizens in 1870. In 1922 the U.S. Supreme Court ruled that Japanese immigrants were not eligible

for citizenship in the United States.

Japanese children were sent to segregated schools in a number of towns in California. The attempt by the San Francisco School Board, however, to segregate Japanese children in the San Francisco schools after the 1906 San Francisco earthquake brought immediate coverage by the newspapers in Japan and an investigation initiated by President Theodore Roosevelt. The Japanese ambassador maintained that the Treaty of 1894 provided the right of Japanese students to attend public schools without being segregated. Japan had achieved international status after defeating Russia in the RUSSO-JAPANESE WAR (1904-1905). Roosevelt was concerned that the incident would harm international relations between the United States and Japan. By the early part of 1907 Roosevelt had negotiated an agreement with the San Francisco School Board and California politicians. In exchange for revoking the segregation order and the tabling of anti-Japanese legislation, Roosevelt would work toward the exclusion of Japanese laborers to the United States and drop a judicial challenge to the school board order.

In 1913 the California legislature passed the ALIEN LAND LAW, which prevented Japanese immigrants from purchasing land and obtaining leases for more than three years on the basis that they were aliens ineligible for citizenship.

In 1920 efforts by four major anti-Japanese groups crystallized in a state initiative placed on the ballot to fortify the 1913 Alien Land Law. A number of Japanese immigrants had purchased farmland in their children's names and thus avoided the restrictions of the 1913 law.

Novelist Jack London, a socialist, staunchly opposed Japanese immigration to America. (AP/Wide World Photos)

One of the most powerful lobbying groups in California, the Native Sons of the Golden West, a nativist group, for the first three decades of the twentieth century believed that the Japanese should be segregated. Unlike the nativist group, the American Legion was a relatively new organization, established in 1919. The national policies of the American Legion included the exclusion of Japanese immigrants and the denial of citizenship of the Nisei. The third group supporting the anti-Japanese movement in the 1920's was organized labor, although labor at that time was not in economic competition with the Japanese. The fourth group, the farmers, opposed the Japanese as independent farmers and as laborers for Japanese farmers.

Immigrant Japanese women laborers often worked alongside their husbands on the plantations of Hawaii. (Hawaii State Archives)

A final push from the anti-Japanese forces came from the state government itself. In 1920 the State Board of Control issued the results of a study of Japanese land use, *California and the Oriental*. The report was meant to convince Californians to vote for the 1920 Alien Land Law, which would prevent Japanese immigrants from serving as guardians of their children who held title to property and would have prevented the immigrants from holding a majority interest in landholdings. The initiative was overwhelmingly passed on December 2, 1920.

Restrictions on Immigration. On March 14, 1907, Roosevelt issued an executive order that prevented the immigration of Japanese from Hawaii, Mexico, and Canada. In 1907 the Gentlemen's Agreement between Japan and the United States established that Japan would no longer issue visas to laborers bound for the United States. Congress passed the Immigration Act of 1924, which established quotas on immi-gration based upon national origins but in a separate section eliminated immigration for those ineligible for citizenship. In effect, Japanese were excluded from immigrating to the United States. By 1924 the anti-Japanese groups that had formed a coalition in the form of the California Oriental Exclusion League had achieved five out of the six goals stated in 1919: passage of restrictive Alien Land Laws, annulment of the 1907 Gentlemen's Agreement, the prohibition of picture brides, the exclusion of Japanese immigrants, and the denial of citizenship to Asians. Efforts to achieve the sixth goal, the removal of the citizenship rights of Nisei, although ultimately unsuccessful, were to be sustained up through the 1940's.—*Alexander Y. Yamato*

Suggested Readings: • Chuman, Frank F. *The Bamboo People: The Law and Japanese-Americans.* Del Mar, Calif.: Publisher's Inc., 1976. • Daniels, Roger. *Asian America: Chinese and Japanese in the United States Since 1850.* Seattle: University of Washington Press, 1988. • Daniels, Roger. *The Politics of Prejudice: The Anti-Japanese Movement in California and the Struggle for Japanese Exclusion.* 1962. 2d ed. Berkeley: University of California Press, 1978. • Herman, Masako. *The Japanese in America: 1843-1973.* Dobbs Ferry, N.Y.: Oceana Publications, 1974. • Ichioka, Yuji. *The Issei: The World of the First Generation Japanese Immigrants, 1885-1924.* New York: Free Press, 1988.

Anti-Korean incidents: Several reports released by the Los Angeles County Human Relations Committee in the early 1990's indicated a rise in hate crimes against people of Asian ancestry. The reports also revealed that Koreans became the target of hate crimes more often than any other Asian group in Los Angeles County. For example, a study published in March, 1991, indicated that thirteen Koreans were the targets of hate crimes in 1990, accounting for 27 percent of total hate crimes against all Asians in the county. This trend continues despite the fact that there are fewer Koreans in the county than there are members of several other Asian groups.

No official studies of anti-Asian hate crimes are available for the New York City area. Yet newspaper reports there suggest that Koreans were the most frequent target of racial assaults despite not being the largest Asian ethnic group in the city.

Rise of Hostility. A close examination of cases of anti-Asian violence shows that economic factors have added significantly to the increase of such inci-

In Brooklyn, protesters rally in support of the 1990 boycott against two Korean American grocery stores. (AP/Wide World Photos)

dents. This is especially true of anti-Korean violence. Since the late 1970's, when the living conditions of the African American underclass began to deteriorate, a large number of Korean migrants have established businesses in low-income black neighborhoods. Many in these neighborhoods blamed their economic woes (such as job losses) on Korean merchants. As a result, Korean merchants have been exposed to verbal and physical assaults, boycotts, arson, and murder.

The New York Boycotts. African American violence against Korean merchants has spread to other parts of the United States since about the early 1980's. It was especially severe during the 1990 boycott of two Korean stores in Brooklyn, New York, and for two years prior to the LOS ANGELES RIOTS OF 1992. During the time that the Brooklyn boycott was drawing national media attention, many Korean stores and their owners in Brooklyn and Manhattan were subjected to various kinds of attacks by African Americans. Two weeks after the start of the boycott, the wife of one of the store owners was beaten inside her own establishment by a picketer. Several months later, a young Vietnamese man who lived close to the boycott site was mis-

taken for a Korean and severely beaten. In August, a Korean merchant was robbed of several thousand dollars and beaten by a group of about thirty blacks after he accused a black girl of stealing cherries.

Tensions in Los Angeles. In the summer of 1990, similar violence broke out in Los Angeles. In June a Korean man was beaten and shot by two African American youngsters in South Central Los Angeles, a predominantly black section of the city. Since the perpetrators called their victim a "yellow monkey" but did not rob him, police considered the incident an anti-Korean hate crime. In another case, several Korean swap meet owners in South Central were attacked inside their stores by African American gang members, and anti-Korean pamphlets stressing the elimination of Korean merchants from the black community were widely distributed in South Central. Incidents of arson arose in late 1990 and early 1991.

Two incidents in particular served to escalate black anti-Korean violence in Los Angeles during the latter half of 1991. In March, a fourteen-year-old African American girl in South Central was shot to death by a Korean store owner after the two had briefly scuffled over whether the girl had paid for a bottle of orange juice. Months later, again in South Central, a Korean liquor owner shot and killed a black man during a robbery attempt.

In October, a nine-year-old Korean girl was critically wounded by gunfire at a gas station minimart in South Central. Since the shooting took place after the assailant had first robbed the market of three thousand dollars, the assault was considered racially motivated. In December, a Japanese American woman was mistaken for a Korean, dragged from her car, and beaten with a baseball bat by two black youths. Later in the month, a Korean liquor store owner in KOREATOWN was shot to death by two black men. Since they cursed the victim before shooting him eight times and did not take any money from the store, the police considered it a hate crime.

The Los Angeles Riots. As racial and economic ten-sions skyrocketed, African American hostility toward Korean merchants was expressed most vociferously during the riots of 1992—the worst urban violence to hit the United States since the Watts riots of Los Angeles in 1965. The disturbances began after an all-white jury, in April, acquitted white police officers who had been videotaped beating Rodney King, a black man. The announcement triggered the release of a flood of pent-up anger over racist and brutal police practices and perceived prejudice against African and Latino Americans generally.

Some twenty-four hundred Korean-owned stores in South Central and KOREATOWN were looted and/or burned. Edward Jae Song, a Korean American, was killed, and forty-six other Koreans were injured. The property damage incurred by the merchants was estimated at more than $350 million, approximately 45 percent of total property damage caused by the rioting.

The unidentified owner of a Los Angeles clothing store reacts to seeing her business burning, a day after the acquittal. (AP/Wide World Photos)

In Koreatown, Chung Kwon Ko, of Garden Grove Christian Church, appeals for an end to violence in the wake of the Los Angeles riots. (AP/Wide World Photos)

The fact that a disproportionately large number of Korean stores were located in the area may partially explain why so many of them were attacked. Other evidence suggests that black rioters selectively targeted Korean-owned stores for reprisal. The Anti-Violence Coalition, a Los Angeles-based civil rights organization, had been monitoring one of the city's major black radio stations and reported that station personnel incited listeners to push Korean merchants out of black neighborhoods and to target Korean-owned businesses once the rioting started.

Other Ethnic Groups. Although most of the assaults against Korean merchants were inflicted by African Americans, Latino and white Americans also participated. They have all continued to take part in hate crimes against Korean merchants. In September, 1993, a group of white, Latino, and African American teenagers assaulted the owners of a Korean liquor store in Orange County, California, and then burned the building. The latter was located in a white middle-class neighborhood.—*Pyong Gap Min*

SUGGESTED READINGS: • *Amerasia Journal* 19, no. 2 (1993). Special issue: "Los Angeles—Struggles Toward Multiethnic Community." Edward T. Chang, guest editor. • Min, Pyong Gap. "Ethnic Business, Intergroup Conflicts, and Ethnic Solidarity: Korean Immigrants in New York and Los Angeles." Unpublished manuscript, Department of Sociology, Queens College of CUNY, 1993. • United States Commission on Civil Rights. *Civil Rights Issues Facing Asian Americans in the 1990s.* Washington, D.C.: Government Printing Office, 1992.

Antimiscegenation laws: Laws that prohibited marriage between individuals of different races and that affected, among other groups, the Chinese. Antimiscegenation laws have a long history in the United States. The first American colonies did not prohibit marriage between individuals of different races, and marriages between white persons and American Indians or African Americans occurred in Colonial times with some frequency. After American independence, however, many states, not all of them Southern, prohibited marriages between white people and African Americans or between white people and "colored" persons, including Chinese. Because of the U.S. federal system, all such antimiscegenation laws were state laws.

Early Chinese immigrants to the United States were principally males, and the CHINESE EXCLUSION ACT OF 1882 and other discriminatory legislation that followed blocked immigration of Chinese females whose arrival might have redressed the imbalance. Lacking suitable marriage partners among their ethnic group, Chinese men sometimes married women of other races, but increasingly these marriages were prohibited by state law.

As late as the middle of the twentieth century, fourteen states (Arizona, California, Georgia, Idaho, Mississippi, Missouri, Montana, Nebraska, Nevada, Oregon, South Dakota, Utah, Virginia, and Wyoming) prohibited marriages specifically between white persons and Chinese or "Mongolians." In South Carolina, a white woman could not marry a Chinese man, but a white man could marry a Chinese woman. Some other states prohibited marriage between a white person and any "colored" person, so the total number of states barring white-Chinese marriages was even higher.

The 1868 passage of the Fourteenth Amendment, which prohibited the states from denying to any person the "equal protection of the laws," should have prevented antimiscegenation laws, but the U.S. Supreme

Although once prohibited by federal law, into the 1990's mixed marriages are increasingly common in American society. (Mary LaSalle)

Court did not enforce this view until almost a century later. The California antimiscegenation laws were frequently challenged as unconstitutional and were finally declared void in 1948. In the Southern states, antimiscegenation laws remained in effect until the 1960's Civil Rights movement, when they were finally declared unconstitutional throughout the United States by the Supreme Court.

Anti-Southeast Asian incidents: Between 1975, when the countries of Indochina fell under Communist rule, and 1990, more than one million immigrants from Vietnam, Laos, and Cambodia arrived in the United States; of these, more than 90 percent were classified as refugees. Soon after arriving, refugees began to encounter hostility from black, white, and Hispanic Americans; incidents continued into the 1990's, raising concerns not only among Southeast Asians in the United States but also throughout the Asian American community. These incidents should not obscure the selfless assistance that many Americans have given to the refugees, nor the fact that many refugees ultimately have succeeded in gaining acceptance from their new neighbors. Nevertheless, the persistence of such vio-

lence (accompanied by countless acts of intimidation and harassment that are never reported) suggests the need for increased public awareness of the problem. The following overview of anti-Southeast Asian violence cites representative incidents only; it is not comprehensive.

Incidents Against Vietnamese. The first reported outbursts were against Vietnamese. In Denver, Colorado, in September, 1979, fights and rock-throwing took place between Vietnamese refugees and Mexican Americans in a housing project. Similar clashes took place in the Allen Parkway Housing Project in Houston, Texas, this time between blacks and Vietnamese.

On the Gulf Coast of Mississippi, Florida, Louisiana, and Texas, and on the Pacific Coast of California, conflicts arose between Vietnamese refugee fishers and whites already established in the fishing industry. In Seadrift, Texas, tensions ran so high that, in late 1979, a Vietnamese killed a white man in self-defense. In 1981, the Ku Klux Klan harassed the Gulf Coast Vietnamese by burning their boats. The conflict between refugees and Gulf Coast white fishers eventually died down as the latter came to appreciate the refugees' work ethic. Harassment of refugee fishers in California took the form not only of the burning of boats (at Moss Landing, in Monterey County) but also of arbitrary enforcement of the law. The latter did not end until 1990, when Congress passed a law guaranteeing resident aliens' fishing rights.

In 1982, some whites in Oklahoma City, Oklahoma, became upset when a Vietnamese Buddhist temple was located in their neighborhood. Racial remarks were hurled at the communicants, some of whom were threatened with a baseball bat.

In Oakland, California, between January, 1985 and the end of 1986, there were more than fifty reported instances of verbal abuse of, or physical violence against, Indochinese refugees. One refugee was shot; several were beaten. Many of the perpetrators were black; toward the end of the period, there was retaliatory violence against blacks by Vietnamese teenagers.

In Houston, Texas, on August 9, 1990, in the early morning hours, two eighteen-year-old white men, Derek Hilla and Michael Allison, caught sight of a fifteen-year-old Vietnamese boy, Hung Truong. They beat him so severely that he died as a result. On January 23, 1991, Hilla was convicted by a jury of murder, and Allison of manslaughter.

On the Saturday evening of August 15, 1992, in Coral Springs, Florida (a suburb of Fort Lauderdale), Luyen Phahn Nguyen, the first-born son of a Vietnamese refugee physician and himself a pre-medical student, went with some friends to a party held in an apartment. At this party, an argument about the history of the VIETNAM WAR turned violent, and several drunken partygoers beat Nguyen senseless; as a result of the beating, he died. Seven young white men were charged in the beating; in December, Bradley Mills, a nineteen-year-old maintenance worker, was sentenced to fifty years in prison.

Incidents Against Hmong and Other Refugees from Laos. The Hmong, who had been hill people in Laos, encountered both severe difficulties in adapting to the American economy and intense hostility from some of their new neighbors. The worst incidents occurred in a tough Philadelphia neighborhood that had been largely black until about five thousand Hmong arrived in 1981. In 1984 the Hmong of Philadelphia endured muggings and pistol whippings, apparently all carried out by about twenty teenagers in the neighborhood. In 1986, some Hmong teenagers tried to wreak revenge on black teenagers who had vandalized their car. In the melee that resulted, one of the Hmong was beaten unconscious; the leader of the black youths involved in the violence, Anthony Starks, was sentenced to a long prison term. As a result of all the harassment, many of the Hmong fled Philadelphia.

The Philadelphia incidents were not the last cases of harassment of refugees from Laos. In September, 1990, in Richmond, California, eight cars parked outside an apartment building where some Laotian refugees lived were severely damaged; this incident followed incidents of egg throwing and BB gun shots.

Vietnamese American men fishing in Galveston Bay, Texas, on the Gulf Coast. Beginning in the late 1970's, Vietnamese refugee fishers competing with their white counterparts were the targets of racial hostility in the Gulf region. (Mary LaSalle)

Incidents Against Cambodians. When Cambodian refugees settled in New England in the early 1980's, they were greeted with hostility by many of their new white neighbors. In 1981, in Portland, Maine, a Cambodian father of small children, who had recently moved into a new house, was hit by a rock hidden in a snowball thrown by his neighbors while he played with his children in the snow. Between 1983 and 1987, Cambodians living in Revere, Massachusetts, a working-class suburb of Boston, met with acts of violence and endured vandalism against their homes, including arson fires (one of which made twenty-eight refugees homeless) and rocks thrown at windows. In April, 1986, Revere resident Robert Lee Stephens drew a prison term for assaulting members of refugee families. By no means, however, were all perpetrators of such violence punished. The same year (1986) saw the acquittal of one man, and the mistrial of another, charged in the beating death of a Cambodian refugee in Medford, Massachusetts.

The second-largest Cambodian community in the United States, exceeded only by that of Long Beach, California, is located in Lowell, Massachusetts, and the surrounding area. There were numerous incidents of harassment, intimidation, and violence directed against Cambodian Americans in Lowell in the 1980's and 1990's, creating a climate of suspicion and intolerance. On September 15, 1987, Vandy Phorng, a thirteen-year-old Cambodian American, was assaulted by an eleven-year-old white boy who began with racial insults, then hit Phorng in the face, pulled him down a flight of stairs to a canal, and threw him in the water, where he drowned.

On August 14, 1993, in Fall River, Massachusetts, two Cambodian men, Sam Nang Nhem and Sophy Soeng, were attacked by a group of white youths who yelled racial insults at the two Cambodians while kicking and beating them. Nhem died two days later; Soeng recovered from his injuries.

Violence against Cambodians has not been limited to the Northeast. In Stockton, California, on January 17, 1989, a young white drifter, Patrick Edward Purdy, fired a rifle into the schoolyard of an elementary school that enrolled many children of Cambodians and other Indochinese refugees. Five children were killed; four were Cambodian, and one was Vietnamese. When he saw the police coming, Purdy killed himself.

Cases of Mistaken Identity. Since many white, black, and Hispanic Americans cannot tell by sight the difference between various East Asian nationalities, some hate crimes are based on mistaken identity. On

July 29, 1989, in Raleigh, North Carolina, Jim (Ming Hai) Loo, twenty-four, a Chinese immigrant restaurant worker, was fatally beaten by someone who mistook him for a Vietnamese and blamed him for American deaths in Vietnam. On May 13, 1990, in Brooklyn, New York, a crowd of black youths attacked some Vietnamese whom they mistook for Koreans; a black boycott of Korean-owned stores was going on at the time.

Causes and Consequences of Anti-Indochinese Incidents. Most incidents of anti-Indochinese violence have been committed by teenage or young adult males, whether black, white, or Hispanic. One common motive is suspicion and hatred of those who differ in race and language. Thus, the two Houston youths who killed a Vietnamese boy in 1990 belonged to a white supremacist group. Fear of Indochinese refugees as competitors for scarce jobs and housing, and resentment of the help refugees received from the federal government, undoubtedly inflamed some perpetrators of anti-Indochinese violence, especially those who were black or Hispanic. The sheer volume and suddenness of the Indochinese refugee influx undoubtedly aggravated matters. In addition, widespread frustration over the loss of the Vietnam War may have caused some Americans to lash out at a convenient scapegoat.

The various anti-Indochinese incidents have not aroused the wave of national soul-searching unleashed by white hate crimes against blacks. Many Asian Americans, however, regardless of their particular ethnic background, have come to see anti-Indochinese violence as a potential threat to themselves. Thus, the failure of the courts to punish all of the perpetrators of the Medford, Massachusetts, beating death of a Cambodian refugee, in 1986, led to a protest by Asian American civil rights activists. The harassment suf-

Mourners attend the funeral ceremonies for four of the five Southeast Asian schoolchildren killed during the Stockton schoolyard shooting of 1989. (AP/Wide World Photos)

fered by Southeast Asians in America has been a goad to action for such groups as the NATIONAL ASIAN PACIFIC AMERICAN LEGAL CONSORTIUM.

Efforts to help Americans of Southeast Asian ancestry and other Americans understand each other better are another way to deal with the problem of violent hostility against Indochinese refugees. Thus, in Stockton, California, long-term residents joined the local Southeast Asian refugee community in expressing horror at the schoolyard massacre of January 17, 1989; a refugee scholarship fund was set up in memory of those children who died. At the same time, the Stockton Southeast Asian Community Development Foundation was established, with the goal of educating the wider public about refugees from Cambodia, Vietnam, and Laos, so as to create greater empathy for them.—*Paul D. Mageli*

SUGGESTED READINGS: • Auerbach, Susan. *Vietnamese Americans.* American Voices. Vero Beach, Fla.: Rourke, 1991. • Clary, Mike. "Dream Turns to Tragedy." *Los Angeles Times.* February 2, 1993. • Fuchs, Lawrence. "Xenophobia, Racism, and Bigotry." In *The American Kaleidoscope: Race, Ethnicity, and the Civic Culture.* Hanover, N.H.: Wesleyan University Press/University Press of New England, 1990. • Gupta, Udayan. "From Other Shores." In *The Problem of Immigration*, edited by Steven Anzovin. New York: H.W. Wilson, 1985. • Johnson, Terry E. "Immigrants: New Victims." *Newsweek* 107 (May 12, 1986): 57. • Rutledge, Paul James. *The Vietnamese Experience in America.* Bloomington: Indiana University Press, 1992. • Stengel, Richard. "Resentment Tinged with Envy." *Time* 126 (July 8, 1985): 56-57. • United States Commission on Civil Rights. *Civil Rights Issues Facing Asian Americans in the 1990s.* Washington, D.C.: Government Printing Office, 1992. • Zinsmeister, Karl. "Prejudice against Asians: Anxiety and Acceptance." *Current* 297 (November, 1987): 37-40.

Aoki, Brenda Wong (b. July 29, 1953, Salt Lake City, Utah): Performance artist. In 1988, she became the first Asian American performer featured at the National Storytelling Festival in Jonesborough, Tennessee. A cofounder of the performance group Sound-Seen, she has performed solo works throughout the United States, Canada, and Japan. Aoki's works fuse elements of classical Japanese theater with Western traditions of theater and dance. Her solo theater piece *Street Stories: Random Acts of Kindness* premiered in 1994 at La Pena Cultural Center in Berkeley, California. Aoki's debut album, *Dreams and Illusions: Tales*

The works of award-winning performance artist Brenda Aoki combine classical Japanese and western elements. (Courtesy Brenda Wong Aoki)

of the Pacific Rim, won the National Association of Independent Record Distributors award for Best Storytelling and Spoken Word Recording (1990).

Aoki, Dan: Political figure. Aoki was a Japanese American veteran of World War II. As a core member of Governor John A. Burns's faction of the Democratic Party in Hawaii, Aoki participated in the 1950's "revolution" that destroyed the Republican dominance in Hawaii and brought about greater equality for nonwhites. His career covered about thirty years of Democratic Party politics in Hawaii.

The eldest child of a Congregational church minister, Aoki was, from the age of eight, raised on Maui. Aoki joined the famed 442ND REGIMENTAL COMBAT TEAM during World War II and rose to the rank of first sergeant. On his return home he became president of the 442nd Veterans Club. It was through a club function that Aoki met Burns. Impressed with Burns's understanding of the Japanese American veterans' deep desire for equality, Aoki became a Burns supporter. Except for the 1948 campaign in which Burns ran for delegate to Congress but lost, Aoki helped to manage all of Burns's campaigns for office.

When Burns was elected as Hawaii's delegate to Congress in 1956, Aoki served as his administrative aide. When Burns was elected governor of Hawaii in 1962, Aoki again served as his administrative aide. Aoki became a trusted confidante to Burns. Aoki never ran for public office, but his influence was recognized by a political analyst, who called him "one of the founding fathers of the modern Democratic Party in Hawaii." A fellow Democrat said of Aoki, "Dan was a foot soldier who organized other foot soldiers to move Hawaii."

In 1984 Aoki claimed, "Since becoming the majority party in the State Legislature and capturing the governorship, the Democrats with Jack Burns as their leader have focused all of their efforts on breaking down the so-called wall of prejudice against the nonwhites."

Aoki, Hiroaki "Rocky" (b. 1940, Tokyo, Japan): Restaurateur. A flamboyant promoter, he came to the United States in 1960 and sold ice cream from a truck in Harlem, New York. He saved enough money to start a small four-table restaurant, which he parlayed into a chain of restaurants called Benihana in the United States and Japan. He is also known for his love of the sport of hot-air ballooning.

APEC. *See* **Asia-Pacific Economic Cooperation**

Appenzeller, Henry G. (Feb. 6, 1858, Suderton, Pa.— June 11, 1902, Kunsan, Korea): Missionary. Arriving at Inchon, Korea, in 1885, he began serving Korean Christians and encouraged them to take advantage of the labor opportunities on Hawaiian plantations in the early 1900's. He also believed that exposure to Western civilization would improve the condition of these immigrants. In 1885 he and his wife became parents of the first white child born in Korea.

Application for Leave Clearance. *See* **Loyalty oath**

April Revolution (1960): Series of mass demonstrations by university students and other activists in Seoul that toppled the authoritarian rule of South Korean president Syngman RHEE. Popular unrest triggered by Rhee's administration and the practices of his corrupt Liberal Party culminated in the presidential elections of March, 1960, and the election-rigging and police brutality stemming from them. Following a series of incidents involving student demonstrators either killed or wounded by police, on April 19 thousands of students of all ages took to the streets to protest prevailing conditions and to demand justice. As martial law ensued, about 140 people were killed and more than 1,000 wounded by army militia. Less than a week later, the tide of outrage again swelled in the wake of a demonstration by university professors calling for Rhee's resignation. After government troops refused to fire on the protestors, Rhee resigned office, on April 26. New elections were followed by a brief period of democratic rule.

Aquino, Corazon (Corazon Cojuangco; b. Jan. 25, 1933, Tarlac Province, Philippines): Philippine president. Born into one of the wealthiest landowning families in the Philippines, Corazon Cojuangco studied at exclusive girls' schools in Manila, Philadelphia, and New York City. A French major, she graduated from the College of Mount St. Vincent in New York (B.A., 1953). Returning home, she abandoned law studies to marry a young politician, Benigno S. Aquino, Jr. She remained in the background as her husband became a governor and senator and the most prominent oppo-

Corazon Aquino, first woman to serve as Philippine president. (AP/Wide World Photos)

nent of President Ferdinand E. MARCOS. After Marcos declared martial law, Benigno Aquino was imprisoned (1972-1980), but he was finally allowed to leave for the United States to have heart surgery. Upon his return to Manila (August, 1983), he was assassinated at the airport, an event widely believed to have been planned by the Marcos government. Corazon Aquino became a symbol of opposition to Marcos and ran for president in the special election called for February, 1986. The election, marked by widespread fraud and intimidation of Aquino supporters, was "officially" won by Marcos, but he faced growing domestic and international pressures to resign. After he and Aquino held rival inaugurations (February 25, 1986), Marcos fled the country for exile in the United States, and Aquino established a new government.

Aquino, the simple housewife turned first woman president of the Philippines, was the moving spirit behind the Filipinos' newfound courage to fight for democracy. She was sworn into office as the seventh president of the Philippines at Club Filipino in Greenhills, Manila. In 1991, she was one of only eight elected women heads of state or government in the world.

Aquino was brought into power by PEOPLE POWER. Upon assumption of duty, she resolved to articulate the country's yearning for justice and economic progress by pure dedication and involvement. The battle cry was peace and reconciliation. Her rise to power was facilitated by the perception of her male counterparts that she would be a pliable and temporary leader, easily manipulated by the traditional male leaders. Her unexpected strength and popularity and her commitment to democratic procedures belied this judgment, and she was able to withstand several attempted coups.

Nepotism plagued Aquino's administration. During her tenure, about half a dozen of her relatives sat in Congress. Government departments were stacked with her friends. Accusations of corruption, while not leveled at her personally, hounded her brothers and other relatives from the day she took office. Her government was accused of sometimes descending to mafia-style thuggery to get its way. It has been claimed that under Aquino, government-sanctioned vigilantes killed more left-wing priests and lawyers than perished during the whole of Marcos' twenty-year rule. Moreover, the landlord-dominated Congress gutted Aquino's ambitious land-reform program, which it was hoped would end centuries of agrarian unrest and the twenty-year-old communist insurgency. Honoring tradition, members of Congress squandered scarce money on patron-

Philippine president Corazon Aquino welcomes some 170,000 people at a 1987 rally in Manila for the new national constitution. (AP/Wide World Photos)

age and themselves. Aquino's powerlessness in the face of so much "horse trading" and corruption weakened her leadership.

Aquino was succeeded by her defense minister, Fidel V. Ramos, who became president of the Philippines on June 30, 1992. Under former president Ferdinand E. Marcos, he had directed the brutal and corrupt Philippine Constabulary. He rebelled against Marcos in 1986, however, and supported Aquino's run for office. Ramos came to power despite winning only 23.6 percent of the vote in the May, 1992, election. One of his six opponents was Marcos' widow, Imelda, who won 10.3 percent.

Arai, Clarence Takeya (1901—1964): Lawyer and community activist. A law graduate of the University of Washington in 1924, he was a founding member of the JAPANESE AMERICAN CITIZENS LEAGUE (JACL). Early on he urged the establishment on the West Coast of a coalition of Nisei citizens leagues. The result of that push for a national federation, in 1930, was a convention in Seattle, Washington, out of which sprang the JACL. That year he married Yone Ut-

sunomiya. In Seattle, Arai also practiced law and participated actively in local politics, until he and his family were interned at MINIDOKA in southern Idaho during World War II.

Arai, Ryoichiro (July 19, 1856, Japan—?): Silk trader. He arrived in the United States in 1876, started as a silk trader in New York the same year, and continued trading silk for the next fifty years. One of the first Japanese to settle in New York, he was awarded the Fourth Class National Treasure from the Japanese government in 1939.

Arakawa's: Department store in Waipahu, Oahu, Hawaii. The founder, Zempan Arakawa, came to Hawaii from Okinawa, Japan, in 1904 to work on a sugar plantation. As soon as his contract expired in 1909, however, he left the plantation to open a tailor shop, to which he later added general merchandise. Arakawa's grew into one of the most successful stores in Hawaii.

Zempan Arakawa's initial success was based largely on the manufacture and sale of items that plantation workers needed. One of his greatest successes was the development of a process of waterproofing muslin to make raincoats. His raincoats were considered the best because they were not tacky and, unlike others, were not highly flammable when packed in bulk. He also made denim *tabi* (footwear) that was strong yet flexible and sold denim pants, lunch bags, and *palaka* (checkered) shirts.

In 1960, Arakawa received the George Washington honor medal from the Freedoms Foundation at Valley Forge, Pennsylvania, for his community service and his belief in American principles. In fostering the entrepreneurial spirit in his children, he often quoted the Japanese saying that is the equivalent of "Nothing ventured, nothing gained." He also emphasized family solidarity. One of his favorite sayings was, "One chopstick is easy to break; two, harder; three, more difficult; and four, impossible." In other words, a family gains strength in unity.

Arakawa's continues to be a family-owned and family-managed store. It is said to be "the closest thing to the plantation store of old Hawaii that sold everything." In fact virtually everything is sold at Arakawa's, including food items, garden equipment, jewelry, clothing, household appliances, electronic items, even old-fashioned wooden washboards.

A leading institution in Waipahu, Arakawa's has actively promoted the rich cultural heritage of the community. Beginning in the 1970's it has honored the Filipino, Okinawan, Japanese, Puerto Rican, and Portuguese groups with a celebration of their culture. Arakawa's also was an early supporter of the WAI-PAHU CULTURAL GARDEN PARK, a collection of plantation homes and other structures established to preserve the memory of plantation life.

Argonauts: Nonnative Californians who came to California during the gold rush period to strike it rich. In 1860, 95 percent of the state population were argonauts from other parts of the United States and different nations, including China. Chinese argonauts in particular were singled out and persecuted.

Ariyoshi, George R. (b. Mar. 12, 1926, Honolulu, Territory of Hawaii): Governor of Hawaii. In 1974 Ariyoshi became the first American of Japanese ancestry to be elected governor of Hawaii—and the first American of Asian descent in U.S. history to serve as governor. Ariyoshi served three consecutive terms (1974-1986).

Ariyoshi was born to Japanese immigrants in Honolulu's Chinatown district. His parents, Ryozo and Mit-

George Ariyoshi's election as the United States' first Asian American governor capped a lifetime of public service. (AP/Wide World Photos)

sue Ariyoshi, were working-class people. During World War II his family was evicted from its home because people of Japanese ancestry were forbidden from living near the waterfront.

Ariyoshi attended public schools. He graduated from McKinley High School in 1944 and attended the University of Hawaii. He interrupted his education to serve in the MILITARY INTELLIGENCE SERVICE. Ariyoshi returned to college in 1947. Enrolling at Michigan State University, he earned his B.A. degree in history and political science in 1949. He received his J.D. degree in 1952 from the University of Michigan.

Ariyoshi practiced law after returning to Hawaii. He found, however, that despite the sacrifices and battlefield accomplishments of Japanese Americans in World War II, nonwhites in Hawaii were still being denied equal opportunities. In an effort to change what he viewed as unjust, Ariyoshi got involved in Hawaii's then-fledgling Democratic Party. In 1954, he ran for the Territorial House of Representatives. His election marked the start of a political career that spanned thirty-two years and included no election defeats. In all, Ariyoshi served as a territorial representative and senator, state senator, 1968 State Constitutional Convention delegate, lieutenant governor, acting governor, and governor.

Perhaps Ariyoshi's most noted accomplishment as governor was the drafting of the Hawaii State Plan, a comprehensive "blueprint" for Hawaii's future direction in the areas of land use, education, agriculture, tourism, water, health, energy, housing, and transportation. He believed the plan would ensure a "preferred future" for Hawaii's people. Hawaii became the first state in the nation to adopt such a plan, which became a model for other states.

Ariyoshi and his wife, Jean, were married in 1955. They have three children: Lynn, Todd, and Donn. Ariyoshi returned to the practice of law and other business interests following his retirement from government service. He has received numerous honors and awards.

Ariyoshi, Koji (Jan. 30, 1914, Kona, Territory of Hawaii—Oct. 25, 1976, Honolulu, Hawaii): Editor. He was the founding editor of the left-wing weekly newspaper, the *Honolulu Record*, which supported the unions in their struggles against the big employers of Hawaii in the late 1940's and early 1950's.

Ariyoshi was born to an immigrant Japanese couple who had come to Hawaii to labor on a sugar plantation and who subsequently became coffee farmers. For six years after graduating from high school, he worked on the family coffee farm, as a laborer on road construction, and as a store clerk in the plantation community.

Ariyoshi then moved to Honolulu and made his debut as a newspaper reporter with an article in *The Honolulu Star-Bulletin* about coffee farming. He worked as a stevedore, but, bent on becoming a journalist, he matriculated at the University of Hawaii. While there, he won a scholarship to the University of Georgia, from which he was graduated with a degree in journalism.

When Japan attacked Pearl Harbor on December 7, 1941, Ariyoshi was working as a stevedore in San Francisco, and he suffered INTERNMENT with others of Japanese ancestry. From the MANZANAR relocation center in California, he volunteered for the Army and trained at the Military Intelligence Institute in Minnesota. He led a ten-man psychological-warfare team in the China-Burma-India theater. Profoundly impressed by his experiences in China, he returned to Honolulu in 1948 and founded the *Honolulu Record*.

In 1952 a jury convicted Ariyoshi and six codefendants of violating the Smith Act, which makes it a criminal offense to advocate the overthrow of any government in the United States by force or violence. On January 20, 1958, the U.S. Ninth Circuit Court of Appeals reversed the conviction and acquitted the seven. (See HAWAII SEVEN.)

When the *Honolulu Record* ceased publication in 1958, Ariyoshi opened a floral shop. After the visit of

U.S. president Richard M. Nixon to China in 1972 opened the way for relations with that country, Ariyoshi became sought after as an expert on communist China. He served as president of the UNITED STATES-CHINA PEOPLE'S FRIENDSHIP ASSOCIATION of Hawaii, which he founded, and as president of the Hawaii Foundation for History of the Humanities.

Arjuna: Hero of the *Mahabharata* (c. fifth century B.C.E.; great epic of the Bharata Dynasty), an epic tale of the struggle for supremacy between two related families, the Pandavas and the Kauravas. Prince Arjuna is the best archer among the five Pandava brothers and a skilled warrior, but as the great war between the two warring families is about to begin, he hesitates. Seeing many of his friends and kin numbered among the enemy, he ponders whether it would not be better to refuse to engage in a just, but cruel, war. Lord Krishna then reminds Arjuna of the meaning of duty, explaining that Arjuna's responsibility as a warrior is to carry out his duties on the battlefield. The dialogue that follows is collectively known as the Bhagavadgita (the Lord's song), India's most celebrated religious text.

Aruego, Jose Espiritu (b. Aug. 9, 1932, Manila, Philippines): Illustrator and author of children's books. Son of a prominent lawyer and legal scholar, Aruego completed his undergraduate education at the University of the Philippines before earning a law degree in 1955. Aruego passed the bar examination but decided to abandon a legal career after losing his first case. A love of drawing and an interest in comic books convinced Aruego to move to New York City to pursue a degree in graphic arts at the Parsons School of Design. After graduating from Parsons in 1959, Aruego worked for various design studios and advertising agencies while submitting cartoons to many magazines. He was married to another artist, Ariane Dewey, who encouraged him to devote his full attention to illustration. Shortly after the birth of his son, Aruego completed writing and illustrating his first children's book, *The King and His Friends*, which was published in 1969. Aruego's illustrations appeared in Robert Kraus's award-winning book *Whose Mouse Are You?* (1970), and his own *Juan and the Asuangs* (1970) was honored as an outstanding picture book of the year by *The New York Times*. In addition to working on his own picture books, Aruego collaborated with his wife in illustrating many books written by other authors, from *The Chick and the Duckling* (1972) through *Alli-*

gators and Others, All Year Long! A Book of Months (1993). Many of Aruego's stories have drawn upon Philippine folklore, and his illustrations incorporate tropical motifs and decorative touches that reflect his Filipino heritage.

Asahis: Japanese American baseball team, organized in 1905, which dominated Hawaii leagues in the years preceding World War II. Beginning league play in 1907, the team captured the first of a string of championships at various levels in 1911. Moving up from Junior League competition to the more powerful Senior League division of the Honolulu Baseball League, the Asahis took the championship title in 1925. In the newly established Hawaii Baseball League, comprising teams of different ethnic groups, the Asahis won titles in 1925 and 1926. The team kept playing during the war but, pressured by anti-Japanese sentiments throughout the islands, added a few white players to its roster while taking a new name, the "Athletics." Play-

During the early years of the twentieth century, baseball was especially popular among Hawaii's immigrant Japanese population. (University of Southern California East Asian Studies)

ing once again as the Asahis after the war, the team—now a mixture of both Japanese American and white players—added five more league championships during the 1960's.

Asakura v. City of Seattle (1924): U.S. Supreme Court ruling that struck down a Seattle, Washington, city ordinance because it violated a federal treaty with Japan. The statute in question provided that pawnbroking licenses could be granted only to American citizens. Enacted in July, 1921, its sole purpose was to keep aliens from obtaining such a license. Asakura, a legal alien and Seattle pawnbroker, argued that the law violated the U.S.-JAPAN TREATY OF COMMERCE AND NAVIGATION (1911), which allowed citizens of each nation to conduct trade and commerce in the other. The Court declared that all U.S. treaties become the supreme law of the land and are therefore binding on all states in the union; consequently, no state may enact laws that violate federal treaties.

Asawa, Ruth (b. 1926, Norwalk, Calif.): Sculptor. One of seven children of an Issei truck farmer, Asawa and her family were interned during World War II. After the war she attended Black Mountain College, an experimental college in North Carolina that produced many prominent artists, and Milwaukee State Teachers College, but did not take a degree. While raising a family in San Francisco—she and her husband, architect Albert Lanier, had six children—Asawa became an accomplished sculptor. Her work has been exhibited at the Museum of Modern Art in New York and at other prestigious museums. She has been commissioned to do several prominent public art works in San Francisco, including the fountain at Grand Hyatt Union Square and the mermaid at Ghirardelli Square.

Asawa was also commissioned to sculpt the Japanese American Internment Memorial in San Jose, California, which was unveiled on March 5, 1994. The memorial, which measures five feet by fourteen feet with panels on both sides, is a visual history of the Japanese American experience, including the wrenching experience of relocation and internment.

Asia-Pacific Economic Cooperation (APEC): Association of economies on the Pacific Rim, founded in 1989 to promote economic cooperation and development. Members include Australia, Brunei, Canada, China, Hong Kong, Indonesia, Japan, Malaysia, Mexico (added in 1993), New Zealand, Papua New Guinea (added in 1993), the Philippines, Singapore, South Korea, Taiwan, Thailand, and the United States; Chile is scheduled to be added at the annual meeting at the end of 1994. In 1993, the gross domestic output of APEC members was more than $12 trillion, half the world's total output; APEC members also account for more than one-third of the world's trade, creating the potential for a free-trade zone that would have an enormous international impact.

Asia-Pacific Triangle: Component of revised U.S. immigration policy in the immediate post-World War II period, providing for small numbers of Asians to come to the United States following a lengthy exclusion. First proposed in 1948 by U.S. representative Walter JUDD, who had spearheaded the successful campaign to repeal Chinese exclusion in 1943 (see IMMIGRATION ACT OF 1943), the Asia-Pacific Triangle encompassed most of South and East Asia. Nations within this region were eligible for annual quotas of at least one hundred immigrants to the United States. The triangle was legitimized by the U.S. Congress as part of the MCCARRAN-WALTER ACT OF 1952, remaining in force until the national-origins quota system was abolished by the IMMIGRATION AND NATIONALITY ACT OF 1965.

Asia Society: Organization founded in 1956 in New York City to assist Americans' understanding of Asia and its increasingly important role in U.S. and world relations. Toward this endeavor the society sponsors research, publications, and public education programs on Asia.

The society has a staff of experts on the various regions of Asia who prepare educational materials and other resources on Asian culture, history, politics, and economics for teachers in secondary education and universities. The society also supports exchange programs with Asian countries and publishes the research of scholars on Asia. Asia House, the headquarters of the society in New York City, houses a library and an art gallery open to the public. The society also hosts performing artists from Asia, periodic lecture series, forums, and specialized conferences.

Asian, Inc.: Nonprofit technical assistance and research organization incorporated in San Francisco, California, in 1971, committed to helping Asian Americans achieve socioeconomic equality. The group began by developing social programs and providing assistance to small businesses; its activities expanded to include developing affordable housing, rehabilitating privately owned residential properties, and offer-

ing technical assistance and strategies to enhance the community's economic competitiveness.

Asian American Arts Alliance: Organization founded in 1983 to increase support, recognition, and appreciation of Asian American arts through information, networking, and advocacy services and related special projects.

Services include information referral, publications, and a resource library. Special projects include *Beyond Boundaries*, a resource book that is a follow-up to the national Asian American arts conference held in December, 1993; regrant/technical assistance initiative to help New York City-based arts groups increase their organizational capacity; presenting-spaces pilot program to cultivate opportunities with New York City area theater, performance, and gallery venues; and a national outreach and policy project to examine the state of Asian American arts around the country.

Asian American Arts Centre: Organization founded in 1974 to promote Asian American artists and arts throughout the United States. The Arts Centre's ongoing programs include folk arts research and documentation, performance presentations, exhibitions, educa-

The Asian American Arts Centre sponsors a wide variety of programs and exhibits that advance the arts and artists of Asian America. The exhibit displayed here is from May of 1993. (Asian American Arts Centre)

tion, and services and advocacy.

Each year the center produces programs featuring living Chinese American folk artists of New York. These programs combine lectures, performances, workshops, and master classes. Activities result in scholarly research papers and oral history documentation. The highlight is the Chinese Lunar New Year Festival, which includes hands-on activities for the public. In 1992 the center's video documentation of NG SHEUNG CHI, *Singing to Remember*, was shown at the Margaret Mead Festival at the American Museum of Natural History. Ng was the first Chinese American to receive a National Heritage Fellowship from the National Endowment for the Arts.

Ng Sheung-chi singing at his home. (Liu Chyun Lin/Asian American Arts Centre)

The Arts Centre includes the ASIAN AMERICAN DANCE THEATRE. Throughout the United States this performance ensemble presents the dances of China, Japan, Indonesia, India, Korea, and the Philippines, as well as new works by Asian American choreographers.

In 1984 the Arts Centre began its annual series of exhibitions and panel discussions of works by contemporary Asian American and culturally diverse artists. Since then hundreds of artists have participated in more than thirty exhibitions, and more than eighteen catalogs have been published. The center also initiated

a research project on senior Asian American artists, 1945-1965, as part of a major exhibition slated for 1994.

In collaboration with the New York City Board of Education, the Arts Centre's award-winning, cross-cultural arts-in-education program has introduced the Asian pointed brush and the traditional dances of Asia to New York's public school children.

The center houses a historic archive of more than five hundred Asian American visual artists. This public service, the only one of its kind in the United States at the time of its creation, is used by the Museum of Modern Art, the Metropolitan Museum of Art, curators, galleries, and scholars. To support emerging artists the Arts Centre awards eight-month fellowships in its Artist-in-Residence program. The organization's annual publication, *Artspiral*, is a critical cultural forum for the arts.

Asian American collections: These comprise materials relevant to the history, culture, and experience of Asians in America. Such collections can include published literature, music, films, art and artifacts, such public media items as newspapers, magazines, and journals, and such archival materials as manuscripts, letters, photographs, posters, legal documents, and so forth.

The distinction between Asian American and East Asian collections is crucial for effective and efficient research. East Asian collections, such as those of Stanford University's Hoover Institution on War, Revolution, and Peace and Harvard University's Harvard-Yenching Library, focus mainly on the People's Republic of China, Japan, Korea, and the Philippines. Asian American collections, by contrast, chronicle the lives of Asian Americans—their history, living conditions, politics, culture, and response to contemporary issues. Within the latter category, for example, objects of historical interest are the documents and other records pertaining to the CHINESE EXCLUSION ACT OF 1882 and the GENTLEMEN'S AGREEMENT of 1907 to exclude, respectively, Chinese and Japanese laborers from coming to the United States. Contemporary issues include topics such as university admission politics, the myth of the MODEL MINORITY, and the glass ceiling for Asian American employment.

Historical Development. The gathering and presentation of information on Asian America began to occur in earnest following student-led strikes at San Francisco State College and the University of California, Berkeley during the late 1960's. Demonstrators demanded the establishment of ethnic studies departments or Third World colleges and the teaching of ethnic studies courses in higher education. The ASIAN AMERICAN MOVEMENT's purposes were threefold: to develop the ethnic studies curriculum; to reevaluate the history and contributions of Asian Americans in the United States and to tell their story from their perspective; and to help the American public understand accurately the contributions made by these individuals, with the hope of securing equality in the United States for all people of color.

Establishing Asian American collections became one of the keys to achieving these goals. The development of such collections, which began in 1970, was divided roughly into three stages. In the "student-care" stage of the early 1970's, there were no budgets, salaried employees, or separate spaces allotted to the creation and maintenance of Asian American collections. Rather, resources were donated by individuals and overseen by the students themselves. During the "paraprofessional" period of the late 1970's, paid library assistants were employed to take charge of the collections. Since both the students and the assistants lacked professional library training, resources were not organized appropriately. Overseers were not able to satisfy the demand for access to the materials. Finally, the "professional" era was inaugurated in 1979 when the University of California, Berkeley's ASIAN AMERICAN STUDIES Library employed a full-time professional librarian to systematically develop and organize the collection—the first such position in the United States. This was the turning point for greater recognition of the value of Asian American collections.

Status in the United States. Since 1980, separate and sizable Asian American collections have grown, but many such materials have become integrated with the more generalized collections of numerous institutions. For example, the Bancroft Library at Berkeley contains a substantial amount of important early Asian American resources as part of its collection on the history of the Western states.

Most institutions or organizations that accumulate Asian American materials can be placed in one of four categories. Academic libraries that maintain such collections concentrate primarily on research materials that support their institutions' course offerings or programs. Public libraries that offer Asian American resources commonly stock items that serve general public interest in such topics as holidays, customs, and travel guides. Federal repositories, such as the National Archives and Records Service in Washington, D.C., and its archive branches in eleven federal-records centers, contain Asian American immigration records and documents of that nature. Most other nonprofit organizations, the fourth category, tend to concentrate on specific Asian American groups or special subject areas or interests.—*Wei Chi Poon*

SUGGESTED READINGS: • Backus, Karen, and Julia C. Furtaw, eds. *Asian Americans Information Directory*. Detroit: Gale Research, 1992. • Gall, Susan B., and Timothy L. Gall, eds. *Statistical Record of Asian Americans*. Detroit: Gale Research, 1993. • Josey, E. J., and Marva L. DeLoach, eds. Ethnic Collections in Libraries. New York: Neal-Schuman, 1983. • Miller, Wayne Charles, with Faye Nell Vowell, Gary K. Crist, et al. A Comprehensive Bibliography for the Study of American Minorities. 2 vols. New York: New York University Press, 1976. • Poon, Wei Chi. The Directory of Asian American Collections in the United States. Berkeley: Asian American Studies Library, University of California, 1982. • Poon, Wei Chi. A Guide for Establishing Asian American Core Collections. Berkeley: Asian American Studies Library, University of California, 1989. • Scarborough, Katharine T. A., ed. *Developing Library Collections for California's Emerging Majority: A Manual of Resources for Ethnic Collection Development*. Berkeley, Calif.: Bay Area Library and Information System, 1990. • Thernstrom, Stephen, ed. *Harvard Encyclopedia of American Ethnic Groups*. Cambridge, Mass.: The Belknap Press of Harvard University Press, 1980.

Asian American Dance Performances: Community-based organization founded in 1974 by several San Francisco Asian American choreographers and dancers. Formerly known as the Asian American Dance

Under sponsorship of Asian American Dance Performances, Mitzie Abe performs a piece. (Asian American Dance Performances)

Collective, the group supports works of Asian American performing artists that reflect the richness and diversity of Asian American culture.

Asian American Dance Theatre: Dance company dedicated to the support and development of Asian and Asian American arts and culture, founded in 1974. Two distinct repertoires, one traditional and one modern, are combined. As the professional dance company of the ASIAN AMERICAN ARTS CENTRE, the company performs traditional dances from the People's Republic of China, Korea, India, Japan, Indonesia, the Philippines, and other parts of Asia, as well as contemporary choreography inspired by Asian forms and sensibilities. The traditional repertory draws on a roster of artists professionally trained in their chosen traditional styles, while the contemporary company consists of core and affiliated dancers trained in modern, ballet, and Asian dance techniques.

Featured artists and choreographers have included Marie Alonzo from the Philippines; Najma Ayasha, a kathak dancer in the Jaipuri tradition; Luna Borromeo, dancer and television star who joined the organization in 1976; Chen Guo, a principal dancer and choreographer with the Chinese theater in Beijing; and Sun Ok Lee, a well-known Korean dancer and choreographer.

The Asian American Dance Theatre's community school of dance expanded to include visual arts as well. In 1980 the visual arts program became the Asian Arts Institute. Other activities include performances, lecture/demonstrations, workshops, master classes, and residencies throughout the United States in such diverse settings as elementary schools, museums, botanical gardens, universities, conferences, concert halls, and outdoor festivals. The dance company has performed at the Metropolitan Museum of Art, Lincoln Center for the Performing Arts, the Statue of Liberty, Amherst College, the Riverside Dance Festival, Urban Fest in Winston Salem, North Carolina, Mid Fest in Ohio, and various other places. As part of the Arts in Education Program, the company presents lecture/performances and workshops for children in the New York City public school system throughout the school year.

Asian American International Film Festival (AAIFF): Oldest American film festival dedicated to the cinematic achievements of Asians and Asian Americans, founded in 1978. The festival was started by Asian CineVision (ACV), a nonprofit media arts organization that promotes the appreciation and growth of Asian and Asian American films and video arts.

The first festival, in the winter of 1978, was a three-day-long exhibition of fifty films at the Henry Street Arts for Living Center in the Lower East Side of New York. During the next fourteen years the festival had to expand its central facilities and its levels of financial support to accommodate a growing audience and increasing artistic diversity. From 1978 to 1992 the popular festival exhibited more than five hundred Asian/Asian American films from Asia, North America, Europe, Australia, the Soviet Union, and the Middle East.

Through the years the festival has provided the initial screenings of numerous films and has provided many filmmakers with a larger audience. Films such as *Rouge* (1988), *Iron Man* (1989), and *The Elephant Keeper* (1989) had their first screenings at the AAIFF, and the festival has showcased the works of artists such as Christine CHOY, Wayne WANG, Ismail Merchant, Gregg Araki, Roddy Bogawa, and Jon Moritsugu.

Each year the festival opens in New York, with a gala opening night reception, and then begins an international tour. The festival has toured cities such as Taipei, Tokyo, Turin, Vancouver, and Victoria, as well as cities in the United States, such as Amherst, Bloomington, Boston, Boulder, Chicago, Denver, Honolulu, Houston, Iowa City, Ithaca, Jacksonville, Lawrence, Los Angeles, Minneapolis, Northampton, Philadelphia, San Francisco, Seattle, and Washington, D.C.

In 1992 there was a special milestone fifteenth-anniversary celebration of the AAIFF. The event paid special tribute to the AAIFF Founding Committee: Daryl Chin, Fern Lee, Thomas Tam, and Dan Yung. Also, the Asian American Media Award was presented to director Mira Nair, and a special retrospective program, "East Through the Looking Glass: Asian Americans in Hollywood," featured screenings of *Flower Drum Song* (1961) and *Enter the Dragon* (1973). The opening night also included a screening of Nair's *Salaam Bombay!* (1988).

Asian American Journalists Association (AAJA): National, nonprofit organization comprising print and broadcast journalists, students, and other supporters, founded in 1981. The association seeks to increase employment of Asian Pacific American journalists; assist students pursuing journalism careers; encourage fair, sensitive, and accurate coverage of the Asian community; and provide support for Asian Pacific American journalists.

Los Angeles news anchor Tritia Toyota, cofounder of the Asian American Journalists Association. (AP/Wide World Photos)

The AAJA began when a few Los Angeles-based journalists, led by *Los Angeles Times* reporter Bill Sing and KNBC-TV anchor Tritia Toyota, came together in an effort to address issues of concern to Asian American journalists. Within a few years several additional sister groups formed, all following the basic goals established by the Los Angeles group. Then in 1987 the organizations met at the first national convention and formally agreed to establish a national association, of which they would all be chapters. The group established its national headquarters in San Francisco in 1988.

The group has chapters in several areas that have large populations of Asian Pacific Americans, including Los Angeles, the San Francisco Bay Area, New York, Hawaii, Seattle, Chicago, and Washington, D.C. Its more than one thousand members are currently (or have formerly been) involved in television and radio or with magazines and newspapers throughout the country and in other parts of the world.

Among the services that the AAJA provides are job referrals and counseling, scholarships for students, advanced skills and management training fellowships, mentor programs, and a speaker's bureau. It produces publications including a national newsletter, a handbook on how to cover the Asian Pacific American community, and analyses of media coverage, and holds chapter events, including workshops, fundraisers, lectures, and social events. The largest event the association offers is its annual convention, which includes speakers, panels, workshops, a job fair, student print and broadcast projects, and other activities.

The association is also one of the founders—along with the National Association of Black Journalists, the National Association of Hispanic Journalists, and the Native American Journalists Association—of Unity '94, a coalition that seeks to address issues common to all four national minority journalism groups. Issues include equitable hiring, retention and promotion of minority journalists, better coverage of communities of color, and better treatment of minority employees.

Asian American Movement: The Asian American Movement emerged during the social ferment of the 1960's. It was and is mainly a reformist movement that unites diverse Asian ethnic groups to work toward racial equality, social justice, and political empowerment in a culturally pluralist society. The emergence of the Movement implies that Asians of different national backgrounds share a common ethnicity and experience in America. Collectively, Asian Americans have sought to develop Asian American Studies and community-based organizations as well as to fight racism and sexism through a combination of radical and conventional politics.

Origins. The birth of the Movement can be traced to the confluence of two historical phenomena: the development of a generation of college-aged Asian Americans (predominantly Chinese Americans and Japanese Americans) and public protests against the Vietnam War. Because exclusion laws limited the number of Asian Americans and segregated schools limited their education, it was not until the late 1960's that there were statistically and socially significant numbers of Asian Americans attending colleges and universities. Politicized by their participation in the Civil Rights movement, the New Left, women's liberation, and other social movements of the period, Asian American activists began protesting the Vietnam War as both unjust and racist. When they tried to publicize their perspective on the war, however, they were roundly rebuffed by fellow antiwar dissidents, who considered the issue of race to be both divisive and distracting. As a result, Asian American activists became increasingly disillusioned with the white-dominated antiwar movement. Though they continued to oppose the war, they did so on their own terms. Usually that meant organizing Asian American coalitions to participate in major antiwar demonstrations, as in November, 1969, when several hundred of them marched as a separate contingent in San Francisco, or in April, 1971, when they decided to march apart from the main body of protesters because the coordinating committee of the protest in Washington, D.C., was unwilling to adopt a statement against racism. In short, the antiwar movement crystallized these Asian Americans' understanding of racial discrimination against Asians in America and convinced them that an inter-Asian coalition was an effective way to oppose it. In bringing Asian American activists together to participate in a common cause that transcended the separate college campuses and Asian ethnic communities, the Movement helped to transform previously isolated instances of political activism into a nationwide social movement.

On the basis of a pan-Asian identity, Asian American activists have been involved in many significant struggles. Employing a combination of protest politics (organizing in the communities and campuses and engaging in militant demonstrations) and conventional politics (passing legislation and bringing lawsuits), activists have been able to improve the circumstances of the Asian American community. These struggles have proved the political effectiveness of Asian Americans and their ability to set a common agenda despite their diversity as a community.

Early Phase. Asian American political activism began spontaneously on college and university campuses and in Asian ethnic communities throughout the country. Though often initiated by a specific Asian ethnic group to address a single issue, these activities quickly attracted broader support because of their implications

The rise of the Asian American Movement is credited largely to politically active Asian American college and university students. (James L. Shaffer)

for all Asian Americans. Asian American student activists participated in the Third World strikes at San Francisco State College (1968) and at the University of California, Berkeley (1969). As members of the Third World Liberation fronts on both campuses, they decried the absence of their history and culture from the college curricula and demanded that their story be told. They sought to give voice to a collective experience that began in Asia but developed mainly in America; to define their racial identity as a people of color, rather than simply as another immigrant group; and to participate in the development of a pan-Asian culture that is an integral part of a culturally pluralist America.

For that purpose, these individuals founded ASIAN AMERICAN STUDIES (AAS), a new field of inquiry that has been from its inception consciously antiestablishment. AAS has emphasized a history of racial oppression and resistance and has challenged the glaring omissions and misrepresentations in existing texts and curricula. It has instilled in Asian American students the self-confidence and self-esteem necessary for personal achievement and social activism in the community as well as on the campus.

Asian American students joined community activists to study the deplorable conditions in Chinatowns and other Asian ethnic enclaves and to seek ways to improve the lives of local residents. One of the earliest and best-known struggles was the effort, beginning in 1968, to save the International Hotel in San Francisco's Manilatown from destruction and the predominantly elderly Filipino American bachelors living there from eviction. For Asian Americans, especially Filipino American students, the hotel symbolized the history and cultural legacy of Asian immigrants, their parents' generation. The hotel also came to represent the right of senior citizens and others to decent, low-cost housing in their own communities. After a protracted struggle involving militant protests, the INTERNATIONAL HOTEL was torn down in 1977.

Shorter and more successful was the 1974 Confucius Plaza struggle being waged on the eastern side of the country. Though CONFUCIUS PLAZA, a 764-unit cooperative that included a school, a day-care center, and some commercial outlets, was being built in New York City's Chinatown, no Chinese Americans were employed in its construction. Community activists organized the local population to protest racial discrimination in the construction industry in general and at the Confucius Plaza site in particular. Several months of picketing and demonstrations led to a settlement that resulted in more jobs for Chinese American workers.

Community activists also went to the courts. In 1970, after years of trying to get the school system to provide an adequate education for Chinese immigrant children in San Francisco, parents of non-English speaking students filed a class-action suit against the San Francisco Board of Education on behalf of nearly eighteen hundred Chinese-speaking students. The parents argued that their children were being denied a meaningful public school education because the school board was not providing the necessary assistance, specifically help with English. In 1974, in the case of *LAU v. NICHOLS*, the U.S. Supreme Court ruled that the San Francisco school system had indeed violated the civil rights of these students and had discriminated against them when it failed to recognize their special educational needs. This landmark legal decision has become the foundation of bilingual-bicultural education for children who speak limited English. An important complement to the *Brown v. Board of Education* decision, which ended the racial segregation of African Americans in the U.S. school system, *Lau v. Nichols* addressed the issue of equal education for non-English speakers, such as recent Asian and Latino immigrants and refugees, and affirmed the linguistic and cultural diversity of American society.

Identity and Culture. Working alongside student and community activists were cultural activists dedicated to the development of an Asian American identity and culture. Unlike European Americans, who found it easier to incorporate their personal identity into their sense of being American, many Asian Americans believed that it was necessary to create an entirely new one. Asian Americans resolved their "identity crisis" by directly challenging the distorted images that have diminished them as individuals and denigrated them as a group, replacing them with more accurate ones based on historical knowledge about themselves. They also created a pan-Asian counterculture that reflected their values and experience. In so doing, they instilled pride and self-esteem in their generation. This process in turn awakened ethnic sensibilities and led to a sense of cultural freedom that gave birth to distinct artistic expressions of the Asian American experience, enriching the multicultural mosaic that is America. Playwright Frank CHIN has written provocative works dealing with the angst and alienation of being Asian American, attracting a loyal following in Movement cultural circles while upsetting the white literary establishment. Others, such as the novelist Maxine Hong KINGSTON, who has written on the Asian American experience from a decidedly feminist perspective, have generated controversy within the Movement but attracted acclaim from mainstream society.

Though this process is still unfolding, it is at least clear that Asian Americans have transcended the cultural limits of particular Asian ethnic groups to identify with the past experiences, present circumstances, and future aspirations of all Asians in America. By developing an integrated identity and a coherent culture, they have begun to build the foundations for a pan-Asian solidarity that will enable them to approach mainstream society on a more equal footing and participate more effectively in a culturally pluralist society.

Community-Based Organizations. In the process of mobilizing Asian Americans around social justice, educational equality, and pan-Asian cultural issues, activists have founded, developed, and institutionalized numerous community-based organizations. These organizations have largely been of two types: social service organizations, such as the Chinatown Planning Council in New York City and the Little Tokyo Service Center in Los Angeles, that deliver services and resources to mainly working-class Asian immigrants and refugees, and alternative grassroots organizations, such as the BASEMENT WORKSHOP in New York City and the ASIAN AMERICAN RESOURCE WORKSHOP in Boston, that address such significant issues as civil rights and helped to develop Asian American culture.

These new organizations have contributed to the social stability of the Asian American community by providing counseling services, welfare assistance, recreational facilities, and employment opportunities. They have mitigated the deprivations of the ghetto, helping individuals to survive, families to remain intact, and communities to thrive. Moreover, they have become a political force in their own right, challenging the control of traditional conservative organizations such as the CHINESE CONSOLIDATED BENEVOLENT ASSOCIATION (CCBA) and democratizing the community. As traditional leaders and their organizations have become increasingly irrelevant in the community, the new community-based organizations have assumed the role of intermediaries to the dominant society. Perhaps most important, these organizations have contributed to the Asian American community's cohesion, a necessary condition for collective action and advancement in a pluratist democratic society.

Women's Movement. As women activists grappled with the problem of racial inequality in U.S. society, they became acutely aware of the problem of gender inequality within the Asian American Movement. Almost from the beginning, they became conscious that Asian American WOMEN suffered from dual forms of oppression. Even if they successfully ended racism, they would still suffer from sexism. Recognizing the need for gender solidarity among Asian American women, concerned activists began to organize among themselves and to engage in collective action. Like the larger Movement, the Asian American women's movement began with small informal groups for personal support and political study and then evolved into large formal organizations that addressed the status and concerns of Asian American women throughout the nation. This development has benefited the Movement in important ways: By actuating the potential of women activists, it has widened their participation in the Movement; and by politicizing formerly inactive women, it has moved them to participate in the common struggle for equality and empowerment.

Sectarianism. While reformist members of the Movement established a host of new institutions as a basis for asserting themselves in the wider society, Asian American revolutionaries considered the existing social, economic, and political order corrupt and irredeemable, needing to be replaced by an entirely new order. Maoist sects, such as the RED GUARDS and Wei Min She (Organization for the People) in San Francisco, and the I WOR KUEN (Righteous and Harmonious Fists) and the Asian Study Group in New York City, tried to exploit these reformist institutions to obtain resources and influence in the community, as they prepared for the social revolution that was always looming over the political horizon.

In the early years, these Maoist sects attracted alienated Asian American youth searching for an explanation for their oppression and a way to overcome it. Without fully realizing it, these youths changed their focus from racism to capitalism. They came to believe that racial oppression was merely a tool of capitalists to divide the working class and that the fundamental solution was socialism. They exchanged their heightened consciousness of themselves as Asian Americans for what would finally prove to be a false consciousness of themselves as Maoist revolutionaries.

With the end of the Vietnam War in 1975, the Maoist sects began to decline. The dissipation of antigovernment sentiment and dwindling numbers of alienated youths made it increasingly difficult for the sects to sustain themselves, let alone grow, and they became bitter rivals for power within the Movement as well as the radical community. The resulting sectarian wars spilled over into various Movement struggles. A case in point was the Chol Soo LEE campaign. In June,

President Ronald Reagan signs the bill releasing more than a billion dollars in compensation to surviving Japanese American internees. (Ronald Reagan Library)

1974, Chol Soo Lee, a Korean immigrant, was convicted of murdering a Chinatown gang leader; in 1977, he received a death sentence for killing another inmate in self-defense and was sent to San Quentin's death row. The Asian American community, especially the Korean Americans, believed that he was innocent and organized a defense committee to obtain justice for him. This effort was marred by sectarian conflict between the Communist Workers Party and the League of Revolutionary Struggle, both of which eventually ceased working on the case altogether, but Chol Soo Lee's other supporters carried on and successfully obtained his freedom in 1983.

Sectarianism poisoned the Movement's atmosphere, tainting Asian American radicals of every political persuasion. For those who survived the sectarian conflicts and continued to be active in the Movement, it was no longer possible to work with others without wondering about their hidden political agenda.

Electoral Politics. By the 1980's, Asian American

radical politics had declined as the nation entered a conservative political era. Under the Reagan Administration, there was an assault on the liberal reforms of the previous two decades: The U.S. Civil Rights Commission was weakened, affirmative action programs were diluted, and social and human services programs were dismantled. Recognizing the futility of confrontational politics in this conservative climate, Asian American activists, including erstwhile Maoists, began participating in electoral politics, particularly Jesse Jackson's Rainbow Coalition and his bids for the presidency in 1984 and 1988. Many saw his political rallies as protest demonstrations reminiscent of an earlier era; Jackson seemed to be leading a social movement as well as an electoral campaign.

The 1980's also saw increasing numbers of Asian Americans running for political office, participating in partisan politics, and being appointed to government boards and commissions. In Los Angeles, for example, Michael Woo became the first Asian American to be

The rise in hate crimes in the United States has forced Asian Americans to embrace the goal of interethnic solidarity. (Frances M. Roberts)

elected to the City Council (1985) and Warren Furutani to the Board of Education (1988).

Ironically, it was during this difficult decade that Asian Americans achieved one of their most important victories—REDRESS and reparations for Japanese Americans interned in CONCENTRATION CAMPS during World War II. Ever since the camps were closed, there had been attempts to correct this injustice. With the coming of the Movement, this effort was reinvigorated. In 1981, President Jimmy Carter's federal COMMISSION ON WARTIME RELOCATION AND INTERNMENT OF CIVILIANS (CWRIC) held public hearings to investigate the camps and their effects on prisoners. The commission concluded that internment had not been justified by military necessity; instead, the incarceration was attributed to racial prejudice, war hysteria, and a failure of political leadership. On August 10, 1988, President Ronald Reagan signed the CIVIL LIBERTIES ACT, authorizing $1.25 billion in reparations payments to an estimated seventy thousand Japanese American camp survivors. Each internee was to receive $20,000 and a formal letter of apology from the president of the United States.

Anti-Asian Violence. During the conservative 1980's, ANTI-ASIAN VIOLENCE increased. In 1982, on the eve of his wedding, Vincent CHIN, a young Chinese American draftsman, was beaten to death with a baseball bat by an unemployed autoworker and his stepson, who apparently thought Chin was Japanese and blamed him for the auto industry's economic woes. In the ensuing trial, Chin's assailants were each sentenced to three years' probation and fined $3,780. Outraged by the light sentence, Chinese Americans and other Asian Americans demanded justice for Chin. Led by AMERICAN CITIZENS FOR JUSTICE (ACJ), Asian Americans were able to bring one of the perpetrators to court again for violating Chin's civil rights. In 1984, he was sentenced to twenty-five years in prison. However, his conviction was overturned on a technicality during the appeal process.

Meanwhile, harassment of and violence against Asian Americans continued unabated. One of the worst instances occurred at the end of the decade: In 1989, Patrick Purdy's hatred for Vietnamese sent him on a bloody rampage at an elementary school in Stockton, California, where he killed or wounded thirty-six children and one teacher. Of the five children killed, four were Cambodian Americans, and one was Vietnamese. Of the thirty-one wounded, twenty-two were Southeast Asian Americans.

Inter-Ethnic Conflict. As the Movement entered the 1990's, Asian Americans faced interethnic strife with other racial groups, indicating that the solidarity that existed among so-called Third World people during the late 1960's and in Jesse Jackson's Rainbow Coalition during the 1980's had all but disappeared. The underlying cause of these racial tensions and violent outbreaks has been growing economic injustice and social disintegration in the urban ghettos, and the failure of American society to deal with racial inequality.

Interethnic conflict has been especially marked between Korean Americans and African Americans, most destructively in the LOS ANGELES RIOTS OF 1992. Displaying the sort of race-driven hatred that has been visited upon them all too frequently in American history, African American and Latino rioters, aided by smaller numbers of whites, destroyed more than eighteen hundred Korean-owned businesses in KOREATOWN and South Central Los Angeles. The police ignored Korean Americans' pleas for protection, forcing them to use firearms to protect themselves, their families, and their businesses.

While the precipitating cause of the riot was the unexpected acquittal of four white policemen in the brutal beating of Rodney King, an African American, the underlying cause was economic competition and cultural misunderstanding. Korean Americans were singled out as scapegoats by African Americans who had become increasingly frustrated by rising unemployment and police brutality. Like other immigrants before them, notably Jews fleeing anti-Semitism in Europe, Korean American families have opened marginal businesses in poor and dangerous neighborhoods, where they put in long hours for small profits. Unfortunately, the Koreans have been mistakenly perceived as a privileged group receiving help from the government by an African American community that has been experiencing declining public assistance and that has blamed the paucity of black-owned businesses in the area on the government's unwillingness to provide equal help for African Americans.

Perhaps the only positive result of these anti-Asian incidents has been to raise the political consciousness of previously apathetic Asian Americans who had, unwittingly, bought into the MODEL MINORITY thesis that argues that Asian Americans have advanced in American society through hard work rather than through militant protest as other people of color, notably African Americans, have done. Indeed, in certain quarters, the idea of "Asian American activism" is inconceivable and its usage an oxymoron. Now, however, Asian Americans have realized the need for political empowerment, recognizing that on most issues it is mutually beneficial for Asian ethnic groups to unite with one another—to be part of the ongoing Asian American Movement. Beyond that there is the realization that Asian Americans must participate in interethnic coalitions working for equal rights and social justice. They must also engage in a meaningful dialogue with other people of color if the misperceptions and misunderstandings that have fueled interethnic animosities are to be avoided.

Significance of the Movement. Without necessarily intending to do so, the Asian American Movement has validated ethnic pluralism. Early on it recognized that the dominant society had failed to include, let alone integrate, Asian Americans. This exclusion had resulted in ethnic enclaves such as the CHINATOWNS, Little Tokyos, KOREATOWNS, and Little Saigons and had continued the cultural divisions inherited from Asia. Instead of increasing social fragmentation and racial tribalism, as some pundits feared, the Movement has contributed to greater cohesion and inclusivity by giving Asian Americans an effective means to assert, on their own terms, their right to belong to the mainstream society and to be treated as respected and responsible members of it. The Movement is a necessary step toward full membership in the national community and is part of the ongoing process of redefining the national identity, so that in the twenty-first century the latter will no longer be equated with only European American traditions, values, and institutions.

Though American cultural pluralism has hardly met its ideal specifications, it remains a viable concept and certainly one worth pursuing. To that end, a new generation of Asian American student activists has emerged to participate in the multicultural education movement, revitalizing the Movement on the eve of the twenty-first century. Multiculturalism traces its lineage to ethnic studies and is based on the belief that the country's common culture results from the interaction of its subsidiary cultures, of which the Asian American culture is one. In other words, America's common culture is itself multicultural in nature. Multiculturalism repudiates the "melting pot" perspective, which predicted the eventual disappearance of ethnic differences in American society and the emergence of a homogeneous dominant white culture, in favor of the "pluralistic" perspective, which accepts and affirms ethnic pluralism as a positive phenomenon. Ethnic pluralism has been a source of America's strength and a salient feature of its democratic tradition, protecting it from those who have advocated social revolution as the solution to its problems. In a milieu where ethnic diversity is valued—in itself or in its results—Asian Americans have done their share to oppose racial oppression, protest against social injustices, and participate in the political process, helping to build a stronger and more perfect union.—*William Wei*

SUGGESTED READINGS:

• Espiritu, Yen Le. *Asian American Panethnicity: Bridging Institutions and Identities.* Philadelphia: Temple University Press, 1992. A case study of how a panethnic group develops, this sociological work explores how diverse Asian national groups have submerged their differences and assumed a common Asian American identity. The author argues that panethnicity was able to develop only after the first generation had children who were born in the United States.

• Omatsu, Glen, ed. "Commemorative Issue: Salute to the 60s and 70s, Legacy of the San Francisco State Strike." *Amerasia Journal* 15, no. 1 (1989). *Amerasia Journal* dedicated this issue to the early years of the Movement. Focusing primarily on the San Francisco State strike, a defining event in the history of the Movement, it also includes articles on Asian American literature, education, communities, and students as well as reminiscences of Movement activists.

• Wei, William. *The Asian American Movement.* Philadelphia: Temple University Press, 1993. This is the only book-length study of the origins, development, and significance of the Asian American Movement. It is a social history that focuses on the salient aspects of the Movement, such as Asian American identity and culture, Asian American Studies, the Asian American alternative press, the Asian American women's movement, community-based organizations, Maoist sects, and electoral politics.

Asian American Political Coalition (AAPC): Private, nonpartisan, nonprofit New Jersey-based organization dedicated to raising political awareness among Asian Americans. The AAPC publishes a bimonthly newsletter, *The Asian American Voice*, which is distributed to members.

Asian American population: According to the 1990 U.S. census, Asian Americans make up the third-largest ethnic minority group in the United States. While their total population, between 7.2 and 7.3 million, is far below that of the two largest minority groups—African Americans, at about 30 million, and Hispanics, 22.4 million—Asian Americans are the fastest-growing group. Moreover, even though African

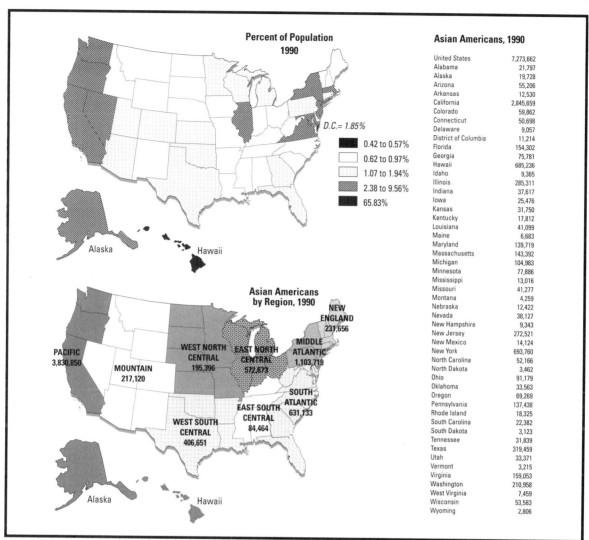

Percent of Population 1990

D.C.= 1.85%

- 0.42 to 0.57%
- 0.62 to 0.97%
- 1.07 to 1.94%
- 2.38 to 9.56%
- 65.83%

Alaska

Hawaii

Asian Americans by Region, 1990

PACIFIC 3,830,850

MOUNTAIN 217,120

WEST NORTH CENTRAL 195,396

EAST NORTH CENTRAL 572,673

NEW ENGLAND 231,656

MIDDLE ATLANTIC 1,103,719

SOUTH ATLANTIC 631,133

EAST SOUTH CENTRAL 84,464

WEST SOUTH CENTRAL 406,651

Alaska

Hawaii

Asian Americans, 1990	
United States	7,273,662
Alabama	21,797
Alaska	19,728
Arizona	55,206
Arkansas	12,530
California	2,845,659
Colorado	59,862
Connecticut	50,698
Delaware	9,057
District of Columbia	11,214
Florida	154,302
Georgia	75,781
Hawaii	685,236
Idaho	9,365
Illinois	285,311
Indiana	37,617
Iowa	25,476
Kansas	31,750
Kentucky	17,812
Louisiana	41,099
Maine	6,683
Maryland	139,719
Massachusetts	143,392
Michigan	104,983
Minnesota	77,886
Mississippi	13,016
Missouri	41,277
Montana	4,259
Nebraska	12,422
Nevada	38,127
New Hampshire	9,343
New Jersey	272,521
New Mexico	14,124
New York	693,760
North Carolina	52,166
North Dakota	3,462
Ohio	91,179
Oklahoma	33,563
Oregon	69,269
Pennsylvania	137,438
Rhode Island	18,325
South Carolina	22,382
South Dakota	3,123
Tennessee	31,839
Texas	319,459
Utah	33,371
Vermont	3,215
Virginia	159,053
Washington	210,958
West Virginia	7,459
Wisconsin	53,583
Wyoming	2,806

Source: Mark T. Mattson, *Atlas of the 1990 Census.* New York: Macmillan, 1992.

Americans and Hispanics outnumber Asian Americans, Asian Americans are more widely distributed geographically.

(Note that exact numbers cited for total Asian American population and population of specific Asian American national or ethnic groups may vary depending on the source. In general, although not across the board, statistics drawn from the Bureau of the Census publication *1990 Census of the Population: Asians and Pacific Islanders in the United States* [1993] are slightly smaller than the corresponding figures in the bureau's *General Population Characteristics* reports. For example, the total Asian American population in the former is 7,226,986, while in the latter it is 7,273,662.)

Between 1980 and 1990, the Asian American population more than doubled. (Paul Ong and Suzanne J. Hee, "Twenty Million in 2020," in *The State of Asian Pacific America: Policy Issues to the Year 2020*, LEAP Asian Pacific Public Policy Center and UCLA ASIAN AMERICAN STUDIES CENTER [1993], use slightly larger figures for 1980, resulting in an increase of 95 percent rather than 108 percent.) Chinese experienced the largest growth in total number, about 840,000, followed by Filipinos, whose population in the United States increased by about 630,000. In terms of percent growth, the fastest-growing group among the six largest Asian American groups was the Vietnamese, 135 percent, followed by Asian Indians and Koreans, both around 125 percent. Among the smaller Asian American groups there were some with even higher percent growth. The Cambodian population in the United

States, for example, went from 16,000 in 1980 to 150,000 in 1990—an increase of more than 800 percent.

Much of the increase in the Asian American population can be attributed to high levels of immigration following the IMMIGRATION AND NATIONALITY ACT OF 1965, coupled with the exodus of refugees from Southeast Asia in the wake of the Vietnam War. In 1991 the United States admitted more than 1.8 million immigrants—almost four times the 1972 total. In that twenty-year span, immigration from Asia has transformed existing Asian American communities and created entirely new ones. Of the top ten sources of immigration to the United States in 1991, five were Asian nations: the Philippines (#2, behind Mexico; 63,600), Vietnam (#4; 55,300), India (#7; 45,100), China (#9; 33,000), and South Korea (#10; 26,500). If the figures for Taiwan (#21; 13,300) and Hong Kong (#25; 10,400) were added to China's total, China would move ahead of Vietnam.

Projections for the future growth of the Asian American population must reckon with many factors, not least the question of whether immigration will continue into the twenty-first century at anything like current levels. Ong and Hee offer three projections, each based on a different set of assumptions regarding immigration and birthrate; two of their scenarios project an Asian American population of 17.9 million in 2020, while the third, their "preferred projection," estimates that by 2020 the Asian American population will have reached 20.2 million. In any case, it is certain that Asian Americans will be an increasingly significant presence in the multicultural society of the United States.

Asian American Renaissance: Community-based Asian American arts organization, founded in Minnesota in 1991. In addition to artists—writers, musicians, visual artists, and others—the organization includes members from many other segments of the Asian American community. The group held its first conference, the Asian American Cultural Renaissance Conference, in St. Paul, Minnesota, in 1992.

Asian American Resource Workshop (AARW): Community-based strategic planning group. Established in 1979 and having more than five hundred members, the AARW is the only organization in the New England area with an Asian American Board of Trustees and staff addressing issues from a pan-Asian perspective.

AARW founders include community activists, educators, and students who saw the need to take a comprehensive approach in solving the problems of the Asian American community in the greater Boston area. The organization's mission is the empowerment of the community in defining issues and the development of effective strategies to address those issues. The board of the AARW is composed of persons active in the Asian American community who are committed to the goals and mission of the organization. The board is managed by an executive director who supervises the staff, and by interns, volunteers, and consultants.

AARW projects and activities strive to promote and document the Asian American experience: community control over land use, REDRESS and reparations for Japanese Americans, ANTI-ASIAN VIOLENCE, civil rights, community development, media stereotypes, voter education, and debunking the MODEL MINORITY myth. Members participate in developing and implementing projects, presenting workshops, producing the AARW newsletter, and serving as board members.

The AARW's resources include a library of books and visual media, and referral and research assistance on Asian American issues. Other programs include community support work such as serving as a fiscal agent, providing meeting and work space, and speaking out on community issues. AARW publications include *The Asian American Comic Book*, an annual Massachusetts Asian/Pacific American directory, a newsletter, and a monthly calendar of events.

Asian American Studies: Asian American Studies can mean two related, though slightly different, things. In one sense, Asian American Studies can refer to that academic discipline—and the institutional programs—devoted to the investigation of the Asian American experience, including the social, cultural, and political issues involving Asian Americans. It can also refer to the body of scholarly research concerning Asian Americans, which has now become rather substantial.

Beginnings. Asian American Studies is a relatively new field of study. It grew out of the social unrest of the 1960's, when the Civil Rights movement, the antiwar movement, and women's liberation led to demonstrations at college campuses across the United States. One result of this conjunction of forces was a heightened sense of ethnic identity among those groups who were excluded from full participation in American society. William Wei's study, *The Asian American Movement* (1993), shows how this student activism led to the development of Asian American Studies.

The advent of Asian American Studies is traceable, in part, to the demands voiced by minority students on U.S. college and university campuses for curricula more relevant to their racial backgrounds. (Ben Klaffke)

Originating in the late 1960's, Asian American Studies is now solidly established as a legitimate academic discipline. (James L. Shaffer)

In November, 1968, minority students at San Francisco State University, as well as at the University of California, Berkeley, demanded more relevance in their classes and a greater voice in the administration of their school. Asian American activist groups, such as the Intercollegiate Chinese for Social Action, the Asian-American Political Alliance, and the Philippine-American Collegiate Endeavor, protested alongside other members of the Third World Liberation Front (TWLF). At San Francisco State, the student strike lasted five months (one of the longest in American history) amid much violence and civil unrest.

The TWLF strikes in 1968-1969 led to the first courses on Asian American Studies being taught in the United States. In 1969 San Francisco State University established its School of Ethnic Studies and the University of California, Berkeley its Department of Ethnic Studies. The following year, the University of California, Los Angeles (UCLA) began its ASIAN AMERICAN STUDIES CENTER. The early days of these programs were difficult, as funding was hard to find and conservative academics were often suspicious of the appropriateness and rigor of ethnic studies as a discipline. Some people outside the academic community felt that programs such as Asian American Studies were only attempts to placate unappreciative, though highly vocal, students—that is, concessions made by weak administrators.

Asian American Studies programs continued to develop, however, and by the 1990's the field was solidly established as an academic discipline. More than five hundred researchers generally attend the annual meetings of the ASSOCIATION FOR ASIAN AMERICAN STUDIES. In 1993 there were more than twenty Asian American Studies programs at universities in the United States. UCLA offers a master's degree in Asian American Studies and publishes several germane journals and research reports, and Berkeley often offers more than two dozen courses a year on Asian American issues. It is difficult to sum up a whole field in a few paragraphs, but the following are some of the areas in which important work is being done in Asian American Studies.

Labor History. Labor history is one of the oldest concerns in the discipline of Asian American Studies. It is now well documented, for example, that nineteenth century Asian immigrants played a vital role in the building of America. Alexander Saxton's *The Indispensable Enemy: Labor and the Anti-Chinese Movement in California* (1971) was a pioneering book in this area. Sucheng Chan's *This Bittersweet Soil: The Chinese in California Agriculture, 1860-1910* (1986), shows how Chinese laborers, farmers, and entrepreneurs contributed to the development of agriculture in California. At the same time, many scholars are turning their attention to recent immigrants: Chinese in the garment industry, Vietnamese in the fishing industry, Filipino health-care workers, Indian motel managers, Korean grocers. Labor history promises to remain one of the most fruitful areas of Asian American scholarship.

Oral History and Folklore. Beginning in the 1970's and 1980's, many Asian American scholars started extensive and far-reaching oral history projects, attempting to capture the essence of the Asian American experience in the participants' own words. Victor and Brett Nee's *Longtime Californ': A Documentary Study of an American Chinatown* (1973) and Linda Tamura's *The Hood River Issei: An Oral History of Japanese Settlers in Oregon's Hood River Valley* (1993) are only two among many works that make extensive use of oral history. Ronald TAKAKI's influential and controversial *Strangers from a Different Shore: A History of Asian Americans* (1989) also relies heavily on oral history. In turn, this scholarly activity has contributed to the revitalized interest in oral history by mainstream American folklorists and anthropologists.

Literature. There is a rapidly growing body of—as well as a market for—Asian American novels, short stories, poetry, and works in other literary forms. Asian American writers such as Maxine Hong KINGSTON and Amy TAN have had a major impact on contemporary American literature. At the same time time, there is a growing recognition of the historical sweep and the breadth of Asian American writing, attested by King-Kok CHEUNG and Stan Yogi's *Asian American Literature: An Annotated Bibliography* (1988). In works such as Sau-ling Cynthia WONG's *Reading Asian American Literature: From Necessity to Extravagance* (1993) and essay collections such as *Reading the Literatures of Asian America* (1992), edited by Shirley Geok-lin LIM and Amy LING, scholars are beginning to map this rich field.

Women's Issues. From the beginning, Asian American Studies has had a strong feminist component, in part rooted in the particularities of the Asian American experience. Asian American WOMEN share the con-

cerns of other women in a sexist society; moreover, many Asian immigrants come to the United States from cultures that are strongly male-dominated and even more discriminatory against women. At the same time, Asian American women experience racism, distinguishing them from mainstream feminists. A good sampling of what Sucheta MAZUMDAR describes as "A Woman-Centered Perspective on Asian American History" can be found in *Making Waves: An Anthology of Writings By and About Asian American Women* (1989), edited by ASIAN WOMEN UNITED of California, with an introduction by Mazumdar.

Education. Asian American researchers are also interested in theories and models of education. One reason for this is that, historically, Asian Americans have used education as a means for social advancement. More recently, however, Asian American scholastic success has ironically had a negative impact. For example, several of the most prestigious universities in the United States have allegedly set quotas on Asian American admissions. The issue of whether or not

Many Asian Americans have tended to view education as the key component to a successful future. This tendency has been a fertile source of study for scholars researching the Asian American experience. (Unicorn Stock Photos)

students should be admitted purely on scholastic "color-blind" qualifications—or whether a student body should somehow reflect the national population as a whole—is a question that is more than merely academic for Asian American scholars. At the same time, many Asian American scholars have pointed out the damaging consequences of the MODEL MINORITY stereotype for educational policy, calling for greater recognition of the diversity within the Asian American community.

Community Studies. Histories and sociological studies of ethnic communities make up another fertile area of research. Many early works in this area predated the founding of Asian American Studies as a discipline. The post-1965 upsurge in Asian immigration has prompted an explosion of scholarship in this field. Works such as Ilsoo KIM's *New Urban Immigrants: The Korean Community in New York* (1981) focus on new immigrant communities, tracing distinctive patterns of adaptation.

To some extent, this division of the field into distinct areas is misleading. The areas often overlap; oral histories, for example, are often community studies (as in Tamura's oral history of Hood River). Moreover, Asian American Studies has made substantial contributions in many areas not mentioned in this brief overview. Taken as a whole, the work of scholars in this field has called into question the image of the United States as a "melting pot." The Asian American case has shown that the dynamics of race and ethnicity in America are much more complex than many Americans would wish to acknowledge. Asian American Studies has been influential in overcoming racial stereotyping; it has helped people of all backgrounds learn more about the many accomplishments and contributions of Asian Americans. The addition of Asian American Studies to the curriculum has made American education in general more inclusive, equitable, and democratic.— *James Stanlaw*

SUGGESTED READINGS: • Asian Women United of California, eds. *Making Waves: An Anthology of Writings By and About Asian American Women.* Boston: Beacon Press, 1989. *Change: The Magazine of Higher Learning* 28 (November/December, 1989). Special issue on Asian Americans. • Hune, Shirley, et al., eds. *Asian Americans: Comparative and Global Perspectives.* Pullman: Washington State University Press, 1991. • Nomura, Gail, et al., eds. *Frontiers of Asian American Studies.* Pullman: Washington State University Press, 1989. • Okihiro, Gary, et al., eds. *Reflections on Shattered Windows: Promises and Prospects*

for Asian American Studies. Pullman: Washington State University Press, 1988. • Omatsu, Glenn, ed. "Commemorative Issue: Salute to the 60s and 70s Legacy of the San Francisco State Strike." *Amerasia Journal* 15, no.1 (1989). • Wei, William. *The Asian American Movement.* Philadelphia: Temple University Press, 1993.

Asian American Studies, University of California, Berkeley: Academic unit focusing on Asian American history and culture. The Asian American Studies program at the University of California, Berkeley, one of the leading programs in the field, is a direct product of the Third World Students Strike of 1969. The strike was part of a larger response to social upheavals of the 1960's, including changing demographics and attendant new needs in the Asian American community, Asian American students' dissatisfaction with an unresponsive educational establishment and irrelevant curricula, the Civil Rights movement, the Anti-Vietnam War movement, and the Black Power movement on which many early Asian American activists modeled their work. (See ASIAN AMERICAN MOVEMENT and ASIAN AMERICAN STUDIES.)

In fall quarter, 1969, upon establishment of an ethnic studies department, the unit then known as the Asian American Division began formal operations and offered its first courses. Enrollment grew quickly, and the curriculum expanded to include three concentrations: history, community studies, and the humanities. Also offered were community language courses, and courses to satisfy the Subject A (remedial writing) requirement offered as an alternative to Asian-ancestry students, especially immigrant ones. Early courses had close relationships with local community agencies, which the instructors, staff, field work assistants, and students helped to develop with their labor, expertise, and resources. Appropriate teaching materials were seldom commercially available and had to be devised on an ad hoc basis. Despite difficulties, an Asian American Studies major was created as early as 1973. In the mid-1970's, as the need to institutionalize became clear, the program began strengthening its academic component, establishing a stable cadre of regular-rank faculty and systematizing its curriculum.

Over the next two decades, the student population served by the program underwent many changes. In 1971, Asian-ancestry students, numbering 3,100, made up only 12.6 percent of the university's undergraduate population; many of the early students were American-born descendants of "oldtimers," and Chinese and Japanese predominated. By the early 1990's, the Asian American student population had more than doubled, making up more than one-third of the undergraduate population. As a reflection of the diversity of the Asian American community resulting from the immigration reform of 1965, the Berkeley student population includes not only Chinese and Japanese but also large numbers of Filipinos, Koreans, Southeast Asians, and South Asians; it has a much higher proportion of first-generation students; and many students are of middle-class, suburban origin.

The Asian American Studies program has been evolving to address this diversity. In the five-year period from 1990 to 1994 it has served 1,300-1,600 students per year, and now offers some thirty-six courses per year, including courses on the histories of individual ethnic subgroups. Its faculty, numbering 6.5 FTEs (full-time equivalents), has not only been teaching Asian American Studies courses but also contributing to the university's undergraduate major and Ph.D. program in comparative ethnic studies. The Asian American Studies Library, little more than a reading room in the early 1970's, is now a full-service library with a collection of more than 35,000 volumes. The program applied for departmental status in spring semester of 1994.

Asian American Studies, University of California, Irvine: Established on paper in 1992, the fledgling Asian American Studies program at the University of California, Irvine (UCI) made news one year later when almost one hundred Asian American student protesters staged a rotating hunger strike that lasted thirty-five days. The students were protesting the fact that, at the time, only two Asian American Studies courses were regularly being offered, often with waiting lists of more than four hundred names, and that no new faculty had been hired to teach in the program.

Set in Orange County, home to the largest Vietnamese settlement outside of Vietnam, the UCI student body boasted the highest percentage of Asian Pacific American students among universities in the continental United States. Some two-fifths of students and more than half of the first-year class were of Asian Pacific American heritage. Although an East Asian Languages and Literatures Department had been created with great fanfare in 1989, that program focused on Asia rather than Asians in the United States. Until 1993, the school had only one tenure-track Asian Americanist, sociologist John Mei Liu. Liu turned down an offer to head the Asian American Studies

Program at the University of California, Davis, and remained at UCI, where he attained tenure that year.

The hunger strike had been preceded by a student occupation of the administration building in April, 1993, and an effort two years earlier, involving Asian and other ethnic students on campus, to push for curriculum reform. The Ethnic Students' Coalition Against Prejudicial Education (ESCAPE) disrupted UCI's twenty-fifth anniversary celebrations in 1991 by demonstrating for ethnic studies programs and chanting, "Celebrate what?"

The hunger strikers in 1993 had some important allies. A group of area Asian American professionals, calling themselves Community Support for Academic Relevance, garnered widespread support for the program. State Senator Art Torres visited the strikers and hinted he might withhold funding from the university. Asian American Studies faculty and staff members from more than a dozen area colleges, meeting in Irvine, also endorsed the idea of a viable program. The Asian American student alternative newsmagazine, *Rice Paper*, ran editorials on the need to "diversify the curriculum" with an ethnic perspective. Asian American cultures are "unique and deserve to be studied," the paper argued. UCI will never be "world class," one editorial asserted, "until it adopts a comprehensive approach to learning," one that responds to the needs of the students. Hunger strikers also made their pitch for support at Orange County's first Asian Pacific American Film and Video Festival held on campus in May, 1993.

The hunger strikers, whose banners proclaimed, "Bodily Hunger Is Nothing Compared to Intellectual Starvation, " finally overcame the administration's resistance and negotiated in June, 1993, an unprecedented settlement with the administration that guaranteed four tenure-track faculty positions in the program. With a new administrator, Chancellor Laurel L. Wilkening, vowing her support of the program, the future expansion of the program appeared more assured.

Asian American Studies Center, University of California, Los Angeles: Academic unit specializing in research on Asian American history and culture. This University of California, Los Angeles (UCLA) program is one of the leading Asian American Studies programs in the United States. The center offers both an undergraduate minor and a master's degree in Asian American Studies. The M.A. degree is the first graduate degree in Asian American Studies to be offered in

North America. In addition, the center has proposed a B.A. degree in Asian American Studies.

The UCLA Asian American Studies Center is one of the oldest in the United States. It began in 1970, soon after the first program in Asian American Studies began in 1969 at San Francisco State. Besides administering classes, faculty, and curricula, this academic unit is one of the few places in the United States devoted to research on the Asian American experience. Research activities of the center have included Asian Pacific demographics, mental health studies, the assimilation problems of the new immigrant Asian populations, and Chinese and Filipino studies.

The center also publishes *Amerasia Journal*, the only international academic publication devoted to scholarship on the history, literature, and culture of Asian and Pacific Americans. Book reviews and criticism are also included, and each year the journal puts out an annual selected bibliography, usually of more than five hundred entries, of the previous year's scholarship on Asian American Studies and literature, including legal, political, and educational issues of concern to Asian Americans. The center also publishes *CrossCurrents*, a newsmagazine that serves as a forum for Asian American social, cultural, and political affairs. The center also offers textbooks, curriculum guides, and various research reports from its ongoing projects. A reading room with an extensive collection of research materials is also available to the public. The reading room has many primary and secondary sources, including a collection of several hundred newsletters from more than one hundred cities and colleges.

Besides research and academics, the Asian American Studies Center also provides social and cultural activities for Asian American UCLA students and others in the community. It also acts as a clearinghouse for available job opportunities, fellowships, internships, and research grants.

Asian-American Theatre Company: Originally established in San Francisco, California, in 1972 as the Asian American Theatre Workshop (AATW) with backing from San Francisco's American Conservatory Theatre (ACT). The organization changed its name to the Asian-American Theatre Company (AATC) in 1977 shortly after the somewhat acrimonious departure of Frank CHIN, its first artistic director. Chin had envisioned an Asian American theater that would serve Asian American artists and their communities and raise issues of concern to them while ignoring the desires of the non-Asian audience marketplace. Chin

Plays by such notable Asian American playwrights as Philip Kan Gotanda have premiered at the Asian-American Theatre Company. (Chester Yoshida)

believed that only in such a purely Asian American environment could a uniquely Asian American aesthetic emerge. While many continue to praise AATW's early productions of his *The Chickencoop Chinaman* (1974-1975 season) and *The Year of the Dragon* (1976-1977 season), Chin's radical position and unwillingness to make concessions to the dominant culture audience created tension with more pragmatic factions in the group. Accordingly his departure and the renaming of the group marked a new beginning.

The Asian-American Theatre Company, then, while continuing to support Asian American talent and its community, aimed to be more mindful of the broader spectatorship of San Francisco. To the organization's credit it has successfully addressed the broader audience, with many productions traveling to venues in the East Bay San Francisco area. Notable in the AATC's productions are important pieces by Wakako YAMA-

UCHI, Philip Kan GOTANDA, David Henry HWANG, R. A. SHIOMI, Velina Hasu HOUSTON, Lane NISHIKAWA, and Sumio Kubota. In addition, through performance series such as *Tsunami: The Next Wave*, the AATC has shown a clear desire to embrace and encourage younger generations of artists such as Philippine-born Hang Ong, Korean American Florence Yoo, Kelly Diem Nguyen, and Judy Weng.

Asian Americans for Community Involvement(AACI): Nonprofit organization founded in 1973. It provides comprehensive social and human services to Asian Pacific immigrants and refugees in Santa Clara County, California.

With a budget of more than three million dollars and with seventy-five staff members, the AACI is the largest multiservice organization addressing the needs of people of all ages from different Asian American ethnic populations. Its staff members are proficient in twenty-one Asian Pacific languages and dialects and include physicians, psychiatrists, psychologists, social workers, family counselors, specialists in recreation, and teachers. The organization's services include counseling, crisis intervention, education, information and referrals, case management, advocacy, social and recreational programs, and training of service providers.

The AACI serves more than thirty thousand people each year. Its stated goals are to advocate for equal rights and opportunities for Asian Pacific Americans; eliminate racial stereotypes in communication, media, and education by promoting the history, culture, and concerns of the Asian Pacific American community; provide culturally and linguistically appropriate human services; train culturally competent service providers; and empower Asian Pacific Americans, individually and collectively, to participate fully in American society.

Formed by a group of community activists, educators, professionals, and concerned individuals, the AACI's first major effort centered on textbook reform in California, an effort that lasted more than three years. The campaign resulted in the State Board of Education's 1976 directive (which eventually became a legislation) that textbooks had to be screened and recommended by local multiethnic committees prior to adoption by the state.

Educational issues remained a priority for the AACI in subsequent years, with the organization sponsoring various presentations on Asian Pacific American culture and history. AACI board members have conducted courses at local colleges on Asian Pacific American

history and contemporary issues. The AACI also works to ensure representation for Asian Pacific Americans within the educational system.

The AACI's programmatic operations are largely based on the philosophical orientation of founder and Executive Director Allan Seid. Seid believes that the AACI is based on the notions of ethnic pride and dignity, individual and collective self-help, and community empowerment. Once the community is empowered, it can be responsible for and capable of responding adequately to its needs. The AACI strives to be client-centered; its services are not acts of charity but vehicles for establishing social and economic justice.

Asian Americans for Equality (AAFE): Organization founded in 1974 in New York by a group of Asian community activists, the organization was originally known as Asian Americans for Equal Employment. These activists first banded together as a group and organized a protest when they learned that a 764-unit housing complex, CONFUCIUS PLAZA, was being built in the heart of New York's Chinatown with no Asians employed. After a six-month struggle, twenty-four jobs were won. The victory signaled the entry of Asians into the construction industry.

Thus inspired, the AAFE moved to fight against injustice and discrimination in New York's CHINATOWN. It led the fight against police brutality on behalf of Peter Yew, who was badly beaten over a traffic incident. It organized tenant and rent strikes. It rallied support for Vincent CHIN, a young man bashed to death by disgruntled auto workers in Detroit. It provided social services in the form of after-school activities, English-language classes, referral assistance, and translation services.

These activities were run by volunteers until 1983, when a small grant enabled the AAFE to hire paid staff. After that, the AAFE began receiving grants from other sources to enable it to move its activities from a reactive one of demonstration and protest to a proactive one of renovating housing and stimulating the economy.

Starting in 1986, with grants from New York State and New York City, the AAFE moved to upgrade rundown tenement apartments for senior citizens and low-income families. From 1986 to 1992, 145 housing units were renovated. This upgrading of the housing stock in lower Manhattan improved the neighborhood and provided much-needed housing for residents in the community. Instead of confronting landlords for their poor services or lack of them to tenants, the AAFE taught landlords how to obtain loans from the Rental Rehabilitation Program of New York City and assisted them in that process.

To stimulate business and provide jobs in Lower Manhattan, the AAFE has operated a red trolley bus that travels between Little Italy, Chinatown, and the South Street Seaport. For a one-price ticket, tourists and visitors can board or get off the trolley at any of these attractions, stimulating the area's business.

The AAFE, located in New York's Chinatown, has grown from a volunteer organization to an established community institution that looks after the interests of its people and works to better their lives.

Asian CineVision (ACV): Nonprofit national media arts center founded in 1976 by Peter Chow, Christine CHOY, and Tsui Hark. ACV is committed to the development of Asian American film and video arts.

ACV's original goal was to provide video training workshops for the New York Chinese community, which could then create programs for the new public access channel on Manhattan Cable. In 1977 ACV video producers were able to produce thirty minutes of programming per week, and by 1982 they were producing a nightly news program for the Chinese-speaking community. Meanwhile ACV had greatly expanded its scope to include exhibitions, media archival and information services, production services, and publications.

In 1978 ACV organized the first ASIAN AMERICAN INTERNATIONAL FILM FESTIVAL (AAIFF), a three-day long exhibition of 50 films by Asian Americans. Since then, this popular festival has expanded to include films by Asians as well as Asian Americans and as of 1993 exhibits fifty-plus films over a six-day period. Each year the AAIFF premieres in New York, before beginning an international tour. By 1992 the AAIFF had presented more than five hundred Asian/Asian American films.

Other projects include the Asian American International Video Festival (AAIVF), the Children's Film Series, and the Asian Film Series. The AAIVF annually presents creative videos by Asian/Asian Americans; it has featured artists such as Nam June PAIK, Arturo Cubacub, and Bruce and Norman Yonemoto. The Children's Film Series, "The Picture Train," co-sponsored with the New York Public Library, is an annual eight-week-long series of films for and about Asian American children. Each autumn the Asian Film Series, "Cinema and Society," combines a scholarly seminar with screenings of the best Asian films, such

as those of Ishmael Bernal, Shohei Imamura, Lino Brocka, Nagisa Oshima, and Wu Tianming.

The ACV Media Archive/Library is open to on-premise use by the public. The Media Information Service provides information and referrals related to Asian American media arts. ACV's Production Services provide low-cost access to video production equipment.

ACV published the *Asian American Media Reference Guide*, a catalog of Asian film and video programs, and *CineVue*, issued five times a year.

Asian Immigrant Women's Advocates: Nonprofit, membership-supported community organizing agency in Oakland and San Jose, California, dedicated to improving the socioeconomic conditions of immigrant women, founded in 1983. The group began by offering translation services and workplace literacy programs to immigrant women. It expanded its services to include vocational English classes, legal referral, leadership training programs, a food production/packaging cooperative, and bilingual workshops on employment rights and occupational health/safety.

Asian Indian businesses in the United States: Immigration of business people and professionals from South Asia to the United States was minimal prior to World War II. The first South Asian immigrants to the United States were largely farm laborers, some of whom ultimately became farmers. Most of the immigrants who came from South Asia after the immigration reform of 1965 aimed, initially at least, at careers as salaried professionals, not as independent businesspeople. Yet by 1980 the U.S. census listed 6.6 percent of Asian Indian males as self-employed. This was slightly below the percentage among Caucasians (7.4 percent) and well below the percentage among Koreans (16.5 percent) but well above the percentage among African Americans (3.0 percent).

South Asians in the Import-Export Business. One early immigrant South Asian businessman, one of the relatively few pre-World War II middle-class immigrants, was Gobindram J. WATUMULL, a Hindu born in 1891 in Hyderabad, in Sind (The Hindus of Sind, who became refugees after the partition of British India in 1947, are known for their entrepreneurial talent). In 1917 he joined forces with an older brother, who ran an export-import business in Hawaii. The two brothers, whose business expanded after 1930, designed and sold the first aloha shirts. After the bombing of Pearl Harbor in 1941, branches of the business were set up in

Asian Indian Businesses in the U.S. by Type and Receipts, 1987

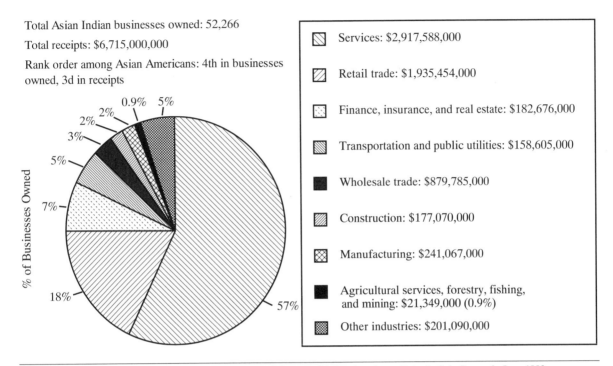

Total Asian Indian businesses owned: 52,266

Total receipts: $6,715,000,000

Rank order among Asian Americans: 4th in businesses owned, 3d in receipts

% of Businesses Owned

5%
0.9%
2%
2%
3%
5%
7%
18%
57%

Services: $2,917,588,000

Retail trade: $1,935,454,000

Finance, insurance, and real estate: $182,676,000

Transportation and public utilities: $158,605,000

Wholesale trade: $879,785,000

Construction: $177,070,000

Manufacturing: $241,067,000

Agricultural services, forestry, fishing, and mining: $21,349,000 (0.9%)

Other industries: $201,090,000

Source: Susan B. Gall and Timothy L. Gall, eds. *Statistical Record of Asian Americans.* Detroit: Gale Research, Inc., 1993.

California. With the wealth gained from the business, Gobindram Watumull set up the WATUMULL FOUNDATION, designed to give intelligent young people from the Indian subcontinent a chance to study in America.

Even for post-1965 South Asian immigrants, the import-export business remained an important outlet for entrepreneurial talents. By the early 1980's, post-1965 South Asian immigrants in Southern California, at one time mostly salaried professionals, included a significant number of people engaged in this business.

South Asians in the Restaurant Business. A major area of endeavor for post-1965 South Asian immigrant entrepreneurs has been the restaurant business. These entrepreneurs have taken advantage of the more adventurous palate developed by many Americans as the latter became better-educated and better-traveled after World War II. Indeed, Indian restaurants are not confined to cities such as New York and Los Angeles; by the early 1990's there were, for example, five Indian restaurants in the middle-sized metropolitan area of Buffalo, New York, in the so-called Rustbelt. In New York City, the restaurant business has become an important source of income not only for Hindus and Sikhs but also for Muslim immigrants from Bangla-

desh. As yet, however, Indian restaurants have not developed the fast-food-market momentum that Mexican restaurants enjoy. In the late 1980's, the Sikh immigrant Sant Singh Charwal tried to set up a chain of Indian restaurants, called the "Bombay Palace," aimed at the fast-food market. Although he at first seemed to have a good chance of success, he eventually ran into serious financial difficulties.

South Asians in High-Technology Enterprises. South Asians of the post-1965 immigrant wave have scored notable successes as entrepreneurs in high technology, where their university training and early experience as salaried professionals have paid off handsomely. In 1980 Subramonian Shankar, who was a director of personal-computer research and development at a large conglomerate in India, migrated to the United States. In 1985, with a partner, he founded American Megatrends, a firm based in Norcross, Georgia, that manufactured personal-computer motherboards and software. By 1991, when Shankar was still in his early forties, the company had registered sales of $70 million and employed 130 workers, both immigrants and native-born Americans. By early 1993, a Pakistan-born electrical engineer, Safi Ur-

This South Asian Indian market in Northridge, California, specializes in food items native to Indian culture. (Martin A. Hutner)

rehman Qureshey, also in his early forties, had carved out a profitable niche for himself as president of AST Research. The company introduced such things as upgradable personal computers, twenty-four hour computer bulletin board and facsimile customer support, and a segmented product line.

In 1990 the Silicon Valley of California boasted several hundred South Asian immigrant millionaires, who had helped found such high-technology enterprises as Sun Microsystems. One prominent Silicon Valley entrepreneur of South Asian background was Akram Chowdry, the Pakistani immigrant head of Mylex Corporation, a San Jose-based manufacturer of computer circuit boards. Although Chowdry himself was Muslim, his engineering staff was largely Hindu; he made a habit of importing Indian engineers to work with his manufacturing staff.

South Asians in the Hotel and Motel Business. The best-known area of South Asian immigrant en-

trepreneurial endeavor is probably the hotel and motel business, entered into by Hindu immigrants from the western Indian province of Gujarat. These Gujaratis, almost all of whom bore the surname of Patel, began arriving in California in the late 1940's. They bought up dilapidated hotels, often in deteriorating neighborhoods, which their original owners had given up as a loss; using inexpensive family labor, the Patels were able to make these hotels turn a profit. By the mid-1980's, Patel-run hotels were common in the state of California and had spread to the East Coast.

Miscellaneous Indian Enterprises. Exploiting a niche neglected by established businesspeople also proved a winning strategy for such immigrants as Tushar Kothari, Pravin Mehta, and Arun Bhansali, all members of the Jain sect, from the Bombay area of India, and all diamond traders. In the United States, in the 1960's, established diamond traders, mostly Jewish, monopolized the market for expensive gems; they showed little interest, however, in the cheaper diamonds. The Jain immigrant traders found a market for these cheaper diamonds, which they imported from India (where labor costs were low).

One Indian immigrant, Shashikant Jogani, born near Bombay, was even able to make a great deal of money in real estate. Jogani, who migrated to America as a university student in engineering in 1969, started out in the family business of diamond trading. Beginning in 1979, Jogani, with the aid of profits from the diamond business and money borrowed from his family, accumulated properties in Los Angeles, California, by pyramiding his debt. Avoiding the investment in expensive properties that ultimately doomed so many native-born American real estate investors, Jogani, who bought run-down properties and fixed them up, stuck to providing apartments for blue-collar workers and others who could not afford to buy their own homes. Buying buildings for as little as $20,000 per unit, Jogani was eventually able to rent some of them for as much as $6,500 a year in the tight Los Angeles market. In 1990, Jogani was one of the city's largest residential landlords. In 1994, one of his Northridge apartment buildings collapsed in a major earthquake, killing sixteen people.

Asian Indian-owned gem dealership in the "Little India" section of Artesia, California. (Martin A. Hutner)

By the mid-1980's, the newsstand business in New York City had become practically monopolized by Indian and Pakistani immigrants; about 70 percent of the city's kiosks are estimated to have been under their control at that time. One of the largest operators was Punjab-born Bhawness Kapoor, who in 1983 won a fifteen-year license to run all the stands in the city's subway system. By the early 1990's, however, immigrants from the Middle East were moving into the business as the children of South Asian newsstand owners moved into different lines of work.

South Asian immigrants have become involved in many other enterprises as well, including machine shops, photography studios, laundries, gift shops, and even the garment industry. By the early 1990's, nearly 40 percent of New York City's gas stations were owned by Punjabi Sikh immigrants, many of them from blue-collar rather than professional backgrounds. In 1993 the commercial district of 74th street, in the Jackson Heights district of New York City, was teeming with Indian-owned electronics and jewelry businesses. It was still unclear, however, to what extent the American-born generation of Asian Indians would carry on the South Asian immigrant entrepreneurial tradition.—*Paul D. Mageli*

SUGGESTED READINGS: • Bagai, Leona B. *The East Indians and the Pakistanis in America.* Rev. ed. Minneapolis: Lerner, 1972. • Greenwald, John. "Finding Niches in a New Land." *Time* 126 (July 8, 1985): 72-73. Gupte, Pranay. "Inner Patience." *Forbes* 139 (January 26, 1987): 74-75. • Helweg, Arthur W., and Usha M. Helweg. *An Immigrant Success Story: East Indians in America.* Philadelphia: University of Pennsylvania Press, 1990. • Jain, Usha R. *The Gujaratis of San Francisco.* New York: AMS Press, 1989. • King, Ralph, Jr. "From Bombay to L.A." *Forbes* 146 (November 12, 1990): 124. • Kotkin, Joel. *Tribes: How Race, Religion, and Identity Determine Success in the New Global Economy.* New York: Random House, 1993. • Lorch, Donatella. "Between Two Worlds: New York's Bangladeshis." *New York Times*, October 10, 1991. • Lorch, Donatella. "An Ethnic Road to Riches: The Immigrant Job Specialty." *New York Times*, January 12, 1992. • Mandel, Michael J., and Christopher Farrell. "The Immigrants: How They're Revitalizing the U.S. Economy." *Business Week*, no. 3274 (July 13, 1992): 116-122.

Asian Indian women in the United States: The first Indian women to come to the United States in the nineteenth century came as students and political ac-

Educational Attainment, Labor Status, and Occupation of Asian Indian Women, 1990

Education of Women 25 Years or Older	
	Percent
High school graduate	14%
Some college or associate degree	16%
College graduate	27%
Advanced or professional degree	22%
Total high school graduate or more	79%

Women 16 Years or Older	
	Percent
In labor force	59%
(Unemployed	8%)
Not in labor force	41%

Employed Civilian Women 16 Years or Older

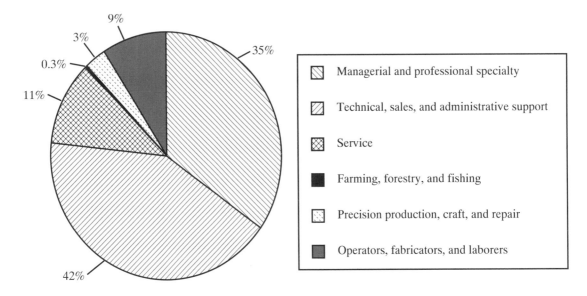

9%
3%
0.3%
11%
35%
42%

- ▨ Managerial and professional specialty
- ▨ Technical, sales, and administrative support
- ▨ Service
- ■ Farming, forestry, and fishing
- ▨ Precision production, craft, and repair
- ▨ Operators, fabricators, and laborers

Source: U.S. Bureau of the Census, *1990 Census of Population: Asians and Pacific Islanders in the United States,* 1993.

tivists involved in women's issues and the struggle for political independence. Anandibai Joshi became the first Indian woman to study Western medicine. She graduated from the Women's Medical College in Philadelphia in 1886. Her cousin, Ramabai, also came to Philadelphia in 1886 and spent the next two years addressing more than three hundred meetings in the Untied States on the condition of women in India. Ramabai had come to the United States to raise money for a home for widows in India and to establish schools for women. A Ramabai Association was formed in Boston with sixty-four branches all over the country. Between 1886 and 1888 Ramabai managed to raise

$30,000 from her lectures, a book on Indian women that she wrote and published in Philadelphia, and from donations.

Hostile Reception. Little is known about the wives of the Indian merchants who were in the United States. Most of the Asian Indian immigrants were young unmarried men; but it was not easy for them to either marry American women or marry and bring wives from India. For those who were married, the expensive process of paying for the passage was complicated by anti-Asian sentiment. Anti-Asian exclusionists were determined to prevent the migration of women. There were three wives in California by 1910, but when the fourth one arrived, newspaper headlines declared, "Hindu women next swarm to California." Wives and children arriving in Canada and the United States typically faced deportation proceedings, and only a few were allowed to stay after lengthy court battles. As a result it is thought that there were fewer than thirty Asian Indian women in the United States prior to 1945. One of the women was Padmavati Chandra, who had come with her husband in 1913. Both husband and wife were involved with the Ghadr (Revolution) Party, an organization that was very active in the struggle for Indian independence and that was supported financially by the Punjabi farm laborers. Padmavati Chandra graduated from high school in Washington and studied at Berkeley. Nand Kaur, a woman who emigrated in the 1920's, was also involved with GHADR activities in the Yuba City area of California.

Interracial Marriage. The second generation of Asian Indians prior to 1949 comprised the children of interracial marriages. Of the 304 marriages of Asian Indians recorded in California between the years 1913 and 1949, more than 200 Punjabi men married Mexi-

can women, 48 married white women, and 15 married African American women. Nineteen of the Punjabi-Mexican daughters also married Punjabi men. Elsewhere, as on the East Coast, several of the professional men also married white women.

ANTIMISCEGENATION LAWS passed in 1922, however, provided that white American women marrying aliens ineligible for citizenship (such as the Indians and other Asians) would lose their American citizenship. Therefore such marriages were rare.

Post-1965 Immigration Profile. Asians Indian immigration has been predominantly male even in the post-1965 period. After acquiring U.S. resident status, most men return to India, get married, and bring their wives back with them to the United States; most Asian Indian women enter the country as wives. Female-headed households are relatively less numerous among Asian Americans than among other ethnic groups, and this is also true for Asian Indians. Asians Indians also have the lowest level of family dissolution through divorce and widowhood among the foreign-born immigrant groups. The percentage of divorced and wid-

The majority of Asian Indian immigrant women coming to the United States do so as wives or mothers of Indian men who have already achieved U.S. resident status. (Richard B. Levine)

owed females in the Asian-born category is, however, almost three times as high as the number of divorced and widowed Asian-born males, suggesting that males remarry far more quickly than the females. The national aggregate data also disguise local realities; in both New York and Chicago, state and community service agencies have found numerous cases of Asian Indian women abandoned by their husbands. Domestic violence also has been a subject of community concern. Several community organizations initiated by Asian Indian women have evolved as a result; these include Manzi (New Jersey), Sakhi (New York), and Narika (Berkeley).

Because the vast majority of Asian Indian women are from middle-class and upper-middle-class urban backgrounds, most are highly educated. The 1980 U.S. census found that 52 percent of Asian Indian women were college graduates and that 46 percent had four or more years of postsecondary education. In 1983 almost 57 percent of Asian Indian women were found to be in the American labor force. Some Asian Indian women have been extremely successful in their careers. One example is Arati Prabhakar, who has been appointed director of the National Institute for Standards and Technology at the U.S. Commerce Department, and Geetha Ann Natarajan, who has been named New Jersey state medical examiner. Other well-known Asian Indian women include film director Mira Nair and actor Persis Khambatta. The vast majority of those in the labor force (42 percent), however, are in the clerical and sales and service sector jobs. Less than 28 percent of the women were found in administrative and professional job categories in 1983. Many women work in family businesses such as grocery or clothing stores and in the hotel and motel business. More than 28 percent of all motels in the United States are owned by Asian Indians. The vast majority of these establishments are small hotels and motels, with up to fifty rooms. Women, often the wives and sisters of motel owners, do the work of cleaning the rooms and laundering the sheets and towels in addition to tending the hotel desk.

Social Activism. Asian Indian women are very active in maintaining the community organizations, from fund-raising for religious causes and temple building to cooking for the community functions to choreographing the dance and entertainment programs that usually accompany these functions. More unexpect-

Since 1965 Asian Indian American women have entered the U.S. labor force in significant numbers. At this New York City public school, a Bengali teacher's aide does volunteer work. (Hazel Hankin)

Among the Asian Indian immigrant population in America, the women have played a central role in preserving the religious traditions of their native land. The woman pictured has entered a Hindu temple in Chatsworth, California, to offer a sprinkling to the gods. (Martin A. Hutner)

edly, perhaps, they have also been active in fighting against discrimination. In 1973 Shymala Rajendar, an assistant professor of chemistry, when denied tenure on the basis of gender and ethnic origin, filed a class-action suit against the University of Minnesota on behalf of women and minority faculty. In a landmark decision settled in 1980, the university agreed to pay Rajendar $100,000 and to pay $2 million in attorney's fees; it also settled almost three hundred claims with other women and minority faculty. A complaint brought by Sarvamangala Devi to the federal Equal Employment Opportunity Commission (EEOC) against the National Institutes of Health (NIH) in 1993, charging discrimination based on national origin, religion, and gender, is another pathbreaking case addressing issues faced by many minority and immigrant scientists. Other activists include Urvasi Vaid, former director of the Gay and Lesbian Task Force.—*Sucheta Mazumdar*

SUGGESTED READINGS: • Asian Women United of California, ed. *Making Waves: An Anthology By and About Asian American Women.* Boston: Beacon Press, 1989. • Leonard, Karen Isaksen. *Making Ethnic Choices: California's Punjabi Mexican Americans.* Philadelphia: Temple University Press, 1992 • Thaker, Suvarna, and Sucheta Mazumdar. "The Quality of Life of Asian Indian Women in the Motel Industry." *South Asia Bulletin* 2, no. 1 (1982): 68-73.

Asian Indians in the motel/hotel business: Family ownership and operation of small, inexpensive motels and hotels by immigrants from India became widespread in the United States during the latter half of the twentieth century. The trend began in the 1940's with one individual and accelerated rapidly in the 1970's, so that by the 1990's there were few if any American cities of populations larger than twenty-five thousand that did not have at least one motel or hotel owner-operator from India.

Causes. A major attraction the lodging business has had for Indians entering the United States has been the prospect of keeping families together, as one economic unit, with all family members contributing toward the success of the business. The place of business is also the place of residence for the owner and family, with experience gained in one operation serving well for those who decide to expand by buying other lodging facilities.

A contributing factor in the success of Indian-born hoteliers was the overall shift of the American economy during the latter half of the twentieth century

toward more service-oriented jobs, such as restaurants and lodging. A more direct cause was American immigration law.

First, the IMMIGRATION AND NATIONALITY ACT of 1965 ended discriminatory immigration policies based on color, religion, and other ethnic criteria. Then a 1978 amendment eliminated quota preferences given to Western Hemisphere immigrants. Possibly the most important factor was a clause in the 1965 law that exempted foreign business investors from quotas entirely and made such entrepreneurs eligible for immigrant visas before entering the United States and for permanent resident status afterward.

Some stipulations applied. First, the prospective investor had to invest a minimum of $40,000 in a business that produced either goods or services. Second, the business had to expand the labor market by hiring other people. Third, the investor had to be the primary manager of the business. Although the foregoing conditions were subject to thorough documentation before exemptions were granted, this clause must be considered as a significant factor in drawing immigrants from India into the lodging business. Once the business was established, the hotelier then needed only to comply with other immigration laws in order to bring in the rest of the immediate family, via a favorable immigration preference category.

Profiles. Sikhs, Punjabis, and Gujaratis are the three largest general groups of Indian hotel owners in the United States, with the Gujaratis (from the Indian state of GUJARAT) constituting by far the largest single ethnic group of hoteliers in the United States. Many Gujaratis carry the family name of "Patel"; the first known Indian-American hotel owner of that name, Nanlal Patel, got his start in Sacramento, California, during World War II.

Most Indian hoteliers in the United States operate small businesses. For example, the number of small lodging establishments owned and operated by Indian-American immigrants in California alone during the 1980's has been estimated at well above one thousand, with many hundreds more spread throughout the United States. (Other states with large numbers of Indian immigrants include New York, Illinois, and Washington.)

A mid-1990's estimate provided by the executive director of the Atlanta-based Asian American Hotel Owners Association (AAHOA) indicates that some 95 percent of the Asian hoteliers in the United States are from India. Even in California, with its large populations of Korean, Chinese, and Japanese Americans, the vast majority of hoteliers are Indian immigrants. Various sources place the number of Indian hoteliers in the United States at approximately six to seven thousand, with 35 to 40 percent of all American motels and hotels owned by Asian Indians. Through the early 1990's, at least half of that percentage—some 20 percent of the overall total—were owned by individuals with the last name of "Patel."

One of the larger Indian-owned chains, JHM Enterprises of Greenville, South Carolina, is reportedly operating as many as eighteen hotels with a total of nineteen hundred rooms. An independent Indian hotelier in Lebanon, Tennessee, is listed as the owner of twelve motels in four states. Many franchise owners operating within the larger motel chains, such as Howard Johnson's, Super 8, Holiday Inn, and an estimated 40 percent of the Days Inn motels, are Indian immigrants.

The foregoing statistics should not be surprising, considering demographic estimates that the fifth largest group of immigrants at the end of the twentieth century would be from India. Far from suffering in the United States, this immigrant group has the highest personal income and the highest level of education of all American racial/ethnic groups, including white Americans. About half of the adult Indian immigrants work as managers or professionals, with more than half holding college degrees—twice the rate of Americans in general.

Success Factors. Although some Indian American hoteliers have worked as managers or clerks in Indian hotels, very few were hotel owners before coming to the United States. To explain their phenomenal American success, three basic characteristics of Indian hoteliers are often cited: a strong work ethic, ability to raise money, and family commitment. Indian American businesspeople are also described as aggressive, perhaps daring, entrepreneurs. The Gujaratis, for example, are known throughout India for their industriousness and business acumen.

Indians are not absentee owners, for the most part, but run their businesses personally, working hard to satisfy their customers. Possibly that is why many have described the Indian culture as naturally hospitable; guests are made to feel welcome and comfortable. Similarly Indians have helped one another generously in getting established, providing expertise and advice whenever needed.

Problems. Prejudice still exists. Insurance policies have been canceled because the owner's name was recognizably Indian. Franchises have also been denied

to Indians, especially to those who employ few white workers, for fear that business may be lost to narrow-minded customers. That fear has occasionally been borne out by anecdotes of would-be customers refusing to patronize establishments with Indians behind the desks. Fortunately those types of encounters have dwindled, as Indian hoteliers' reputation for clean, affordable lodging has spread among American travelers. By all objective measures the history of Indian immigrants in the hotel/motel business is impressive.—*William Matta*

Suggested Readings: • Greenwald, John. "Finding Niches in a New Land." *Time* 126 (July 8, 1985): 72-73. • Papademetriou, Demetrios G., and Mark J. Miller, eds. *The Unavoidable Issue: U.S. Immigration Policy in the 1980's.* Philadelphia: Institute for the Study of Human Issues, 1983. • Romeo, Peter. "Opening the Door to the Largest Family in Lodging." *Hotel and Motel Management* 197 (November, 1982): 7. • Shaw, Russell. "Asian-American Owners May Organize." *Hotel and Motel Management* 204 (November 27, 1989): 2, 40. • U.S. Immigration and Naturalization Service. *Guide to Immigration Benefits.* Rev. ed. Washington, D.C.: Government Printing Office, 1982.

Asian Indians in the United States: Asian Indians are the most numerous of the immigrant groups from South Asia. Prior to 1947, when the independent states of India and Pakistan were formed (in 1971 the province of East Pakistan became the independent state of Bangladesh), the term "Indian" was used for all immigrants from the subcontinent. There are also immigrants of Indian origin from Fiji, Guyana, Great Britain, and Africa. The U.S. census of 1990 counted 815,447 Asian Indians, making them the fourth-largest group among the Asian Americans. There was probably an undercount of the Asian Indian population because the term "Asian Indian" is a self-identified census category; many who are of Indian origin but are from Africa and the Caribbean likely did not identify themselves as such.

Early History in the United States. The first Asian Indians came to the United States with sea captains and traders involved in the American trade with India in the 1790's. Some came as indentured servants, others as slaves who were later indentured. Although indentured labor was common in many parts of India and as many as two million Indians went to work in the plantations of the Caribbean and the Pacific between 1830 and 1870, the total number of indentured individuals who came to the United States is not known.

Asian Indian American Statistical Profile, 1990

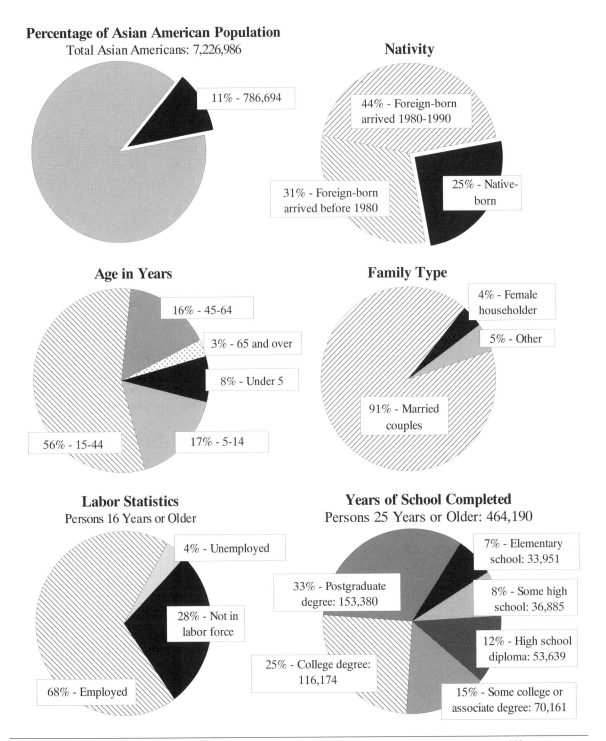

Percentage of Asian American Population
Total Asian Americans: 7,226,986

11% - 786,694

Nativity

44% - Foreign-born arrived 1980-1990

31% - Foreign-born arrived before 1980

25% - Native-born

Age in Years

16% - 45-64

3% - 65 and over

8% - Under 5

56% - 15-44

17% - 5-14

Family Type

4% - Female householder

5% - Other

91% - Married couples

Labor Statistics
Persons 16 Years or Older

4% - Unemployed

28% - Not in labor force

68% - Employed

Years of School Completed
Persons 25 Years or Older: 464,190

7% - Elementary school: 33,951

33% - Postgraduate degree: 153,380

8% - Some high school: 36,885

12% - High school diploma: 53,639

25% - College degree: 116,174

15% - Some college or associate degree: 70,161

Source: U.S. Bureau of the Census, *1990 Census of Population: Asians and Pacific Islanders in the United States,* 1993.

By the end of the nineteenth century, there were also around five hundred Indian merchants, several dozen religious teachers, and some medical professionals in the United States; for example, the doctor for the port of Boston in the 1880's was an Asian Indian. In 1900 there were around two thousand resident Indians.

A dramatic increase in Indian immigration began after 1905. Between 1907 and 1917 almost six thousand Indians arrived on the West Coast of the United States; during the same period more than three thousand were barred from entry by immigration officials. Several hundred also entered (illegally) via Mexico and stayed on as immigrants. Most of the immigrants were from the province of PUNJAB (now divided between INDIA and PAKISTAN). The majority were adherents of the SIKH religion, but there were also Hindu and Muslim immigrants. On the West Coast the major-

ity of the immigrants worked in California and Oregon agriculture and horticulture, some in the lumber mills of Washington or on the Pacific railroad. Others moved from California to settle in Colorado, Utah, Texas, Arizona, and New Mexico. Professionals, several of whom were active in the INDIAN INDE-PENDENCE movement, were located primarily on the East Coast.

Among immigrants from India to the United States have been a number of Sikhs. Near a New York City park a member of the Guardian Angels tries to recruit two Sikhs. (Richard B. Levine)

As Indian immigration increased, however, ANTI-ASIAN VIOLENCE, which had been common in the West Coast states, now targeted Asian Indians. There were riots and other cases of violence starting in 1907. With the support of the ASIATIC EXCLUSION LEAGUE, as early as 1911, California legislators started pushing for bills to exclude Indians. The federal BARRED ZONE ACT OF 1917 barred virtually all immigration from South and Southeast Asia. This terminated Asian Indian immigration. In 1923 the U.S. Supreme Court ruled that Asian Indians, like all other Asians, were ineligible for naturalized citizenship; simultaneously, the ALIEN LAND LAWS passed by several states prevented all Asians, including Indians, from owning land. In this hostile environment several thousand Indians chose to go back to India. The 1940 census counted only 2,405 Indians living in the United States; most were to be found in the area around Yuba City in central California and in the Imperial Valley in Southern California. Several of the Punjabis (Sikh, Hindu, Muslim) living in the Imperial Valley married Mexican women and formed the nucleus of the Punjabi-Mexican community.

A new phase of immigration started in 1946. Legis-

Occupation

Employed Persons 16 Years or Older	Percentage
Managerial and professional specialty	44%
Technical, sales, and administrative support	33%
Service	8%
Farming, forestry, and fishing	0.6%
Precision production, craft, and repair	5%
Operators, fabricators, and laborers	9%

Income, 1989

Median household income	$44,696
Per capita	$17,777

Household Size

Number of People	Percentage
1	12.1%
2	18.6%
3	19.9%
4	27.8%
5	12.6%
6	5.4%
7 or more	3.6%

Source: U.S. Bureau of the Census, *1990 Census of Population: Asians and Pacific Islanders in the United States,* 1993.

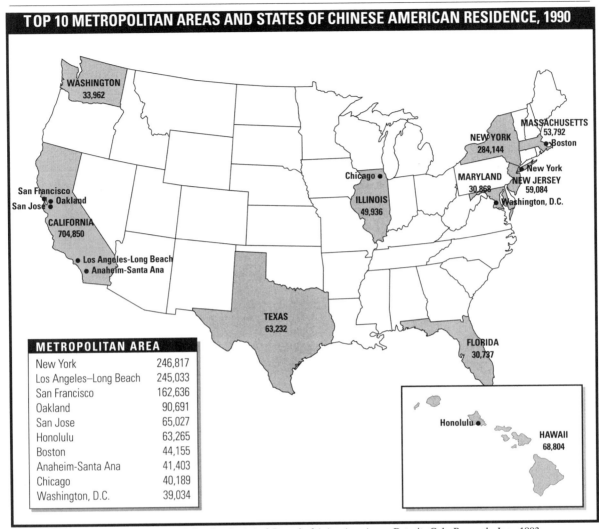

TOP 10 METROPOLITAN AREAS AND STATES OF CHINESE AMERICAN RESIDENCE, 1990

WASHINGTON
33,962

MASSACHUSETTS
53,792
Boston

NEW YORK
284,144

New York

Chicago

MARYLAND
30,868

NEW JERSEY
59,084

ILLINOIS
49,936

Washington, D.C.

San Francisco
Oakland
San Jose

CALIFORNIA
704,850

Los Angeles-Long Beach
Anaheim-Santa Ana

TEXAS
63,232

FLORIDA
30,737

Honolulu

HAWAII
68,804

METROPOLITAN AREA	
New York	246,817
Los Angeles–Long Beach	245,033
San Francisco	162,636
Oakland	90,691
San Jose	65,027
Honolulu	63,265
Boston	44,155
Anaheim-Santa Ana	41,403
Chicago	40,189
Washington, D.C.	39,034

Source: Susan B. Gall and Timothy L. Gall, eds., *Statistical Record of Asian Americans.* Detroit: Gale Research, Inc., 1993.

lation giving Indians the right to naturalized citizenship was passed and a quota system of immigration established permitting one hundred Indians to enter the United States each year. This allowed family reunification for some of the earlier immigrants. Rights to citizenship removed the barriers to landownership, and within a short time some PUNJABI immigrants in the Imperial Valley in particular were able to become quite wealthy farmers. In 1956, Dalip Singh SAUND, a Punjabi from the Imperial Valley, became the first Asian American to be elected to the U.S. Congress. Since then, both the Yuba City and the Imperial Valley communities have grown through new immigration that started in 1965; Asian Indian farmers are heavily involved in peach, kiwi, and cotton cultivation. Between 1948 and 1965, 6,474 Asian Indians entered the United States as immigrants.

Contemporary Immigration. Changes in the U.S. immigration laws in 1965 raised the immigration from India to twenty thousand admissions per year. Asian Indians live predominantly in metropolitan areas; 70 percent of them live in eight major industrial-urban states—New York, California, New Jersey, Texas, Pennsylvania, Michigan, Illinois, and Ohio.

The majority of the post-1965 immigrants from India were professionals because the new legislation provided preferential categories for professionals. There was also a large pool of potential immigrants; while there had been an enormous expansion in educational facilities for training professionals in medicine and engineering in India, the slow-growing economy could not accommodate the graduates. The 1980 census found that 52 percent of Asian Indian women and almost 80 percent of the men were college graduates; the Association of American Physicians from India suggests that there are approximately twenty-six thousand physicians of Indian origin in the United States. Among the ranks of the professionals, engineers are the most numerous, followed by physicians. Overall, 47 percent of Asian Indians are found to be in the high-status categories of managers, executives, and other professionals. Yet this pattern of immigration is changing. In 1990, although 1,016 Indians came to the United States under the third preference category of immigration (professional and highly skilled workers), the vast majority of the 19,157 Indian immigrants entering that year came under other preference categories such as family reunification. These immigrants may not have the same level of professional training as their sponsors. The economic downturn in the United States

has also meant that some immigrants, while entering the country with professional degrees, have not been able to find regular employment and are working in the service sector. In economic terms the community is therefore diverse and ranges from the very wealthy to the approximately 10 percent who live below the poverty level.

Throughout the 1980's there was a rapid increase in the number of Asian Indians going into small businesses. As of 1987 there were some 52,266 Asian Indian businesses with receipts of $6.715 billion. Many Indians are involved in the lodging and motel industries; 28 percent of all U.S. motels were owned by Asian Indians in 1987. In both New York and California many Asian Indians operate 7-11 Stores. On the East Coast many Asian Indians also work as cab drivers. Asian Indian cab drivers account for 43 percent of the drivers in New York City and 15 percent of the

At a multicultural festival in Queens, New York, an Asian Indian family visits with a family of immigrants from El Salvador. (Odette Lupis)

drivers in the boroughs. Gas stations have been another major area of investment and employment. In New York City, 40 percent of the city's gas stations are owned and operated by South Asians.

Except for raising funds for major political candidates, the Asian Indian community was not particularly active in electoral politics in the 1980's. Most were involved only with community-based religious organizations, yet that seems to be changing with the 1990's. Four Asian Indians ran for congressional seats in the 1992 elections; two others ran for county supervisor in their states of residence. Although none was elected, the effort to win electoral office continued with Asian Indian candidates running for congressional seats in Tennessee, Maryland, and California in 1994.

Asian Indian political involvement may have also come as a result of awareness regarding racial discrimination. In the late 1980's, anti-Indian gangs such as the Dotbusters and the Lost Boys developed in New Jersey, where many Indians have settled. There were numerous assaults against Asian Indians in New York and New Jersey; some ended with serious injuries, and there was one death. Forty anti-Asian bias-related incidents were reported in Hudson County (New Jersey) in 1991 alone, and statewide fifty-eight such incidents against Asian Indians were reported the same year. Similarly, on the West Coast, Indian homes and businesses have been vandalized, property destroyed, and racial epithets spray-painted in Fremont, Union City, and Artesia, California; in Springfield, Washington; and Portland, Oregon.

The high level of immigration from South Asia in the 1980's made Asian Indians a far more important and visible component (almost 19 percent) of the Asian American population. As the Asian Indian community establishes itself and continues to grow numerically through both immigration and the growth of the second generation, new forms of political activism and alliances are becoming necessary. In New York and New Jersey as well as in Virginia and Mississippi, a few Asian Indians have begun to work with the

During a New York City parade, two Indian women perform a Sikh Kathar, or story-telling dance. (Richard B. Levine)

The Asian Indian immigrant population in the United States includes a number of Hindus. At this Indian temple in Queens, New York, Hindus celebrate the Festival of Ganesh. (Hazel Hankin)

National Association for the Advancement of Colored People (NAACP); in California some have formed alliances with other Asian American groups.—*Sucheta Mazumdar*

SUGGESTED READINGS: • Jensen, Joan M., *Passage from India: Asian Indian Immigrants in North America*. New Haven, Conn.: Yale University Press, 1988. • Leonard, Karen Isaksen. *Making Ethnic Choices: California's Punjabi Mexican Americans*. Philadelphia: Temple University Press, 1992. • Mazumdar, Sucheta. "Punjabi Agricultural Workers in California, 1905-1945." In *Labor Immigration Under Capitalism: Asian Workers in the United States Before World War II*, edited by Lucie Cheng and Edna Bonacicih. Berkeley: University of California Press, 1984. • Mazumdar, Sucheta. "South Asians in the United States with a Focus on Asian Indians." In The State of Asian Pacific America: A Public Policy Report, Policy Issues to the Year 2020. Los Angeles: LEAP Asian Pacific American Public Policy Institute and UCLA Asian American Studies Center, 1993. • Melendy, H. Brett. Asians in America: Filipinos, Koreans, and East Indians. New York: Hippocrene, 1981.

Asian Law Alliance: Nonprofit legal organization founded in 1977 in San Jose, California. The alliance is dedicated to providing equal access to the legal system and promoting self-reliance, self-initiative, and a better way of life for Asian Americans. It provides multilingual and culturally sensitive legal services that include programs in legal counseling, community education, and community organizing. In 1991-1992 these three programs served almost ten thousand clients.

Asian Law Caucus: Nonprofit organization formed in 1972 in Oakland, California, to provide low-cost, culturally sensitive legal services to low-income people, primarily those in the Asian American community. The first law office of its kind in the country, it served as a model for several community-based law offices in Asian and other communities.

Now based in San Francisco, the caucus provides legal representation—particularly in cases that may have a broad impact—educates the community about the law, and organizes support on community issues. The areas in which the caucus has focused its activities are civil/constitutional rights, employment/labor, housing/land use, and immigration/immigrant rights.

The caucus has been involved in many cases significant to the Asian American community. These include Chann v. Scott (1972), which stopped the San Fran

cisco police practice of massive race-based arrests of Chinese youths; Ping Yuen Tenants Association v. San Francisco Housing Authority (1978), which led to public housing improvements and formation of tenant associations in San Francisco's Chinatown; and *Korematsu v. United States* (1942; 1982), *vacated*, which vacated the World War II conviction of Fred T. KOREMATSU, who had refused to obey federal orders forcibly relocating Japanese Americans. *International Molders and Allied Workers Union, Local 164 v. Nelson* (1982) led to the termination of Immigration and Naturalization Service (INS) factory raids and to a requirement that the INS must use specific warrants to enter workplaces. *Ha, et al. v. T & W Fashion* (1983), which sought to hold a garment manufacturer liable for wage violations of its contractor, ended three years later with the manufacturer and contractor jointly paying more than $80,000 to thirteen workers. *EEOC v. Tortilleria La Mejor* (1987) affirmed that federal civil rights laws protect undocumented workers. Finally, *Vietnamese Fishermen's Association of America v. Admiral Paul Yost* (1989), a case that sought injunctive relief against enforcement of a federal law prohibiting noncitizens from piloting fishing vessels in U.S. fishing waters, led to the passage of a bill granting permanent residents the right to fish commercially.

The group has worked on many important efforts outside the courtroom, including fighting to protect bilingual ballots; helping workers through the unionization of workplaces, the establishment of fair minimum wages, and the recovery of back wages; preserving and upgrading existing tenant housing; and supporting immigrant rights.

Asian Pacific American Labor Alliance: Labor activist organization formed in 1922 by Asian Pacific American labor activists and the AMERICAN FEDERATION OF LABOR-Congress of Industrial Organizations (AFL-CIO). It addresses the needs of Asian Pacific American labor by organizing workers and training union leaders. Initial chapters were located in Washington, California, New York, the District of Columbia, Massachusetts, and Hawaii.

Asian Pacific American Legal Center of Southern California (APALC): Legal assistance bureau founded in 1983 to provide the growing Asian Pacific American community with culturally sensitive legal services and education. Funded by private donors, foundation grants, and state allocations, the APALC offers free legal help to indigent and low-income groups, especially those of Asian and Pacific Islander origin. Headquartered in Los Angeles, the organization is equipped to dispense advice regarding family law and domestic violence; immigration; government benefits, housing, and unemployment; landlord and tenant disputes; and consumer matters. The APALC also actively pursues civil rights issues, including monitoring and publicizing race-related crimes and incidents and influencing court cases and legislation.

Asian Pacific American Librarians Association (APALA): Organization founded in 1980 to serve the interests of librarians and information specialists of Asian Pacific descent working in the United States. The association's purposes include providing a forum for discussing problems and concerns, supporting and encouraging library services in Asian Pacific communities, recruiting Asian Pacific Americans for the field of library and information science, and job placement. The APALA publishes a newsletter as well. With an increasing membership representing almost every state in the nation, the APALA has become one of the most prominent organizations of its kind.

Asian Pacific Democratic Club (APDC): Political empowerment group formed in November of 1992. It was founded by a group of Asian Pacific American activists who were involved in electoral politics in the San Francisco Bay Area. Their goal was to unite a cross section of Asian Pacific Americans in forging a multiethnic alliance based on progressive and democratic politics.

The APDC seeks to advance the political empowerment of the Asian Pacific community. It hopes to achieve this goal by identifying, developing, promoting and supporting Asian Pacific American political candidates. With more Asian Pacific American candidates running for elected office, the needs of the community will be better heard. The APDC also sees its role as an active political advocate at the local, state, and national levels, bringing attention to issues of particular concern to Asian Pacific Americans.

By bringing activists together from different Asian Pacific American communities, the APDC hopes to nurture a pan-Asian agenda that promotes their common concerns. This pan-Asian formation can promote an increase in coordination of resources.

The APDC also believes that strong political participation by a broad diversity of ethnic groups will lead to the long-term strength and stability of democracy and thereby benefit the population and the society at large. The group seeks to accomplish this aim by cooperating with other ethnic groups to identify issues of common concern.

Asian Pacific Health Forum: National nonprofit membership-supported health organization formed in 1986. Headquartered in San Francisco, California, the group, formerly known as the Asian American Health Forum, addresses the diverse health needs of the Asian American community. In an effort to empower the community, it conducts health-related research; compiles, analyzes, and disseminates critical data; and assists in the development of government policies and programs.

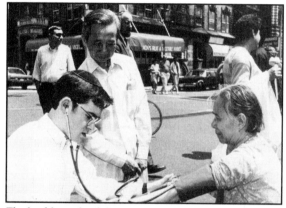

The health needs of the Asian American community are diverse. The Asian Pacific Health Forum strives to ensure that the health-related issues involving Asian Americans become a governmental priority. (Frances M. Roberts)

Asian/Pacific Women's Network (APWN): U.S. organization founded in 1979 to promote issues of interest to Asian Pacific women nationwide. The APWN began with a group of Asian Pacific women who were inspired by other marginalized communities that were working toward social justice and economic mobility. Through a federal grant from the Women's Educational Equity Program of the U.S. Office of Education, Tyn Maing Thein, an immigrant from Myanmar (Burma), was able to secure funds for a series of nationwide conferences aimed at promoting educational equity for Asian Pacific women. Under the leadership of Irene HIRANO and Thein, California became the flagship state for this national series. The first conference, chaired by Patricia Lin, was held at the University of Southern California. It drew more than eight hundred Asian Pacific women and became a rallying point for the formation of a national organization. Subsequent conferences modeled after the Los Angeles conference were held in Hawaii, New York, and Washington, D.C. Under the leadership of Hirano a national APWN was established with state and local chapters in several states.

The organization's threefold emphasis has been to promote public awareness regarding Asian Pacific women's issues, to sponsor educational programs for Asian Pacific women, and to build networks both within and without the Asian Pacific community. In more than a decade since its founding, several members of APWN have become well-known advocates for Asian Pacific women's rights. Others have distinguished themselves in the workplace, civic and community groups, business, and the popular media.

Over the years APWN has worked to forge linkages with other women's organizations such as NOW, comision femina, Black Women's Forum, Filipino Women's Network, ORGANIZATION OF CHINESE AMERICAN WOMEN (OCAW), Asian American Drug Abuse Program, and Asian Pacifics for Choice.

Each year the network presents its annual Woman Warrior Award (named after Maxine Hong KINGSTON's 1976 book *The Woman Warrior*) to Asian Pacific women who have distinguished themselves as educators, artists, entertainers, civic leaders, entrepreneurs, and media figures. Past awardees have included Justice Joyce Kennard, author Kingston, California state secretary March Fong EU, and architect Maya LIN.

Asian Week: San Francisco-based weekly newspaper, founded in 1979 by John FANG. The only English-language weekly covering the diverse Asian American community, *Asian Week* supplements news stories with profiles, reviews, information regarding Asian Pacific American organizations, a calendar of upcoming events, and other regular features. Circulation in 1993 was 30,000 (about 20,000 in California), with an estimated readership of 135,000.

Asian Women United: Organization dedicated to promoting educational equity for all women, especially for Asian Pacific American women, founded in 1976. It produces research and writing relevant to community concerns and also creates educational materials that help eradicate stereotypes and that help eliminate barriers to equal educational opportunities. To help achieve this goal, the group has produced several books and videotapes, which have become key resources in schools and universities, and has sponsored or cosponsored activities in the Asian Pacific American community.

Asian Women United, located in the San Francisco Bay Area, began when several women from diverse ethnic, educational, and career backgrounds came together to address the issue of discrimination against Asian American WOMEN. The women had been active with Asian American community groups, but they believed that women additionally faced different types of issues because of their gender.

The group's most widely viewed videotape, *Slaying the Dragon*, uses film and television clips to describe stereotypes of Asian American women and to illustrate how those stereotypes have affected these women. In 1989 Asian Women United's major anthology, *Making Waves: Writings By and About Asian American Women*, was published. Containing short stories, essays, articles, and poems, the book is used widely as a resource in public libraries and colleges.

Its first large-scale project, the "With Silk Wings" project, began in the early 1980's and included a major survey of the education and employment aspirations of more than six hundred local Chinese, Filipino, Japanese, and Korean American girls and young women. It spawned four videotapes and three books, featuring women from different ethnic backgrounds who combine community service, work, and family life. *With Silk Wings: Asian American Women at Work* (1983) profiles Asian American women in nontraditional jobs. *Dear Diane: Letters from Our Daughters* (1983), written bilingually in English and Chinese or English and Korean in a question-and-answer format, deals with questions facing immigrant families; its companion book, *Dear Diane: Questions and Answers for Asian-American Women* (1983), looks at issues of concern to young women beginning jobs or going to college. The "With Silk Wings" videotapes include *On New Ground*, *Four Women*, *Talking History*, and *Frankly Speaking*.

Asiatic Exclusion League: Organization that existed in San Francisco from 1908 until 1913. Its efforts were aimed at eliminating Japanese immigration to the United States and engaging in activities to disrupt the lives of those residing there.

The organization first started in May, 1905, as the Japanese and Korean Exclusion League. A league report claimed a California membership of 110,000 in February, 1908, as well as members in Oregon, Washington, Idaho, Colorado, and Nebraska. Moreover, out of 231 member organizations in 1908, 195 were labor unions.

At a June, 1906, meeting, the league supported a

Foreigners targeted for exclusion by the Asiatic Exclusion League included the Chinese, as illustrated by this political cartoon. (Asian American Studies Library, University of California at Berkeley)

union boycott of Japanese and Chinese restaurants. The league even threatened to photograph patrons of the Asian restaurants. The picketing did not begin until October. It lasted for about three weeks until the restaurant owners agreed to pay the boycotters $350.

Also in October, 1906, the league lobbied the San Francisco Board of Education to exclude the Japanese and Korean students from the regular public schools and to require them to attend the racially segregated school for Chinese. The resolution passed, but U.S.

president Theodore Roosevelt interceded and the board rescinded the order in exchange for a federal restriction on Japanese immigration. In the meantime the Japanese students boycotted the segregation order and attended a private school until they were allowed to return to the public schools in March, 1907.

Political supporters of the league introduced anti-Japanese bills on both the federal and the state levels, although none of these bills was ever enacted. The organization soundly criticized the failure of the 1909 California legislature to enact any of the anti-Japanese legislation that was introduced. Yet in an about-face two years later, league president Olaf Tvietmoe wrote a letter to the California legislature opposing the pending anti-Japanese legislation. This change was made to support San Francisco as the site of the 1915 Panama-Pacific International Exposition. Had California passed any anti-Japanese laws, the federal government would not have allowed San Francisco to host the exposition.

Asiaweek: Hong Kong-based weekly newsmagazine. Its 1975 mission statement, printed in every issue, summarizes the magazine's purpose: "To report accurately and fairly the affairs of Asia in all spheres of human activity, to see the world from an Asian perspective, to be Asia's voice in the world." The magazine is a distinctive combination of hard-hitting reporting, state-of-the-art graphics, business news, and irreverent wit. While its focus is on Asia, many of the events, people, and issues it covers are relevant to the rapidly changing Asian American community.

Assembly centers: Temporary detention centers. During the internment of Japanese Americans during World War II, the U.S. government began the process of evacuation, in which persons of Japanese ancestry were required to move from designated military areas, or zones. At first Japanese Americans were allowed to move on their own from the prohibited areas. After March 29, 1942, however, mandatory evacuation was established when General John DeWitt issued Public Proclamation No. 4; it prohibited Japanese Americans from independently leaving Military Area No. 1, which included western Washington, Oregon, California, and southern Arizona.

Japanese Americans were placed in so-called assembly centers under the direction of the Wartime Civil Control Administration (WCCA). The Army authorized the removal of Japanese Americans into the

Evacuees both young and old were forcibly trundled off to the assembly centers en route to the more inland relocation centers. Three-year-old Donald Okji rolls into the Portland, Oregon, assembly compound atop his tricycle. (AP/Wide World Photos)

Japanese evacuees arrive at the Santa Anita assembly center after traveling by train from San Pedro, California. (National Archives)

assembly centers and oversaw the operation of the centers.

From March 31 to August 7, 1942, approximately ninety-two thousand Japanese Americans were placed in assembly centers while more permanent facilities, the RELOCATION CENTERS, were being constructed. Many of the sites for the sixteen assembly centers were fairgrounds and racetracks. The assembly centers in California were located in Fresno, Manzanar, Marysville, Merced, Pinedale, Pomona, Sacramento, Salinas, Santa Anita, Stockton, Tanforan, Tulare, and Turlock. There were also assembly centers in Puyallup, Washington; Portland, Oregon; and Mayer, Arizona.

The assembly centers were plagued by severe overcrowding and deteriorating conditions. Housing in some of the centers consisted of converted horse stalls. In some cases four couples had to share one room. The housing conditions and toilet facilities were constructed with little consideration for the privacy of the internees. Each facet of daily life was regulated. Internees had to line up at the mess halls, laundry rooms, toilets, showers. An effect of these regimented conditions was the deterioration of the family bond among the internees.

Guard towers and barbed-wire fences surrounded the centers. The military police, armed with machine guns, were responsible for securing the perimeter of the camps. The internal police, many of whom were deputized, were responsible for enforcing the laws within the centers. At many of the centers the internal police would enforce curfews and roll calls.

Japanese Americans began to be transferred from the assembly centers to the relocation centers in May, 1942.

Assing, Norman (Norman Asing; Norman Ah-Sing; Yuan Sheng; c. 1800's, Sanzao, Guangdong Province, China): Merchant and early leader of the San Francisco Chinese community. In an 1852 letter rebutting California Governor John Bigler's speech against Chinese immigration, Assing claimed to be "a naturalized citizen . . . of Charleston, South Carolina, and a Christian too." He probably arrived in San Francisco prior to 1850 since the 1850 *City Directory* listed him as proprietor of the Macao and Woosung Restaurant at Kearny and Commercial streets.

On August 28, 1850, Assing served as interpreter at the first public appearance of the Chinese when they received Christian tracts at Portsmouth Square. The next day he led the Chinese at a procession commemorating the death of U.S. president Zachary Taylor. Assing's presence was very much in evidence on other occasions such as the 1850 parade celebrating admission of California into the Union and the July 4th parade in 1852. On the first reported celebration of the Chinese New Year in the United States on February 1, 1851, Assing gave a grand feast at his home. Assing was listed in the 1854 *City Directory* as the Chinese representative among "Foreign Consuls in San Francisco."

In 1852 Assing, Cai Libi, and Liu Zuman led in the founding of YEONG WO COMPANY, of which Assing became the head. Later that year, however, an attack of hemorrhages forced him to relinquish this position to Tong K. Achik.

As head of the company, Assing "taught [members] like a father and teacher, and punished by flogging those who were disobedient. . . . " After he relinquished his post in the company, he continued to try to use his coercive powers. He soon found, however, that there were limitations. In 1853 Assing lost a suit involving the personal freedom of Ah Toy, a prostitute who charged that Assing intended to abduct and deport her to China. Shortly afterward he was foiled in a move to use the San Francisco Vigilance Committee to place into his custody two Chinese men he charged as being persons of bad character and two women associated with them who he claimed were whores. An 1853 grand jury report charging repressive conditions in the companies further curbed Assing's naked exercise of power. Soon afterward his name disappeared from the news.

Association for Asian American Studies (AAAS): Independent, nonprofit educational organization founded in 1979 to promote teaching and research in the academic discipline of ASIAN AMERICAN STUDIES.

The Association for Asian American Studies plays an important role in U.S. colleges and universities by encouraging them to recruit Asian American students. (James L. Shaffer)

The AAAS is open to all interested scholars, educators, professionals, and members of the public sector and the Asian American community at large. The association sponsors national and regional conferences, promotes understanding among the various groups of Asian Americans, facilitates communication among educators in the field, advocates and represents the interests of Asian Americans, and educates the general population concerning Asian American issues.

Publications include an annual thematic anthology of conference proceedings, occasional papers, and the quarterly AAAS *Newsletter*. The latter contains news of the association and of the various Asian American Studies programs in academia, reviews of recent publications in the field, descriptions of recent research, job announcements, and news of individuals. Numerous book awards are given annually in the categories of lifetime scholar, cultural studies, history and society, and literature. Awards for papers or articles are given for graduate and undergraduate students.

The association plays an advocacy role on university and college campuses by helping to define tenure qualifications in the field of Asian American Studies and by ensuring the availability of special services and compliance with affirmative action for recruiting and retaining Asian American undergraduate and graduate students. It strongly supports the founding and continuation of programs and departments of Asian American Studies. The association offers its help in monitoring and rectifying the treatment of gay and lesbian Asian Americans. It also fosters public commemoration of important events in Asian American history.

Association for Asian Performance (AAP): Organization founded in 1986 by a small group of university educators and theater professionals to promote the appreciation, study, and performance of Asian theater and drama. Two years later, at the Association for Theatre in Higher Education Conference in San Diego, the AAP sponsored its first exclusively Asian American theater panel. "The Search for a Voice: The Emerging Asian American Theatre Movement" featured artistic directors from the three professional Asian

Actors rehearse a play at Los Angeles' East West Players. (Michael Yamashita)

American theater companies: The PAN ASIAN REPERTORY THEATRE's Tisa Chang, the ASIAN-AMERICAN THEATRE COMPANY's Eric HAYASHI and Lane NISHIKAWA, and MAKO, then artistic director of EAST WEST PLAYERS. The AAP subsequently expanded its original focus to include Asian American and crosscultural and intercultural performance in publications, conference programming, consulting, speakers, and guest artists.

Association for Asian Studies (AAS): Nonprofit, nonpolitical association open to all individuals interested in Asia, founded in 1941. The AAS was established as the Far Eastern Association and reorganized in 1957 under its present name. A member of the American Council of Learned Societies and the National Council of Area Studies Associations, the AAS is the major professional association for persons with scholarly and professional interests in Asia, such as teachers and scholars, diplomats, journalists, and businesspeople.

The association is divided into four area councils— China and Inner Asia, Northeast Asia, South Asia, and Southeast Asia—that sponsor special conferences on research problems and other issues of topical interest. The United States is divided into eight regional conferences that hold annual meetings.

The association hosts a national annual meeting at which research is presented and panel discussions held on a wide range of topics in the various fields of Asian Studies. A placement service is sponsored for scholars and others seeking employment in educational, research, and other institutions.

To promote scholarship on Asia, the association publishes the *Journal of Asian Studies*, the *Bibliography of Asian Studies, Doctoral Dissertations on Asia*, and a scholarly monograph series. The *Asian Studies Newsletter*, published five times yearly, contains association news as well as information on conferences and exhibits, publications, grants and fellowships, and professional placement.

Association for the America-Bound: Japanese organization founded in Tokyo in 1902 to encourage Japanese citizens to visit the United States. During this campaign to stimulate enthusiasm about America, the group published travel guidebooks as well as its own magazine and provided letters of introduction and employment assistance to potential emigrants. The association even purchased a huge tract of land in Texas in the hope of starting a Japanese-populated rice-farming colony there, but the venture ultimately failed.

Association of Asian/Pacific American Artists (AAPAA): Nonprofit educational and cultural organization whose primary mission is to promote "the balanced portrayals and realistic images of Asians, Asian Pacifics, and Asian Americans in the mainstream media," founded in 1976. The active membership includes camera operators, performers, writers, technicians, and executives in the entertainment industry, while the supporting membership consists of individual and corporate friends of the organization. The Advisory Council and Honorary Board consist of representatives from a variety of professional and political groups.

The AAPAA is dedicated to monitoring the media in its portrayal of all Asians, encouraging positive Asian/Pacific role models, seeking more opportunities for Asians in the entertainment industry through ongoing dialogue with decision makers, increasing primetime visibility of Asian/Pacific Americans, developing scholarship funds in the creative and theater arts, and establishing community outreach programs.

To achieve these goals, the AAPAA sponsors numerous programs. The Advocacy Program educates the media and voices a stance regarding stereotypes and unrealistic portrayals of Asians. The Education Program publishes a quarterly newsletter and conducts ongoing dialogue with decision makers in the entertainment industry to ensure that Asian Pacific Americans are given equitable opportunities. The Talent Showcase Program presents special events, such as concerts and plays. The association also sponsors a Writers Workshop and a Speakers Bureau.

The Jimmie Media Awards Program was established in 1985 to recognize individuals, corporations, production companies, and others who have helped portray Asian Pacific Americans realistically and sensitively in film, television, theater, and print. This popular and prestigious annual event was named after the Oscar-winning cinematographer James Wong HOWE. Jimmie Lifetime Achievement Award recipients have included Howe, Hawaii senator Daniel K. INOUYE, famed Japanese film director Akira Kurosawa, and actors Keye LUKE, Pat MORITA, and Beulah Kuo.

The AAPAA publishes the *Directory of Asian/ Pacific American Artists (annually) and Association of Asian/ Pacific American Artists—Inside Moves (quarterly). In 1989 the AAPAA, the National Conference of Christians and Jews, and the* ASIAN AMERICAN JOURNALISTS ASSOCIATION *(AAJA) published* Asian Pacific Americans: A Handbook on How to Cover and Portray Our Nation's Fastest Growing Minority Group.

Chinese teachers and educators formed the Association of Chinese Teachers in 1969 to respond to the educational needs of the Asian American community. (James L. Shaffer)

Association of Chinese Teachers: Community-based organization comprising San Francisco Bay Area Chinese teachers and educators, formed in 1969. The group targets its programs to address specific educational needs of the Asian American community; advocates and implements programs for underrepresented, limited-English-proficient Asian students; promotes equal employment opportunities for Chinese teachers; and produces and distributes curriculum materials that more accurately portray the Chinese American experience.

Association of Indians in America (AIA): Oldest national association of Asian Indians in the United States, founded on August 20, 1967. It was established after passage of the IMMIGRATION AND NATIONALITY ACT OF 1965, which admitted Asian Indians to the United States in unprecedented numbers, and was incorporated in 1971. The association has grown on a scale that parallels the growth of the nationwide Indian

immigrant community. Its purpose is to involve Indians living in the United States in the progress and development of their mother country as well as to facilitate their involvement in mainstream American community life.

The AIA is a tax-exempt, nonpartisan, and nonpolitical organization headquartered in Glendale, New York, with chapters and membership throughout the United States. It is a grassroots organization that claims to represent the hopes and aspirations of all Indians united by the common bond of their Indian heritage and American commitment. The AIA promotes its objectives through charitable, cultural, and educational activities and works actively to represent Indian immigrant interests before congressional committees at the federal, state, and local levels of government.

Among the more notable achievements of the AIA are reclassifying immigrants from South Asian countries as Asian Pacific Americans and obtaining minor-

One of the goals of the Association of Indians in America is to give its members a powerful, unified voice and a strong identity in American society. (Richard B. Levine)

ity status for immigrants from South Asia for civil rights purposes. Its most significant act has been to get a separate enumeration of Asian Indians as an independent category for the first time in the U.S. census of 1980. The AIA addresses issues of bias or discrimination against Indians in the United States, setting up funds for the defense of victims of ethnic and religious bigotry and violence.

The AIA also seeks to promote economic and cultural cooperation between India and the United States. It sponsors voter registration drives and celebrates the national events and festivals of both countries for mutual understanding. Given that the Indian community in the United States is so diverse socioeconomically and so widely scattered geographically as to be called the "invisible" minority, the AIA gives Indians a strong, unified voice and a distinct national identity. It articulates and defends the special interests of all Indians and keeps alive their Indian heritage while encouraging their full participation in American society.

Association of Korean Political Studies in North America (AKPSNA): Professional organization founded in 1973 as the Association of Korean Political Scientists in North America. In 1985, in order to open and expand membership to non-Korean political and social scientists, its name was changed to its present form. It is made up of political and social scientists in the United States whose research and professional interests include Korean political studies.

During the 1950's, at the height of the KOREAN WAR (1950-1953), a generation of KOREAN STUDENTS came to the United States to attend American universities, and by the 1960's and 1970's, most of these students had completed their education. The military regimes in Korea at that time did not respect such values as freedom of expression and human rights, which are essential for social scientists to function as true professionals. Consequently many Korean political and social scientists remained in the United States to pursue their professional career, and individuals from this early group formed the association.

The group had two motives: professional interaction and the advancement of Korean Studies at American colleges and universities. The AKPSNA held its first general meeting on March 31, 1973, and on April 1, 1973, Young C. Kim, a professor at George Washington University, was elected the association's first chairperson.

The AKPSNA's general meetings are held annually in conjunction with either the American Political Sci-

ence Association or the ASSOCIATION FOR ASIAN STUDIES. During these conferences, the AKPSNA has sponsored panels and roundtable workshops. In addition, seven joint Korean Political Science Association and AKPSNA conferences have been held in Seoul biannually.

In 1989 the AKPSNA began actively cooperating with the Korean Political Science Association in the biannual World Conference of Korean Political Studies, which developed from previous American-Korean joint conferences. The AKPSNA has been in the forefront in its push for diversity in faculty recruitment. Tenured senior members of the AKPSNA provide informal career guidance to younger scholars of Korean and Asian descent as well as all others with a Korean specialty. The association has more than one hundred members.

Atman: Hindu philosophical concept. It found its currency essentially in the *Upanishads* (1000 B.C.E.), which were written in the Sanskrit language in ancient India and which are as central to HINDUISM as the New Testament is to Christianity. No single word exists in the English language that can capture the essence of the term *atman*. Therefore it is often translated as "spirit," "self," "essence," and "soul," but its most widely accepted translation in literary, religious, and philosophical literature is "self."

In the *Upanishads*, human beings are viewed as one of the objects of the world with several layers of reality—matter, life, mind (*mana*), reason (*buddhi*), and *atman*. Hence within each individual, there is a core self that is called *atman*. This hidden and underlying self is not the body, the mind, or the individual ego but the silent and formless depth of being within each person. *Atman* is infinite in the sense that it never dies. It is that part of each individual that is the ultimate reality, the Brahman, "the supreme God." Failure to recognize the inner self results in failure to grasp the full meaning of life.

The ultimate finding of *atman* leads to a state called *moksha*. Before *moksha* is reached, however, one must encounter the following four types of desires: pleasures, worldly success, desire to be useful, and infinite being. The task of achieving the ultimate last step is not accomplished in one lifetime. Therefore, one must go through the cycle of reincarnation. The freedom from the cycle of reincarnation is achieved only when one is able to recognize one's true underlying self, the *atman*. The *atman* concept, along with other concepts of the *Upanishads*, has dominated Hindu thought from

Buddha to Mahatma Gandhi and Kabir and will continue to dominate the Hindu way of life.

August Moon Festival. *See* **Moon Festival**

Aung San Suu Kyi, Daw (b. June 19, 1945, Rangoon, now Yangon, Burma, now Myanmar): Human rights activist. Since 1988 Aung San Suu Kyi has devoted her life to resisting the military regime in Myanmar and fighting for human rights and the right of self-determination for the people of her native country. Although her political opposition party scored a decisive victory at the polls in 1990, she remained under house arrest. In honor of her nonviolent campaign for democracy and human rights, she was awarded the Nobel Peace Prize in December, 1991.

Aung San Suu Kyi is the daughter of General U Aung San, the father of Burmese independence and a national hero. He was assassinated in 1947, on the eve of Burma's obtaining its freedom from British rule, which he had helped negotiate. She left Burma in 1960, after her mother, prominent diplomat Daw Khin Kyi, was made ambassador to India. Aung San Suu Kyi attended Oxford, studying political science, philosophy, and economics. She also met Professor Michael Aris, a scholar of Tibetan anthropology; they married in 1972, and have two sons, Alexander and Kim. After Oxford she worked for the United Nations (UN) for several years before returning to England with her husband. The years following were spent tending to her family and writing books, including *Burma and Japan: Basic Studies on Their Cultural and Social Structure* (1987), *Burma and India: Some Aspects of Intellectual Life Under Colonialism* (1990), and *Aung San of Burma: A Biographical Portrait by His Daughter* (1991).

After her mother suffered a stroke in 1988, Aung San Suu Kyi went back to Burma to care for her and there was caught up in the revolutionary political and protest movements sweeping the country. Student-led demonstrations had broken out against the autocratic and isolationist military regime of General Ne Win, a socialist who had overthrown Burma's democratically elected government in 1962 and had remained in power ever since. Ne Win was forced to resign as head of the Burma Socialist Programme Party in the summer of 1988, but the military regained power following a bloody coup (possibly controlled by the "retired" Ne Win) staged in September.

In response, Aung San Suu Kyi cofounded the National League for Democracy (NLD), an opposition political party, and began mounting massive rallies throughout the country to denounce the junta and its imposition of martial law and to mobilize worldwide support for her party and its drive for a democratically controlled civilian government. A year later, in 1989, she was placed under house arrest; arrests followed for other NLD members as well. Her husband and two sons returned to London months later. Even after the NLD party won nearly 82 percent of the parliamentary seats in the 1990 elections—the nation's first multiparty parliamentary elections in almost thirty years—the government cancelled the results and refused to transfer power to the NLD. Aung San Suu Kyi, whom the government had barred from running for office or participating in the elections, remained under confinement.

Following the announcement of the million-dollar Nobel Peace Prize for 1991, much of the world rallied in support of Aung San Suu Kyi. A UN resolution called upon the Myanmar military regime to relinquish power and allow her to assume office. The U.S. government, citing Myanmar's dismal record on the matter of human rights, cut off all aid (except that attached to certain humanitarian projects) to the country. Media coverage, particularly in the West, cast new light on the brutalities and other abuses charged to the regime. In recognizing Aung San Suu Kyi, the Nobel Prize committee characterized her struggle for human rights as "one of the most extraordinary examples of civil courage in Asia in recent decades." *Freedom from Fear and Other Writings*, a collection of her articles and speeches, was published in 1991.

Austronesian languages: Languages spoken in a vast and highly diversified region of the world. This region stretches from Madagascar (Africa) and the Fiji Islands to Southeast Asia (Taiwan, Thailand, Indonesia, the Philippines), Hawaii, the Pacific Islands (Fiji, Samoa), and New Zealand.

Austronesian languages represent one of the largest family of languages in the world in two respects: first, the number of languages grouped under this family (as many as five hundred) and, second, the number of speakers (approximately two hundred million). Malayo-Polynesian and Austro-Tai are two other names given to this language family.

The important languages that belong to this group are as follows: Malagasy (Madagascar), Thai (Thailand), Bahasa Indonesian (Indonesia), TAGALOG (Philippines), Malay (Malaysia, Singapore), Lao (Laos), Cambodian, Fijian (Fiji Islands), Hawaiian, Tahitian, and Maori (New Zealand). In spite of its proximity to Africa, Malagasy shows little African influence, apparently because traders from Indonesia settled in Madagascar around the first millennium C.E. Languages such as Bahasa Indonesian and Bazaar Malay (Bahasa Malay) developed as pidgin languages that later became the languages of wider communication, that is, lingua francas. Therefore, they were influenced by the languages of India, China, and Europe. Actually, the modifier ibahasa is derived from the Sanskrit word *bhasha*, which means "language." Many pidgin languages are still spoken in the area.

Archeological and linguistic evidence reveals that Austronesian languages have their origins in the New Guinea region, and their history can be traced back to four thousand years ago. Although extensive research in this region continues to alter modern understanding of Austronesian languages, the linguistic picture is still far from clear. Therefore, the classification and subclassification of many languages of this language family are still subject to disputes by linguists. Despite these limitations, linguists classify Austronesian languages into two subgroups: The Eastern group and the Western group. The Eastern group embodies approximately three hundred languages spoken mostly in New Guinea and the more than ten thousand islands of Polynesia, Micronesia, and Melanesia. The Western group represents about four hundred languages spoken in Madagascar, South East Asia, and Western New Guinea.

The structural differences between the Austronesian languages are quite sharp, ranging from tonal languages (Thai) to nontonal (Hawaiian) ones. The Austronesian languages of Southeast Asia have a rich history of folk and written literature.

Avalokitesvara: The *bodhisattva* of compassion, perhaps the best-known figure in BUDDHISM aside from the historical Buddha Sakyamuni. *Bodhisattvas* are beings who, out of compassion, have postponed their own complete enlightenment in order to remain in the world to help all other beings move toward enlightenment. For this reason, all *bodhisattvas* are compassionate figures, but Avalokitesvara is believed to embody compassion, which is one of the two aspects of buddhahood (the other is wisdom). Avalokitesvara, who is known in both male and female forms, is almost universally popular in Buddhism, and is known as Chenrezig in Tibet; Kannon, Kwannon, or Kanzeon in Japan; and Kuanyin in China.

B

Bainbridge Island: Island in Puget Sound, near Seattle, Washington. Its large population of Japanese Americans owned or leased land for farming before World War II (1939-1945). Shortly after the attack on Pearl Harbor (December 7, 1941), it was the first area from which Japanese Americans were relocated because of the community's proximity to the Bremerton Navy Yard north of Seattle. Only about half of the Japanese Americans incarcerated chose to return to live on the island following the war.

Baisakhi Day (Apr. 13): Most important festival of northern India. It falls on the first day of the month of *Baisakh* (April 13 in the Gregorian calendar) and marks the beginning of the Hindu New Year.

Celebrated with gaiety and jubilation all over northern India, the festival holds special significance for farmers. On Baisakhi Day, the reaping of the winter crop begins and village communities all over Punjab, India's fertile granary, sing and dance the *bhangra*, a vigorous Punjabi folk dance renowned for its rhythm and energy. The dances depict the toil of the farmer from ploughing to harvesting and celebrate nature's bounty with joy and abandon.

Baisakhi Day has a deep religious significance for Hindus and Sikhs. Hindu mythology has it that Ganga descended to earth on this day, and millions of Hindus throng to Hardwar on the banks of the Ganges River

The typical Sikh observance of Baisakhi Day includes a visit to a gurdwara, or temple, such as this one in Hollywood, California. (Martin A. Hutner)

for the religious fair called the *Kumbha Mela*.

For the Sikhs, *Baisakhi Day* is one of the holiest of holy days. On this day in 1699, the tenth and last *guru*, Gobind Singh, founded the *Khalsa* brotherhood, a Sikh militant fraternity, at Anandpur, admitting the Sikhs into a new religious order with the baptism of the sword, and naming them *Singh*, meaning "lion." Sikhs everywhere observe this day of initiation by visiting a *gurdwara* (Sikh temple). Many flock to the Golden Temple at AMRITSAR and its major shrine, the Harminder Sahib. They take a holy dip in the *amrit-sarovar* (pool of nectar), the lake that surrounds the Golden Temple. The main religious service is the *Ak-hand Path*, the continuous reading of the holy *Granth Sahib* (the scriptures). The holy book is taken in a religious procession, and five leaders of the congregation, representing the *Panch Pyare*, or Beloved Five of Guru Gobind Singh, walk in front of the *Granth Sahib* with drawn swords.

Like so many major festivals in India, *Baisakhi Day* has a religious, social, and cultural significance that transcends its origins. Though it has its most profound religious significance for the Sikhs, it has a truly national character since it is celebrated in different parts of India in distinctive ways.

Baishakunin: Japanese term for a go-between. In arranged marriages, the parents of the couple would employ a go-between to bring the bride and groom together. Issei in the United States also employed them to arrange marriages for their Nisei children.

Balch, John A. (July 6, 1876, San Francisco, Calif.—May 15, 1951, San Francisco, Calif.): Businessperson. Though based in San Francisco, he invested in Hawaii businesses and became extremely influential in the Territory. Starting in 1906, he bought the Territory's telegraph company, which later dominated telephone companies on the islands. He wrote the book *Shall the Japanese Be Allowed to Dominate Hawaii?* (1943).

Balut: Fertilized duck egg in which the duckling is partially formed. It is considered a Filipino delicacy. The province of Rizal in the Philippines, considered the center of the balut industry, annually celebrates the River Festival at Pateros on July 29 in honor of Santa Maria, who saved the town's ducks from a crocodile.

Bamboo Ridge: The Hawaii Writers' Quarterly: Literary journal founded in 1978 by coeditors Eric CHOCK and Darrell H. Y. LUM to foster writing by and about Hawaii's people. Its name is taken from a favorite fishing spot where the long poles used to cast for ulua are so numerous as to make the lava ledge appear like a bamboo forest. Begun by Bamboo Ridge Press as part of the same literary groundswell in Hawaii that produced the watershed TALK STORY CONFERENCE, *Bamboo Ridge* has been published quarterly. From 1987, however, the press has alternated between single subscription issues following the literary journal format and double issues that feature the work of a single author or single theme.

Over the years *Bamboo Ridge* has provided a forum for a wide range of authors and interests, such as Hawaiian legends, Native Hawaiian rights issues, children's poetry, the screenplay of *Chan Is Missing* (1982), and *tanka* written by Hawaii Issei internees of World War II. The core of the press's publications is its single-author books by major local writers (Chock, Lum, Susan Nunes, Wing Tek LUM, Juliet S. Kono, Rodney Morales, Gary Pak, and Lois-Ann Yamanaka). An anthology of selections from the first twenty-nine issues was published as *The Best of Bamboo Ridge* (1986); other notable anthologies have been *Sister Stew* (1991), an issue of contemporary women writers, and *Pake* (1989), a collection of Chinese writers in Hawaii past and present.

Bamboo Ridge acknowledges the long history of literature created by Hawaii writers, a rich tradition that has only recently been recognized by scholars. (See Stephen H. Sumida's *And the View from the Shore: Literary Traditions of Hawaii*, published in 1991.) It has served as an alternative to academic journals as well as to mainland publications that often have been unreceptive to Hawaii's Asian Americans, Pacific Islanders, *hapas*, women, or PIDGIN speakers. Though the writers, their themes, and their writing styles are diverse and not solely focused on island issues, their works when viewed as a growing body of literature share common characteristics: a rejection of the "paradise," "assimilation," and "melting pot" myths; a centering on Hawaii's unique island geography and environment; an understanding of its colonial history, notably the paternalistic plantation and "divide and conquer" immigration experiences; an honest acknowledgment of the conflicts within a multicultural society; and the commitment to a pluralism born from a grudging tolerance of others' differences. Typically this "local literature" asserts a worldview that both converges upon and diverges from Asian traditions and the mainland Asian American experience. It includes a strong sense of place, an expansive notion of time, and hard-won personal relationships (especially of family) noted for respect, reciprocity, deference, and an indirectness that is seemingly nonconfrontational. In literary terms such a worldview is manifested in the use of Pidgin English, clear concrete images, and a narrative ("talk story") style.

Ban, Shinzaburo (1854, Tokyo, Japan—Jan. 18, 1926): Labor contractor and businessman. After college, he entered foreign service in 1885 and was stationed in Hawaii. Years later, he resigned his post to start an emigration company back in Japan. Returning to the United States, in 1891 he formed the S. Ban Company of Portland, a labor-contracting business. As one of the region's three biggest firms, the company imported many Japanese immigrants to work on American railroads. Expanding his mercantile base, Ban also opened other business ventures, including a lumber mill, with branches in several states. In 1893 he helped to found Portland Japanese Methodist Church. Ban's company went bankrupt in 1924.

Ban Vinai refugee camp (Loei Province, Kingdom of Thailand): Hmong and Lao refugee camp in northeastern Thailand. It was established in 1975 and is located along the Mekong River. The camp is important for the approximately one hundred thousand Hmong living in the United States because most Hmong who fled Laos spent several years living in Ban Vinai and because large numbers of Hmong continue to live there. In addition, most Hmong Americans have families and friends living in Ban Vinai, and they often send them money to help them lead a better life, despite the camp's austere conditions.

In addition to the Hmong, small numbers of ethnic Lao lived in Ban Vinai just after the fall of Laos in 1975. Small groups of Mien and Tin were also transferred to Ban Vinai in 1983 and continued to live there. In 1986, a total of forty-five thousand people lived in Ban Vinai, of whom approximately forty-three thousand were Hmong, nine hundred were Mien, and nine hundred were Tin.

Like other refugee camps for Laotians in Thailand, Ban Vinai is operated by the Thai Ministry of Interior, which uses money from the Office of the United Nations High Commissioner for Refugees (UNHCR) to purchase food and housing materials for the refugees. Much of the housing in Ban Vinai is made of bamboo and thatch and is built by the refugees themselves. Community facilities such as schools, a hospital, and headquarters for the UNHCR and the Ministry of Interior are made of more durable cinder-block construction.

Camp refugees have not been allowed to leave Ban Vinai without special permission from Thai authorities and, as a result, are usually restricted to the camp area. Visitors need special permission to enter. In general, the refugees were not allowed to work in the Thai economy. The only major exception is the large-scale production of Hmong reverse appliqué quilt art (*paj ntaub* in Hmong). *Paj Ntaub* is a specialty product produced for sale both in Thai markets and through relatives living in the United States and other countries. One consequence of Ban Vinai's isolation from the Thai economy is that the Hmong refugees do not mix much with the Thais who live in the area which means that although the Thai control the camp, the day-to-day cultural life is primarily Hmong.

A number of other agencies besides the Thai Ministry of Interior are involved in the camp's administration. At different times, a number of foreign and Thai voluntary agencies known as *volags* have provided medical care, opium detoxification, instruction in English, sanitation, occupational training, and other services to the refugees. The Thai Ministry of Education also conducts classes for refugee children using a Thai elementary-school curriculum. Classes are also conducted in the Hmong and Lao languages for the children.

Like Ban Vinai, the Phanat Nikhom camp is another compound housing Southeast Asian refugees in Thailand. Here two Indochinese refugees are about to depart from Phanat Nikhom. (A. Hollmann/UNHCR)

The number of refugees housed in Ban Vinai remained stable from 1981 to 1986, even though streams of people arriving from Laos declined and departures for the United States, France, and other resettlement countries continued. The stable population number is a result of the camp's high birthrate. In 1986, the camp's birthrate was more than 4 percent, which is higher than that of most developing countries.

Bandaranaike, Sirimavo Ratwatte Dias (b. Apr. 17, 1916, Ratnapura, Ceylon, now SRI LANKA): Prime minister of Ceylon. Her party's victory in the 1960 general election made her the world's first female prime minister of any country. She married Ceylon statesman S. W. R. D. Bandaranaike in 1940; he served as prime minister from 1956 until 1959, when he was assassinated by a Buddhist monk. The following year, with the backing of the Sri Lanka (blessed Ceylon) Freedom Party (SLFP), she won election as the country's seventh prime minister and vowed to continue her husband's policies of socialism and foreign neutrality and his pro-Buddhist and pro-Sinhalese leanings. She was defeated in the 1965 election but regained power in 1970, holding office until 1977. During her second term, backed by her Socialist coalition, the United Front, she launched a more radical political platform that included the nationalization of important industries and diplomatic recognition of major communist world powers. Her administration was, however, marred by the impact of repressive measures and failure to revive the economy and to resolve issues concerning minority rights.

Bandung Conference (Apr. 18-24, 1955): Meeting of several Asian and African states in Bandung, Indonesia. The conference represented more than half of the world's population and was attended by twenty-nine Asian and African countries. Its purpose was to forge a unity among the newly independent Asian and African countries so that they could play an assertive and independent role in international affairs. Attending the conference were such leaders as Achmed Sukarno of Indonesia, Jawaharlal Nehru of India, Zhou Enlai of China, U Nu of Burma, and Gamal Abdel Nasser of Egypt.

Since former European colonies, especially in Africa, had not yet gained independence, the conference had hoped to make a bold stand on this question. Because, however, some pro-Western countries also pointed to Soviet domination of many Eastern European countries and Central Asia as a new form of colonialism, the conference eventually adopted a com-

Chinese premier Zhou Enlai. At the Bandung Conference he assured delegates of China's cooperation on the matter of international solidarity. (AP/Wide World Photos)

promise formula under which "colonialism in all its manifestations" was condemned.

The conference especially helped Zhou Enlai, the prime minister of China, to project a more moderate view of the new Beijing regime, which was widely suspected of backing several local Asian communist parties. In his speech to the conference, Zhou spoke of China's readiness to respect the independence and sovereignty of all Asian and African countries, to cooperate with them for mutual benefit, to stop all hostile propaganda against them, and to advise overseas Chinese to give up their dual citizenship. On China's border disputes with its neighbors, he assured the delegates that China would maintain the status quo until all disputes were resolved by peaceful negotiations.

At the insistence of Prime Minister Nehru of India, the conference also endorsed *Panchshila*, the five principles of peaceful coexistence, embodying such concepts as mutual respect for territorial integrity and sovereignty, nonaggression, noninterference in one another's internal affairs, equality, and mutual benefit. Some pro-Western countries such as Ceylon (now Sri Lanka), Thailand, and the Philippines doubted the usefulness of such a declaration, as they were skeptical of the adherence to such principles by a country such as China.

More than the ten-point declaration that represented the group's stand on various international issues in general terms, the conference marked an important stage in the emergence of what was called the "Bandung Spirit," which later resulted in the formation of the Asian-African group at the United Nations. On many issues, such as colonialism, the group often found itself working closely with the Soviet Union. The United States, which at one time almost controlled the majority vote, now had to scramble for votes. A new political alignment had upset the clear Cold War divide between Washington and Moscow.

Bangladesh, People's Republic of: Independent South Asian republic. It is bounded to the east, north, and west by India, to the southeast by Myanmar (Burma), and to the south by the Bay of Bengal. Formerly known as East Pakistan, it became an independent nation in 1971. Two-thirds of Bangladesh constitutes the low-lying delta of the Ganges River and is ravaged by annual floods and tidal waves generated by cyclones that originate periodically from the Bay of Bengal. The climate is warm and humid most of the year, with cool and dry winters.

The region was ruled as part of British India from 1857 to 1947, when it was given independence as East

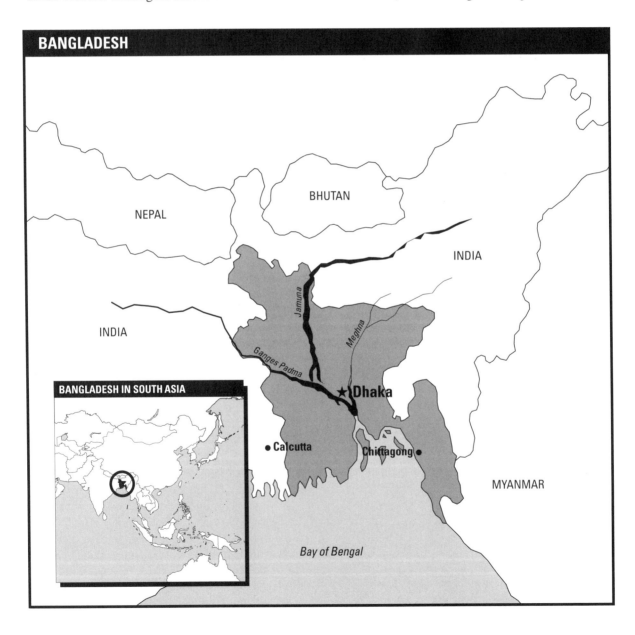

Pakistan. Its government, however, was located in West Pakistan until 1971, when Bangladesh declared its independence. War with PAKISTAN ensued, and Pakistan did not recognize Bangladesh as a nation until 1974.

Bangladesh is comparable in size to the state of Wisconsin, but, with a population of about 117 million people (1991 estimate), it is the eighth most populous country in the world. The population is made up of migrants from north India, Tibet, and Myanmar, but many in Bangladesh share cultural attributes with the people of West Bengal. About 85 percent of the population is Muslim and most of the rest are Hindu.

With a population density of 2,028 persons per square mile, it is one of the most crowded countries in the world. The overcrowding, frequent floods, and low agricultural productivity contribute to widespread poverty. About 80 percent of the people live in the rural areas, and most of them are poor farmers struggling to survive on small plots of land. Dacca, the capital and the largest city, has two million people. Only about 70 percent of the population is literate. World-renowned poet Rabindranath TAGORE is a prominent figure revered by many in Bangladesh.

The government is a civilian democracy, and Khaleda Zia, wife of the deposed leader General Ziaur Rahman, became the first woman prime minister of Bangladesh in 1991. Zia's political party, the Bangladesh Nationalist Party, and the Awami League constitute the two dominant parties in the nation.

Agriculture is the mainstay of the economy, and the main crops are rice and jute, a fiber for making sacks and carpets. Bangladesh does not produce enough rice to feed its large population, which suffers from famine and poverty. Industrial production is largely confined to the processing of agricultural products, such as jute. Despite natural disasters, such as the 1991 cyclone that killed more than 131,000 people, and economic problems, Bangladesh has a long and rich urban and folk heritage, depicted in poetry, dance, and music.

Bango: Copper disk that served as a means of identification for laborers on Hawaii plantations. The term is thought to be derived from the Japanese word for "number." Contract laborers would present their disks for inspection by plantation security police before receiving a sealed envelope containing their pay.

Bank of the Orient: First U.S. commercial bank to establish a branch in the People's Republic of China. Founded in San Francisco, California, in 1971, the bank has four branches in the San Francisco Bay Area and one overseas branch in Xiamen, China.

Bannai, Paul (b. July 4, 1920, Delta, Colo.): Politician. A realtor and the first Japanese American elected to the California state legislature, in June, 1973. He had served previously on the Gardena City Planning Commission and the Los Angeles County Assembly, representing the Sixty-seventh District. Later he was appointed to a position in the U.S. government to oversee national cemeteries.

Baohuanghui (also Chinese Empire Reform Association; Protect the Emperor Society; as of 1907, Constitutionalist Party): Chinese nationalist movement founded in Victoria, British Columbia, Canada, in 1899. As one of the first Chinese political parties, the China Reform Association spread rapidly throughout Chinese communities in the United States as well as Southeast Asia and elsewhere. Related organizations sprang up in China. The party and its affiliates were very influential in Chinese American communities through 1909 or 1910, losing influence rapidly after that. A few very small branches continued in existence as late as the 1980's.

The Chinese Empire Reform Association, founded by KANG YOUWEI, at its height had more than sixty branches in the United States as well as Hawaii. At first, membership and leaders came from all segments of the Chinese American community. Leadership soon fell to entrenched community leaders, however, but this included heads of certain groups that had earlier been only of secondary importance. Around 1910 community leadership came generally under challenge, and the party suffered in consequence. In addition, political currents in China outstripped the party's ideas, and China's republican revolution of 1911 dealt the party a blow from which it never recovered.

The association stood for radical reform, economic modernization, national strength, and constitutional monarchy (except briefly in 1900 and 1902, when revolution was considered). Kang Youwei and party leaders first tried to use the party to help the reform-minded Guangxu Emperor, who had lost power in a coup d'état in 1898. These efforts, including attempts to field an army and representations to U.S. president Theodore Roosevelt, failed. When the emperor died in 1908, the party still favored a British-style constitutional monarchy for China.

To demonstrate modern economic and industrial methods, the party early launched a commercial cor-

Members of the Baohuanghui gathered at party headquarters, circa New Year's Day, 1909. (Library of Congress)

poration; U.S. branches played an active role. Sometimes advised by Kang's American friend Charles Ranlett Flint ("father of the trust"), the corporation established financially interlocked ventures including a hotel in Chicago, a bank in New York, and a Chinese-language newspaper in San Francisco. Outside the United States, there were streetcar lines, a rice brokerage, other banks, mining companies, and the like. These ventures collapsed between 1908 and 1910, however, amid charges of corruption and mismanagement.

In 1903, the party organized a cadet training corps in the United States (the Western Military Academy). The cadets were intended either to help implement the party's aims directly or to modernize China's national army. Led by the American Homer Lea and with several hundred (Chinese) cadets, at its height the program operated in twenty-two American cities and towns. Lea used his connections with U.S. Army officers to ensure that American law would not close down the program. In 1908, Lea became disaffected with Kang Youwei, however, and moved with the cadets into a rival, prorevolutionary organization.

Barred Zone Act of 1917: Common term for the Immigration Act of 1917, which severely restricted Asian immigration to the United States.

The act of 1917 was based on the recommendations of a joint congressional commission appointed in 1907 to review the then existing U.S. immigration system and propose reforms. The commission submitted its report in 1911.

The Immigration Act of 1917 retained all the preceding barriers to immigration from China and Japan and imposed more severe restrictions on Asian regions not included previously. It created a zone that included India, Indochina, the Malay states, the Asian part of Russia, most of Arabia, Afghanistan, and the present-day island states of Polynesia and Southeast Asia. The natives of this zone were barred from immigrating to the United States (although exceptions permitted small numbers of immigrants from the barred zone to enter even during the period of exclusion). Filipinos, and Japanese and Chinese immigrants not barred by previous legislation were not affected by the 1917 act.

Another controversial clause of the Barred Zone Act, which affected Asian Americans and other immigrants who were not natives of Northern or Western Europe, pertained to the establishment of literacy tests for those over the age of sixteen as a precondition for their admission.

Historically viewed, the Barred Zone Act was merely another manifestation of anti-Asian bias in U.S. IMMIGRATION POLICY, which during the late nineteenth century became heavily influenced by nativist sentiments. The 1917 act was preceded by the CHINESE EXCLUSION ACT OF 1882, the latter's subsequent renewals, and the GENTLEMEN'S AGREEMENT (1907) between the U.S. and Japanese governments. Moreover, these restrictions were accompanied by provisions that left Chinese and Japanese immigrants ineligible for naturalized citizenship.

The Barred Zone Act adversely affected the lives of Asian Americans for almost half a century. It resulted in the separation of families and contributed to gender and generational imbalance. This act remained essentially unaltered until the passage of the MCCARRAN-

WALTER ACT OF 1952, which abolished all racial and ethnic barriers to immigration and naturalization and provided for family reunification. The 1952 act, however, provided only tiny quotas for Asian immigration, and it was not until the passage of the IMMIGRATION AND NATIONALITY ACT OF 1965 that such barriers to Asian immigration were removed.

Barrio: Primary form of settlement in the Philippines. This Spanish term is used in that country to mean "place of settlement" or "village." Within these small, rural, integrated villages, kinship groups play a central role. Children born in the *barrio* often have extended families of in-laws and godparents. Most of the Philippine population still lives in *barrios*.

Barroga, Jeannie (b. Sept. 30, 1949, Milwaukee, Wis.): Playwright. She is best known for her plays *Eye of the Coconut* (pr. 1987), about growing up Filipino American in Milwaukee, and *Walls* (pr. 1989), about architect Maya Lin's struggle to execute her design for the Vietnam Veterans Memorial in Washington, D.C.

Other scripts include *Kenny Was a Shortstop* (pr. 1991), *The Revered Miss Newton* (pr. 1991), and *Talk Story* (pr. 1991). Barroga was instrumental in founding the Discovery Project for Palo Alto's TheatreWorks in 1989, an organization that identifies and develops new American playwrights.

Basement Workshop: Influential community organization established in 1971, in New York City, as an outgrowth of individuals who researched and compiled data for Columbia University's *Chinatown Report* (1969). The group continued compiling information about Asian American communities and subsequently incorporated materials on the arts and the media as well as other historical documentation. From 1971 to 1979, the Basement Workshop funded *BRIDGE* magazine. The New York Chinatown History Project (now the CHINATOWN HISTORY MUSEUM) also had its roots in the group. The workshop is no longer in existence.

Bataan Death March: March forced upon seventy thousand U.S. and Filipino prisoners of war captured

During the Bataan Death March, numerous American prisoners of war endured brutal treatment inflicted by their Japanese captors. (Library of Congress)

Filipino dancers perform the Tinikling, the national dance of the Philippines. This form is one of various dances that the Bayanihan Dance Company strives to preserve and popularize. (Martin A. Hutner)

by the Japanese in the Philippines in 1942, during World War II. Following the taking of Bataan, a peninsula bordering the western shore of Manila Bay, on April 9, the prisoners were ordered to walk more than sixty miles north to Camp O'Donnell. About fifty-four thousand prisoners reached the camp; as many as ten thousand died because of the horrible physical conditions, while others managed to escape their captors.

Bataan News: English language weekly newspaper published in Sacramento, California. This national journal for Filipino Americans has covered national and international news and carried in-depth community news and analyses on subjects that mainstream newspapers have ignored.

Bayanihan: Filipino term that means "working together." As applied to Filipino society, the term emphasizes such values as tradition, authority, and the importance of the group as opposed to the individual.

Bayanihan Dance Company: Troupe of professional folk dancers organized in the Philippines. The company tours internationally hoping to preserve and popularize traditional Filipino dance forms reflecting Malay, Muslim, and Spanish influences. The group began as a joint project of the Bayanihan Folk Arts Association and Philippine Women's University and reflects the latter's desire to revive folk art forms native to the Philippine Islands.

Bayard-Zhang Treaty (1888): Unratified treaty between the United States and China that attempted to resolve certain immigration-related issues involving the two nations. The Chinese Qing government had become increasingly alarmed by reports of recent violence perpetrated against Chinese laborers in the United States. In response the Chinese government contacted the U.S. government and proposed to limit severely the emigration of its laborers abroad in exchange for assurances of better protection for those

Soldiers of the People's Liberation Army inside the Forbidden City, Beijing. (Edwin Bernbaum)

already overseas. The Americans were represented by Secretary of State Thomas Bayard, the Chinese by minister ZHANG YINHUAN.

The new treaty, a draft of which was signed on March 12, prohibited the migration of Chinese laborers to the United States for twenty years; it did not bar from returning to the United States any laborer having a "lawful wife, child, or parent in the United States, or property of the value of $1,000 or debt of like amount due him."

Both sides, however, immediately demanded that the proposals be recast, and from there the situation continued to deteriorate. Failure to ratify the treaty eventually resulted in the U.S.-drafted Scott Act of 1888, which stipulated that any Chinese laborer, having once left the United States, could not return.

Beche-de-mer. *See* **Sea cucumber**

Beekman, Alan (b. Jan. 16, 1913, Utica, N.Y.): Writer. He became resident of Honolulu in 1935 and has written extensively about Japanese immigrants and their descendants in Hawaii. He also contributed a column in the *Pacific Citizen* newspaper for eight years, reviewing books of interest to Nikkei. He authored *Hawaiian Tales* (1970), *The Niihau Incident: The True Story of the Japanese Fighter Pilot Who, After the Attack on Pearl Harbor, Landed on the Hawaiian Island of Niihau and Terrorized the Residents* (1982), and *Crisis: The Japanese Attack on Pearl Harbor and Southeast Asia* (1992).

Beijing: Capital of China. It is located in an extensive plain in northeastern China and is China's second largest city. It occupies an area of about sixty-five hundred square miles and has a population of about 10,819,407 (1990 estimate). It is a cultural and administrative center and boasts several universities. Among its major industries are iron and steel manufacturing and machine building.

Bellingham incident (1907): First in a spate of riots by white American labor against Asian Indian immigrant workers, mostly Sikhs, in the lumber and railroad towns of the Pacific Northwest.

On the night of Thursday, September 5, 1907, more than five hundred white workers raided the lumber mills of Bellingham, a frontier town in Washington State about fifty miles south of Vancouver, broke into the waterfront tenements and bunkhouses occupied by Indian workers, dragged them from their beds, looted their belongings, and tried to drive them out of town. Several hundred terrified Indians sought protective custody in the village hall and city jail. Fearing for their lives, about 750 of them fled northward to the Canadian border on the Great Northern Railroad.

The cause of the rioting is attributed to the strong anti-Asian sentiment prevalent in North America at the time. Bellingham already had a twenty-year history of anti-Chinese rioting when the first Indian immigrants showed up looking for jobs in the lumber mills. Mill owners, anxious for cheap labor, hired the Indians eagerly, but white workers resented the competition. Goaded by the ASIATIC EXCLUSION LEAGUE, whose stated goal was to focus hostility against Asians, white mill workers targeted the "Hindus" or "ragheads," as they called the Sikhs, denouncing them as unclean, immoral, and lustful. In August of 1907, white mill workers warned mill owners not to employ Indians and on Labor Day paraded down the main streets of Bellingham in a show of solidarity.

The first reports of sporadic violence against Indians on the day after Labor Day were ignored by the police. The next day, two white youths were arrested for stoning Indians in a mob attack but were quickly released by the police chief. Encouraged by this seeming acquiescence on the part of the authorities (whose dominant sentiment was support for exclusion and the ideology of white supremacy), a mob of white mill workers and townspeople assaulted the Indians and drove them out of town. Though the mayor assured the Indians that they would be protected since they had not broken any law, the Indians preferred to leave town en masse. By the end of September, 1907, there were no Asians left in Bellingham.

Benevolent assimilation: Earliest statement of U.S. colonial policy concerning the Philippines. President William McKinley's proclamation of benevolent assimilation declared that limited self-rule rather than outright independence should govern the American government's relationship with the Philippine Islands. Up to the time of his assassination in 1901, McKinley opposed completed self-government for the Filipino people.

When the United States decided to retain the Philippines in 1898, Admiral George Dewey, worried about potential hostilities between American and Philippine forces, pressed McKinley to ease the tension by asserting an official American policy for the archipelago.

McKinley was aided by Dean Worcester of the University of Michigan, who, despite his ignorance of the Philippines, helped to write the policy statement. Benevolent assimilation as proclaimed on December 21, 1898, expressed the American government's desire to gain the favor of the Filipinos in order to demonstrate that its task was well intentioned. Filipino inhabitants could be officeholders if they conceded U.S. domination over the islands. American power would, however, be exercised to keep peace and to surmount every obstruction hindering the creation of a benign and firmly established regime. According to the declaration, the United States was sovereign in the Philippines

William McKinley's policy of benevolent assimilation, offering the Philippines limited self-government instead of full independence, incited further revolution in the Philippines. (White House Historical Society)

because Spain had relinquished the archipelago through treaty.

Upon being informed of the stated U.S. policy, General Elwell Otis, stationed in the Philippines, refrained from issuing the document. Otis realized Filipino revolutionaries were ready to fight and feared inciting them to battle. The general decided to reword McKinley's proclamation, substituting bland language for some provocative terms.

Misfortune, however, befell the Americans when General Marcus Miller, occupying Iloilo on Panay Island, publicized the original statement. Local Filipino authorities dispatched the text to President Emilio Aguinaldo of the Philippine Republic, who complained about American violations of Philippine sovereignty and threatened a resort to force.

Yet regardless of the Filipino desire for independence and the outbreak of war, McKinley more clearly defined benevolent assimilation in a letter of April 7, 1900, and the U.S. Congress incorporated its idea of evolutionary self-government in the first Philippine Organic Act two years later.

Bengal: Region situated in the northeast of India. Bengal is divided between the Indian state of West Bengal (since 1947) and the People's Republic of BANGLADESH, the name for East Pakistan since 1972. The original non-Aryan inhabitants of the region must have been avid traders, as their land was mentioned in the *Mahabharata* as well as in several Greek sources.

Bengal was a part of the Gupta Empire from the fourth century through the seventh. From the eighth century onward, it was ruled by the Buddhist Pala Dynasty, with its headquarters at Gaur. From the middle of the twelfth century, the Hindu Sena Dynasty ruled the region from the capital at Nadia. In the thirteenth century, Bengal was absorbed into the Turko-Afghan Empire of India. It became a province (*suba*) of the Mughal Empire in the sixteenth century. The eighteenth century saw the area come under the incompetent rule of the *nawabs* (chiefs), who had been provincial governors (*subadars*) under the Mughals. By this time, European traders such as the Dutch, Danes, French, and British had begun to establish trading posts in Bengal. Especially after the defeat of the last *nawab*, Siraj-ud-Daulah, by the British East India Company's force at the Battle of Plassey in 1757, Bengal passed under de facto British rule.

As Bengal was the first Indian region to come under British domination, it was also the first region to absorb Western culture and undergo a renaissance in the nineteenth century. It also was the first to rebel vocally and violently against the British at the beginning of the twentieth century.

Bengali language and cuisine have an unusual charm of their own. Bengali folk songs, devotional song (*kirtana*), wandering minstrels songs (*baul*), and the modern melodies named after their composers, such as Rajanikanto Sen, Dwijendralal Roy, Atulprasad Sen, Kazi Nazrul Islam, and, above all, Rabindranath TAGORE, are all testimonies to the rich culture of the people. Bengalis are by nature gregarious and given to communal celebration of holy days and holidays. The most popular communal religious festivals (*baroaripuja*) of the region are those dedicated to the goddesses Durga and Kali, the two manifestations of the Divine Mother principle most widely worshiped by Bengalis.

Bengali: Modern Indo-Aryan language. It is spoken primarily in two South Asian countries: India and Bangladesh. Approximately 150 million people speak Bengali as either a first or a second language. It is ranked among the ten most widely spoken languages of the world, and it is the national language of Bangladesh and the official language of the state of Bengal in India. It is also quite prominent in the Indian state of Assam. The eastern variety, spoken in Dacca, the capital of Bangladesh, is distinct from the Western variety spoken in Calcutta (India). The variety of Bengali spoken in Chittagong (southeast Bangladesh) is so distinct both from the eastern and western Bengali that it can be characterized as an independent language.

In contrast to the case of Hindi-Urdu, which Hindus call Hindi and Muslims call Urdu, religious identity does not take precedence over linguistic identity in the Bengali speech community. The Bengali Hindus and the Muslims show more affinity to their language than to their religion.

Bengali, which is a descendant of the Sanskrit language, belongs to the eastern group of Indo-European languages spoken on the Indian subcontinent. It has undergone three stages of development: Old Bengali (1000-1300), Middle Bengali (1375-1750), and Modern Bengali (1750-   ).

Bengali is written in a script that is a descendant of the Brahmi script, which was well-established in India before 500 B.C.E. The script is phonetic in nature and shows a fairly regular correspondence between the letters and their pronunciation. It is written from left to right.

Bengali represents one of the richest literary traditions of all South Asian languages. Its literary history goes back to the tenth century. The oldest literary work, *Caryaapada*, composed during the period 1000-1200 C.E., contains the celebrated Buddhist hymns. Rabindranath Tagore brought international visibility to Indian literature in general and Bengali literature in particular when he received the Noble Prize in Literature in 1913.

Benshi: Male narrators for Japanese silent films. Often becoming more famous with community patrons than the films themselves, these men frequently accompanied the films whenever they were shown in other places. At times, they were accompanied by *bansho*, women who supplied sound effects and music during the film.

Berger v. Bishop (1903): U.S. district court case filed by Frederick V. Berger against businessman E. Faxon Bishop. Berger claimed that Bishop had violated a U.S. law, enacted in March, 1903, that prohibited assisting the immigration of contract laborers into the United States or any of its territories by paying money to these individuals prior to their arrival in America. The law also gave any private citizen the right to file suit alleging such unlawful assistance and by so doing to earn financial rewards stipulated by the law.

Earlier, in late 1902, Bishop had been instrumental in finalizing an agreement between the Hawaiian Sugar Planters' Association (HSPA) and the Korean government to bring Korean contract laborers to the United States to work on Hawaii plantations. Those who agreed to emigrate were prepaid a sum of money by the HSPA—$100 each, half for passage to America, the other half for incidental expenses. Workers then began arriving in Hawaii by ship shortly thereafter.

The Honolulu arrival in April, 1903, of the *Nippon Maru*, with more than a hundred Koreans aboard, triggered a special investigation by American authorities, which concluded that illegal immigration assistance had been rendered. Under questioning, Bishop admitted that payments had been made—but a legal technicality ultimately saved him. The district court found that because those aboard the ship had been recruited before March of 1903, when the act was adopted, Bishop therefore was not guilty.

Berssenbrugge, Mei-mei (b. Oct. 5, 1947, Beijing, China): Writer. An American citizen born abroad, she earned her B.A. degree at James Reed College (1969) and an M.F.A. degree at Columbia University (1974). She has published several books of poetry—among them are *Fish Souls* (1971), *Summits Move with the Tide* (1974), *Random Possession* (1979), *The Heat Bird* (1983), *Empathy* (1989), and *Sphericity* (1993)—and authored the one-act play, *One, Two Cups*, which was first produced by New York's Basement Workshop in 1979. She has contributed to many periodicals, including *East-West Journal*, *Yardbird Reader*, *Gidra*, *Bridge*, and *Conjunctions*.

Bhachu, Parminder Kaur (b. Oct. 20, 1953): Scholar. Much of Bhachu's work has focused on Sikhs in Great Britain—see for example *Twice Migrants: East African Sikh Settlers in Britain* (1985). With other scholars of the diaspora experience, she has contributed to the growing recognition of the need for comparative and global perspectives in Asian American Studies.

Graduated with honors in anthropology from University College, London in 1976, Bhachu received a Ph.D. in 1981 from London University. In 1991, she became Henry R. Luce Professor of Cultural Identity and Global Processes at Clark University. She coedited

Enterprising Women: Ethnicity, Economy, and Gender Relations (1988, with Sallie Westwood) and *Immigration and Entrepreneurship: Culture, Capital, and Ethnic Networks* (1993, with Ivan Light).

Francis Biddle. (AP/Wide World Photos)

Biddle, Francis (May 9, 1886, Paris, France—Oct. 4, 1968, Hayannis, Mass.): U.S. Attorney General. During the "yellow peril" hysteria preceding the internment of Japanese Americans, Biddle received angry criticism from white Americans for his nonevacuation policy. Succumbing to demands for a mass relocation of Japanese Americans, he supported transferring authority from the U.S. Justice Department to the War Department.

Big Five: Five powerful corporations that acted as intermediaries between the plantations of the Hawaiian Islands and the markets. By the end of the nineteenth century, large corporations such as the Big Five had come to dominate the economic and political life of the islands. In 1879, for example, there were nine such agencies for sixty plantations; four such firms failed to survive into the twentieth century. The story of the rise and fall of the Big Five tells in microcosm why Hawaii developed a prosperous, multicultural society.

C. Brewer & Company. In 1818 and again in 1924, Captain Andrew Blanchard bartered a ship for a shipment of sandalwood from the Hawaiian Kingdom, leaving crewman James Hunnewell to await the wood in order to complete the transaction. In 1826 Hunne-well started a trading company. Two years later he hired Henry Pierce, who bought him out in 1833. Pierce formed a partnership with Captain Charles Brewer in 1836. After Pierce left for Boston in 1842, the firm became C. Brewer & Company. When Brewer retired to Boston, he sold one-third interest in the company to J. F. B. Marshall, who started Lihue Plantation. Thus, C. Brewer & Company was the first of five sugarcane agents that soon dominated the economy of the Hawaiian Islands.

Starting costs for large-scale plantation agriculture required bank loans from the mainland, but C. Brewer & Company and the later sugarcane companies lacked collateral, such as land. Accordingly, pressure was applied on the king of Hawaii to privatize land ownership, which was traditionally held in common by the crown. The so-called GREAT *MAHELE* of 1848 distributed land to Hawaiians, and the Kuleana Act of 1850 permitted non-Hawaiians to own land. Since Hawaiians did not enjoy sugarcane cultivation, the white owners recruited laborers from China, Japan, Korea, the Philippines, Portugal, Puerto Rico, and other countries, who by the beginning of the twentieth century outnumbered both Hawaiians and whites.

Theo H. Davies & Company. The second Big Five firm arose from a branch office of a trading firm, Starkey, Jannion & Company of Liverpool, first established at Honolulu in 1845. After Starkey sold his share of the business, Jannion formed a new partnership, Jannion, Green & Company. Davies came to work as a clerk in 1857, and he bought the business in 1867.

American Factors. Captain Henry Hackfeld, a German who had traded with Hawaii for some time, decided to start a mercantile business in 1849 under the name H. Hackfeld & Company, renting a building from the owner of two sugar plantations. He later purchased the plantation with capital from lucrative trading with Bremen, Germany. During World War I (1914-1918) Congress froze all German assets, the firm was declared enemy property, and in 1918 a group of Americans with interests in the sugar industry bought the company, renaming it American Factors.

Castle & Cooke. Samuel Northrup Castle and Amos Starr Cooke, ordained ministers, were sent to Hawaii by the American Board of Missions in 1837 to keep a tight rein on finances of the growing missionary com-

H. Hackfeld & Co., the predecessor of American Factors, at Kailua-Kona, circa 1900. (Lyman House Memorial Museum)

Japanese and other laborers at a sugar plantation in Kilauea, circa 1890. (Hawaii State Archives)

munity. In 1851, they opened a store under the name Castle & Cooke, and from 1858 they began to buy stock in sugar plantations that were started by friends in the missionary community. As the partners had considerable business acumen, they in time secured controlling interests in several large plantations.

Alexander & Baldwin. Samuel Alexander and Henry Baldwin, both sons of missionaries, opened a sugar plantation at Paia in 1871. The firm, Alexander & Baldwin, sold subscriptions of stock to get started and soon became the fifth of the Big Five firms.

Capital Accumulation Strategies. As the economic and political fate of the small white community in Hawaii came to depend on the Big Five, the commercial leaders realized that they should devote less attention to competing among themselves and more to assuring markets for sugarcane abroad. Initially their capital came from elsewhere, and the repayment of loans was a debit on their account books. Yet in 1858

the first bank in Hawaii opened, and by the 1920's the island merchants accumulated enough capital to be independent of outside funds, a remarkable achievement.

Markets in England and Germany were farther away than the United States, affecting shipping costs, so trade with the United States became dominant. Tariffs on Hawaiian sugar after the Civil War (1861-1865) stimulated the Big Five to lobby for a free-trade agreement with Washington, D.C., and the Reciprocity Treaty of 1875 resulted. When the McKinley Tariff Act of 1890 put sugar on the list of duty-free goods, Hawaii began to compete with other sugar-producing countries, and Big Five leaders increasingly sought annexation, which came in 1898.

The Big Five overcame the mainland sugar trust and dependence on outside shipping by buying its own refinery and launching its own shipping fleet, but the same economic prowess was used to control banking, insurance, and shipping to supply other firms, notably those led by nonwhite entrepreneurs, who sought to link up with businesses in China and Japan. The Big Five also gave few concessions to nonwhite workers who struck for better working conditions on the plantations.

The Decline of the Big Five. So odious was the reputation of the Big Five as an instrument of white dominance that during the territorial elections of 1954 the landslide defeat of the white-dominated Republican Party by the nonwhite-led Democratic Party was viewed as a repudiation of the Big Five. After 1959, when Hawaii became a state, the ruling Democratic Party made no effort to put the Big Five out of business but rather sought to facilitate the ability of new entrepreneurs to compete.

As the world economy became more important than the national economy, the Big Five diversified its holdings; most of these holdings became multinational corporations and moved headquarters elsewhere. American Factors and Theo. H. Davies sold out to become subsidiaries of giant corporations. C. Brewer & Company and Alexander & Baldwin continued to maintain home offices in Honolulu.—*Michael Haas*

Suggested Readings: • Cooper, George, and Gavan Daws. *Land and Power in Hawaii: The Democratic Years.* Honolulu: Benchmark Press, 1985. • Kent, Noel. *Hawaii: Islands Under the Influence.* New York: Monthly Review Press, 1983. • Smith, Jared G. *The Big Five.* Honolulu: Advertiser Publishing, 1942.

Biggers, Earl Derr (Aug. 26, 1884, Warren, Ohio— Apr. 5, 1933, Pasadena, Calif.): Writer. After graduating from Harvard University in 1907, he worked as a journalist, writing humor columns and drama reviews for the Boston *Traveler.* His first novel, *Seven Keys to Baldpate* (1913), a mix of mystery, melodrama, and farce, was well received; adapted for the stage by George M. Cohan, it became a hit, the inspiration for five movies.

Biggers' greatest success came with a series of six novels featuring a Hawaii-based Chinese American detective named Charlie CHAN. The first book in the series, *The House Without a Key*, was published in 1925, and the last, *Keeper of the Keys*, in 1932; all six novels were serialized in *The Saturday Evening Post.* Like earlier works by Biggers, the Charlie Chan novels combined mystery with humor. Very successful in book form, the series was even more popular when adapted for the screen. In all, more than thirty films

taking off from the series were released. For many Asian Americans, however, the Chan character has become a symbol of the racist stereotyping that historically has shaped depictions of Asians and Asian Americans in the media.

Bilingual education: A course of instruction that uses two languages (English and the students' native language) for classroom communication. Such school-based programs have been a critical yet controversial component of the education of Asian American children in the United States. Asian and Pacific Islander enrollment in American public schools was expected to rise by 60 percent over the ten-year period 1985-1994, from 940,000 students to 1.6 million. In states with large numbers of new immigrants, including refugees from Southeast Asia, the demand for bilingual education is steadily increasing; in California, the need is particularly acute.

Background. Bilingual education is not new to the United States. Nineteenth century Ohio, for example, supported bilingual English-German public schools in districts where there was sufficient demand for German-language instruction. In the twentieth century, how-

Asian Americans and Languages Spoken by Limited-English Proficient (LEP) Students in California Public Schools, 1990

Percent of Asian American students	10.6%
Asian students as percent of LEP students	17%

Top 11 Languages Spoken by LEP Students	Percent
Spanish	76.0%
Vietnamese	4.0%
Cantonese	2.5%
Cambodian	2.2%
Hmong	2.1%
Filipino	1.9%
Korean	1.6%
Lao	1.4%
Armenian	1.0%
Mandarin	0.8%
Japanese	0.6%

Source: Laurie Olsen, ed., *California Perspectives.* San Francisco: California Tomorrow, Inc., 1991.

Immigrant Southeast Asian students learn English at a class in Madison, Wisconsin. (James L. Shaffer)

ever, linking language policy to patriotism, Ohio, like adjacent states Indiana and Illinois, approved an English-only, anti-German law regarding school instruction, a legislative enactment declared unconstitutional by the U.S. Supreme Court in *Meyer v. Nebraska* (1923). More recently the federal Bilingual Education Acts of 1968, 1974, 1978, 1984, and 1988, together with federal judicial opinion in the landmark *LAU v. NICHOLS* (1974) and *Serna v. Portales Municipal Schools* (1974) cases, have encouraged state legislatures to mandate bilingual education.

Lau addressed the barriers to equal opportunity confronting non-English-speaking Chinese American students in the San Francisco public schools whose needs were not being met by existing programs. As a result of the Supreme Court decision, the school district established bilingual/bicultural programs for Chinese-language students and other students whose first language was not English.

Such programs, in which students' native cultures and languages are viewed as assets and are included in their instruction, were special targets of criticism by those who in the 1980's called for the United States to return to a Eurocentric, back-to-basics curriculum. Congressional reauthorization of the Bilingual Education Act, Title VII of the Elementary and Secondary Education Act of 1988, has followed what Sonia Nieto terms "the zigzag of support and rejection of languages other than English" in the United States. This legislation sharply reduced federal funding for bilingual/bicultural education and increased federal support for immersion bilingual education.

Still, many educators would endorse the statement of purpose issued by the Philadelphia School District in 1988, defining the district's bilingual education obligation to its sizable Southeast Asian refugee population as easing "the linguistic, academic, and cultural transition of language minority students . . . while maintaining and fostering an appreciation and respect for the cultures and languages of language minority students."

Bilingual Education: Variations. Granted a commitment to bilingual education, the question of what type of program best assures meaningful opportunity remains controversial. The term "bilingual education" denotes numerous competing educational agendas.

Two of the most popular bilingual education programs are developmental, or maintenance, bilingual education and transitional bilingual education. The aim of developmental bilingual education is the attainment of fluency and literacy in both the student's native language (the language normally used by the individual and by the individual's parents) and English. Developmental programs provide content-area instruction in one's native language and the opportunity to learn English as a second language. With a similar instructional strategy, transitional programs are designed to help students become English-proficient as quickly as possible so that they may graduate to classrooms where only English is used. Easily the most common system of bilingual education in the United States, transitional bilingual education in recent years

English Proficiency of Asian Americans, Selected Statistics, 1990

Asian Americans 5 Years or Older Who:

Speak a language other than English: 73%

Do not speak English "very well": 38%

Are in linguistically isolated households: 24%

Are children in linguistically isolated households: 6%

Asian Americans 5-17 Years Who Speak an Asian Language at Home and Report Speaking English "Not Well" or "Not at All" in Top 10 States of Asian Residence

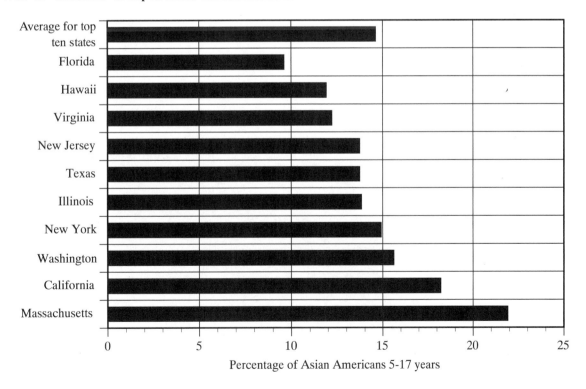

Sources: Susan B. Gall and Timothy L. Gall, eds., *Statistical Record of Asian Americans.* Detroit: Gale Research, Inc., 1993. U.S. Bureau of the Census, *1990 Census of Population: Asians and Pacific Islanders in the United States,* 1993.

has had competition from "special alternative instructional programs."

Special alternative programs provide structured English-language instruction aimed at fostering achievement in English competency in order to meet promotion and graduation criteria. An increasingly popular alternative bilingual education program is immersion bilingual education, in which students are immersed in their second language, English, prior to the introduction of their native language as a means of instruction. Unlike two-way bilingual education, where the aim is the integration of non-English-speaking and English-speaking students and the development of bilingualism in both, immersion programs may or may not provide instruction in both the native language and English. Immersion is viewed by many researchers as inappropriate for language minority students in the United States.

Bilingual Education for Asian Americans: Issues. Choosing the most suitable bilingual education program depends on a number of factors. The spoken home language is only one criterion. Students' cultural and socioeconomic background and the language preferences of their parents and community are also critical to program selection.

Asian American children, especially those of low socioeconomic status—who stand to gain the most from educational environments that are not exclusively monocultural or monolingual—are underserved by bilingual/bicultural education programs. A 1987 California Department of Education investigation found no certified bilingual teachers in the state for Cambodian, Hmong, and Mien students. Similar shortages exist in other areas where there are substantial Southeast Asian refugee populations. Moreover, some Asian American students, because of their limited En-

In transitional bilingual education programs, students attempt to learn English as fast as possible so as to graduate to English-only classrooms. (James L. Shaffer)

glish proficiency, are inappropriately placed in programs for learning-disabled children.

Meanwhile, support for developmental programs for Asian American children has wavered, as documented, for example, in Grace Pung Guthrie's ethnographic study of bilingual education for Chinese children at King School in the Little Canton community of Cherrywood, California. As King School faced an end to the cycle of federal funding for its maintenance bilingual program, teachers in both bilingual and non-bilingual classrooms disagreed sharply over the placement of 431 ethnic Chinese students in bilingual education programs. The school environment became increasingly hostile to the use of Chinese in the classroom.

Advocates of increased funding for bilingual education and other bilingual services note that in 1990, the Asian Pacific American population was approximately 65 percent foreign-born. Continuing high levels of immigration in the 1990's ensure that bilingual education will remain a critical issue for Asian Americans into the twenty-first century.—*Malcolm B. Campbell*

SUGGESTED READINGS: • Baron, Dennis. *The English-Only Question: An Official Language for Americans? New Haven, Conn.: Yale University Press, 1990. •* Colangelo, Nicholas, Dick Dustin, and Cecelia H. Foxley, eds. *Multicultural Nonsexist Education: A Human Relations Approach.* 2d ed. Dubuque, Iowa: Kendall/Hunt, 1985. • Cummins, James. *Bilingualism and Minority-Language Children.* Toronto: Ontario Institute for Studies in Education, 1981. • Guthrie, Grace Pung. "An Ethnography of Bilingual Education in a Chinese Community." Ph.D. diss., University of Illionis, Urbana-Champaign, 1982. • Nieto, Sonia. *Affirming Diversity: The Sociopolitical Context of Multicultural Education.* New York: Longman, 1992. • Saravia-Shore, Marietta, and Steven F. Arvizu, eds. *Cross-Cultural Literacy: Ethnographies of Communication in Multiethnic Classrooms.* New York: Garland, 1992. • U.S. Commission on Civil Rights. *Civil Rights Issues Facing Asian Americans in the 1990s.* Washington, D.C.: Government Printing Office, 1992.

Bilingual Education Act of 1974: U.S. legislation enacted to advance the federal mandate of equal educational opportunity among disadvantaged schoolchildren. Signed into law by President Gerald R. Ford on August 21, 1974, the act continued an American federal government policy of establishing equal educational opportunity for limited-English-speaking students, a policy first enunciated in the Bilingual

Education Act of 1968, the first BILINGUAL EDUCATION congressional bill. Like its predecessor, the Bilingual Education Act of 1974 did not seek to promote minority languages in a pluralistic American society. The focus, rather, was on helping economically disadvantaged, low-income students overcome cultural, environmental, and linguistic barriers to success.

The Bilingual Education Act of 1974, like the succeeding Bilingual Education Acts of 1978, 1984, and 1988, was based not on a celebration of non-English languages; adherence to the Civil Rights Act of 1964 guideline prohibiting exclusion from participation in, denial of benefits of, or discrimination under federally funded programs was its motive. While Congress recognized in the Bilingual Education Act of 1974 that "children of limited English-speaking ability benefit through the fullest utilization of multiple language and cultural resources," the act's force centered on limited-English-speaking students becoming English-proficient. The act authorized the federal funding of preschool, elementary, and secondary school programs to help these students learn English while not abandoning their native languages. This congressional policy has created a number of bilingual education issues that subsequent congressional legislation has failed to resolve, especially the questions of appropriate clientele and what constitutes appropriate bilingual education: cultural and linguistic enrichment, maintenance of first language, restoration of languages in danger of extinction, or programs with an objective of making the transition from first language to English competency.

The recent past of federal support for bilingual education programs in U.S. preschools, elementary schools, and secondary schools includes funding at or near 1974 levels (approximately $135 million), predominance of English as a Second Language (ESL) programs, and Bilingual Education Act support for early-exit transitional bilingual education. In the latter program 20 to 30 percent of the initial instruction (reading, in particular) is in a child's first language. By the second grade of elementary school most instruction is in English, and at the beginning of the third year limited-English-speaking students are placed in regular English-only classrooms. This development is a direct legacy of the Education Amendments of 1974, Title VII: The Bilingual Education Act of 1974.

The Bilingual Education Act of 1974 was viewed by groups such as the National Advisory Council on Bilingual Education as a means of providing Asian American children with in-school instructional programs designed to meet their particular needs. This

Bindi worn by a Bangladeshi girl in New York City. (Richard B. Levine)

and subsequent legislation, the Bilingual Education Act of 1988, for example, obligated school districts receiving federal funds to provide bilingual education and ESL programs. Yet in many cases these programs have not worked to the advantage of Asian American immigrant children.

Several factors contribute to the lack of success of bilingual education programs for Asian American immigrant children: conflicting values of home, peer group, and school; high dropout rates of some groups of Asian American students, for example, Southeast Asians; racial tensions and ethnic hostility targeted at Asian American, and especially Asian American immigrant, children; severe shortages of bilingual counselors and teachers; and the lack of information for parents of Asian American immigrant children concerning American public schools, coupled with these schools' lack of information concerning Asian American immigrant children. A 1989 California Tomorrow report stressed that public schools need programs to help Asian American and mainstream students bridge their cultural differences. Bilingual education, recognized in the Bilingual Education Act of 1974, is pivotal to this endeavor.

Bindi: Decorative red dot made of paste and worn by Hindu South Asian women. The mark is placed in the middle of the forehead and slightly above the eyebrow line. Historically indicating the married status of a Hindu woman, this brightly colored dot is often worn today as a fashion accessory.

Bing cherry: Dark red, heart-shaped fruit developed by Chinese American horticulturist Ah Bing.

Bing Kung Tong (Bingkongtang): Secret society (*tong*) headquartered in San Francisco. During the mid-1870's a dispute arose during an audit of accounts in the Los Angeles lodge of the CHEE KUNG TONG. A group of fourteen members led by Lo Yuk (Luo Yu) and Won Tsang (Wen Zeng) withdrew from the lodge; in 1878 they and their band of more than twenty supporters founded the Tuk Kung Tong (Dugongtang). The latter organization considered itself part of the Triads. Its English name was Second Independent Order of Chinese Free Masons, and it used the same symbols, ceremonies, and regulations as the parent organization.

Feeling that the Chinese name of the group was insulting to it, the Chee Kung Tong pressured the new group to change the name, even bringing the matter to court in 1882. Finally the name was changed to Bing Kung Tong.

Shortly after its founding, Wong Du King convinced the leaders of the new group to move its headquarters to San Francisco. Wong soon became its leader, and the group expanded to become one of the largest secret societies on the Pacific Coast. Lodges began to appear in towns in California's Central Valley and along the southern coast. At the *tong*'s height, lodges were founded as far east as Denver, Salt Lake City, and Billings (Montana) and as far north as Seattle, Washington. One of the few cities in which it failed to gain a foothold was San Jose, where it was unable to dislodge the Hip Sing Tong in a *tong* war.

As the bachelor society disappeared the power of the *tongs* also declined. From the second quarter of the twentieth century onward, Bing Kung lodges began to close as *tong* wars became history. From a total of twenty-one lodges in the mid-1940's, the number had dropped to fourteen by 1991.

During the republican era a number of members joined the Guomindang. Ties were strengthened in the 1930's when leader Wong Goon Dick (Huang Jundi) became part of the party clique loyal to Chiang Kai-shek and also was instrumental in negotiating a settle-

Nineteenth century San Francisco Chinatown was largely a bachelor society. As the number of women increased, the power wielded by such Triads as the Bing Kung Tong declined. (Asian American Studies Library, University of California at Berkeley)

ment of the eight-year boycott called by the Ning Yung Association against the Guomindang organ *Young China*. His successor, Doon Wong, was a key figure ensuring community support for Taiwan during the Cold War and was given the title of advisor on national policy by the Chiang Kai-shek government on Taiwan. Doon Wong was followed by Wallace Lee, who was also an important party official.

Birthday, first: Korean celebration one year after the birth of a baby, when the baby is considered two years old. At this occasion, various objects are placed on the floor, and the one to which the baby crawls signifies the baby's future. Appropriate gift objects include a spool of thread for long life, a bowl overflowing with rice for wealth, a silver set of spoon and chopsticks, and money.

Birthday, one-hundredth day (*paek il*): Korean celebration observed one hundred days after the birth of a baby.

Birthday, sixtieth: In Korean tradition, the day of one's completed life span. This milestone is marked by a celebration, *hangap*, commonly arranged by the children of the celebrant. Sometimes this is observed on the sixty-first birthday instead.

Bishop, E. Faxon (Oct. 27, 1863, Naperville, Ill.— Feb. 11, 1943, Honolulu, Territory of Hawaii): Businessperson. He began working for C. Brewer & Company in 1883, eventually serving as secretary, treasurer, and president. As president of the HAWAIIAN SUGAR PLANTERS' ASSOCIATION (HSPA) (three terms in all), he helped negotiate an agreement between the HSPA and the Korean government to bring Korean contract laborers to the United States to work on Hawaii plantations. Those who agreed to emigrate were prepaid a sum of money by the HSPA. In 1903, however, he was accused of violating a U.S. law that made it illegal to assist the immigration of contract laborers into the United States or any of its territories by paying money to these individuals prior to their arrival in America. Later that year he was cleared of the charge by the U.S. district court. (See *BERGER V. BISHOP*.) In 1904 he won election to the Territory of Hawaii Senate, becoming its president in 1907.

Bishop Estate: Largest private land owner in Hawaii. As of 1991, the estate controlled 337,000 acres, or about 15 percent of all privately owned land in Hawaii. The estate was created by the will of Ke Alii Pauahi (Bernice Pauahi Bishop), who died in 1884 as the last direct descendant of Kamehameha I. Its sole beneficiary is the KAMEHAMEHA SCHOOLS, dedicated to the education of children and youth of indigenous Hawaiian ancestry. It is venerated by indigenous Hawaiians as the principal legacy of the *alii* (chiefs). As its income increased greatly in the 1980's, it became increasingly controversial. Non-Hawaiians criticized its policies with regard to residential leasing, while Hawaiian beneficiaries criticized the selection of estate trustees, the amount of their compensation, and the estate's educational policies.

In the first decades following its creation, the estate leased it lands to sugar producers and invested its capital in sugar production. Subsequently, lands were leased for residential and tourist-related real estate development. By the time low initial lease rents came up for renegotiation in the 1980's, the vast inflation of land values in Hawaii created an overwhelming political demand for forcible conversion of the estate's residential lands to freehold. Income from the sale of these residential lands since 1978 has amounted to about $733 million. This is less than the lands are worth, causing great resentment among Hawaiians. In response the trustees have withdrawn from further residential leasing, investing instead in commercial real estate in Hawaii and overseas.

In 1971 many Hawaiians protested the appointment of yet another non-Hawaiian as a trustee. All six subsequent appointees have been of Hawaiian ancestry. In 1991 the five trustees received $3.5 million in commissions, about 65 percent of the amount allowed by law. Nevertheless many Hawaiians feel that the trustee's income is excessive, in view of the dire educational needs of the majority of the state's Hawaiian youth. Others charge that appointments are made as political rewards.

Bishop Museum: Founded in 1889 (opened in 1892) as a memorial to Princess Bernice Pauahi Bishop and to preserve the cultural heritage of Hawaii. The museum was officially established by her husband, Charles Reed Bishop, a prominent island resident originally from New York. Bernice Pauahi was a great-granddaughter of Kamehameha the Great, the warrior chief unified the Hawaiian Islands in 1810 and laid the foundations for the kingdom of Hawaii. She was the last direct descendant of the Kamehameha family.

Before King Kamehameha V died without heirs in 1872, he entreated Pauahi, his daughter, to ascend the throne, but Pauahi declined. Instead she arranged for her land, about one-ninth of the kingdom, to be dedicated as the Bernice Pauahi BISHOP ESTATE. In her will she established the KAMEHAMEHA SCHOOLS as the sole beneficiary of the estate, dedicating her considerable wealth to educating the native youth of Hawaii.

Charles Bishop inherited her collection of Hawaiian antiquities and turned this "treasure house" into a valuable cultural and educational resource. He built the museum on the original grounds of the Kamehameha Schools in suburban Honolulu. The museum operates

under deed of trust drawn in 1896, which further describes the institution's scientific and historical purposes.

The main historical structure of the museum, the three interconnected exhibition buildings, began construction in 1888. It includes a grand entrance memorial tower in neo-Romanesque style; the Polynesian Hall to display and store natural history and ethnographic material from the rest of the Pacific region; and the Hawaiian Hall in Victorian style as the premier gallery.

Later additions include a planetarium/science center in 1961, a children's Hall of Discovery in 1979, and the Atherton Halau in 1980, an open-air Polynesian longhouse.

The museum's unique geographic position in the Pacific has contributed to its long history of area-focused research. It has collected more than twenty-one million specimens under the anthropology, botany, entomology, and zoology research departments. The Bishop Museum Library contains thousands of rare Pacific region manuscripts, photographs, maps, and files. The Bishop Museum Press, one of the oldest

The Bishop Museum was built on the original grounds of the Kamehameha Schools, named after Hawaii's greatest monarch, King Kamehameha. This statue of him adorns the front of the Honolulu Circuit Court Building. (National Archives)

continuing scientific publishers in the Western Hemisphere, is known internationally for its systematic documentation of the natural and cultural diversity of Hawaii and the Pacific.

In 1988 the Bishop Museum was designated as the "State of Hawaii Museum of Natural and Cultural History." Under this new status the museum is now qualified to receive state funding.

Black Dragon Society. *See* **Kokuryukai**

Blaisdell, Richard Kekuni (b. Mar. 11, 1925, Honolulu, Territory of Hawaii): Hematologist and Native Hawaiian activist. He became the first Native Hawaiian professor at the University of Hawaii's John A. Burns School of Medicine. Between 1959 and 1961 he served as chief hematologist of the Atomic Comb Casualty Commission in Japan. He has authored articles on Native Hawaiian medicine and has actively participated in the Pro-Hawaiian Sovereignty Working Group and in Ka Pakaukau, another Native Hawaiian sovereignty group.

Boat people: Southeast Asian refugees who, at the end of the Vietnam War in 1975 and in the years immediately following, fled in boats that were often old, crowded, and unsafe. Approximately 800,000 refugees from Vietnam (including large numbers of ethnic Chinese and smaller numbers of other minorities) reached camps in Malaysia, Thailand, Hong Kong, and elsewhere in Southeast Asia; ultimately the majority of these refugees were admitted by the United States. (See REFUGEE CAMPS IN SOUTHEAST ASIA and SOUTHEAST ASIAN EXODUS TO THE UNITED STATES.)

Bok Kai Temple: Only surviving Chinese Taoist temple in the United States, located in Marysville, California. Marysville was established during California's mid-nineteenth century gold rush days. The Chinese called it "the fourth town" because among the Chinese it was the fourth most populous California town, after San Francisco, Sacramento, and Stockton. Marysville continues to be remembered for its Bok Kai Temple and its annual celebration of the Bok Kai Festival. The festival has been a civic tradition there since the 1930's.

The Chinese built the temple sometime after 1850. It was destroyed by a flood in the 1860's. The present temple was rebuilt in 1880 along the Yuba River. The festival itself is always held on the second day of the second month of the lunar calendar. According to early

Southeast Asian refugees aboard the Tung An, *docked in Manila Bay, the Philippines, 1978. Those who clambered onto the Hong Kong-based cargo vessel try to find space to walk, sit, or sleep atop the stern of the sixty-eight meter vessel.* (AP/Wide World Photos)

Chinese tradition, the celebration is held in honor of the "god of water and flood control." During the event local legend recalls how this god of the Bok Kai Temple has protected the town from floods. A special parade with golden dragon, lion dance, floats, and firecrackers, along with thousands of tourists, highlights the festival.

Inside the temple, the Bok Kai god is represented by a small figure placed in the central altar. Many other Chinese deities are represented by beautiful handcrafted figures. This temple is filled with worshipers throughout the festival weekend.

The Bok Kai Temple continues to sponsor "Bomb Day." Bomb Day derives its name from the shooting off of bombs or firecrackers that contain "good fortune" rings. When the firecrackers explode, the rings fall out. It is believed that whoever can get one of these rings will be prosperous that year.

The Bok Kai Temple is listed as a California State Historical Landmark and appears on the National Register of Historic Places. (See CHINESE TEMPLES IN CALIFORNIA.)

Bombay: Capital of the state of Maharashtra, India. Bombay is the largest metropolis in India and functions as the premier port on the nation's west coast. The Portuguese bestowed this trading post on King Charles II of England in 1661 as a wedding gift for marrying a Portuguese princess. Bombay, which occupies a peninsula, is linked to two islands in the north to form Greater Bombay. It is hot and humid most of the year and receives summer monsoon rainfall.

With its modern skyline, it is one of India's more advanced, progressive, and cosmopolitan cities. Its southern part retains the wide boulevards, spacious parks, and massive stone buildings of the colonial period. This section also contains most of the businesses, commercial enterprises, and several cultural and educational institutions. To the west of the city are the palatial homes and beautiful gardens of the Malabar Hills, which overlook a series of beaches. The rest of the city is crisscrossed by narrow streets and contains pavement shops, bazaar areas, small houses and tenements, and thousands of small factories and workshops. The northern part of the city is dominated by major industrial establishments and numerous slums.

Bombay's economy is based on manufacturing, commerce, banking, government, transportation, and port functions. Its major industries include cotton textile manufacturing, engineering, food processing, motion-picture production, chemical and drug manufacturing, and petroleum refining.

The densely populated metropolitan area of 13.3 million people (1992 estimate) consists of a Marathi-speaking majority, Gujarati- and Hindi-speaking minorities, and other smaller linguistic and religious groups. The majority of the people are Hindus, and the rest are divided among Jains, Muslims, Christians, and Buddhists. Violence erupts occasionally between the Hindu majority and the Muslim minority. The Gujaratis, the most skillful merchants and entrepreneurs of India, are the most successful retailers and businesspersons among Asian Americans of Indian origin. Zubin MEHTA, the music director of the New York Philharmonic, is a member of the Parsi community of Bombay. While Bombay, the nation's financial center, has a booming economy, a substantial percentage of its population resides in slums.

Bon odori: Or *bon* dancing, part of the Japanese Buddhist *O-bon* celebration, an annual festival honoring the dead. Sanskrit religious texts of India relate the origin of *bon odori* to the meritorious actions of Mokuren, a Buddhist disciple who saved his departed mother from suffering in the netherworld. According to the old texts, when her salvation occurred she danced for joy, as did Mokuren and the people around him.

In Japan *bon odori* is most typically done outdoors near temples, where it usually takes the form of circle dances, and in the streets of large cities, where it becomes processional line-dancing. Both forms may be found among Japanese communities in the United States. In San Francisco and Los Angeles, for example, elaborate street dances are held during the summer. Throughout Hawaii *bon* dances are held at Buddhist temples all summer long on weekend evenings. Dancing takes place around a tower (*yagura*) that houses musicians or playback equipment for recorded music. Most dances are done to recorded music. Most are also imported from Japan, but some are choreographed to incorporate new, and often local, themes such as baseball or, in the 1950's in Hawaii, doing the hula during the day and *bon odori* at night.

Although still done in many parts of the country by Japanese Americans in conjunction with celebrations to honor the dead, some dances associated with *O-bon* are also done as a kind of Japanese identity marker. As such they are included in May Day celebrations to represent the Japanese population of public schools, at community events celebrating the various ethnic groups constituting the local population, and in physical education classes as dances representative of the Japanese people.

The dances are typically done to a moderate tempo, duple rhythm; contain short, simple movement phrases that are continuously repeated; do not involved any physical linking (such as hand-holding) between dancers; and include basic stepping and toe-touching without elevation. Arm gestures occasionally mimic activities mentioned in accompanying songs.

Dancers generally wear *yukata* (a light weight, summer *kimono*) or slacks and shorts with a *happi* coat (a *kimono*-style jacket).

Bonacich, Edna (b. Mar. 30, 1940, Greenwich, Conn.): Scholar. A professor of sociology at the University of California, Riverside. Working from a Marxist perspective, she has researched the historical and contemporary Asian American experience. In *Labor Immigration Under Capitalism* (1984), coedited with Lucie Cheng, she examined early Asian immigration in the era of America imperialist expansion. Bonacich has also published community studies including *The Economic Basis of Ethnic Solidarity: Small Business in the Japanese American Community* (1980), with John Modell, and *Immigrant Entrepreneurs: Koreans in Los Angeles, 1965-1982* (1988), with Ivan Light.

Bose, Sudhindra (1883, Keotkhali, Bengal Province, India, now Bangladesh—May 26, 1946, Cedar Rapids, Iowa): Scholar, journalist, and lecturer. Bose was one of the first Asian Indians to receive a Ph.D. degree in the United States. He became a lecturer in political science at Iowa State University, where he developed courses in world politics, imperialism, and Asian politics and civilization. He was the American correspondent for the Indian newspapers the *Hindu* (Madras) and *Amrita Bazar Patrika* (Calcutta). He lectured widely on Asian politics, civilization, art, and culture.

Bose attended college in Calcutta, India, before coming to the United States in 1904. He received his undergraduate and master's degrees from the University of Illinois. After completing his Ph.D. degree at Iowa State University in 1913, he joined its faculty as a lecturer in political science. Bose, a noted Asia specialist, held an untenured position at Iowa State until his death in 1946.

Making the United States his home, Bose became a naturalized citizen. He lost his citizenship papers in 1923, however, when the U.S. Supreme Court ruled that Asian Indians were ineligible for naturalization (*UNITED STATES V. BHAGAT SINGH THIND*). Bose went to court and won back his rights in 1927. During the same year he married Anne Zimmerman of St. Gall, Switzerland, who had also been a student at Iowa State.

Bose wrote extensively about both the United States and India. His books include *Some Aspects of British Rule in India* (1916), *Fifteen Years in America* (1920), *Glimpses of America* (1925), and *Mother America* (1934). A critic of British imperialism, Bose frequently lectured to university audiences and civic groups about the negative impact of colonialism on countries such as India. He advocated independence for India and other colonized nations.

In 1915, the Asian Indian community chose Bose as one of its representatives to Washington, D.C. There he spoke before a House immigration committee on behalf of immigration rights for Asian Indians. Bose later worked with the INDIA LEAGUE OF AMERICA and served on the advisory board of the WATUMULL FOUNDATION. He was also a member of several American professional and civic organizations such as the American Political Science Association and the Iowa State Historical Society.

Bow On Guk (Self-Defense Society): Association formed in 1887 to help safeguard the lives and property rights of the Chinese in Hawaii. The society, composed of Chinese islanders, was set up to raise money from within the community to carry out its work. The Bow On Guk was born in response to the rising tide of anti-Chinese sentiment spearheaded by such political agitators as the Anti-Asiatic Union and the Workingmen's Party of California in protest against unfair Chinese economic competition.

Boxer Indemnity Fellowship: American portion of the Boxer indemnity remitted back to China to enable it to send Chinese students to the United States.

At the conclusion of the BOXER REBELLION (1900), forty-five thousand foreign troops occupied north China, the court had fled to Xi'an, and China appeared on the verge of partition. China's acceptance of the Boxer Protocol in 1901, though stopping short of completely surrendering imperial sovereignty, promised to hobble the economy for decades to come. In addition to requiring the Chinese to punish Boxer collaborators and acquiesce in a long-term military occupation, an indemnity of $333 million at 4 percent interest was imposed. The repayment schedule, projected to 1940, meant that China would pay a total of $739 million in yearly installments that exceeded the annual revenue of the imperial government. The need for foreign loans to help service the debt burdened the country further.

The weakness of China's position, however, also created the possibility for extensive reform. The Empress Dowager Cixi, who had crushed attempts at reform in 1898, now reluctantly sanctioned modernization in the military, government, and education. In the last category Meiji Japan provided a convenient model. Since 1872, ambitious programs of sending Chinese students abroad, first to the United States, and then to Europe, had also been tried. The legacy of these American "returned students," the general cordiality of Sino-American relations in the wake of the Hay notes and the Open Door policy, and U.S. eagerness to influence the direction of reform in China prompted the Roosevelt Administration to propose the return to China of the American portion of the indemnity on the condition that the funds be used to send Chinese students to the United States. In 1908 the Chinese government agreed.

The fellowship proved both popular and successful.

Chinese Boxer, circa 1900. (National Archives)

Thousands of Chinese students were the direct beneficiaries of the funds, and the United States would have a hand in training a large percentage of China's leaders during the latter's republican and Nationalist eras. Following the American example, Great Britain, in 1930, similarly returned its portion of the indemnity in exchange for science education and railroad construction.

Boxer Rebellion (1900): Last attempt of the Qing Dynasty (1644-1911) to expel foreigners from China. Although some reforms were implemented in the decade following the rebellion, this conflict marked the effective end of China's last imperial dynasty, the Qing.

Events of the nineteenth century had eroded both the sovereignty and the prestige of China's Qing Dynasty. The TREATY OF NANJING (1842), the product of Great Britain's defeat of China in the First Opium War, (1839-1842), provided the model for continual foreign incursion and the extraction of a wide range of foreign privileges. By the 1890's, despite Chinese efforts at "self-strengthening," foreigners maintained enclaves in dozens of Chinese cities, controlled foreign trade and the Chinese customs, dispensed justice in consular courts, and later extended this control over Chinese Christian converts.

New powers had entered the arena as well, and the competition for concessions from the Qing government intensified. In 1894-1895, Japan humiliated China in a war over influence in Korea, and in 1897, Germany acquired a naval base at Jiaozhou Bay, which was swiftly expanded into control of Shandong Province. The speed and vigor of German expansion, the threat to Chinese culture from Western missionaries, and the impotence of the imperial government all worked to encourage the activities of secret societies. The most prominent of these societies was the *Yihe chuan*, or the Association of Righteousness and Harmony, nicknamed "Boxers" by foreigners because its members practiced certain calisthenic rituals.

By the summer of 1898, Boxer attacks on missionaries and converts had become alarmingly frequent. The Qing EMPRESS DOWAGER, after attempting to suppress the movement, now decided to use it to drive all foreigners out of China. On June 21, 1900, the Qing government declared war on the treaty powers, and Boxer and Chinese army units besieged the diplomatic compound in Beijing and seized key points in northern and northeastern China.

By July, an international relief force had landed in Tianjin, and on August 14, following several sharp clashes, advance units entered the city and relieved the legations. Following a bloody suppression campaign around the capital, the powers then imposed the most severe of the "unequal treaties," the Boxer Protocol, on China. Its provisions called for the punishment of Boxer collaborators, posting of foreign troops in key cities, and a crushing indemnity of $333 million.

Boys' Day. *See* **Children's Day**

Bratt, Robert K.: Government administrator. He was the first director of the U.S. Department of Justice's Office of Redress Administration (ORA), which administered the government's redress and reparations program. The agency processed payments to Japanese Americans and others interned during World War II. He also served as executive officer in the Civil Rights Division of the U.S. attorney's office. This office was responsible for implementing that section of the CIVIL LIBERTIES ACT OF 1988 extending restitution to the Japanese internees.

Bridge: Magazine that first appeared in 1971, growing out of New York's BASEMENT WORKSHOP. Originally aimed at the overseas Chinese community, the magazine gradually shifted to a broader Asian American orientation. In addition to political and social issues, it addressed cultural topics and included contributions by leading Asian American writers. With a peak circulation of about seven hundred, and virtually no advertising, the magazine struggled financially. When the Basement Workshop stopped supporting *Bridge* in 1979, the magazine suspended publication until 1981, when it was taken over by Asian Cinevision. The last issue of the magazine appeared in 1985.

Bridge generation. *See* **1.5 generation**

British East India Company: European trading organization established in 1600 and dissolved in 1858. It was the most powerful of the government-chartered, privately capitalized, semiautonomous European trading organizations.

Its origins lay in the competition among the Atlantic maritime states to tap the wealth of Asia in the sixteenth century. Chartered by Queen Elizabeth I in 1600, company ships had, by 1634, inaugurated trade with Mughal India's wealthy province of BENGAL. Following the pattern of other European traders, company traders established a system of fortified outposts, the most famous of which, Calcutta, was founded in 1690.

Because of the vast distances involved, and the equally vast profits flowing into English coffers, the organization enjoyed a political and economic position unique in the early modern world. Along with the growing power of its international trade in Indian, Southeast Asian, and Chinese commodities, its formidable army, with European officers and Indian Sepoy troops, soon proved to be a decisive factor in Bengali politics. Against the backdrop of the Maratha rebellions of the mid-eighteenth century, company forces first eliminated French competition from India (1744-1748), then broke the power of the Nawab of Bengal following the Battle of Plassey in 1757. By the start of the nineteenth century, the company ruled the province outright and exercised crucial influence over northern and central India.

Though India remained the focus of the company's activities, India was by no means the company's sole theater of operations. In 1699, English vessels first called at the Chinese port of Canton. European taste for tea and luxury items, coupled with Chinese desire to control the trade, led to the development of the Cohong merchant guild system by 1760. British conquest of Java and the acquisition of Singapore in the early nineteenth century created a continuous band of possessions and dependencies from Afghanistan to the South China Sea.

The movements for reform and free trade in the post-Napoleonic era spelled change and, ultimately, the end of the company monopoly of the China trade in 1834 and of company rule itself in 1858. Resistance to British expansion, heavy-handed attempts to reform Indian institutions, the dislocations of new technologies, and British insensitivity toward Indian religious sensibilities exploded in the Indian Mutiny of 1857. Following a bloody suppression campaign, the British government took direct control of India, and the company's charter was dissolved in 1858.

Bruyeres: Town located in the northeastern part of France near the German border. During World War II it was also the site of a fierce battle between the United States' all-Nisei combined 100TH INFANTRY BATTALION/442ND REGIMENTAL COMBAT TEAM and the German army.

The battle for Bruyeres began on October 15, 1944. In contrast to 100th/442nd's recent battles in Italy, where the Germans had surrendered territory in order to preserve their dwindling ranks, at Bruyeres the Nisei soldiers encountered an enemy determined to hold what it had taken. Crucial to victory were four hills located to the north and to the west of Bruyeres. All four were occupied by the Germans. After one full day of battle, the 100th/442nd cleared out four machine gun nests, captured twenty prisoners, and advanced a hard-fought five hundred yards.

The next day, October 16, the Germans launched three counterattacks in an attempt to regain the land that they had lost and also to preserve their strategic location in the hills above Bruyeres. Their efforts, however, were to no avail. For two days, the 100th/442nd held its ground and then continued the advance toward the hills. Along the way the combined forces captured more enemy soldiers and neutralized some farmhouses that the Germans had transformed into machine gun nests. On October 18, after hours of heavy artillery fire, the hills were finally captured by the men of the 100th/442nd, and Bruyeres was liberated from German hands.

The citizens of Bruyeres have never forgotten the heroics of their Nisei liberators. Besides hosting a special reunion for these soldiers in the mid-1980's, the town also organized a massive letter-writing campaign in 1987 to urge U.S. president Ronald Reagan to support the redress bill for Japanese Americans who had been interned in American concentration camps.

Bryan, William Jennings (Mar. 19, 1860, Salem, Ill.—July 26, 1925, Dayton, Tenn.): Politician. As U.S. secretary of state in 1913, he refused to consider Japanese ambassador Chinda Sutemi's appeal for naturalization rights for Japanese immigrants.

William Jennings Bryan. (AP/Wide World Photos)

Buaken, Manuel: Writer. Born in the Philippines to a family with ties to India, Buaken was educated in the Philippines before traveling to the United States in 1927 to attend Princeton University on a theology scholarship. After his arrival, however, Buaken decided to give up the scholarship and sought employment in a variety of jobs to finance his education. During the time he spent as a domestic servant, janitor, dishwasher, and farm worker, Buaken came in contact with many other Filipino laborers. In World War II he served with the U.S. Army's FIRST FILIPINO INFANTRY REGIMENT, Drawing on these experiences, he wrote a book entitled *I Have Lived with the American People* (1948). His memoir presents, in painstaking detail, the poverty, racial prejudice, and mistreatment endured by Filipino immigrants and the ethnic solidarity within the Filipino American community that helped support them during their struggle.

Buck, Pearl S. (Pearl Comfort Sydenstricker; June 26, 1892, Hillsboro, W.Va.—Mar. 6, 1973, Danby, Vt.): Writer. Buck is best remembered for her novels on China and the Chinese. She was taken to China as an infant, where her father was a Presbyterian missionary. She began writing short stories and articles about China in 1922 for American magazines.

Buck's most famous work is undoubtedly *The Good Earth*, published in 1931. *The Good Earth* depicted the enduring strength of Chinese peasants and particularly the courageous tenacity of its central woman character, O-lan. The book was an immediate best-seller—more than two million copies were sold, and the work has been translated into more than thirty languages. It inspired a Broadway play and a Hollywood movie starring Luise Rainer and Paul Muni. Buck was awarded the Pulitzer Prize for *The Good Earth* in 1932.

Following *The Good Earth*, Buck went on to publish both original fictional works on China as well as translations of such Chinese classics as *Water Margin* (c. fourteenth century; *All Men Are Brothers*, 1933). Her other works include *Dragon Seed* (1942), which was also made into a Hollywood movie starring Katharine Hepburn, *Pavilion of Women* (1946), *The Hidden Flower* (1952), *Of Men and Women, 1941* (1971), as well as dozens of articles, interviews, and children's fiction. Using the pen name "John Sedges," Buck also published five novels between 1945 and 1953. In 1938, she became the first American woman to win the Nobel Prize in Literature.

Buck also established institutions in aid of children. She founded Welcome House, an adoption agency for

American-born novelist Pearl Buck became a best-selling author with the publication of The Good Earth. *(AP/Wide World Photos)*

AmerAsian children in 1949, and in 1964 she established the Pearl S. Buck Foundation to support Asian children of unknown American fathers. Far in advance of her time, she also advocated women's rights as well as global peace.

Buddha Amida: Japanese name for the Buddha Amitabha, the great savior deity worshipped principally by members of the Jodo (PURE LAND) sects. Followers of Amida believe that after death they will be reborn in Sukhavati, the Pure Land, Amida's western paradise. Such passage is ensured, they believe, by chanting, "Namu Amida Butsu" (homage to Amida Buddha), a formula that acknowledges the compassionate working of Amida. (See AMIDISM.)

Buddhahead: Slang term dating from World War II that was used to identify Japanese Americans from the Hawaiian Islands. Nisei servicemen, such as those of the 442ND REGIMENTAL COMBAT TEAM, coined the term to distinguish members born in Hawaii from those born on the U.S. mainland, who were designated as "kotonks." Initially considered to be derogatory because of its implied disrespect for Buddhist tradition as well as its pun on the Japanese term "buta" or "pig," "buddhahead" eventually took on a positive connotation for some Japanese Americans, when used as a term of self-identification, but others continue to regard it as unacceptable.

Buddhism: One of the world's major religions. Founded in North India in the sixth century B.C.E. by Siddhartha Gautama, Buddhism eventually spread to all of southern and eastern Asia. In the twentieth century, significant numbers of Buddhists were living in Europe and North America as well. It is estimated that there are some 300 million Buddhists in the world.

Early Buddhism. About 560 B.C.E., Siddhartha Gautama was born to a family of the warrior class living in a small republic in an area that is now the border of Nepal and India. Although he married, had one son, and lived comfortably, he was dissatisfied with human life, particularly with the fact that human life is subject to old age, disease, and death. Contemplating the impermanence of human life and all things, he decided to seek enlightenment through meditation and self-denial. He left his wife and child in the care of his family and went to a forest to learn meditation and practice the ascetic discipline of self-denial. Six years later, still troubled by the nature of human life, he abandoned the path of self-denial, realizing that the body and mind required nourishment to function well. Shortly thereafter, he achieved a series of meditative insights that climaxed in an experience of enlightenment that he called "Nirvana." From this time onward, he was called "the Buddha," a title that means "Awakened One" or "Enlightened One."

He began to teach a set of ideas and practices that are the heart of Buddhism and that are known as the Four Noble Truths: First, life is characterized by suffering and dissatisfaction because of the impermanence of all things, including life itself; second, this sense of discontentment is a result of one's desire to cling to and want impermanent things, which leads to desires being unfulfilled and in turn results in rebirth and suffering over and over again; third, this cycle of desire and suffering can be stopped, if one stops desiring; fourth, the method that helps one achieve this stopping of desire is called the "Eightfold Path" and consists of the right views, the right intentions, the right speech, the right action, the right livelihood, the right effort, the right mindfulness, and the right concentration. With this practice, anyone can attain Nirvana, ending the cycle of suffering and rebirth. This is the essential teaching of early Buddhism.

The Spread of Buddhism. As hundreds of people

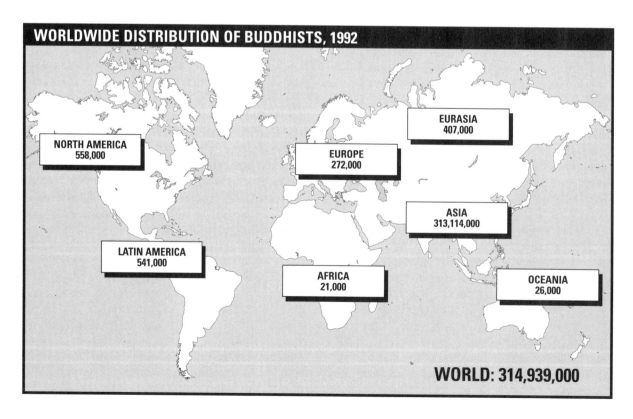

WORLDWIDE DISTRIBUTION OF BUDDHISTS, 1992

NORTH AMERICA 558,000

EURASIA 407,000

EUROPE 272,000

ASIA 313,114,000

LATIN AMERICA 541,000

AFRICA 21,000

OCEANIA 26,000

WORLD: 314,939,000

Japanese statue of Buddha, situated in Kamakura, Japan. (Diane C. Lyell)

San Francisco Joss House (Buddhist temple). (Asian American Studies Library, University of California at Berkeley)

The Byodo In Buddhist temple of Oahu, Hawaii. (John Penisten, Pacific Pictures)

began to gather around the Buddha to hear his teachings and follow them, it became necessary to organize them into a community. For this purpose, rules were formulated on how to live together as a community, the men as monks, the women as nuns. After instruction, they were sent out to teach Buddhist ideas and practices to others. In this way, Buddhism spread throughout North India during the lifetime of the Buddha. After his death in about 480 B.C.E., the monks and nuns continued the tradition. His teachings are recorded in the Pali canon, a collection of scriptures many volumes in length. The varieties of Buddhism found in South and Southeast Asia (Sri Lanka, Burma, Thailand, Laos, and Cambodia) regard the pali canon as the complete teachings of the Buddha.

Mahayana Buddhism. Several centuries after the death of the Buddha, new scriptures began to appear that emphasized the importance of compassion and the ideal of the *bodhisattva*, who, because of his great compassion, voluntarily accepts rebirth repeatedly to aid others on the path to Nirvana. Monks and nuns spread Mahayana Buddhism into China beginning in the first century. One feature of Mahayana Buddhism that made it popular was greater opportunity for leadership and participation by laity, Buddhists who were not monks or nuns. From China, Buddhism spread into Vietnam, Korea, and Japan. The most influential varieties of Buddhism in East Asia are the Pure Land (Jingtu, or Jodo) and Meditation (Chan, or Zen) traditions. Pure Land Buddhism emphasizes the importance of faith, while Chan /Zen emphasizes meditation and discipline.

Tantric Buddhism. Another development of the Buddhist teachings is the Tantric tradition. Tibetan Buddhism is one example of this variety; Japanese Shingon is another. Tantric Buddhism emphasizes that all aspects of human life must be used in the effort to attain Nirvana, and it has developed numerous practices to aid in the effort. Chanting mantras (words and phrases regarded as powerful), drawing and visualizing mandalas (meditation diagrams regarded as powerful), and performing rituals are important aspects of Tantric traditions.

Buddhism in North America and Europe. All these varieties of Buddhism are represented in North America, and most in Europe. As a result of emigration of

Asians from their home countries in the nineteenth and twentieth centuries, substantial populations of Asian heritage live in the West, where temples for the worship of laity have been built. Buddhism in the West is different from Asian Buddhism in two major respects: Women are more heavily involved and more often found in leadership positions, and the laity are engaging in meditation practices to a greater extent. Of the hundreds of Buddhist groups in North America, many are led by laity. Tibetan, Japanese Pure Land, and Zen traditions appear to be the best-organized and most numerous groups in North America in the late twentieth century. In addition to Buddhist groups that are based on one sect or nationality and could be described as denominational, nondenominational groups have also come into existence, such as the Buddhist Peace Fellowship, which is dedicated to social activism in the cause of world peace. Buddhism will be an important part of the religious life of North America in the late twentieth and twenty-first centuries.—*Bruce M. Sullivan*

SUGGESTED READINGS: • Boucher, Sandy. *Turning the Wheel: American Women Creating the New Buddhism.* San Francisco: Harper & Row, 1988. • De Bary, William T., ed. *The Buddhist Tradition in India, China, and Japan.* New York: Vintage Books, 1972. • Fields, Rick. *How the Swans Came to the Lake: A Narrative History of Buddhism in America.* 3d ed. Boston: Shambhala, 1992. • Morreale, Don, ed. *Buddhist America: Centers, Retreats, Practices.* Santa Fe, N. Mex.: John Muir, 1988. • Robinson, Richard H., and Willard L. Johnson. *The Buddhist Religion: A Historical Introduction.* 3d ed. Belmont Calif.: Wadsworth, 1982. • Schumann, Hans W. *The Historical Buddha.* Translated by M. Walshe. London: Arkana/ Penguin, 1989.

Buddhist Churches of America (BCA): Incorporated, nonprofit religious organization of JODO SHINSHU Buddhist churches on the mainland United States.

Jodo Shinshu, literally meaning "True Pure Land Religion," was founded in the thirteenth century by Shinran Shonin, who is widely regarded as one of the most important and innovative religious thinkers in Japanese history. By radically reinterpreting PURE LAND teachings and rooting them in fundamental Mahayana Buddhist thought in which compassion for all beings is another face of supreme enlightenment, Shinran Shonin spread his teachings among the common people, revealing a path to religious awakening that is accessible to all in daily life.

The history of the BCA dates back to September, 1899, when two ministers arrived in San Francisco, California. Appointed by the Lord Abbot Myonyo Shonin, twenty-first Abbot of the Jodo Shinshu Hongwanji-ha Hongwanji in Kyoto, Japan, they were the first official missionaries sent to serve the religious needs of the growing Japanese population in the United States. In 1994, almost one hundred years later, Buddhist Churches of America comprised sixty independent temples or churches, twenty-seven branch temples, and six less formally organized fellowships in the United States.

Until 1944, the affiliation of American Jodo Shinshu Churches and groups was known as the Buddhist Mission of North America (BMNA). Ministers were trained in Japan and then sent to America to work in various communities. The ministers assigned as Bishop also came from Japan. In 1944, during the World War II internment of approximately 120,000 persons of Japanese ancestry living on the West Coast, the BMNA was newly incorporated as the Buddhist Churches of America. This significant event took place in the Topaz Relocation Center in Utah, where the "Articles of Incorporation of Buddhist Churches of America" was written and signed by forty-seven members of the board of directors on April 6, 1944. Prior to this time, administration, ministerial services, and membership in the BMNA were dominated by Japanese immigrants (Issei) living in the United States. With the incorporation of BCA, the second generation (Nisei) Japanese Americans, who were American citizens, began to get more involved. Greater emphasis was placed on starting publications and writings in the English language, as well as the growing necessity for English-speaking ministers.

The 1950's saw an expansion of programs for the English-speaking membership. To further this end, the BCA initiated the BCA Study Center at the Berkeley Buddhist Church in 1954. In 1966 the Study Center became the Institute of Buddhist Studies (IBS), Graduate School and Seminary. The IBS is authorized by the State of California to grant a master's degree in Buddhist Studies and a fully accredited master of arts degree through its affiliation with the Graduate Theological Union (GTU), the world's largest consortium of religious educational institutions. The first non-Judeo-Christian educational institution to be admitted to the GTU, the IBS also offers a master in Jodo Shinshu Studies, the professional degree program for the Jodo Shinshu Buddhist ministry, as well as sponsoring various programs promoting Buddhist understanding and education to both ministers and the general public.

In the early years of the Institute, most of the students were Japanese American. The trend in the 1980's and 1990's, however, has been for people of other ethnicities to receive education in Buddhist Studies or training for the priesthood. The Institute of Buddhist Studies is affiliated with Ryukoku University, the main institution in Kyoto, Japan that trains Jodo Shinshu priests. The university provides support for the IBS through a library grant and the provision of Shinshu scholars who annually lecture at the IBS as exchange faculty members. Since 1973 the IBS has been recognized as fully accredited to qualify students for ordination as Jodo Shinshu priests, although the candidate is still required to go to the main temple of the sect in Kyoto for approval. In Japan, Jodo Shinshu is divided into ten branches. The Nishi Honganji is by far the largest of those in North America and is represented in the form of the BCA.

In 1994, the BCA maintained sixty independent churches or temples with the following geographical distribution: forty-three in California; two in Oregon; five in Washington; three in Utah; and one each in Arizona, Colorado, Illinois, Ohio, New York, New Jersey, and Virginia. Branch temples are affiliated with the nearest BCA temple—not all temples have branches, and some have more than one (e.g., the Fresno Betsuin Buddhist Temple has ten branch temples).

The American Shin Buddhists within the state of Hawaii have a separate jurisdiction and administration because at the time of the Hawaiian mission's founding, Hawaii was not a part of the United States. In 1989, the year that marked the centennial of the Hawaiian mission, there were thirty-seven Shinshu temples in Hawaii.

The national headquarters of the BCA has always been in San Francisco and, since 1971, occupies a four-story office building which houses the Office of the Bishop and other administrative offices, including the Department of Buddhist Education, the Endowment Foundation, a publications division, and the Buddhist Bookstore, which offers numerous titles on Buddhism in general and Jodo Shinshu Buddhism in particular.

It is estimated that there are more than 100,000 Buddhists of Shinshu faith throughout the United States, and although they all may not be official members of the BCA, the organization is available to address their spiritual and educational needs.—*Deborah Malone*

SUGGESTED READINGS: • Buddhist Churches of America. *Buddhist Churches of America.* 2 vols. Chicago: Nobart, 1974. • Kashima, Tetsuden. *Buddhism in America: The Social Organization of an Ethnic Religious Institution.* Westport, Conn.: Greenwood Press, 1977. • *Pacific World: Journal of the Institute of Buddhist Studies,* 1982-   . (Published in Berkeley, California). • Tuck, Donald R. *Buddhist Churches of America: Jodo Shinshu.* Lewiston, N.Y.: Edwin Mellen Press, 1987. • *Wheel of Dharma,* 1974-   . (Official monthly bilingual newspaper of the BCA, published in San Francisco, California.) • Yamaoka, Seigen H. *Jodo Shinshu: An Introduction.* San Francisco: Buddhist Churches of America, 1989.

Bul kogi: Korean entrée of seasoned, thinly sliced lean beef either roasted or grilled.

Bulosan, Carlos (Nov. 24, 1913 or 1914, Binalonan, Luzon, Philippines—Sept. 11, 1956, Seattle, Wash.): Writer and union activist. When Bulosan was born, U.S. rule since 1898 had already transformed the Philippines into a colonial dependency, a source of raw materials and cheap labor. From 1907 to 1926 more than 100,000 Filipinos toiled in the Hawaiian sugar plantations. Driven by poverty and feudal oppression at home, Filipinos under imperial tutelage began migrating to the United States to pursue the "dream of success" via thrift and hard work. Neither citizens nor aliens, they soon became the victims of exploitation and discrimination by labor contractors, farmers, gamblers, racist vigilantes, and state laws (for example, prohibiting their marriage with whites). They also, however, developed a rich and complex culture of resistance. When Bulosan arrived in Seattle, Washington, in 1931, little did he imagine that after his death he would be acclaimed as the militant chronicler and prophetic tribune of the multiracial workers in the West Coast farms and canneries whose struggles for equality and justice would define an era of unprecedented social change in U.S. history.

Apprenticeship. Laboring in restaurants and farms at the height of the Depression, Bulosan was exposed to the suffering and survival craft of migrant workers from California to Alaska. His friendship with a compatriot, Chris Mensalvas, involved him in Congress of Industrial Organizations (CIO) organizing of the UNITED CANNERY, AGRICULTURAL, PACKING AND ALLIED WORKERS OF AMERICA (UCAPAWA). As editor of *The New Tide* in 1934, he became acquainted with progressive authors such as Richard Wright, William

Carlos Bulosan (center). (Filipino American National Historical Society)

Saroyan, Carey McWilliams, and Sanora Babb. When Bulosan was confined at Los Angeles General Hospital for tuberculosis and kidney problems, it was Babb and her sister Dorothy who helped Bulosan discover through books a new "world of intellectual possibilities—and a grand dream of bettering society for the working man."

Bulosan's partisan experience as journalist and activist laid the groundwork for shaping his imagination as an "organic intellectual" of the masses (in Antonio Gramsci's sense). His adventures in the Los Angeles Public Library—reading the writings of authors ranging from Walt Whitman, Theodore Dreiser, Pablo Neruda, Nazim Hikmet. Jorge Guillén, Agnes Smedley, and Lillian Hellman to Mahatma Gandhi, José Rizal, Karl Marx, and others—supplemented his rudimentary high school education and endowed him with an astute social conscience.

Encouraged by Harriet Monroe, editor of *Poetry*, Bulosan began composing the comic fables satirizing patriarchal authority and the tyranny of the colonial elite that would later become the best-selling *The Laughter of My Father* (1944). Responding to critics who accused him of commercializing folk humor, Bulosan confessed in a letter: "My politico-economic ideas are embodied in all my writings. *The Laughter* is not humor; it is satire; it is indictment against an economic system that stifled the growth of the primitive. . . ." Tales found in *The Philippines Is in the Heart* (1978) celebrated the indigenous revolutionary tradition that mobilized "popular memory" and the carnivalesque resources of subaltern subjects.

Turning Point. When the Japanese struck Pearl Harbor in 1941 and subsequently occupied the Philippines, Bulosan "rediscovered' his homeland as the fountainhead of his creative originality and strength. Earlier he had written verses in sympathy with the defenders of the Spanish Republic fighting reactionary forces. His commitment to a global "popular front" against capitalism in its fascist phase (exemplified by the expansionist militarism of Germany, Italy, and Japan) afforded a philosophical orientation that gave coherence and direction to the uprooted and nomadic existence of his people. In the late 1930's he summed up their collective predicament: "Yes, I feel like a criminal running away from a crime I did not commit. And the crime is that I am a Filipino in America."

During the war Bulosan affirmed his support of the war against fascism in his volume of poems *Chorus for America* (1942), in *Letter from America* (1942), and in *The Voice of Bataan* (1943); most of them were broad-

cast overseas by the Office of War Information. Invited by the exiled government of the Philippine Commonwealth to work in its Washington, D.C., office, Bulosan opted to remain in the "battlefront" of the unions. He contributed to numerous magazines, among them *New Masses, Harper's Bazaar, Town and Country, The New Yorker*, and *Arizona Quarterly*. He also corresponded with Filipino progressive intellectuals such as Amado V. Hernandez and Salvador P. Lopez.

In such representative texts as "Be American," "Story of a Letter," and "As Long As the Grass Shall Grow" (anthologized in *If You Want to Know What We Are*, 1983), Bulosan narrated the vicissitudes of fragmentation and alienation of the migrant's life in a bourgeois milieu. In the process he also unfolded those moments of solidarity (especially with enlightened American women) and other progressive elements from all races and classes. His quasi-autobiographical account of his life from birth to the outbreak of World War II, *America Is in The Heart* (1946) distills half a century of resistance by people of color. It pays homage to grass-roots democracy found, for example, in the 1931 Tayug uprising of peasants in the Philippines and the strikes of multiethnic farmworkers in California. This classic text of immigrant "failure" is essentially a critique of the dominant assimilationist ideology that underwrites the continuing exclusion of Bulosan and other counterhegemonic artists from the mainstream literary canon.

Achievements. Blacklisted by the media and threatened with deportation at the outset of the Cold War, Bulosan persevered in the project of radical social transformation as editor of the 1952 *Yearbook* of the International Longshoremen's and Warehousemen's Union (ILWU). How could the government deport this alleged "communist" who was commissioned by U.S. president Franklin D. Roosevelt to celebrate one of the "four freedoms" with an essay displayed at the Federal Building in San Francisco in 1943? By this time Bulosan was internationally famous, listed in *Who's Who in America* and *Current Biography*. In an entry in *Twentieth Century Authors* (supp. 1955) he expressed the guiding principle of his art: "What impelled me to write? The answer is—my grand dream of equality among men and freedom for all. To give a literate voice to the voiceless one hundred thousand Filipinos in the United States, Hawaii, and Alaska. Above all and ultimately, to translate the desires and aspirations of the whole Filipino people in the Philippines and abroad in terms relevant to contemporary history."

One of Bulosan's last manuscripts, the novel *The*

Families of Filipino sugarcane laborers near their living quarters, a plantation in Pahala, on the island of Hawaii, circa 1916. The lives of such individuals were a subject of great concern to Bulosan. (Lyman House Memorial Museum)

Cry and the Dedication (published as *The Power of the People*, 1986), returns to the Philippines to explore the linkage between the Huk guerilla struggle and the Filipino diaspora. In numerous letters (gathered in *The Sound of Falling Light*, 1960) and essays such as "I Am Not a Laughing Man," "My Education," and "How My Stories Were Written," Bulosan assumed the responsibility of remapping the U.S. multicultural landscape: "What really compelled me to write was to try to understand this country, to find a place in it not only for myself but my people."

Bulosan's poems, among them "If You Want to Know What We Are" (1940), and his aforementioned novel of national-popular insurgency, dramatize in symbolic action the democratic socialist vision that animates his entire life-work. Long before Frantz Fanon, Che Guevara, and others articulated the politics of Third World liberation, Bulosan had already enacted in life and letters the necessary connections of class, gender, race, and ethnicity, as well as the mediations of value and ethos integrating the struggles of people in the metropolis with those in the periphery. His search for the "heart" of America may be conceived as the paradigmatic quest for a just, equal, and free society where individual happiness coalesces with the common good. Bulosan the Filipino exile thus returns to the true if utopian homeland of all humanity.—*E. San Juan, Jr.*

SUGGESTED READINGS: • Bulosan, Carlos. *If You Want to Know What We Are: A Carlos Bulosan Reader.* Albuquerque, N.Mex.: West End Press, 1983. • Bulosan, Carlos. *The Philippines Is in the Heart.* Quezon City: New Day Publishers, 1978. • Bulosan, Carlos. *The Sound of Falling Light.* Edited by Dolores Feria. Quezon City: University of the Philippines Press, 1960. • Bulosan, Carlos. *The Power of the People.* Manila: National Book Store, 1986. • San Juan, E., Jr. *Bulosan: An Introduction with Selections.* Manila: National Book Store, 1983. • San Juan, E., Jr. *Carlos Bulosan and the Imagination of the Class Struggle.* Quezon City: University of the Philippines Press, 1972.

Burakumin (also, *buraku*): Japanese word for a class of individuals within Japanese society who have violated certain social and religious beliefs and are therefore subjected to various forms of discrimination. The *burakumin* have traditionally resided in the Kyoto-

Osaka region and in western Japan generally; typical population estimates number in the range of two million (although precise figures are hard to ascertain).

The most commonplace historical terms used to describe the *buraku* are *eta* (great filth) and *hinin* (non-person). The label *eta* seems to have been affixed to those members of early Japan who had been in contact with unclean objects, such as dead bodies (animal or human). Such behavior was, according to Buddhist beliefs and popular superstition, defilement. Thus the *eta* have commonly been linked with the making of leather products. The name *hinin* arose during the Tokugawa period (1600-1867) and referred to those who were not strictly *eta* but who were still the objects of discrimination. *Hinin* were usually beggars or those involved in disreputable types of entertainment.

Although the Meiji government (1868-1912) legally "raised" the *eta* and *hinin* to the level of commoner, societal distinctions and prejudices remain nevertheless.

Burlingame Treaty (1868): Reciprocal most-favored-nation treaty between the United States and China, dealing with the two countries' citizens in each other's land.

American policy in the mid-nineteenth century looked to the development of trade and economic relations with China in a cooperative spirit (unlike the "gunboat" diplomacy of European nations). The United States sought the tea, silk, porcelains, and lacquers of China while seeking to market its own goods. The inauguration of the Pacific Steamship Line and the opening of the transcontinental railroad promised limitless opportunities for such expansion. To facilitate this, American diplomats forged the Burlingame Treaty, granting reciprocal most-favored-nation treatment between the two countries.

Anson Burlingame became the American representative in the Chinese imperial court in 1860, and later a trusted friend and adviser to the Chinese government. He was about to leave his post in 1866 when the Chinese officials made a most unusual request. Burlingame was asked to represent China as the Chinese envoy to the United States and the principal European nations. With the consent of the American government, he was in a position to negotiate the treaty of 1868.

The treaty secured reciprocal privileges for citizens of both countries while residing in each other's community. The preamble reads: "The United States of America and the Emperor of China cordially recognize the inherent and inalienable right of man to change his home and allegiance and also the mutual advantage of the free migration and emigration of their citizens and subjects, respectively, from one country to another, for the purposes of curiosity, of trade, or as permanent residents." The treaty also acknowledged reciprocal rights of freedom of worship and conscience, granted reciprocal most-favored-nation treatment to immigrants and travelers, and gave the Chinese "all the privileges of the public educational institutions under the control of the government of the United States."

The treaty at first received good press and was speedily ratified in the U.S. Senate and, in time, by the Chinese imperial court. It was hailed as a triumph for American diplomacy, bringing China out of seclusion. History showed, however, that the American government focused only on the benefits derived from the treaty and not on the obligations it was to assume. Soon, it was clear that the United States was not only unprepared to assume such obligations but also most unwilling.

The ignominious treatment of Chinese immigrants soon after ratification of the treaty bore witness to this fact. In repeated cases of persecution and attack, the U.S. government failed to exert all its powers to secure the protection of Chinese subjects and their property in the United States. For example, in 1871, a group of toughs attacked Chinatown in San Francisco. Twenty-one Chinese were killed, including fifteen lynched in the street. In the end only eight rioters received sentences of two to eight years—a mockery of justice for twenty-one murders. Racial and economic prejudice continued, resulting in revisions and tightening of the provisions of the Burlingame Treaty and finally leading to the CHINESE EXCLUSION ACT OF 1882.

Burns, John Anthony (Mar. 30, 1909, Ft. Assiniboine, Mont.—April 5, 1975, Honolulu, Hawaii): Governor of Hawaii. A major figure in Hawaii's politics, Burns served as a delegate to Congress from Hawaii from 1956 to 1959 and as governor of Hawaii from 1962 to 1973. A Democrat credited by many for engineering the 1950's "revolution" that destroyed the Republican dominance in Hawaii, Burns had one overriding goal: to bring equality to the people of Hawaii. Pre-World War II Hawaii was dominated—politically, economically, and socially—by a Caucasian elite that was mainly Republican. Non-Caucasians were denied the same opportunities granted the Caucasians, or *haoles*, as they were called in Hawaii.

Burns lived in Hawaii for most of his life. During World War II he headed a Honolulu Police intelligence unit, the Morale Contact Group, that worked with the Japanese community. Many in the community came to see him as a sympathetic friend. When World War II ended, Burns formed an informal group that met frequently to discuss political plans for bringing changes to Hawaii. When the Japanese American veterans began to return from the war and from the schools they attended with the help of the GI Bill, the group was expanded to include them. Although the Burns faction that emerged was not the only influential Democratic faction, it is credited for helping to bring the Demo-cratic Party to prominence in Hawaii and equal status to the state's non-Caucasians.

Burns is also remembered for his work as a delegate to Congress, during which he was instrumental in achieving statehood for Hawaii in 1959. Congressional opponents to statehood raised many issues, including that of race. Senator Strom Thrumond, Democrat from South Carolina, for example, claimed that statehood for Hawaii would be the "deathknell of our federated Republic" because of the "Eastern heritage" of a large segment of the population. Burns responded

Hawaii congressional delegate John Anthony Burns outside the U.S. Capitol, making final adjustments to a speech he will deliver on the House floor. (AP/Wide World Photos)

New Jersey Muslim women dressed in the traditional burqah. (Frances M. Roberts)

by pointing to the proven loyalty of the people of Hawaii, including the Japanese Americans, who had fought valiantly in World War II.

Burqah: Long cloak worn by Muslim women to cover the face and body.

Bushido: Japanese "code of the warrior." It contains the ideal philosophical and spiritual tenets of the samurai class as developed during the Kamakura period (1192-1333). The code's guiding principle is absolute loyalty to one's lord, or *daimyo*. It is comparable to the code of chivalry of the Middle Ages in Europe.

C

Ca dao: Vietnamese folk poetry. The poet and translator John Balaban has defined *ca dao* as "short lyric poems, passed down by word of mouth and sung without instrumental accompaniment by ordinary individuals." Many of these oral poems are traditional, but new poems in this form are being created and performed—as attested by the existence of *ca dao* composed in the United States, reflecting the experience of the Vietnamese refugee community. A representative selection of *ca dao* can be found in *"Ca Dao Vietnam": A Bilingual Anthology of Vietnamese Folk Poetry* (1980), edited and translated by Balaban with a helpful introduction.

Cable Act (1922): Federal legislation designed to discourage Chinese Americans from marrying immigrants. More than a century earlier, in 1790, the U.S. Congress had limited the right of naturalized citizenship to white immigrants. Furthermore, when China and the United States signed the BURLINGAME TREATY in 1868, which permitted unrestrained voluntary migration between the two countries, anti-Chinese representatives exchanged their support of ratification for a clause expressly denying naturalization to Chinese immigrants.

In the 1920's, however, as the United States was moving toward more general immigration restrictions, one element in the Chinese American community created a small hole in this policy of discrimination: the American-born. By virtue of their birthplace, such individuals did not require naturalization in order to achieve citizenship. Furthermore, through marriage to a citizen, immigrant males could circumvent laws preventing them from owning land and could establish a permanent home in the United States. Likewise, immigrant women could gain an exemption from naturalization laws by marrying a citizen husband.

Therefore, in September, 1922, Congress sought to close this window of opportunity with the passage of the Cable Act. The law contained three important ingredients. First, it prohibited female immigrants from achieving citizenship through marriage to citizens. Second, American-born women who married individuals ineligible for naturalization lost their citizenship. Finally, marriage to men who could naturalize did not affect the status of citizen wives.

Since white aliens met eligibility requirements, the 1922 law did little to inhibit European immigration. Its contents, however, profoundly affected Chinese Americans. Immigrant wives could never become citizens and thus remained in fear of deportation. Women born in the United States lost all citizenship rights by marrying someone from China. Such restrictions forced the Chinese American community to turn inward and remain a bachelor-dominated society. Without a promise of future protection, male citizens did not bring wives from China, and the small number of American-born women limited their marriage choices to individuals who shared the same status. Thus, until its eventual repeal in 1936, the Cable Act specifically intimidated Chinese Americans and severely restricted their ability to build families in the United States.

Cairo Declaration (1943): Joint proclamation issued by leaders of the United States, Great Britain, and China affirming the goal of a free Korea. The declaration resulted from the Cairo summit conferences held near the close of World War II. It promised Korean independence from Japan while resolving to strip Japan of all of its colonial possessions.

Calcutta: Capital of the state of West Bengal, Calcutta is the second-largest metropolis in India. It is located along the banks of the Hooghly River in the Ganges delta and was the capital of British India from 1773 to 1912. It has a hot and humid climate and receives heavy rains from summer monsoons and winter rains from cyclones.

Calcutta is the commercial hub, the financial center, and the primary port of northeast India. Its busy harbor handles the export of coal, iron ore, and tea from the surrounding states and jute from the immediate neighborhood. Calcutta is one of India's leading manufacturing areas. Its industries include jute milling, engineering, metallurgy, paper, petrochemical, glass, and textiles.

The city, surrounding a large park called the Maidan, is served by a modern, well-kept subway and is connected to Greater Calcutta by a major highway. The commercial and financial centers are located north of the Maidan. Wealthy people reside in neighborhoods near the city's center, while about one-third of the city's population live in slum areas, north and northeast of the commercial center. More than 200,000 people live on the city's streets.

The city, with a density of 82,000 people per square mile, is one of the most crowded metropolises in the world. Many of its slums have electricity, running water, and sewage facilities, and many slums contain small foundries, machine shops, and production units for goods sold to the city's major companies.

Two-thirds of the 11.1 million people of Greater Calcutta speak BENGALI, and the majority of the rest speak either Hindi and Urdu. Hindu and Muslim Bengalis form 66 percent and 14 percent of its population, respectively. Although Calcutta's government, a leftist stronghold, faces endless problems resulting from the high cost of labor, inadequate transportation, poor water supply, and sprawling slums, Calcuttans cherish their city and their Bengali heritage. They are proud of their creativity and the achievements of fellow Bengalis. Rabindranath TAGORE received the Nobel Prize in Literature in 1913; other notable contributors to their heritage are sitarist Ravi SHANKAR and filmmaker Satyajit Ray.

California roll: Variation of a Japanese appetizer. Originating in California, its ingredients include dried seaweed, rice, avocado, cucumber, and crabsticks.

California State Federation of Labor: Organization of major labor unions that was in the forefront of anti-Asian sentiment in California in the first half of the twentieth century. When the federation was established in 1901 by the California legislature, it had a mandate to protect the welfare of the wage earner and to enforce the laws affecting labor conditions. Members of the organization were white Americans who displayed open hostility to Asian Americans. The mandate of the federation was to help Filipino farm workers gain equality in the fields. The reverse occurred, however, as many Asian Americans experienced problems in the labor market as a result of the policies of federation leaders.

In the 1920's, the federation pressured Will J. French of the California Department of Industrial Relations to survey ethnic conditions as they related to Filipinos in the California fields, which resulted in the publication of *Facts About Filipino Immigration into California* (1930). This Department of Industrial Relations' pamphlet publicized a 91 percent increase in Filipino immigration, which created an organized move to rewrite federal immigration laws.

In October, 1927, at the forty-seventh annual convention of the American Federation of Labor (AFL) in Los Angeles, Paul Scharrenberg, the secretary-treasurer of the California State Federation of Labor, delivered a fiery speech demanding the exclusion of Filipino labor. He argued that Filipinos represented the same danger that the Chinese and Japanese had posed to organized labor. The Filipinos worked too cheaply and were resistant to sophisticated union organization. Scharrenberg cooperated with V. S. MCCLATCHY, chairperson of California's Joint Immigration Committee, to begin a decade of anti-Filipino propaganda.

In 1929, the California legislature, encouraged by the federation, pressured Congress to restrict Filipino farm workers because they did not understand the U.S. system. Filipinos, however, enjoyed the unique status of being classified as American nationals, and the exclusionists could not deny them rights in the labor market.

By 1930, the federation had joined with the Commonwealth Club of California, the American Legion, and the California Joint Immigration Committee to plead for federal restrictions on Filipino farm labor. This action precipitated much of the labor violence of the Great Depression against Filipino field workers.

One of the by-products of the California State Federation of Labor and the Department of Industrial Relations fomenting anti-Filipino hostility was that the courts applied a double standard to Filipinos. In 1930, a Los Angeles Superior Court judge ruled that the county clerk could not issue a marriage license to Tony Moreno, a Filipino, and Ruby Robinson, a white woman. The federation had no business involving itself in this matter, but its officials applauded the decision.

Filipino social organizations took exception to this ruling and filed four separate lawsuits in 1931. The Los Angeles Superior Court ruled that Filipino-white marriages did not violate sections 60 and 69 of the California Civil Code. The federation then pressured Will French to make speeches and distribute state-sponsored writings on the "Filipino problem." Soon, French's phrase "unfair competition to American labor" was used to justify anti-Filipino movements. In this atmosphere, Filipino farm workers increasingly turned to unionization. The formation of the Filipino Labor Union (FLU) and successful strikes in Salinas in 1934 and 1936 were the direct result of the attempt by the federation to intimidate Filipino farm labor.

From the WATSONVILLE INCIDENT of 1930, with its five days of anti-Filipino rioting, until the recognition of Filipino labor unions by the AFL in 1937, the federation consistently sought to erode the rights of Filipino workers. Ironically, the lasting significance of the federation is that it was the catalyst to increased ethnic labor unionization.

Calligraphy: The art of writing Chinese characters with brush and ink. Of the "three perfections," or *san jue*, of brush and ink in traditional Chinese culture, namely painting, poetry, and calligraphy, calligraphy has long been the most exalted. As such, the art form spread along with Chinese culture throughout all of East Asia, where it continued to evolve in ever distinctive ways apart from its place of origin.

The first examples of a truly Chinese writing system—one, in other words, that combines pictograms, ideograms, and phonetical and categorical signifiers to create meaning—can be dated to the Shang Dynasty (c. 1766-1122 B.C.E.) in the inscriptions of the ceremonial bronzes of the period and on what have come to be called the "oracle bones," bits of bone upon which questions were inscribed for purposes of divination. From the Shang through the Zhou (c. 1122-221 B.C.E.) and Qin (221-206 B.C.E) dynasties the rounded forms carved on stone seals evolved. Styles appeared that were designed for writing with brush and ink: *li shu* (clerical script), *kai shu* (standard script), *xing shu* (running script), and *cao shu* (grass script). They developed in that order, with varying degrees of cursiveness.

Thus the styles from which a contemporary calligrapher can choose have all been formalized since the fourth century. None has become superannuated but all are always there for selection and inspiration. The order

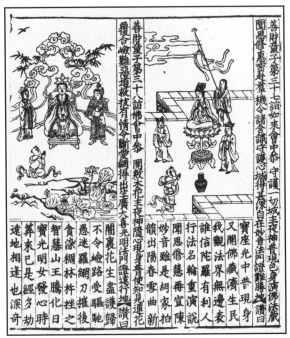

An example of Chinese calligraphy, from a book printed during the Southern Song Dynasty (1126-1279). (Library of Congress)

of strokes in an individual character, and their method of execution, are also all determined: Only so much variation is possible before a Chinese character ceases to be itself and falls from its status as self-sufficient evoker of meaning to mere incoherent gibberish.

A story often told of one of China's greatest calligraphers, Wang Xi Zhi, is that he practiced so long and hard that he turned the waters of a pond black from washing his brushes. To become a great calligrapher

Evolution of the Chinese Character for "Fish"

Oracle-bone script	Bronze script	Large seal script	Small seal script	Clerical script	Standard script	Running script	Cursive script
jiaguwen	*jinwen*	*dazhuanshu*	*xiaozhuanshu*	*lishu*	*kaishu*	*xingshu*	*caoshu*
13th-11th centuries b.c.e.	11th-3d centuries b.c.e.	5th-3d centuries b.c.e.	3d century b.c.e.	2d century	since c. 4th century	since c. 4th century	since c. 4th century

Source: Calligraphy by Shen C. Y. Fu. Reprinted with permission from "A Closer Look: Chinese Calligraphy." Copyright, 1994, Freer Gallery of Art, Smithsonian Institution.

Of the three brush-and-ink art forms of traditional Chinese culture, calligraphy is considered the highest. (Robert Fried)

involves countless hours of mastering the forms until they have become so internalized that one can begin to call them one's own and create something original. The delight a connoisseur feels before a beautiful calligraphic work lies in recognizing flashes of insight and brilliance against a backdrop of tradition and convention. The ideal for which artist and audience search exists, of course, only in the minds of both.

Cambodia: Tropical mainland Southeast Asian country, more than seventy thousand square miles in size. Cambodia lies in a shallow basin between Thailand to its west and northwest, Laos to its northeast, and Vietnam to its east and southeast. The country is bisected by the Mekong River, which flows south through Cambodia into southern Vietnam before exiting into the South China Sea. In northwestern Cambodia the Tonle Sap, the largest lake in Southeast Asia, drains southeastward into the Mekong. During the rainy season the waters back up around PHNOM PENH, the nation's capital, forming wide floodplains where much of the nation's rice is raised.

The overwhelming majority of Cambodia's 1992

Bayon Temple, a Cambodian relic dating from approximately the twelfth century C.E. (Eric Crystal)

population of almost nine million people live in small rural villages. Some 15 percent live in Phnom Penh and in Battambang, the country's second largest city, and the remainder in small towns throughout the country.

People. More than 80 percent of Cambodia's people are KHMER. Almost all practice BUDDHISM, the predominant religion of the country. Cambodia's largest ethnic minorities include the approximately three hundred thousand descendants of Chinese immigrants, most of whom are urban-dwelling traders, together with an equal or greater number of Vietnamese. Cambodia also has a small number of hill tribe groups in the northeastern part of the country and an even smaller number of Moslem Chams.

Today more than half a million Cambodians live outside Cambodia, having fled from the political upheavals that engulfed their country in the 1970's and 1980's.

Early History Through the Post-Angkorean Years. Archaeological evidence shows that Cambodia has been inhabited since at least 5000 B.C.E. From about 200 B.C.E. into the early centuries of the first millennium, Indian traders and priests traveling between India and China brought Hindu and Buddhist concepts of religion, kingship, and statecraft together with Indian writing systems to Southeast Asia. The first historical kingdoms in what is now Cambodia emerged during this period.

The rise in the ninth century of the kingdom of Angkor in northwest Cambodia led to a great flowering of Indianized civilization. At its height the Angkorean empire, which lasted until the mid-fifteenth century, extended over much of present-day central Thailand and southern Laos as well as Cambodia itself. Angkorean temple-pyramids, of which ANGKOR WAT (built by King Suryavarman II around 1130 C.E.) and the Bayon (built by Jayavarman VII) are regarded as the supreme examples, display a mixture of Hindu and Buddhist iconography, with Hindu elements predominating. Many were dedicated to Siva or Visnu. Angkorean rulers also built royal mausoleums, reservoirs, irrigation systems, canals, and even hospitals throughout their domains.

Cambodian classical dance perpetuates images of the goddesses that grace the temples of Angkor. The Khmer regard Angkor as the culmination point of their civilization, and Angkor Wat is pictured on all Cambodian national flags.

The Angkorean Empire collapsed in the fifteenth century, its population exhausted by the heavy labor demands royal building programs had placed upon it.

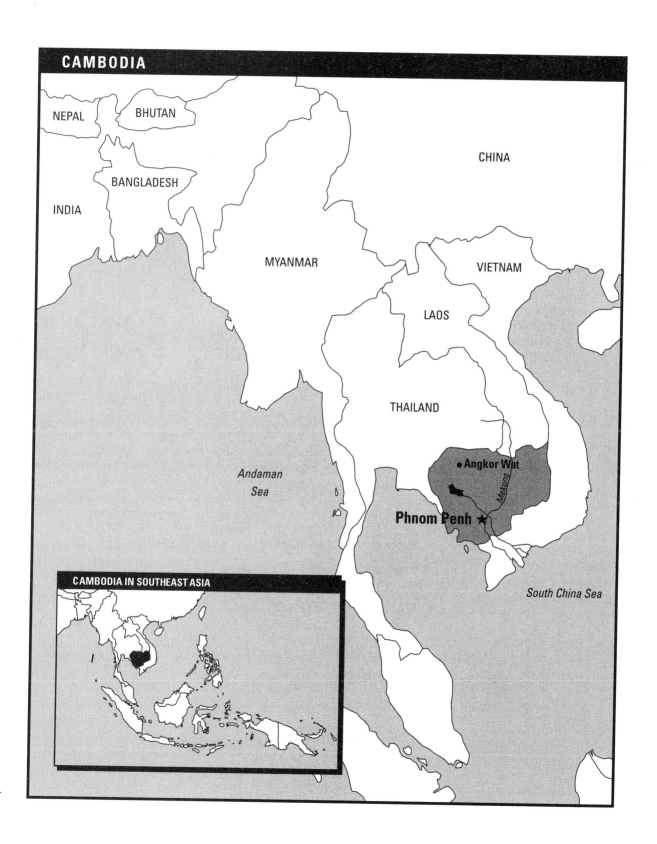

CAMBODIA

NEPAL

BHUTAN

CHINA

BANGLADESH

INDIA

MYANMAR

VIETNAM

LAOS

THAILAND

Andaman
Sea

• Angkor Wat

Mekong

Phnom Penh ★

South China Sea

CAMBODIA IN SOUTHEAST ASIA

In 1430 the Siamese, precursors of the modern Thai, sacked Angkor, and the Cambodian capital moved south to Phnom Penh. Between the mid-fifteenth and the mid-nineteenth centuries, Cambodia was wracked by internal divisions and by wars against its Siamese and Vietnamese neighbors.

French Colonial Domination. In 1863 Cambodia became a French protectorate; for the next ninety years it formed part of French Indochina. Cambodian rulers remained on the throne but had little real power.

The French did little to provide Cambodians with educational or public health benefits; rather they concentrated on developing rice and rubber production for the export market. Large numbers of Vietnamese were brought in to work on the rubber plantations.

During World War II the Japanese conquest of French Indochina showed that French rule could be challenged. After the war Prince Norodom Sihanouk took advantage of Vietnam's struggle against the French to rally Cambodia's growing nationalist forces and gain independence for his country in 1953.

Cambodia in Conflict. Initially Cambodia prospered under Prince Sihanouk, but by the mid-1960's it had become drawn into the VIETNAM WAR, creating internal challenges to his rule. In 1970 Sihanouk was overthrown by a U.S.-supported right-wing military group. Over the next five years fighting between right-wing forces and the Khmer Communists, or KHMER ROUGE, intensified. The United States bombed parts of Cambodia in efforts to destroy both Khmer and Vietnamese Communist strongholds.

The Pol Pot Regime. In April, 1975, the Khmer Rouge under Pol Pot seized control of Phnom Penh and embarked on one of the most radical revolutions in modern history. During the reign of terror that ensued, as many as 1.7 million people were killed or died of starvation and disease. Most members of the country's educated elite were destroyed, and Buddhism was almost eradicated from Cambodia.

Cambodia After Pol Pot. In January, 1979, the slaughter of Vietnamese living in Cambodia, coupled with the Khmer Rouge's aggressive forays into Vietnam, led to fighting with Vietnam in 1977 and 1978. In December, 1978, Vietnamese troops invaded Cambodia. They captured Phnom Penh and forced the Khmer Rouge to retreat to the Thai border. A new Vietnamese-sponsored government, the People's Republic of Kampuchea, was established. For eleven years it was recognized only by members of the Soviet Bloc. During this period more than 500,000 Cambodians fled their country as refugees. More than 250,000 were resettled

Ousted Cambodian despot Pol Pot at a press conference in 1979. (AP/Wide World Photos)

in the United States, France, and Australia; the rest were eventually repatriated to Cambodia.

By 1990 international pressures had led to the withdrawal of Vietnamese troops from Cambodia, but the Kampuchean government, under Hun Sen, remained in power. Cambodians both inside and outside the country, split into different political factions, could not agree on which group should ultimately hold power in Cambodia. To break the deadlock, in 1991 representatives of all major factions, including the Khmer Rouge, signed an agreement allowing the United Nations (UN) to supervise the holding of national elections.

Recent Political and Economic Conditions. In May, 1992, elections were held under the auspices of the UN Transitional Authority in Cambodia (UNTAC). The elections resulted in the formation of a coalition government in which Prince Sihanouk once again became the head of the government.

Cambodia has made a remarkable recovery from the devastation caused during the Pol Pot years. Buddhism has reemerged strongly since 1979, and today there are thousands of Buddhist monks living in temple-monasteries throughout the country once again.

The economy, however, remains fragile. Industry is minimal; as in the past most of the country's foreign exchange comes from sales of agricultural products and natural resources such as rice, rubber, timber, and gems. Despite increases in exports since the late 1980's, especially to Thailand, Cambodia remains a very poor country.—*F. Jane Keyes*

SUGGESTED READINGS: • Chandler, David P. *A History of Cambodia*. Boulder, Colo.: Westview Press, 1983. • Chandler, David. *The Land and People of Cambodia*. New York: HarperCollins, 1991. • Lutheran Immigration and Refugee Service. *Cambodia: The Land and Its People*. New York: Lutheran Council in the USA, 1983.

Cambodian Americans: The Cambodian American community came into being in the United States as a direct result of the VIETNAM WAR. Prior to the end of that conflict in 1975, no discernible community of Cambodian Americans existed in the United States. By the 1990's, Cambodian American communities were spread across the United States, with a few predominant clusters on the East and West coasts manifesting much economic vitality, growth, and cultural strength.

Cambodian Culture. The Angkor Dynasty of Cambodia (802-1453 C.E.) was the predominant power on mainland Southeast Asia in the time of the European Middle Ages. Cambodian territory by the twelfth century C.E. included southern Laos, eastern Thailand, and the southern third of what is now Vietnam. The wealth and glory of that empire are reflected in the archaeological ruins of ANGKOR WAT, long recognized as one of the marvels of ancient building in stone. Cambodian arts of music, dance, song, wood carving, and painting are highly refined and developed. Cambodian silk weaving is a highly developed art, again manifesting the complexity of the arts in this very ancient civilization. The Cambodian language (Khmer) is spoken by about ten million people worldwide, including about eight million residents of Cambodia and between one million and 1.5 million Cambodian minority citizens of Vietnam. One of the first great kingdoms of Southeast Asia, Cambodia has declined in recent centuries to become one of the less populated states of mainland Southeast Asia.

War and Refugees. Despite the efforts of Prince Norodom Sihanouk, last of the Cambodian monarchs to rule that Southeast Asian land, Cambodia failed to remain neutral in the Vietnam conflict. Sihanouk was overthrown in 1970, and the country was soon plunged into war. Vietnamese, American, and Cambodian troops were engaged in this conflict, which soon developed into a bitter civil war. On April 17, 1975, KHMER ROUGE revolutionary armies marched victorious into the capital, Phnom Penh. Almost immediately the Khmer Rouge instituted an unprecedented reign of terror. All inhabitants of the cities were forced to move to the countryside; basic institutions such as the monarchy, Buddhism, and the use of money in commercial transactions were abolished. Forced relocation, starvation, and mass murder resulted in the death of an estimated one million Cambodians during the 1975-1979 regime of the Khmer Rouge. Vietnam invaded Cambodia on December 25, 1978, driving the Khmer Rouge from power. From 1979 to 1981 large numbers of malnourished, ill, and traumatized Cambodian refu-

Cambodian classical dance troupe performing in Arcadia, California. (Alon Reininger, Unicorn Stock Photos)

Cambodian American Statistical Profile, 1990

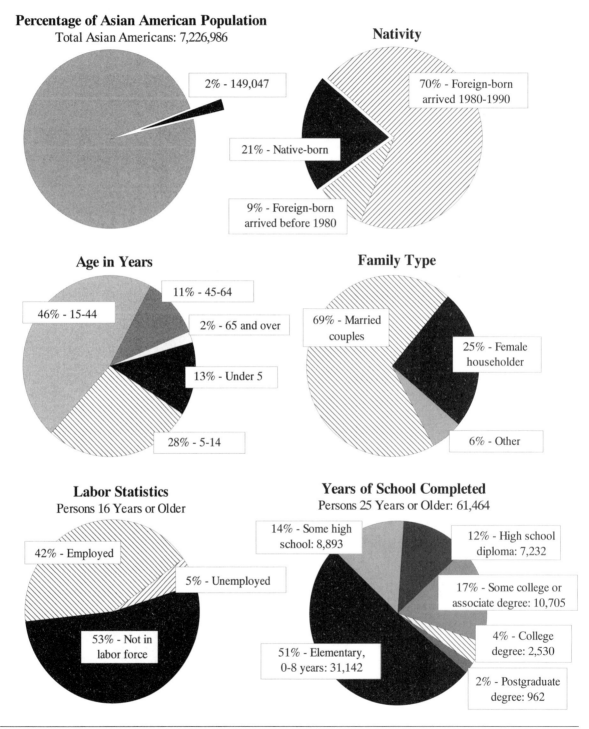

Percentage of Asian American Population
Total Asian Americans: 7,226,986

2% - 149,047

Nativity

70% - Foreign-born arrived 1980-1990

21% - Native-born

9% - Foreign-born arrived before 1980

Age in Years

11% - 45-64

46% - 15-44

2% - 65 and over

13% - Under 5

28% - 5-14

Family Type

69% - Married couples

25% - Female householder

6% - Other

Labor Statistics
Persons 16 Years or Older

42% - Employed

5% - Unemployed

53% - Not in labor force

Years of School Completed
Persons 25 Years or Older: 61,464

14% - Some high school: 8,893

12% - High school diploma: 7,232

17% - Some college or associate degree: 10,705

4% - College degree: 2,530

2% - Postgraduate degree: 962

51% - Elementary, 0-8 years: 31,142

Source: U.S. Bureau of the Census, *1990 Census of Population: Asians and Pacific Islanders in the United States,* 1993.

gees fled their homeland to refugee camps such as Khao-I-Dang in Thailand. Approximately 150,000 Cambodians arrived in the United States between 1975 and 1990. Of these, more than 98 percent were admitted as refugees. Except for a small number of Cambodian officials and their families brought to the United States in 1975, the vast majority of adult Cambodian refugees in the United States are survivors of Khmer Rouge brutality.

Cambodian American Communities. Cambodian American communities of varying size are found across the United States, from Tacoma, Washington, in the northwest to Atlanta, Georgia, in the southeast. The U.S. government instituted a plan to cluster newly arriving Cambodian refugees in areas not previously host to large Asian immigrant or refugee populations

Cambodian American family, Oakland, California. (Eric Crystal)

(Columbus, Ohio, for example). Two major population concentrations of Cambodian Americans are found in Long Beach, California (35,000) and Lowell, Massachusetts (30,000). The refugee population reflects a cross section of Cambodian society. Some refugees originally lived in major urban centers, were accomplished professionally, and were well-educated prior to the assumption of power by the Khmer Rouge. The majority of Cambodian refugees, as is true of the majority of residents of Cambodia, originally hailed from village farming areas. Many adults arrived in the United States with only a rudimentary elementary school education.

Issues Confronting the Cambodian American Community. Adaptation to the United States has been difficult for many adult, first-generation refugees. Many experienced unspeakable cruelties under the Khmer Rouge. Lack of formal education, depression resulting from personal loss, and the absence of widespread effective kin networks have engendered adjustment problems for many middle-aged and older people. Younger Cambodian Americans have adapted with greater ease. Concern for the preservation and continu-

Occupation

Employed Persons 16 Years or Older	Percentage
Managerial and professional specialty	10%
Technical, sales, and administrative support	23%
Service	18%
Farming, forestry, and fishing	2%
Precision production, craft, and repair	17%
Operators, fabricators, and laborers	30%

Income, 1989

Median household income	$18,837
Per capita	$5,121
Percent of families in poverty	42%

Household Size

Number of People	Percentage
1	4%
2	8%
3	12%
4	19%
5	19%
6	15%
7 or more	23%

Source: U.S. Bureau of the Census, *1990 Census of Population: Asians and Pacific Islanders in the United States,* 1993.

ation of their culture motivates many Cambodians to support local dance and music ensembles in the United States, to maintain an active interest in developments in their homeland, and to attempt to ensure that children born in the United States continue to appreciate and participate in their traditional culture. Many Cambodians have secured an economically productive economic niche in the management and ownership of donut shops. In Los Angeles County alone, by 1992 it was estimated that fully half of all donut franchise operations were managed by Cambodian Americans.

Cambodian Americans and the Wider Community. The release of the Academy Award-winning film *The Killing Fields* (1984) informed a great number of Americans about the traumas and tragedies that engendered the refugee flow to the United States. A host of subsequent books by Cambodian American witnesses to the years of Khmer Rouge terror further facilitated communication and understanding of Cambodian Americans by their neighbors. Cambodian restaurants have opened everywhere that large Cambodian populations reside; most have been enthusiastically received by reviewers and patrons alike. The isolation of the Cambodian refugee community will erode as more Cambodian American young people begin to make significant contributions to their newly adopted country. Only time will determine the degree to which the language, religious traditions, and artistic contributions of Cambodia will be successfully preserved in refugee communities throughout the United States.—*Eric Crystal*

SUGGESTED READINGS: • *The Killing Fields*. Film/

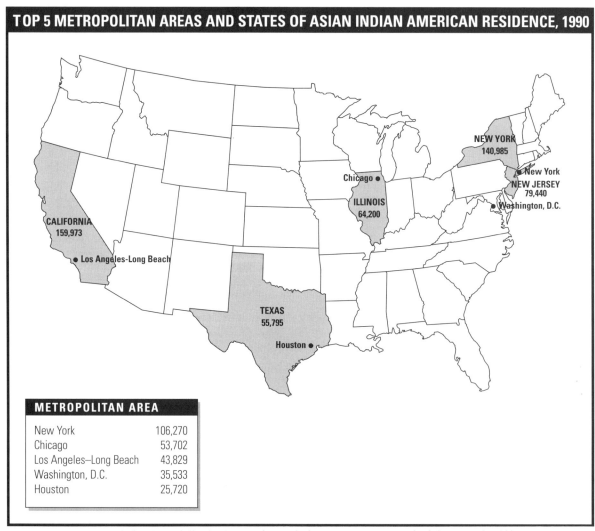

TOP 5 METROPOLITAN AREAS AND STATES OF ASIAN INDIAN AMERICAN RESIDENCE, 1990

NEW YORK
140,985

New York

NEW JERSEY
79,440

Washington, D.C.

Chicago

ILLINOIS
64,200

CALIFORNIA
159,973

Los Angeles-Long Beach

TEXAS
55,795

Houston

METROPOLITAN AREA	
New York	106,270
Chicago	53,702
Los Angeles–Long Beach	43,829
Washington, D.C.	35,533
Houston	25,720

Source: Susan B. Gall and Timothy L. Gall, eds., *Statistical Record of Asian Americans.* Detroit: Gale Research, 1993.

Young Cambodian American dancer dressed for Cambodian New Year festivities. (Claire Rydell)

video. 1984. Warner Bros. • Ngor, Haing. *A Cambodian Odyssey*. New York: Macmillan, 1987. • *Rebuilding the Temple*. Film/video. Florentine Films. 1991. • Schanberg, Sydney. *The Life and Death of Dith Pran*. New York: Penguin Books, 1985. • Shawcross, William. *Sideshow: Kissinger, Nixon, and the Destruction of Cambodia*. New York: Simon & Schuster, 1979.

Cameron, Donaldina Mackenzie (July 26, 1869, New Zealand—Jan. 4, 1968, Palo Alto, Calif.): Teacher, social worker, and human rights advocate. Cameron dedicated her life to aiding, educating, and Christianizing Chinese immigrants.

The youngest of seven children of a New Zealand sheep rancher, Cameron was raised in an intelligent, fun-loving, and staunch Christian family. In 1871 her family moved to the United States, eventually settling in Southern California. After graduating from an Oakland high school she entered teacher training school in 1888. One year later her plans for higher education ended with her father's death.

In 1895 Cameron began her lifetime work for the Chinese Presbyterian Mission Home in San Francisco's Chinatown. She served as superintendent from 1900 until 1934. The home had been established to educate Chinese prostitutes and slave girls who were rescued from abusive masters and slave traders. These girls were taught Christianity, English, and domestic skills in order to help them secure jobs and establish their own economic independence. These Chinese women affectionately called Cameron "Lo Mo," or "old mama."

During the San Francisco earthquake of 1906, Cameron, after moving her "children" to safety, disobeyed martial law and risked being shot by armed troops in order to return to the home. She had done so in order to secure all legal documents so as to prevent the rise of any illegal claims to the Chinese girls later. She was constantly battling the Chinese *tong* associations, which used threats, intimidation, and violence against her and the mission home. Referring to her as "Fahn Quai," or "white devil," the *tongs* warned Chinese girls to keep their distance, claiming Cameron would torture or poison them. Yet she would go on to help rescue more than three thousand Chinese and Japanese women and assist in establishing rescue homes in Oakland, Los Gatos, and Berkeley. During World War II the mission home also helped Chinese war brides and other misplaced war refugees.

During a time when anti-Chinese sentiment was high and exclusion was practiced, Cameron spent her life laboring against Chinese slave traders, the *tongs*, prejudice, violence, and discrimination. Her efforts helped to end the Chinese and Japanese illegal slave trade to the United States. In honor of her dedication the Chinese Presbyterian Mission Home was renamed the Donaldina Cameron House, and after her death, the California State legislature recognized her life work and contributions to the Chinese community in San Francisco by passing a resolution paying tribute to her.

Cameron House: Chinatown "rescue" foundation established in 1873 for the aid and welfare of immigrant Chinese women who had come to the United States as wives, slaves, concubines, or prostitutes. Officially known as the Donaldina Cameron House, it was formerly the Chinese Presbyterian Mission Home. It assumed its present name on June 7, 1942, in honor of Donaldina Mackenzie CAMERON, its superintendent from 1900 to 1934. The current house was designed in 1907 by Julia Morgan, California's first female engineer and licensed architect. The Cameron House is a utilitarian, multiwindowed building, strongly built from bricks recovered from the original building on the same site.

The Mission Home's founder, Margaret Culberston, along with several prominent Christian women, established it in hopes of helping the boarders become economically independent. While living in the home the Chinese girls were taught English, sewing, Christianity, and domestic duties, enabling them to enter mainstream society, supporting and caring for themselves. Some girls attended college and became educators and nurses. Many married, rearing families of their own, and others worked for the Church.

In 1895 the twenty-five-year old Cameron came to work for the home for one year—and stayed for more than forty. She took over the superintendent position after Culberston's death. Cameron dedicated her life to rescuing Chinese girls from the slave and opium dens of Chinatown. She and the Mission Home continually came under attacks from both Chinese and Caucasians. Dynamite was planted more than once outside the home. Yet she successfully battled the violence, slander, and harassment, managing to help more than three thousand girls. She adopted Chinese children or was appointed their legal guardian, and they affectionately called her "Lo Mo" (old mama).

The home was destroyed in the San Francisco earthquake of 1906. A new building was constructed from donations by the Presbyterian Foreign Mission Board and fund drives in 1907. Upon Cameron's retirement the mission board renamed the home in her honor. The Cameron House is still used as a Chinese community center and is a San Francisco Registered Landmark.

Camp McCoy: U.S. Army base. For six months in 1942, this installation, located in the southwest corner of Wisconsin, near the Minnesota border, was the training center for Japanese American soldiers in the 100TH INFANTRY BATTALION.

Camp Shelby: U.S. Army base. In January, 1943, after six months of training at Camp McCoy, Wisconsin, the Japanese American 100TH INFANTRY BATTALION was transferred to Camp Shelby in rural Mississippi, south of Jackson. After further training at Camp Shelby, the 100th embarked for combat in North Africa on August 21, 1943.

Cannery Workers' and Farm Laborers' Union: Labor organization founded in 1933 originally by Filipinos employed in Alaskan salmon canneries. In time, because of the fishing industry, Filipinos became the dominant Asian immigrant group in Alaska and a sizable labor bloc as well. Eager to upgrade the quality of their lives, they began to involve themselves in labor union activities. The establishment of the Cannery Workers' Union was soon followed by official recognition by the American Federation of Labor (AFL). Years later the union became the sole negotiator representing cannery workers headed for Alaska.

Canton: Sixth-largest city in China, and the capital and largest metropolis of Guangdong Province, with a population of almost three million in 1990. It is located at the confluence of the West, East, and North rivers and at the heart of the Pearl River Delta. With railway links to Hong Kong and several major urban centers in China, and with the outport of Huangpu giving it access to the South China Sea, Canton (Guangzhou) is the major transportation node in South China.

Canton has enjoyed a long history as a leading maritime and foreign trade center since the third century B.C.E. Following China's defeat by Great Britain in the First Opium War (1839-1842), Canton lost its monopoly of Sino-Western trade and was replaced by Shanghai as the preeminent port of China. The resultant economic depression induced an emigration wave

among the Cantonese, for whom Canton served as the main port of exit and the central point for the funneling of communications and money back home.

From the 1890's, when revolutionaries staged a series of abortive uprisings against the Qing Dynasty (1644-1911), Canton was a center of revolutionary politics. It was the base of the Nationalist-Communist alliance against northern warlords in the 1920's. Canton also witnessed a major strike and boycott against British imperialists in 1925 and 1926 and a Communist insurrection against the Nationalists in 1927. Such political disturbances along with periodic foreign invasion and occupation (the British from 1857 to 1861 and the Japanese from 1938 to 1945) hampered Canton's commercial development.

Under Communist rule, beginning in 1949, Canton's development continued to lag until the institution of economic reforms in the late 1970's. Since that time Canton has taken advantage of its access to world developments through Hong Kong and links to overseas Chinese investment in trade, industry, and tourism. By 1990 Canton's economic eminence in South China was challenged by the nearby and rapidly growing Special Economic Zone of Shenzhen. Nevertheless, with its central location, semiannual trade fair, and concentration of educational and technical institutions, Canton has remained Guangdong's political and cultural center and South China's point of entry for tourism and business ventures.

Canton Bank of San Francisco: First Chinese banking institution in the United States. Incorporated as a state-registered bank in San Francisco in 1907, within less than a year of operation, it quickly became the most preferred bank for nearly one hundred thousand Chinese throughout the United States and Mexico. The bank, however, eventually failed and closed its business on July 21, 1926.

Cantonese: Natives of Guangdong Province in the southeastern region of the People's Republic of China in the broad sense; sharers of the subdialects and culture of the region surrounding the provincial capital city of Canton in the strict and commonly accepted definition; and the greatest source of Chinese emigrants to the United States, Southeast Asia, and elsewhere.

Because of Guangdong's relatively late incorporation into the Chinese cultural sphere and successive waves of invasions and migrations, it is a region of considerable linguistic and ethnic diversity, reckoning among its natives non-Han ethnic minorities such as the Yao and the Li, and Han Chinese non-Cantonese speakers such as the Chaozhou people and the Kejia (Hakkas). The Cantonese speakers in turn subdivide into various subdialect and regional groups. Among these the Siyi (Szeyup), or four counties of Taishan (Toishan), Xinhui (Sunwui), Kaiping (Hoiping), and Enping (Yanping); the Sanyi (Samyup), or three counties of Panyu (Punyu), Nanhai (Namhoi) and Shunde (Shuntak); and Zhongshan (Chungshan) County contributed the greatest proportion of overseas emigrants.

From the mid-nineteenth century, Cantonese emigration was fueled by economic distress in Guangdong and employment opportunities and prospects of wealth overseas. The Cantonese are especially known for their commercial enterprise, regional pride, and close-knit lineage system. Cantonese immigrants have carved out significant commercial niches in their host countries. Regional and lineage solidarity provided support systems facilitating Cantonese emigration and adaptation to new overseas environments.

Overseas experience with progressive Western ideas and institutions and encounters with anti-Chinese discrimination and agitation predisposed the Cantonese to play leading roles in the radical political movements of late nineteenth and twentieth century China, directed at modernizing China and resisting foreign imperialism. Cantonese emigrants (SUN YAT-SEN being the best known) were especially prominent in the 1911 republican revolution, which overthrew the Qing Dynasty (1644-1911).

Because of their retention of family and sentimental ties to their home communities, Cantonese emigrants have sent a steady stream of money back to Guangdong. Since China embarked in 1978 on a policy of encouraging foreign ties and investment, these emigrants have sent a growing stream of visitors and capital investment in construction, industrial development, and school building.

Capitation taxes: Also known as the "Chinese police tax," discriminatory taxes levied principally on Chinese workers in Western states in the late 1800's; all such taxes were subsequently declared unconstitutional. In 1850 California passed the first such tax, the FOREIGN MINERS' TAX (levied mainly against Chinese). A few years later it was applied exclusively to the Chinese, who throughout the period contributed the vast majority of all revenue raised by the tax. In 1859 Oregon followed suit with a $5 tax per Chinese head, and Washington Territory shortly thereafter levied a quarterly $6 tax on every "Mongolian." Eventually Montana, Nevada, and Idaho had similar taxes.

The Chinese challenged these taxes and gradually succeeded in having them declared unconstitutional, as in the early case of *LIN SING V. WASHBURN* (1863). When California applied the Miners' Tax to all Chinese occupations in 1862, Lin Sing challenged the law, losing in the lower courts but prevailing in the California Supreme Court. California argued that the tax applied to Chinese only after they had left their ships and become California residents, therefore making the law a legitimate exercise of state "police" power that did not interfere with the national government's control over foreign commerce. The California Supreme Court relied on the 1827 *Brown v. Maryland* decision rejecting taxes on the sale of imported goods. The *Brown* case held that the right to import implied the right to sell. Arguing by analogy, the California court maintained that the right to immigrate implied the right not to be taxed. Also arguing that the tax would discourage further immigration into the United States, the court held that this restrained foreign commerce, which could only be done by the U.S. Congress. After the adoption of the Fourteenth Amendment, the Chinese position was reinforced, since such taxes were an obvious denial of due process and equal protection of the laws.

Cariaga, Roman Ruiz (b. 1909, Santo Tomas, Philippines): Anthropologist, journalist, and community leader. Cariaga's scholarly and popular media writings on Filipinos in Hawaii during the 1930's provide rich information on their experiences and struggles in both rural and urban settings. Without his insightful contributions, knowledge and understanding of the Filipino American historical experience in Hawaii, particularly from a Filipino perspective, would be substantially reduced.

Cariaga attended public schools in Santo Tomas and later the St. Thomas Academy in his hometown. In May, 1927, he went to Syracuse University in New York to study business administration. He transferred to the University of Hawaii (UH) in 1931 and was graduated with a B.A. degree in sociology three years later. Cariaga then entered the master's degree program in anthropology at UH and was awarded a research fellowship. He received his M.A. degree in June, 1936, submitting a thesis entitled "The Filipinos in Hawaii: A Survey of Their Social and Economic Conditions." It was published the following year by the Filipino Public Relations Bureau, based in Honolulu, which Cariaga directed.

As a graduate student and research fellow in anthropology, Cariaga conducted "short but intensive" field studies in several plantation communities (such as Aiea, Ewa, and Waialua) between 1932 and 1936. He also did a study of Filipinos in Honolulu during this period. Besides research, Cariaga taught a course on Filipino culture at UH in 1937, very likely as the first Filipino instructor at the university at a time when there were very few Filipino students.

In addition to his academic work, Cariaga wrote articles on Filipinos in Hawaii and the Philippines for magazines and the daily newspapers of Honolulu. During the 1930's, when Filipinos in Hawaii had to contend with widespread negative stereotypes and tremendous prejudice, these articles represented an effort to give the larger society a better understanding of Filipinos and their social and economic problems.

Cariaga served as an officer in several Filipino community organizations, including the Filipino Community Council of Honolulu, of which he was president in 1946. He is believed to have returned to the Philippines sometime after World War II.

Caste: Social stratification in Hindu society. (See VARNA.) The word "caste" originated from the Portuguese *casta*, which means "breed," "race," or "class" and which carries a connotation of "purity." In the earliest Aryan writings, there is no mention of caste. Careful study of the Vedic culture and society suggests that caste is a socioeconomic rather than religious institution.

In traditional Hindu society, each caste or hereditary class was governed by a distinctive set of rules and customs pertaining both to conduct within one's group and to contact with members of other groups. While not as pervasive or rigid as it was for many centuries, the caste system in India is only gradually giving way to political and social reforms at the end of the twentieth century.

Cathay: Name by which China was known during the Middle Ages. It is derived from the Persian word *khitai*, of the Khitans, a Mongol people who conquered parts of Manchuria and China during the tenth century C.E. The thirteenth century Venetian traveler Marco Polo is believed to have introduced the term to Europeans.

Cayetano, Benjamin Jerome (b. Nov. 14, 1939, Honolulu, Territory of Hawaii): Politician. In 1986 Cayetano became the first Filipino American to win election as lieutenant governor of a U.S. state. The son of Bonifacio Marcos Cayetano and Eleanor Infante, he attended the University of California, Los Angeles, and Loyola University Law School, from which he earned a J.D. degree in 1971. Almost immediately thereafter he entered government service. He served as a Hawaii state representative from 1974 until 1978 and as a state senator from 1978 until 1986, when he was named lieutenant governor. From 1975 to 1978 the *Honolulu Star Bulletin* recognized him as one of the ten most effective legislators.

CCBA. *See* **Chinese Consolidated Benevolent Associations**

Celler, Emanuel (May 6, 1888, Brooklyn, N.Y.—Jan. 15, 1981): U.S. representative. Celler's congressional tenure spanned fifty years, from 1922 until 1972. During that time, Celler, of Jewish background and a Democrat, earned a reputation as a staunch advocate of liberal causes, including those targeted toward greater immigration from Asia. He opposed the British colonialist policies in India and supported the Indian independence movement. In 1944 Celler and fellow congressional representative Clare Boothe Luce introduced legislation to enable South Asian Indians to enter the United States and become naturalized American citizens. Later a provision was added to increase the annual number of Filipinos permitted entry and to extend naturalization rights to them. The final result was the LUCE-CELLER BILL OF 1946. Many years later, Celler similarly advocated passage of the IMMIGRATION AND NATIONALITY ACT OF 1965, which rolled back significant barriers governing immigration from Asia.

Center for Korean Studies, University of Hawaii: Institute founded in 1972 to coordinate and develop resources for the study of Korea. The Center for Korean Studies (CKS) is organized to enhance the activities of university faculty interested in Korean studies, develop academic programs related to Korea, encourage research on Korea, and correlate the resources of the university with those of state, national, and international scholarly communities.

CKS faculty represent a wide range of disciplines throughout the university, including language, history, political science, geography, economics, sociology, art, music, and literature. While it does not award academic degrees, the center promotes interdiscipli-

nary and intercultural approaches to the study of Korean affairs. It maintains scholarly resources matched by very few academic institutions outside Korea itself.

The CKS aids in developing academic curricula, hosts scholarly conferences, supports research projects, and publishes an annual research journal, *Korean Studies*, and a colloquium papers series. It also maintains a collection of library materials focusing on disparate aspects of Korean studies. Funding comes principally from the University of Hawaii system but is supplemented by grants and donations from public and private sources in both the United States and South Korea.

The center's programs are guided by several committees composed of faculty, students, and representatives of the Hawaii community. These committees oversee such areas as academic development, research, community service, publications, and fundraising. The center also awards scholarships to students of Korean descent who are attending the University of Hawaii.

The center is located in Honolulu on the University of Hawaii's flagship Mahoa campus. It is housed in two buildings whose traditional Korean architecture reflects its purpose and identity. The main building is an adaptation of the throne hall of the Yi Dynasty's Kyongbok Palace in Seoul. The other building is a detached octagonal pavilion based on another Yi Dynasty design, the Hyangwonjong Pavilion. The methods and materials used in the construction of these buildings were a mixture of the traditional and the modern. Artisans from Korea were imported to put the finishing touches on the structures, adding to their air of authenticity.

Central Japanese Association of Southern California: Immigrant organization formed in 1915, in Los Angeles, to address concerns of Japanese in America. The Japanese Associations were part of a three-tiered system that served as the primary political voice for permanent ISSEI settlers. The central organizations represented an intermediary between local associations and the Japanese consulate.

Central Pacific Bank: Japanese American bank in Hawaii, formed in 1954 by NISEI veterans of World War II and ISSEI investors. The bank was granted its charter in January of that year, with Koichi Iida as chairman of the board. By the mid-1980's the bank had expanded to include sixteen branches and was the fourth-largest bank in Hawaii.

Centre Daily News (*Zhong Bao*): Chinese-language daily newspaper founded in 1980 in Hong Kong by Taiwan newspaperman Fu Chao-chu. In 1982 Fu launched San Francisco and New York editions of the paper in North America. Subsequently he started a Los Angeles edition and in 1986 a short-lived Houston edition as well. The paper tried to maintain a non-partisan position in the political struggle between the People's Republic of CHINA (PRC) and TAIWAN. Although the paper attracted many readers during a period when the United States was developing friendly ties with the PRC and people were seeking more objective reporting on Chinese affairs, the newspaper consistently operated at huge losses in the intense competition for a larger share of the Chinese American market. As losses mounted toward the latter part of the 1980's, the paper's management was marked by great instability. Finally when the editor defended the PRC government's position during the June 4, 1989 TIANANMEN SQUARE INCIDENT, Democracy Movement partisans called for a boycott of the paper and its advertisers. Fu then decided to cease publication on September 18, 1989.

Cha, Theresa Hak Kyung: (March 4, 1951, Pusan, Republic of Korea—Nov. 5, 1982, New York, N.Y.) Filmmaker and writer. Along with her family, Cha emigrated to the United States in 1963 to escape political repression in South Korea. This early experience of immigration and its attendant cultural, geographical, and social displacements would come to mark much of her later creative endeavors. In the early 1970's, she attended the University of California, Berkeley, where she studied in the art department, graduating with a B.A. and an M.A. It was at this time that she began to give performances in the San Francisco Bay Area. She also studied filmmaking and film theory in Paris in 1976.

Among Cha's video works are *Secret Spill* (1974), *Mouth to Mouth* (1975), *Permutations* (1976), *Re Dis Appearing* (1977), *Passages, Paysages* (1978), and *Exilee* (1980). In 1980, she edited *Apparatus: Cinematographic Apparatus*, a collection of theoretical and critical writings by various writers on film. In 1982, she published *Dictee*, a complex, multiform text that addresses the question of representation against various conditions of exile and displacement.

Indeed, much of Cha's work deals with social and cultural alienation and displacement. Often referring to herself as a Korean exile, she explores the ambivalence between the desire for origin, solidity, stability, and connection and the sober awareness that in a heterogeneous and ever-changing world, all of these can be only partially and momentarily achieved. This sense of geographical and cultural uprootedness is a metaphor for the very act of representation, whether through cinematic or textual means. Language and film may give one a sense of wholeness, certainty, and control, but for Cha, all acts of representation and reception are partial and ambiguous, and demand a certain submission to an arbitrary logic. Her works are critical meditations on the form and structure of literary and cinematic transmission. In the preface to *Apparatus*, she wrote about the importance of "making active the participating viewer, reader, making visible his/her position." Her works inhibit an immediate grasp of their significance in an attempt to reveal the active participation of their audience in the process of meaning-making.

Chado: Philosophical and spiritual tenets of the Japanese TEA CEREMONY, or *cha-no-yu*. It is literally translated as the "way of tea." The ceremony was greatly influenced by Zen Buddhism, and the famous tea master Sen no Rikyu contributed greatly to its evolution in the late 1600's. The tea ceremony has had a profound influence on Japanese culture.

Chae Chan Ping v. United States (1889; also recorded as *The Chinese Exclusion Case*): U.S. Supreme Court ruling that upheld the constitutionality of the SCOTT ACT OF 1888, which barred all Chinese laborers from returning to the United States once they had left it. On a broader scale the Court found that as a function of national sovereignty Congress had power and authority to restrict the entry of aliens into the United States. Congress could therefore ban immigration from Asia.

Chae Chan Ping involved a Chinese laborer who lived in San Francisco from 1875 to 1887. In 1887 Chae Chan Ping took a trip to his homeland, having in his possession a certificate of reentry issued by the United States pursuant to the congressional laws of 1882 and 1884. In October, 1888, he came back to San Francisco, presented his certificate, but was denied admission because a week before his return, Congress had passed the Scott Act, by which all outstanding certificates were annulled and the right of reentry abrogated.

Chae Chan Ping applied for a writ of habeas corpus to test the legality of his detention for deportation, arguing that his impending expulsion violated the treaties of 1868 and 1880 between the United States and

China. The unanimous decision of the Court was written by Justice Stephen J. Field. While admitting that the immigration of Chinese laborers into the United States after the gold rush has been "exceedingly useful," Field reflected the hostility of white Californians by characterizing the Chinese as "strangers in the land residing apart by themselves and adhering to the customs and usages of their own country." There was "great danger" that California would be "overrun by them unless prompt action was taken to restrict their immigration." The result had been the treaty of 1880, by which the United States was granted the right to regulate, but not to prohibit, the immigration of Chinese laborers.

Chae Chan Ping had, however, been prohibited from reentering the United States. Field conceded that the Scott Act was in violation of the earlier treaties. He held, however, that Congress by later legislation could modify or abrogate a treaty; the last expression of sovereignty, the Scott Act, must control the relationship between the two countries.

Cham: Indianized people of Indonesian stock who inhabited the ancient Indochinese kingdom of Champa.

The Culture and Civilization of Champa. Champa, situated in coastal areas of what is now VIETNAM, was one of the first of the Indianized states of Southeast Asia. Seafaring and trading kingdoms, the states of Champa adopted Hindu religion as the result of sustained economic relations with Indian maritime entrepreneurs. The several successive Cham states continually competed with Vietnam for territory, control of trade, and influence in mainland Southeast Asia. Cham villagers resided close to the coast, tilling alluvial rice plains, harvesting the sea, and trading with peoples as far afield as Malaysia, Indonesia, and China. Cham rulers erected massive brick towers overlooking their seaports and major settlement areas, thus marking the extent of the territory under their control with distinctive monumental architecture.

The competition between Champa and Vietnam evolved into a contest between a coastal trading state and an inland rice-producing empire (Vietnam). Despite the valor and aggressiveness of Cham warriors, who often sailed in armed craft to do battle with their enemies, Vietnam continually gained ground at their expense. By the dawn of the fifteenth century, Champa was reduced to the small state of Panduranga in the vicinity of the current Vietnamese coastal towns of Phan Rang and Phan Thiet. Vietnam finally defeated

the last Cham kingdom in 1471. At that time, much of the Cham nobility fled over the mountains to the west to find safe haven in Cambodia. Since then, relict Cham minority communities have persisted in coastal southcentral Vietnam, on the Cambodian Vietnamese border at Chau Doc, and in Cambodia.

Cham girl wearing traditional Muslim clothing, Berkeley, California. (Eric Crystal)

The Cham, along with the linguistically affiliated Raglai, Churu, Jarai, and Rhade highland tribal peoples who reside in the vicinity of the Daclac plateau, are the only mainland Southeast Asians who speak Austronesian (Malayo-Polynesian) languages. All of island Southeast Asia and most of Polynesia are peopled with Austronesian speakers. Current research indicates that the relict linguistic communities were first established by migrants to the area from the island of Borneo some eight hundred to one thousand years ago.

In recent centuries, increasing numbers of Cham have converted from Hinduism to Islam. Cham communities in Cambodia are orthodox Sunni Muslims. Cham communities in coastal Vietnam are primarily Hindu. Hinduism in Southeast Asia is practiced by

Cham dancers, Berkeley, California. (Eric Crystal)

indigenous peoples in only two locales today: the Cham minority regions of Vietnam, and the island of Bali, east of Java.

Cham Refugees at Home and Abroad. As indicated above, the Cham nobility fled as refugees to the safe haven of Cambodia half a millennium ago. During the Vietnam War (1965-1975), most Cham were allied with American-supported governments in both Cambodia and Vietnam. As a result of the defeat of the Republic of Vietnam (1954-1975) and the Republic of Cambodia (1970-1975), Cham minority communities found themselves in an exposed position in the spring of 1975.

In Cambodia, the KHMER ROUGE exacted a heavy toll among the Muslim Cham minority community. The prewar Cham population there is thought to have declined by two-thirds as a result of executions, starvation, and lack of medical supplies. In Vietnam, Cham traders and entrepreneurs found their business activities severely constrained by the new Communist government. Approximately 3,500 Cham refugees from both Cambodia and Vietnam now reside in the United States. Additionally, Malaysia has resettled nearly twenty thousand Muslim Cham refugees. The Malaysian program for fellow Muslims from Cambodia and Vietnam is the only instance of a Southeast Asian state accepting Indochinese refugees for permanent resettlement.

Cham Communities in the United States. Cham population concentrations are found largely in Texas (Houston) and California (Santa Ana, Fullerton, San Francisco, San Jose). Muslim Chams have successfully encouraged almost all Hindu Cham to convert to the monotheistic faith preached by the prophet Muhammad. Funds from Saudi Arabia have enhanced such conversion efforts. Cham Americans from coastal Vietnam continue to preserve their ancestral dance, musical, and linguistic heritage. Although the Cham American community is relatively small, its members share a dedication to nurture and preserve Cham cultural traditions. Highly cognizant of the fragility of their culture in the Southeast Asian homeland itself, Cham Americans are dedicated to preserving their linguistic and artistic traditions in the resettlement context.

In 1992, the Cham minority area of VIETNAM began to attract the interest of the international travel industry. It is apparent that this region will be increasingly visited as the tourist flow to Vietnam increases in coming years. Cham Americans have begun to visit their Southeast Asian home villages, contributing to the prosperity of once-isolated farming communities.

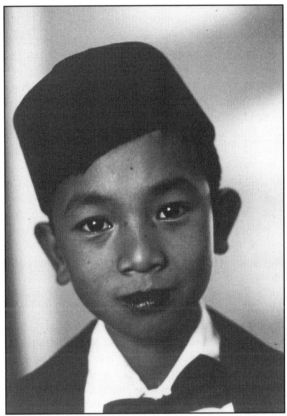

Cham boy wearing traditional Malay hat, Berkeley, California. (Eric Crystal)

Although the largely Muslim Cham community in the United States is destined to remain one of the smallest of Indochinese refugee groups, the Cham are nevertheless an important component of the complex Asian American cultural mosaic. Their history and culture reflect prehistoric seafaring migrations, recall dynastic and imperial conflict in precolonial Southeast Asia, and attest the dynamism of religious and demographic change in Indochina. Several hundred Rhade tribal highlanders have been resettled in Fort Bragg, North Carolina, survivors of a tribal guerilla force that resisted the Vietnamese for fifteen years after American support had been withdrawn. These tribal people are the upland linguistic cousins of the Cham, residing in areas that remained barred to foreign visitors.

The Cham and linguistically affiliated, upland tribal populations are important minority groups in Indochina. Their resettlement in the United States recalls the ethnic diversity, linguistic complexity, and cultural richness of Cambodia and Vietnam, a diversity that is now expressed in American political asylum as well as in the natal homeland.—*Eric Crystal*

SUGGESTED READINGS: • Crystal, Eric. "Champa and the Study of Southeast Asia." In *Le Champa et le monde malais*, edited by P. LaFont. Berkeley, Calif.: Conference on Champa and the Malay World, 1992. • Kiernan, Ben. "Orphans of Genocide: The Cham Muslims of Kampuchea Under Pol Pot." *Bulletin of Concerned Asian Scholars* 20, no. 4 (October, 1988): 2. • Majumdar, Ramesh Chandra. Champa: History and Culture of an Indian Colonial Kingdom in the Far East, Second to Sixteenth Century A.D. Delhi, India: Gian Publishing House, 1985. • Prasad, Ram Chandra. Archaeology of Champa and Vikramasila. Delhi, India: Rammanand Vidya Bhawan, 1987. • Thomas, David, Ernest W. Lee, and Nguyen Dang Liem, eds. Chamic Studies. Canberra: Department of Linguistics, Research School of Pacific Studies, Australian National University, 1977. • Vickery, Michael. "Comments on Cham Population Figures." Bulletin of Concerned Asian Scholars 22, no. 1 (January, 1990): 31.

Chamorros: The Chamorros, who take their name from the word *chamorri*, an ancient term for the highest-ranking Chamorro nobility, are the first known inhabitants of the Mariana Islands. Early European explorers described the Chamorros as tall, athletic, physically attractive, and intelligent—traits that characterize many present-day Mariana Islanders. Their origins, based on linguistic, anthropological, and genetic evidence, are Malayo-Polynesian.

History After 1521. Following European discovery of the Mariana Islands in 1521, during Ferdinand Magellan's famous circumnavigational voyage, the Chamorros lived relatively undisturbed throughout the Marianas for nearly 150 years. In the late 1600's, however, epidemics and subjugation to Spanish military rule decimated the Chamorro population, estimated from archaeological evidence and early Spanish records at between 50,000 and 80,000 before Spanish colonization.

By 1700 only some 3,000 Chamorros survived, confined to the islands of Guam and Rota. By 1784 their numbers were down to 1,583. The remaining ethnically pure Chamorros soon disappeared through intermarriage, primarily of Chamorro women with Spanish colonizers. Many Filipinos, Mexicans, Chinese, Japanese, and Americans have also emigrated to the Marianas and have married into Chamorro families; in any case, anthropologists believe that by 1850 the last full-blooded Chamorro had died.

Guam, home for most Chamorros, became a United States possession in 1898, during the Spanish-American War. By that time, the native Chamorro culture had been heavily Hispanicized. During the twentieth century, under American naval rule (interrupted by the Japanese occupation of 1941 to 1944) and under the U.S. territorial government established after World War II, the Chamorros have become increasingly Americanized.

The Chamorro Language. The 1990 U.S. census identifies the Chamorro language as the first language for about half the Mariana Islanders. Nevertheless, on Guam virtually everyone speaks some English, with the use of Chamorro apparently in the most rapid decline among the youngest and most upwardly mobile: For example, a 1993 survey of 40 first-year students at the University of Guam revealed only one student who considered Chamorro her first language. Most students surveyed, although of Chamorro ancestry, claimed little or no knowledge of Chamorro and identified themselves as speakers of but one language: English.

In an effort to restore the Chamorro language (sometimes spelled Chamoru), a bilingual curriculum has been instituted within the public schools of Guam. Ultimately, however, efforts to preserve the language in anything other than an academic setting are likely to fail. The desire to learn English (usually considered essential for economic success), the pervasive influence of American television, and the need for a common language all contribute to the rise of English and to the fall of other languages, including Chamorro.

Marriage and Social Structures. The Chamorro family hierarchy was traditionally matrilineal. The father directed the family's economic activities, but the mother provided the family name for children (until American rule of Guam began), ruled the home, and managed the family's religious and social affairs.

Before Spanish colonization, single adult males and females lived communally until choosing to marry. Families of newlyweds exchanged gifts, with the more valuable gifts—the equivalent of a dowry—going to the woman's family. Yet the bride remained for life a member of the family into which she was born and, if widowed, returned to her birth family, taking along her children and property.

Some Chamorro traditions have persisted through-out the twentieth century. For example, mother-son ties have remained strong and father-son ties weak. The oldest child, whether male or female, still has many family responsibilities, particularly following the death of his or her parents. Chamorros also remain famous for their displays of generosity and, perhaps infamously, for their obsession with status.

The original Chamorro status system (nobles, commoners, and slaves) discouraged intermarriage between different social classes. By the end of Spanish rule, that system had only two levels: the high people (those of the Chamorro nobility who had married into Spanish families) and the low people (everyone else). That system, while still visible, has largely been converted to the American economic class system.

Diet. Use of corn tortillas, beans, and hot sauces illustrate the Spanish influence on Guam and in other Chamorro communities. The traditional Chamorro diet included rice, yams, taro, Polynesian arrowroot (*gap-gap*), two species of breadfruit, carabao mango, fruit bats (*fanihi*), fish, coconut crabs, and indigenous plants.

Rice, corn, beans, and hot sauces remain dietary staples, but fish, pork, beef, poultry, and garden vegetables are also important. Foods that have supplemented the Chamorro diet since World War II include American fast foods, canned goods, and other modern convenience items.

From the Filipinos, the Chamorros learned to make an intoxicating liquor called *tuba* by fermenting the sap of the coconut flower bud; more potent was the distilled tuba, called *aguayente* or simply *agi*. After War II those beverages gave way to beer and other alcoholic drinks. A much less dangerous traditional drug, the stimulant obtained by chewing betel nut, remains popular among many Pacific Islanders, including the Chamorros.

Demographics. The 1990 census lists about 50,000 Guamanians as Chamorros, almost half the population of Guam. The Northern Mariana Islands sustain an additional 12,500 Chamorros. Finally, between 40,000 and 50,000 Chamorros live abroad, mostly in California and the rest of the United States. Those living abroad usually fall into two general groups: students, military personnel, and other temporary absentees; and retirees from military and civil service, living abroad permanently, often because of the lower cost of living found elsewhere. Many Chamorros from the latter group initially left Guam temporarily, returned, and then left once again on a more permanent basis.

Emigration both to and from the Marianas has created problems in defining the ethnic Chamorro. The

1950 Organic Act of Guam, which allowed all GUAMA-NIANS to become U.S. citizens, defines Chamorros as Spanish subjects living on Guam as of April 11, 1899, and anyone born on Guam thereafter. In the 1980's and 1990's, that definition was expanded further to include not only the previously defined group of individuals but also their descendants, including those born off the island.

Clearly, the legal and scientific definitions clash. A person might be legally (and perhaps philosophically) Chamorro but genetically Irish, African, Korean, or anything else. Or one might have a preponderance of ancestors who were indeed the original Chamorros yet be thoroughly Americanized in language, habits, and thought. For better or worse, it seems likely that continued contact and travel between Guam and the rest of the United States will ultimately result in the loss of a distinctively Chamorro identity.—*William Mata*

SUGGESTED READINGS: • Carano, Paul, and Pedro C. Sanchez. *A Complete History of Guam*. Rutland, Vt.: Charles E. Tuttle, 1964. • Del Valle, Teresa. *Social and Cultural Change in the Community of Umatac, Southern Guam*. Agana, Guam: Micronesian Area Research Center, University of Guam, 1979. • Puyo, Ana Maria. *The Acceptance of Americanization by the Chamorros and Carolinians of Saipan*. St. Louis: St. Louis University, 1964. • Sanchez, Pedro C. *Guahan Guam: The History of Our Island*. Agana, Guam: Sanchez Publishing House, 1986. • Spencer, Mary L., ed. *Chamorro Language Issues and Research on Guam: A Book of Readings*. Mangilao, Guam: University of Guam Press, 1987. • Thompson, Laura. *Guam and Its People*. New York: Greenwood Press, 1969. • Underwood, Robert A. "Excursions into Inauthenticity." In *Mobility and Identity in the Island Pacific*, edited by Murray Chapman and Philip S. Morrison. A special issue of *Pacific Viewpoint*. Wellington, New Zealand: Department of Geography and Victoria University of Wellington, 1985. • Van Peenen, Mavis Warner. *Chamorro Legends on the Island of Guam*. Agana, Guam: Micronesian Area Research Center, University of Guam, 1974.

Chan, Charlie: Fictional Hawaii-based Chinese American detective created by author Earl Derr BIGGERS. Also featured in a long-running series of popular films, Chan became one of the most famous fictional detectives of all time. To many Chinese Americans—and Asian Americans in general—Charlie Chan epitomizes the inaccuracies, misconceptions, and racist stereotyping that have shaped depictions of Asians and Asian Americans in the media.

Biggers introduced Chan in the novel *The House Without a Key* (1925), followed by *The Chinese Parrot* (1926), *Behind That Curtain* (1928), *The Black Camel* (1929), *Charlie Chan Carries On* (1930), and *Keeper of the Keys* (1932). All six novels in the series were serialized in *The Saturday Evening Post*. Adapted to the screen, Chan was portrayed principally by Swedish actor Warner Oland and American actors Sidney Toler and Roland Winters. The popular image of Chan derives more from the films than from the novels. Between 1926 and 1952 more than thirty Chan films were released; in addition, some forty television episodes in a series featuring Chan were broadcast in 1957. Chan was also featured in radio plays and comic strips in the 1930's and 1940's.

The Charlie Chan novels were mysteries with strong elements of romance, exoticism, and humor. While the Chan character was somewhat altered in his various incarnations (the character evolved even in the course of the six novels), much of Biggers' original conception remained throughout. Chan is fat, self-deprecatory, overly polite, speaking with a mixture of flowery and broken English and spouting aphorisms (many of them apocryphal) attributed to Confucius. Rather like the detective Columbo as portrayed on television by Peter Falk, Chan is frequently underestimated by his adversaries.

Not all Asian Americans find Chan objectionable, but the consensus in the 1990's is suggested by the title of a book edited by Jessica Hagedorn, *Charlie Chan Is Dead: An Anthology of Contemporary Asian American Fiction* (1993). Elaine Kim echoes the sentiment in her preface to the anthology: "Charlie Chan is indeed dead, never to be revived. Gone for good his yellow-face asexual bulk, his fortune-cookie English, his stereotypical Orientalist version of 'the [Confucian] Chinese family.'"

Chan, Gordon (b. Feb. 11, 1936, Macao): Horticulturalist. He immigrated to the United States in 1947, served in the Army, and joined his family's chrysanthemum flower-growing business in 1961. The business eventually expanded to growing roses after relocating to San Jose, California. He was the founder of the California Cut Flower Commission, the first Chinese American to serve on the Santa Clara County Farm Bureau, and the first Chinese American planning commissioner in Santa Clara County.

Chan, Jeffery Paul (b. Aug. 19, 1942, Stockton, Calif.): Writer. He attended the University of California, Berkeley (B.A. in English, 1965) and San Francisco State College (M.A. in creative writing, 1973). Chan has authored fiction, essays, and plays, including (as coauthor) the seminal essay "Racist Love" (1972), which deconstructed the ideology behind cultural and sexual stereotypes of Chinese Americans in the American popular consciousness. His play *Chinatown Gangs* was produced by San Francisco television station KQED in 1972, while *Bunnyhop* was presented at East West Players in 1978. He coedited *Aiiieeeee! An Anthology of Asian-American Writers* (1974) and *The Big Aiiieeeee! An Anthology of Chinese American and Japanese American Literature* (1991). A former drama critic for the *Independent Journal* of San Rafael, California (1978-1982), he is a professor of English and Asian American Studies at San Francisco State University, where he began teaching in 1968.

Chan, Kenyon Sing (b. 1948, Oakland, Calif.): Psychologist and scholar. Chan has studied the experience of minority children in the American school system, writing many articles for scholarly journals and such reports as *Dropping Out Among Language Minority Youth* (1982) and *Navajo Youth and Early School Withdrawal: A Case Study* (1983). He has also served as a consultant for children's television, with particular attention to the impact of violence and racial stereotypes. Chan cofounded *Rice Magazine*, a monthly magazine focused on the Asian American community and the Pacific Rim; eighteen issues appeared between 1987 and 1989, when it ceased publication. He is the founding chair of the Asian American Studies Department at California State University, Northridge. In 1993 he began a two-year term as president of the ASSOCIATION FOR ASIAN AMERICAN STUDIES.

Chan, Sucheng (b. China): Scholar. Chan is one of the preeminent figures in Asian American Studies. The author of the award-winning *This Bittersweet Soil: The Chinese in California Agriculture, 1860-1910* (1986) and of *Asian Americans: An Interpretive History* (1991), she has also edited such works as *Social and Gender Boundaries in the United States* (1989), *Income and Status Differences Between White and Minority Americans: A Persistent Inequality* (1990), and *Entry Denied: Exclusion and the Chinese Community in America, 1882-1943* (1991). In addition, she edited and wrote an introduction for *Quiet Odyssey: A Pioneer Korean Woman in America* (1990), by Mary Paik Lee.

Chan is the editor of the Asian American History and Culture series from Temple University Press and

Leading Asian American Studies scholar Sucheng Chan. (Asian Week)

has served as the director of Asian American Studies at the University of California, Santa Barbara. She wrote of her struggle against childhood polio and of living with a physical handicap in the piece "You're Short, Besides!" for *Making Waves: An Anthology of Writings by and About Asian American Women* (1989).

Chan, Wing-tsit (Aug. 18, 1901, Guangdong, China—Aug. 12, 1994, Pittsburgh, Penn.): Scholar. Chan received a B.A. degree from Lingnan University in Canton, China, in 1924 and a Ph.D. degree from Harvard in 1929. He has held professorships with schools such as Lingnan University, the University of Hawaii, Dartmouth College (where he taught Chinese culture and philosophy from 1942 until 1966), and Columbia University. He was, in addition, a Guggenheim Fellow in 1948-1949. Chan has also authored or edited a number of books and more than a hundred book reviews, articles, and abstracts in publications such as the *Encyclopædia Britannica*.

Chandrasekhar, Subrahmanyan (b. Oct. 19, 1910, Lahore, India): Astrophysicist. This naturalized U.S. citizen was awarded a Nobel Prize in Physics in 1983 "for his theoretical studies of the physical processes of importance to the structure and evolution of the stars."

Subrahmanyan Chandrasekhar, Nobel laureate in Physics in 1983. (The Nobel Foundation)

He won the prize for shaping theories of how stars age and collapse. He shared the $190,000 prize with California Institute of Technology physicist William A. Fowler.

Born into an educated upper-middle-class family—his father was a government official, his mother a linguist and literary scholar—Chandrasekhar received his early education at home. After his family moved to Madras, he attended the Hindu High School and Presidency College in the city; he earned his bachelor's degree with honors in theoretical physics. As a young student Chandrasekhar wanted to become a scientist. His uncle Chandrasekhara Venkata Raman, a professor of physics at the University of Calcutta who was knighted in 1929 and won the Nobel Prize in Physics in 1930, became his role model.

In 1930 Chandrasekhar went to Cambridge, on a government of India scholarship, to pursue his graduate studies in theoretical astrophysics; he specialized in the theory of stellar structure. In the early 1930's Chandrasekhar formulated the theory of stellar evolution and collapse that led, decades later, to his winning the Nobel Prize. (When Chandrasekhar first presented his position, it was sweepingly rejected by his mentor, Sir Arthur Eddington.) After earning his doctoral degree in 1933, he remained at Cambridge as a fellow of Trinity College. He joined the faculty of the University of Chicago in 1937, beginning a long association with the school.

In *An Introduction to the Study of Stellar Structure*, published in 1939, Chandrasekhar gave a full account of his theory of white dwarfs. His theory was not however, completely accepted for more than two decades. He has contributed to the theory of stellar dynamics, the theory of radiative transfer, the theory of hydrodynamic and hydromagnetic stability, the general theory of relativity and relativistic astrophysics, and the mathematical theory of black holes. As sole editor of the *Astrophysical Journal* for about twenty years, he maintained the highest standards not only of scientific excellence but also of clarity and elegance in writing.

Chandrasekher has received numerous honors from Asian American organizations and from the government of India in recognition of his scientific achievements.

Chang, Diana (b. 1934, New York, N.Y.): Novelist, poet, and painter. The daughter of a Chinese father and a Eurasian mother, Chang was born in the United States but spent much of her childhood in China with her mother. She was graduated from Barnard College in 1949. Among her many novels are *The Frontiers of Love* (1956), *A Woman of Thirty* (1959), and *Eye to Eye* (1974). Her books of poetry include *The Horizon Is Definitely Speaking* (1982) and *What Matisse Was After* (1984). She has taught creative writing at Barnard, where she is an adjunct associate professor of English.

Chang, Edward T.: Scholar. Chang, who holds a doctorate in ethnic studies from the University of California, Berkeley, has taught at several California universities and is currently an assistant professor of ethnic studies at the University of California, Riverside. Much of his scholarly work has focused on interethnic relations, particularly KOREAN AMERICAN-AFRICAN AMERICAN RELATIONS—the subject of his Ph.D. dissertation, "New Urban Crisis: Korean-Black Conflicts in Los Angeles" (1990). He published a Korean-language book, *Who Are the African Americans?* (1993), to foster greater understanding of African Americans and their history. Chang was the guest editor of *Amerasia Journal* 19, no. 2 (1993), a special issue entitled "Los Angeles—Struggles Toward a Multiethnic Community."

Chang, Gordon (b. June 19, 1948, Hong Kong): Scholar. A member of the Stanford University history department, he has specialized in U.S.-China relations and foreign policy and is the author of *Friends and Enemies: The United States, China, and the Soviet Union, 1948-1972* (1990). In 1988 he participated in symposia in what was then the Soviet Union and in Korea. Before coming to Stanford he taught Asian American Studies and history at the University of California, Berkeley, and the University of California, Irvine.

Chang, John M. (Chang Myon; Aug. 28, 1899, Seoul, Korea—June, 1966, Seoul, Republic of Korea): Politician. Educated in the United States, he led the student revolution that overthrew Syngman RHEE's twelve-year regime in South Korea. He was the prime minister of the subsequent Second Republic from 1960 to May, 1961, when Park Chung Hee seized power by means of a military coup.

Chang, Michael (b. Feb. 22, 1972, Hoboken, N.J.): Tennis player. Chang was born to Chinese parents who had immigrated to the United States. He began playing Ping-Pong as a small child and soon moved on to

Michael Chang shot to worldwide fame in 1989 as the youngest men's player ever to capture the prestigious French Open tennis championship. (AP/Wide World Photos)

tennis. After moving with his family to California, Michael began training seriously with his father and worked with several tennis coaches. At the age of fifteen, he won a match at the U.S. National Junior Championships; at age sixteen, he turned professional. In 1989 Chang became the youngest male player ever to win the French Open and the first American to do so in thirty-four years. That same year he was the youngest player to compete on center court at Wimbledon. In 1990 Chang helped lead the U.S. team to a Davis Cup championship.

Chang, Yum Sinn (Mar. 11, 1888, Guangdong Province, China—Sept. 13, 1966): Educator. He became one of the first two instructors (1911-1915) and later principal (1915-1966) of Mun Lun School in Honolulu, Hawaii. He served as board chair (1961-1963) and managing editor (1941-1961) of *New China Daily Press*, a paper published by the Bow Wong Wui (society to Protect the Emperor); as president of the Oo Shak Village Club; and as adviser to the Sam Heong Village Club and the Chinese Education Association of Hawaii.

Chang Chan v. Nagle (1925): U.S. Supreme Court ruling that denied admission into the United States to four alien Chinese wives of native-born U.S. citizens. Chang Chan and three other men had married the women in China. The latter then sailed by ship to San Francisco, where they arrived in July, 1924. Without immigration visas, the women were denied entrance and detained by immigration officials on the basis of the recently passed IMMIGRATION ACT OF 1924, which excluded the wives of Chinese U.S. citizens if the former were lawfully ineligible for citizenship.

The Supreme Court agreed, citing applicable federal law to explain its opinion. Under the CHINESE EXCLUSION ACT OF 1882, it declared, Chinese women remained ineligible for citizenship; they could not therefore acquire it simply by marrying American citizens. Moreover, under the CABLE ACT of 1922 and the Immigration Act of 1924, such wives were not entitled to admission to the United States.

Chang In-hwan (Mar. 30, 1875, North Pyongan Province, Korea—May 22, 1930, San Francisco, Calif.): Political activist. One of the first wave of Korean immigrants who came to Hawaii as plantation laborers, Chang moved to San Francisco in 1905, where he became active in the Korean independence movement. In 1908, Chang joined other outraged Koreans in San Francisco to counter statements made by Durham White Stevens, an American who had become a foreign affairs adviser to the Korean puppet government installed by Japan. During a struggle between a fellow activist and Stevens, Chang shot and killed Stevens. Despite Chang's plea that he was acting on behalf of Korean independence, he was convicted of murder and sentenced to twenty-five years in San Quentin prison. After serving ten years, he was released in 1919.

Chao, Elaine L. (b. 1954, Taiwan): Government official and business executive. After earning an M.B.A. degree from Harvard University in 1979, she worked for Gulf Oil and Citicorp before entering government service full time in 1986. She served as chair of the Federal Maritime Commission in 1988 and as deputy secretary of transportation from 1989 until 1991, when she left to become director of the Peace Corps. In 1992 she became president of the United Way.

Elaine L. Chao. (Asian Week)

Chao, Rosalind (b. Orange County, Calif.): Actor. She has enjoyed a number of stage, television, and screen roles during her career. She was a regular cast member in such series as *AfterMASH* (1983-1984) and *Star Trek: The Next Generation* (1987-1994). Her feature film roles include *Thousand Pieces of Gold* (1991) and *The Joy Luck Club* (1993).

Chao, Stephen (b. Ann Arbor, Mich.): Entertainment producer and executive. Chao gained a measure of recognition as an innovative but controversial programmer for the Fox network. He is the youngest of three sons born into a middle-class family descended from the Song Dynasty (960-1279 C.E.). His father was an engineer and a physicist at the Massachusetts Institute of Technology (MIT); his mother is a professor of American literature at Bennington College, Vermont. Chao's maternal grandfather had served as China's economic minister to the United States during the 1940's and 1950's.

After attending Phillips Exeter Academy on a scholarship, Chao majored in classics at Harvard, graduating cum laude in 1977. Following a two-year stint as a reporter for the *National Enquirer*, he went back to Harvard, earned an M.B.A. degree, and spent a year and a half as an investment banker. He attempted without success to land a job with a major Hollywood film studio before being hired by Australian media baron Rupert Murdoch and assigned to the mergers and acquisitions unit of Murdoch's Fox News Corporation.

About two years later, Murdoch transferred Chao to the Fox Television Studios in Los Angeles, placing him at the disposal of Barry Diller, then head of Twentieth Century-Fox Film Corporation. Under Diller's mentorship, Chao was told to develop innovative, low-budget television shows. After a few false starts, Chao responded by coming up with such hits as *America's Most Wanted* (1988-   ) and *Cops* (1989-   ), reality-based crime-solving programs that scored high with the younger audiences to which the fledgling network was targeted and revived its ailing prime-time lineup. Other inventions of his, such as *Studs* (a dating-game show), were tagged as trashy and vulgar and despite generating millions of dollars in revenue were eventually cancelled. Programs such as these helped ensure the Fox network's public image as brassy and profane—qualities not unlike those attributed to Chao during his rapid trip up the corporate ladder. As an executive, he attracted a reputation for being brilliant but arrogant, deliberately unconventional, and absolutely uninhibited in his personal management style. In the spring of 1992 he was made president of Fox television and news.

Chao's brief tenure at the top ended in true tabloid fashion, when, at a Fox management conference in Aspen in 1992, he was summarily dismissed after hiring a male model to strip naked in front of assembled executives and their wives. In 1993 he signed a deal to produce independent films for Twentieth Century-Fox. That year he was also hired by Diller to develop programming for Q2, the proposed cable home-shopping channel.

Chao, Yuen Ren (Nov. 3, 1892, Tianjin, China): Scholar. Graduated with a Ph.D. from Harvard University in 1918, he was a professor of East Asian Languages at the University of California, Berkeley, until his retirement in 1960. A specialist in Chinese grammar and logic, he also taught at Cornell University, Harvard University, the University of Hawaii, and Yale University and authored numerous books, including *A Grammar of Spoken Chinese* (1968) and *Language and Symbolic Systems* (1968).

Berkeley professor emeritus Yuen Ren Chao in a photograph taken in 1966. (Asian Week)

Chap chae: Korean entrée consisting of sautéed rice noodles mixed with soy sauce, shredded beef, dried mushrooms, black pepper, sugar, sesame oil, sesame seeds, and shredded vegetables such as carrots, spinach, onions, and scallions.

Char, Tin-Yuke (July 4, 1905, Honolulu, Territory of Hawaii—June 17, 1990, Honolulu, Hawaii): Insurance executive, educator, writer, and researcher. Char began research into the history of his ancestral folk, the HAKKA, while a student at Yenching University in Beijing. This interest would develop into a lifelong avocation of investigating and writing about the history of the Chinese in Hawaii.

One of eight children of immigrant parents, Char attended Wah Mun Chinese-language school and public schools in Honolulu. Touring China with a group of Pacific Coast college students in 1925 and visiting his family's ancestral village in Guangdong Province convinced him to complete his studies in China, where he received his baccalaureate with honors from Yenching University in 1928. His senior thesis, "On the Origin of the Hakka," was published as *The Hakka Chinese: Their Origin and Folk Songs* (1969).

Thereafter he served in administrative and teaching positions at Lingnan University, Canton, and the University of Hawaii, Honolulu. His marriage to Wai Jane Chun in 1934 would produce four children and begin an intellectual partnership and collaboration as well.

Char began his insurance career as a field representative for Home Insurance Company in 1939. In 1952 he became a member of the Chartered Property and Casualty Underwriters, the first person in Hawaii to achieve this distinction. After retiring as president of Continental Insurance Agency of Hawaii in 1969, he devoted himself to community service, research, and writing. He was instrumental in founding the Hawaii Chinese History Center, incorporated in 1971.

In addition to his autobiography, *The Bamboo Path: Life and Writings of a Chinese in Hawaii* (1977), he compiled and edited *The Sandalwood Mountains: Readings and Stories of the Early Chinese in Hawaii* (1975). With his wife he also compiled and coedited *Chinese Historic Sites and Pioneer Families of the Island of Hawaii* (1983) and *Chinese Historic Sites and Pioneer Families of Rural Oahu* (1988).

Char and his wife were supporters and benefactors of Kapiolani Community College in Honolulu. The Tin-Yuke and Wai Jane Char Asian and Pacific Reading Room in the college's library commemorates their patronage.

Chee Kung Tong (Zhigongtang; Hongmen; Heaven and Earth Society; Sanhehui; Sandianhui; Triads): Secret society aiming to overthrow the Manchu regime and restore the Ming Dynasty in China. Membership was widespread in southern China. Members were among early emigrants going abroad, to which was added those fleeing Manchu retribution after the defeat of the Red Turbans and the Taiping Rebellion during the 1850's and 1860's.

Triad lodges existed in San Francisco and in mining camps by the early 1850's. Away from China, the founding political ideals of the organization became secondary as some members engaged in activities on the borderline of social respectability. In 1854 the TRIADS first came to public attention in San Francisco after they had been accused of extortion and police had raided their clubhouse, seizing documents and paraphernalia. In various localities conflicts also erupted as rival lodges vied for control of gambling and prostitution interests.

As Chinese moved throughout the West, into Canada, and east of the Rockies, Triad lodges sprang up wherever there were concentrations of Chinese. Beginning with the 1870's and accelerating in the 1880's and 1890's, however, highbinder tongs that adopted the rituals but not the political objectives of the early Triads gradually eroded the power of the Triads as a whole. In Hawaii and the rest of the Americas, however, secret society lodges remained part of the Triad system.

Early Triad lodges used a number of different names. The name Chee Kung Tong appears to have been a late development, perhaps as late as the 1860's, and for many years was not universally used. When SUN YAT-SEN came to San Francisco in 1904 and won Chee Kung Tong support for the national revolution, the organization reaffirmed its founding political objectives. The group reorganized, ordering all lodges on the U.S. mainland to use the name Chee Kung Tong. By 1919 several Hawaii Triad lodges, but not all, had also changed to this name. During this period the re-politicized Triads also established a network of news organs in the Americas and in Hawaii. After establishment of the republican government in China, the Chee Kung Tong had a falling out with the Guomindang. As the GUOMINDANG rose to power in China, the Chee Kung Tong declined. The latter organized into a political party attempting to play a greater role in China, but without much success. Chee Kung Tong news organs ceased publication one by one, in Hawaii by 1929, in the continental United States by 1966, and in Canada by 1992.

Cheema, Boona: Community leader. Cheema, a Sikh, immigrated to the United States, settling in the San Francisco Bay Area in California, where she organized support services for homeless people. For this project, which served as a model for similar efforts, she was cited by U.S. president George Bush as one of the "thousand points of light" during his nomination acceptance speech at the Republican National Convention in 1988.

Chen, Jack (Bernard Ivan Felix Acham; b. July 2, 1908, Port-of-Spain, Trinidad): Writer. A founding member, in 1983, of the Pear Garden in the West, the San Francisco American Chinese Opera and Performing Arts Center, he is the second son of Eugene Chen, former foreign affairs adviser to Sun Yat-sen. An authority on Sino-American relations, he has published fifteen books, including *New Earth* (1957), *A Year in Upper Felicity* (1973), *Inside the Cultural Revolution* (1975), and *The Chinese of America* (1980).

Chen, Joan (b. Apr. 26, 1961, Shanghai, People's Republic of China): Actor. She has performed in many films, including *Blade Runner* (1982) and *The Last Emperor* (1987), with starring roles in *Heaven and Earth* (1993) and *Golden Gate* (1994). She was a regular on the television series *Twin Peaks* (1990-1991).

Chen, King C. (Oct. 24, 1926, Fujian Province, China—June 9, 1992, Newark, N.J.): Scholar. A professor of political science at Rutgers University for twenty-four years, Chen specialized in Asian political affairs and international relations. A 1948 graduate of National Chengchi University in Nanjing, he fled to Taiwan during the Communist revolution before receiving a scholarship to study in the United States. He attended the University of Virginia and Pennsylvania State University, from which he earned a doctorate in political science in 1962. Eventually, he became a naturalized American citizen. Chen also served as an adviser to the U.S. State Department, on the editorial boards of *Asian Affairs* and the *Central Daily News* in Taipei, and as president of the Chinese-American Academic and Professional Society. His books include *Vietnam and China, 1938-1954* (1969), *China's War Against Vietnam, 1979* (1987), and *China's Policy Toward Taiwan* (1990).

Chen, Lily Lee (b. May 27, 1936, Tianjin, China): Politician. She served as mayor of Monterey Park,

Joan Chen has scored a number of high-profile roles in assorted Hollywood productions since emigrating from her native China to the United States. (AP/Wide World Photos)

California, from November, 1983, until September, 1984—the first Chinese American woman ever to serve as mayor of a U.S. city. She has also served as president of the CHINESE AMERICAN DEMOCRATIC CLUB and the Chinese American Political Action Committee, a planning committee member of the 1984 Democratic National Convention, and national president of the ORGANIZATION OF CHINESE AMERICAN WOMEN (OCAW).

Cheng, Lucie: Scholar. An associate professor of sociology and director of the Center for Pacific Rim Studies at the University of California, Los Angeles, Cheng, formerly known as Lucie Cheng Hirata, served as director of the university's Asian American Studies Center, and coedited the book *Labor Immigration Under Capitalism* (1984).

Chennault, Anna C. (Chen Xiangmei; June 23, 1925, Beijing, China): Chinese journalist and American political lobbyist. The wife of American aviator Claire Lee Chennault, the legendary commander of the Flying Tigers in China during World War II (1939-1945), she was a prominent member of the China lobby in the United States during the Cold War.

Chennault came from a well-to-do cosmopolitan family. Both her father and her maternal grandfather served in the Chinese diplomatic corps. She grew up in Beijing and, after 1935, in Hong Kong. During World War II, she attended Lingnan University at its refugee campus in Guilin, Guangxi; after her graduation in 1943, she worked for the Chinese Central News Agency as a correspondent in Kunming and, after the war, in Shanghai. It was in Kunming that she met her husband. They married in 1947 in Shanghai, where he headed an airline, the Civil Air Transport (CAT), for which she subsequently did public-relations work. She first came to the United States in 1948, soon after her marriage, and became a naturalized citizen in 1950. Until her husband's death in 1958, however, she and her family spent most of their time in Taipei, Taiwan, to which they had evacuated following the Communist takeover of the mainland and where both continued to work for CAT.

As a widow, Chennault resettled in Washington, D.C., where she soon established herself, under the tutelage of influential attorney Thomas G. Corcoran, as a lobbyist. She also became active in Republican Party politics and emerged during the Nixon era as one of the capital city's leading hostesses. She used her political connections especially on behalf of the Chi-

Distinguished reporter and lobbyist Anna C. Chennault, also a published author. (Asian Week)

nese Nationalists on Taiwan and the similarly anticommunist regime in South Vietnam. Despite her ties to President Richard M. Nixon, she opposed his efforts to normalize relations with the People's Republic of China. Eventually, however, she too came to terms with the Communists. In 1981, she returned to Beijing, her birthplace, for the first time since the late 1940's and was accorded a well-publicized reception with China's paramount leader, Deng Xiaoping. Thereafter, she served as an intermediary between the mainland and Taiwan.

Chennault wrote a number of books in English and Chinese. Her English-language writings include the autobiographical works *A Thousand Springs* (1962) and *The Education of Anna* (1980). Her Chinese-language books, published under her Chinese name, include collections of essays written over the years for various Taiwanese newspapers.

Cherry Blossom Festivals: Yearly spring celebrations that typically coincide with the blooming of cherry trees at selected locations, often public parks or gardens.

The ephemeral beauty of the short-lived *sakura*, or cherry blossom, has long been valued in Japan. Since they bloom so briefly and then scatter their petals over the ground or water, cherry blossoms have traditionally been seen as reflecting the Buddhist truth of the

San Francisco's Cherry Blossom Festival celebrates the beauty and transience of Japan's national flower by honoring children. Symbolic of youth, the sakura, *or cherry blossom, blooms fleetingly before spring breezes carry them away.* (San Francisco Convention and Visitors Bureau)

impermanence of all life, and the form and color of the delicate flowers are thought to reflect the traditional Japanese values of simplicity and purity.

One of the oldest flowers in Japan, the cherry is mentioned in historical and poetic texts dating back to as early as the eighth century. One poetry anthology from the late eighth century contains about forty poems praising the cherry tree and its blossoms. Over time the cherry blossom became thoroughly identified with Japanese philosophical and aesthetic traditions.

Annual organized flower-viewing (*hanami*) parties have existed since the reign of Emperor Saga in the Heian period (794-1185), and at this time the word for flower, *hana*, simply came to mean *sakura*, the cherry blossom. The custom of cherry blossom viewing became increasingly popular among the aristocratic classes in subsequent eras and by the Edo period (1600-1868) had spread to the common people.

In modern Japan picnicking under blossoming cherry trees with friends and coworkers is still a popular activity during the month of April. Radio and television stations broadcast hourly reports on local blossoming trees, and trains and other forms of transportation can become packed with people on their way to areas especially noted for cherry viewing. Some of these sites, such as Bizan Park in Tokushima, Maruyama Park in Kyoto, Mount Yoshino in Nara, and Ueno Park in Tokyo, boast a thousand or more trees in beautiful settings. Other spots are famous for very old or unusual trees.

Many of the different varieties of cherry trees around the world were introduced from Japan. It is said that saplings were transported to Europe from Japan by a Swedish botanist in 1822. The most famous trees taken to the United States are the more than one thousand given to the city of Washington, D.C., by the mayor of Tokyo in 1909. Washington's annual spring festival commemorates the blossoming of the Japanese cherry trees first planted along the Tidal Basin. Similar celebrations are held in other U.S. cities such as San Francisco and may include Japanese foods, tea ceremonies, flower arrangements, bonsai displays, dancing and other art forms, and parades.

Cheung, King-Kok: Scholar. Raised in Hong Kong, where she began college, Cheung continued her education in the United States, receiving a Ph.D. in English at the University of California, Berkeley. With Stan Yogi, she coauthored *Asian American Literature: An Annotated Bibliography* (1988), a pioneering work that has been invaluable to scholars and students in the

field. Her book *Articulate Silences: Hisaye Yamamoto, Maxine Hong Kingston, Joy Kogawa* was published in 1993. Cheung edited *"Seventeen Syllables"* (1994) by Hisaye Yamamoto, a volume in the series Women Writers: Texts and Contexts, published by Rutgers University Press. In addition to two stories by Yamamoto, the volume includes critical essays and other materials, including an interview with the author, conducted by Cheung, who also contributed an introduction and one of the critical essays. An associate professor in the English department at the University of California, Los Angeles (UCLA), Cheung has served as associate director of UCLA's ASIAN AMERICAN STUDIES CENTER.

Cheung Sum Shee v. Nagle (1925): U.S. Supreme Court ruling that admitted into the United States the alien wives and children of Chinese merchants legally residing there. Cheung Sum Shee and her children sailed from China and arrived in the United States in July, 1924. They were, however, denied admission by immigration officials on the basis that under law they were not guaranteed entrance simply because of the husband's mercantile status (which was recognized under federal treaty provisions). Were the Chinese wives of lawfully resident merchants mandatorily excluded under the IMMIGRATION ACT OF 1924?

The Supreme Court found otherwise. The act, it declared, must be interpreted and applied so as to preserve the prior treaty rights of aliens, except where such rights have been expressly annulled. Therefore, a treaty provision allowing merchants to enter the United States must extend also to their families, who, moreover, cannot be denied admission under the act.

Chew Heong v. United States (1884): U.S. Supreme Court ruling that readmitted into the United States a Chinese laborer otherwise barred from reentry under recently enacted federal legislation. Under an 1884 amendment to the CHINESE EXCLUSION ACT OF 1882, all Chinese laborers leaving the United States had to present a federal certificate of residence in order to be readmitted. Chew Heong left the United States for Hawaii in 1881, before passage of the 1882 act, remaining there until September, 1884, after passage of the amendment. Upon arrival in San Francisco, he was denied entry for lack of a certificate—which, being out of the country, he could not in any event have obtained in time.

In this first legal challenge to the Chinese exclusion law, the Supreme Court found for the plaintiff. The

Chiang Kai-shek visits troops of the Chinese national army in 1952. (National Archives)

justices agreed with the contention of Chew's attorneys that ANGELL'S TREATY (1880) between the United States and China gave him the right to come and go without being adversly affected by subsequent legislation. The Court affirmed Chew's rights under the treaty and concluded that to hold him to a rule enacted in his absence was, under the circumstances, grossly unfair.

Chiang Kai-shek (Chiang Chung-cheng; Oct. 31, 1887, Zhejiang Province, China—April 5, 1975, Taipei, Taiwan): General and politician. Chiang nominally unified China (1927-1945) before being driven through civil war to TAIWAN, where he presided over an authoritarian pro-Western government and a burgeoning industrial economy until his death.

Chiang first gained distinction for bravery during the revolution against the Manchu government in 1911. During the early 1920's he rose to prominence in Sun Yat-sen's Nationalist Party or GUOMINDANG (GMD), both as a field officer and as a link to the powerful financial and underworld community of Shanghai. In 1924 Chiang founded the Whampoa Military Academy outside Guangzhou, which was to serve as his power base.

After Sun's death in 1925, Chiang gradually consolidated his leadership of the GMD, continuing his mentor's unification of China by subduing regional warlords (1926-1928) and purging Communists from the party (April, 1927). Efforts to modernize China during the 1930's were plagued by Communist insurrection, natural disasters, Japanese encroachments, corruption within the GMD, and a Confucian philosophy that was essentially hostile to radical social change.

When Japan invaded China in 1937, the GMD and the Chinese Communist Party (CCP) formed a united front, maintaining an uneasy truce for the duration of the Sino-Japanese War (1937-1945) while Chiang courted American support. In the West he had maintained the image of a liberal democratic leader, but in China he steadily lost ground to the Communists. With Japan's defeat, civil war resumed.

A decisive Communist victory in 1949 forced Chiang to flee to the island of Taiwan, accompanied by 800,000 troops and two million civilians. The GMD presence was resented by many Taiwanese, who had been freed from Japanese colonial rule only to see Chiang and his forces take control of the island. Resistance against the GMD was brutally suppressed.

Chiang Kai-shek, moments after accepting the U.S. Legion of Merit medal from Lieutenant General Joseph Stillwell, commander of U.S. forces in the China-Burma-India theater. (AP/Wide World Photos)

On Taiwan, Chiang established the government-in-exile of the Republic of China (ROC). Accepting Chiang's claim to be leading the legitimate government of China, the United States refused to acknowledge the newly established People's Republic of China, led by Mao Zedong. Chiang promised to one day lead his forces back to the mainland and overthrow the Communists. Under Chiang, Taiwan engaged in a long-term military build-up. Economic development, gradual at first, increased rapidly as Chiang's son, Chiang Ching-kuo, began to exert greater influence in the 1960's.

Chiang Kai-shek continued to served as president of the ROC until his death in 1975, although failing health limited his effectiveness in the later years of his presidency. Less than four years after his death, the United States officially recognized the People's Republic of China and severed formal diplomatic relations with the ROC. (See CHINA, PEOPLE'S REPUBLIC OF—RECOGNITION.)

Chiang Kai-shek, Madame. *See* **Chiang Soong Mei-ling**

Chiang Kham refugee camp (Chiang Kham, Kingdom of Thailand): Laotian refugee camp located in northern Thailand. The camp opened in 1975 and until 1983 housed refugees from the highlands of Laos. Most of these refugees were Mien from northern Laos, although some were from other highland groups living there at that time.

In 1983 all the pre-1983 "early" arrivals living in the Chiang Kham camp and other northern Thai camps were transferred to the BAN VINAI REFUGEE CAMP in northeastern Thailand. At the same time, the Chiang Kham camp was reopened as a humane deterrence camp for post-1983 arrivals from Laos. The status of Chiang Kham as a "humane deterrence" camp for highland Lao (primarily HMONG) meant that conditions in the camp were austere, and little movement outside the camp was permitted. Most significantly, though, these refugees had a different status under Thai law. Unlike the early arrivals, the refugees housed in Chiang Kham were not defined by Thai law as "refugees" but were called "economic migrants" and, as a result, were not eligible for resettlement in the United States. It was presumed by the Thai government that the "late arrivals" would eventually return to Laos under the Office of the United Nations High Commissioner for Refugees' "voluntary repatriation program." In 1987 there were more than twelve thousand refugees living in the camp at Chiang Kham who had this legal status.

In practice, though, some of the late arrivals sent to Chiang Kham under the humane deterrence policy have eventually migrated to the United States because Thai authorities have periodically relaxed regulations governing third-country resettlement. This flexibility has proved particularly important to those refugees eligible for family reunification resettlement in the United States. The Thai government has relaxed these laws because few highland refugees have volunteered to be repatriated to Laos, which in turn led to Thai fears that a permanent Laotian population was emerging in Chiang Kham.

Chiang Soong Mei-ling (Soong Mei-ling; b. Apr. 14, 1897, Shanghai, China): Widow of the former president of the Republic of China, CHIANG KAI-SHEK, and a leader of Chinese women.

Soong was born into an affluent Chinese Christian family in Shanghai as the fourth of six children and the youngest of three daughters. Her father, Soong Yao-ju, known as Charles Jones Soong, was an American-educated Methodist missionary as well as a successful industrialist and merchant. Her mother, Ni Kuei-chen, received a Western education from Bridgeman girls' school in Shanghai. At the age of ten, Soong Mei-ling attended Wesleyan College for Women, in Macon, Georgia, as a special student. In 1912, she was admitted to Wesleyan as a regular college student. In the following year, she transferred to Wellesley College in Massachusetts and was graduated in 1917 as an English major, a philosophy minor, and several honors and awards.

On December 1, 1927, Soong Mei-ling married Chiang Kai-shek, president of the Republic of China. After their marriage, she assisted her husband's political career as his personal secretary and interpreter. From 1934 to 1937, she directed the women's department of the New Life movement, a program of moral reform based on traditional Chinese virtues. She helped to train young women for wartime jobs and organized relief programs for refugees and shelters for homeless children. Between 1942 and 1943, she visited the United States to plead China's cause. Her grace and eloquence charmed millions of Americans and helped to create a positive image of wartime China and therefore gain American support for the Chinese Nationalist government.

After the Communist Party's victory in 1949, Chiang Kai-shek's Nationalist government took refuge in Taiwan. Soong Mei-ling directed the Chinese Women's Anti-Aggression League in Taiwan. Between 1952 and 1966, she also made four unofficial trips to the United States for medical reasons, but she was still received as a goodwill ambassador and personal envoy of Chiang. After Chiang Kai-shek's death in 1975, she settled on Long Island, New York.

Chick sexing: Occupation that many Nisei adopted, especially during and after World War II (1939-1945). The migratory job involved determining the sex of just-hatched chicks, destroying males, and selecting females for egg laying. This occupation was not desired by others, and, as such, it provided an opportunity for the Nisei, who suffered from racial discrimination in hiring, to work. During World War II, chick sexing enabled Nisei to obtain an indefinite leave from the internment camps.

Children's Day: Japanese and Japanese American holiday. Known as *Kodomo no Hi* in Japanese, it is a festival held annually on May 5. It began as a day dedicated to the general health of everyone, and was used during the Tokugawa era (1603-1868) to encourage a martial spirit. By the 1700's it had been popularized across classes as a holiday dedicated to boys. In 1948 it was renamed Children's Day and designated a national holiday in Japan. Japanese Americans observe the occasion by giving gifts and holding the Chigo Parade for children.

Chin, Frank [Chew] (b. Feb. 25, 1940, Berkeley, Calif.): Writer and editor. Best known as a dramatist, Chin was the first Chinese American playwright to have serious drama produced on the New York stage and on national television. Using techniques that range from surrealistic dreams to naturalistic defecation,

Frank Chin—among Chinese American dramatists, the first to attract broad critical acclaim in the United States. (Nancy Wong)

Chin's verbally exuberant *The Chickencoop Chinaman (pr. 1972) and The Year of the Dragon (pr. 1974) are angry denunciations of white racism in American society and anguished studies of the Asian American search for identity.*

Chin is a fifth-generation Californian who grew up in the Sierras and the Chinatowns of Oakland and San Francisco. He attended Chinese as well as English schools; enrolled at the University of California, Berkeley, where he won several writing prizes; and pursued graduate study in creative writing with a fellowship to the Writers' Workshop at the University of Iowa (1961-1963). Subsequently Chin worked for railroad companies, becoming the first Chinese American brakeman on the rails laid by his forebears. In 1966 Chin left railroading for film and television scriptwriting in Seattle. He also did college teaching in 1969-1970 at San Francisco State University and the University of California, Davis, organizing the COMBINED ASIAN AMERICAN RESOURCES PROJECT (CARP), which collected literary, documentary, and oral history materials about Asian Americans, materials now housed at the Bancroft Library, University of California, Berkeley. In 1972 in San Francisco, Chin founded the Asian American Theatre Workshop with the support of the American Conservatory Theatre (where he was a writer-in-residence). During the 1980's Chin settled in Los Angeles with his third wife and third child; there his research in Asian American history and folklore has been supported by several grants (including a Rockefeller Fellowship) and has led to several important exhibitions.

Chin has also published fiction, including The Chinaman Pacific and Frisco R.R. Co. (1988), a collection of short fiction, and Donald Duk (1991), a novel. With Jeffery Paul CHAN, Lawson Fusao INADA, and Shawn WONG, he coedited a breakthrough anthology of Asian American writing, *Aiiieeeee! An Anthology of Asian-American Writers* (1974). A substantially revised and expanded volume, *The Big Aiiieeeee! An Anthology of Chinese and Japanese American Literature*, appeared in 1991 with a ninety-two-page manifesto by Chin entitled "Come All Ye Asian American Writers of the Real and Fake." In addition, Chin has published a number of other important, provocative, and controversial essays.

Chin, John Yehall (b. Mar. 2, 1908, Toishan, China): School principal. He was the first Chinese American elected to a public office in San Francisco, California. As president of the San Francisco Community College Board, he was appointed to the first Human Rights Commission in Washington, D.C. He served as president of the Chinese Six Companies, the Hop Wo Benevolent Association, and the Yee Fung Toy Family Association. In 1955 he became principal of the Chinese Language School in San Francisco.

John Yehall Chin, the first Chinese American to hold public office in San Francisco, California. (Asian Week)

Chin, Marilyn (b. Hong Kong): Poet and fiction-writer. Raised in Portland, Oregon, Chin was educated at the University of Massachusetts, Amherst, where she majored in classical Chinese literature, and the University of Iowa, where she received an M.F.A. in 1981. In 1994 she was teaching in the English department at San Diego State University. Her first book of poems, *Dwarf Bamboo*, was published in 1987; a second collection, *The Phoenix Gone, the Terrace Empty*, appeared in 1994. Chin has been the recipient of several awards and fellowships, including a National Endowment for the Arts Writing Fellowship and a Stegner Fellowship.

Chin, Vincent, case (1982): Racially motivated murder case in which a twenty-seven-year-old Chinese

American was beaten to death by two white assailants in Detroit, Michigan.

Detroit in 1980 was a city with high unemployment—18 percent, as compared with the national figure of 6 percent. During the past five years, about one out of every three auto workers had lost his or her job. Japanese imports claimed a substantial share of the American automobile market and became the target of anti-Japanese criticism and resentment.

On the night of June 19, 1982, Chin, a draftsman at an engineering firm, was in a bar celebrating his upcoming wedding. There he was accosted by auto workers Ronald Ebens and Michael Nitz (who had been laid off from his job). Mistaking Chin for being Japanese, the two began blaming him for the ailing U.S. auto industry, including the loss of jobs. The three exchanged angry words, then Chin left the bar. After catching up with Chin some twenty minutes later, Nitz held him while Ebens hit him repeatedly with a baseball bat. Chin died four days later.

The Wayne County criminal court initially charged Ebens and Nitz with second-degree murder—unpremeditated homicide—which because of a plea bargain was later reduced to manslaughter. (Nitz pleaded *nolo contendere*, a decision not to contest the charge.) The court eventually sentenced each of them to three years' probation and a $3,000 fine. The lenient terms handed down provoked bitter criticism of the presiding judge, Charles Kaufman. In defending his decision, Kaufman explained that the defendants had no prior criminal record and were not likely to violate the terms of their parole.

In Detroit and across the United States, Kaufman's reasoning outraged Asian Americans, who interpreted it as judicially condoning anti-Asian violence. The widespread outcry that followed sparked public protest and demands for justice. Chin's mother appealed to local Chinese associations for help in prosecuting the case further. She also traveled cross-country to raise money to pay the costs involved in bringing a civil

Ford autoworkers picket a suburban Detroit Toyota dealership in January, 1992, to protest Japanese imports. (Jim West)

suit. More criticism flowed from other, non-Asian quarters as well, including the public declaration of another Michigan judge. Numerous media editorials charged the Wayne County criminal court with legalizing murder.

Concerned Asian Americans in Detroit formed the pan-Asian activist group AMERICAN CITIZENS FOR JUSTICE (ACJ) soon after the killing and, supported by sympathetic Asian Americans nationally, mobilized to demand a retrial. The organization staged rallies and demonstrations locally, initiated a massive national letter-writing campaign to members of the press and government (especially the U.S. Justice Department), and raised money to fund the effort. Various other pan-Asian associations sprang up in major U.S. cities and, guided by the ACJ, similarly began to push for justice. Through it all, the ACJ stressed that what happened to Chin affected Asian Americans everywhere and that it was therefore vital for all of them to back the pan-Asian coalition and present a united front.

In light of the acquittal, and convinced that the attack on Chin had been racially motivated, the ACJ also asked the Justice Department to charge the two men with having violated Chin's civil rights. Following a Federal Bureau of Investigation (FBI) inquiry ordered by the department, federal charges were filed and a federal grand jury indicted Ebens and Nitz in November, 1983, on two counts—one for the violation of civil rights, the second for conspiracy. In June, 1984, Ebens was found guilty only on the first count and was sentenced to twenty-five years in prison; Nitz was freed on both charges.

Ebens' conviction was, however, overturned by a federal appeals court in September, 1986, on a legal technicality (errors made by the court). Responding to heavy public pressure, the Justice Department ordered a retrial, this time in a new venue, Cincinnati. The jury, however, cleared Ebens of all charges in May, 1987. Ebens was freed but in a subsequent civil suit was ordered to pay $1.5 million to Chin's estate as part of a court-approved settlement.

The aftermath of the incident and its attendant publicity galvanized not only the fragmented Asian American community of Detroit but also the national Asian American community. Because of the case, Asian Americans are better prepared to resist violence and much more willing to speak out when it does occur. Throughout the United States, new organizations have arisen to monitor and report violent acts perpetrated against Asian Americans and to lobby for the official and extensive compiling and reporting of anti-Asian crimes. For example, Asian groups (among others) lobbied hard for the passage of the Hate Crimes Statistics Act of 1985. Under the new law, the U.S. attorney general's office must collect and publish statistics on crimes motivated by religious, racial, or ethnic prejudice or that are based on sexual orientation. *Who Killed Vincent Chin?*, a documentary film by Christine Choy and Renee Tajima, was released in 1988.

Chin Bak Kan v. United States (1902): U.S. Supreme Court ruling that authorized the deportation of an illegal Chinese immigrant laborer who failed to prove his American citizenship. Chin Bak Kan entered the United States from Canada unlawfully in May, 1901. After being apprehended, he was ordered deported by the commissioner of immigration.

On appeal, the Supreme Court agreed that the commissioner had authority to deport an individual found to be an illegal alien, under the CHINESE EXCLUSION ACT OF 1882. The deportee, moreover, had the burden of proving to the court any claim to U.S. citizenship.

The opinion extended the range of authority of the executive branch in resolving issues pertaining to aliens. In *FONG YUE TING V. UNITED STATES* (1893), the Court had previously empowered the legislature to require that Chinese laborers produce credible white witnesses. In *Li Sung v. United States* (1901), the justices ruled that an alien had no right to the constitutional guarantee against unreasonable search and seizure.

China: Center of one of the world's oldest civilizations, profoundly influential in Asia and throughout the world. The name of China can be traced to the Qin Dynasty (Chi'in, in the Wade-Giles system of romanization), which in the third century B.C.E. briefly ruled over the entire Chinese world. Since then, China has remained for the most part a single political entity.

Geographic Aspects of Chinese Civilization. Like other countries of continental proportions (e.g., India), China is more than a nation: It is also a distinct civilization. The cradle of Chinese civilization is the middle basin of the Yellow River. Blessed with a temperate climate, fertile alluvial soil, and sufficient precipitation, the ancient Chinese pioneered in the development of productive field agriculture, based on intensive cultivation. In so doing, they laid the foundation of their civilization.

Expanding from their original home, the Chinese assimilated the aboriginal population, eventually fill-

CHINA

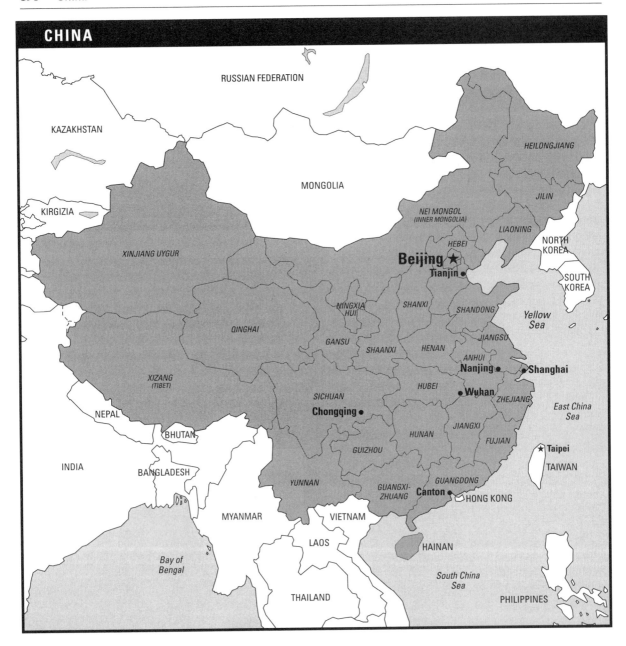

ing up the land within the traditional borders of China. The direction of expansion was primarily to the south and east. South of the Yellow River lands, the vast Yangtze basin offered no ecological barrier to expansion. Initially, however, assimilation was slowed by primitive technology and inadequate manpower. These obstacles were overcome by the fifth century C.E. With a large influx of migrants from the north who brought with them their technology and their culture, the swamps were drained and virgin forests cleared so that the enormous potential of these lands began to be realized. The tempo of development continued unabated in the following centuries, so that by the Song Dynasty (960-1279), the Yangtze basin had clearly outdistanced other parts of China, becoming the economic, cultural, and demographic center of the country. The situation remains the same to the present day. Further south, the assimilation of the provinces of Guangdong, Guangxi, and Yunnan was in full swing only in the second half of the Ming Dynasty (1368-1644).

To the north and west, the Chinese soon reached the

Chinese girl with bound feet. Foot-binding, rooted in antiquity, was not widely abandoned until the twentieth century. (Bancroft Library, University of California at Berkeley)

Worker prepares a Chinese-language typesetting machine. The Chinese writing system comprises more than forty thousand characters, or ideographs. (Asian American Studies Library, University of California at Berkeley)

ecological limits of their expansion. These arid regions with short growing seasons could not support field agriculture; their optimum land use was nomadic pastoralism. In due course, the true nomad emerged. Known successively in Chinese sources as Xiongnu (Huns), Tujue (Turks), and Mongols, these nomads evolved a way of life diametrically opposed to that of the sedentary Chinese agriculturalists in many vital respects. At times when China was strong, the borderlands inhabited by the nomads might be temporarily subjugated. At other times, the northern nomads might conquer parts or even the whole of China. However, due to their essentially different ways of life, a permanent union of agricultural China and the nomadic borderlands was not feasible. With the advent of industrialism in modern times and faster means of communication (railroads, airplanes), the dichotomy might be transcended and a permanent union might eventually materialize.

Historic Achievements. Although intermittent contact was maintained between China and other centers of civilization from Roman times, the Chinese had been living in a universe of their own, little affected by what went on elsewhere, until well into the nineteenth century. Delighting in their amply endowed homeland and well satisfied with their own achievements, they exhibited little interest in peoples and things beyond their immediate ken. This self-centered, parochial outlook is reflected in a popular synonym for their country, *tianxia* (all under heaven) and in their generic name for all non-Chinese people, *yidi* (barbarians).

To a considerable extent, this self-image is justified. With little help from other people, the ancient Chinese successfully tackled the problems that have challenged all civilizations, namely how to organize for production and distribution, propagation of the race, and law and order. In solving these problems, they evolved the ideals, values, and norms they lived by; perfected a family system based on exogamous marriage and patrilineal descent that anchored the individual firmly in the security of the primary group; and developed a sophisticated, literate high culture that found expression in government and law, literature, and science. With their ingenuity, they perfected a style of architecture that combined utility with aesthetic values. Summing up, it may be said that in historical perspective, the Chinese experience amounts to a notable success story: the story of integrating a large segment of the human race, probably a quarter of mankind over the last two thousand years, of endowing their lives with meaning, enabling them to live in dignity and with a decent standard of living.

Much of the success of the Chinese can be attributed to their genius for making well-advised tradeoffs. In the interest of political stability, they were willing to concede to their rulers virtually unlimited powers. In exercising these powers, the latter, however, were exhorted not to indulge in self-aggrandizement but to regard them as a sacred trust to be used for the benefit of the people. This in essence constitutes the principle that legitimated the rule of emperors during the imperial age, a principle known as the Mandate of Heaven. For this reason, among others, the Chinese were blessed with reasonably responsible government and, except for the crises of barbarian invasion or changes of the ruling dynasty, could count on the prevalence of peace in their land.

Much of their success should also be attributed to their mechanical ingenuity. They invented paper, printing, gunpowder, and the mariner's compass—innovations which, when duly transmitted to Europe, initiated revolutionary changes that ushered in the modern age; they could boast of a wide range of breakthroughs in the technologies of metallurgy, mining, shipbuilding, and other manufacturing processes. Their technological prowess together with the productivity of their agriculture and the extent of their commerce explains their affluence in medieval times and the tremendous impression they made on Marco Polo and other foreign visitors.

China's Legacy. Today, the Chinese people can still point with pride to much of their cultural heritage. Their written language, based on a unique system of ideographic signs, is remarkably versatile. In addition to being the vehicle for China's rich literary tradition, it is also a vital component of the written language of Japan and, to a lesser extent, that of Korea. Although much of China's heritage of traditional attitudes and values is obsolete, much still remains valid and in fact constitutes the most valuable part of contemporary Chinese culture. It is from this source that the Chinese derive the character traits that have won them the admiration of the world: discipline, industriousness, respect for authority, and family solidarity. Insofar as traditional Chinese culture, often under the name Confucianism, has been assimilated by other East Asian peoples, notably the Japanese and the Koreans, the

same virtues are also clearly discernible among them.—*Winston W. Lo*

SUGGESTED READINGS: • Fairbank, John King. *China: A New History.* Cambridge, Mass.: Harvard University Press, 1992. • Fitzgerald, C. P. *The Southern Expansion of the Chinese People.* New York: Praeger, 1972. • Gernet, Jacques. *A History of Chinese Civilization.* Cambridge: Cambridge University Press, 1982. • Ho, Ping-ti. *The Cradle of the East: An Inquiry into the Indigenous Origins of Techniques and Ideas of Neolithic and Early Historic China, 5000-1000 B.C.* Chicago: University of Chicago Press, 1975.

China, People's Republic of (PRC): Socialist republic located in east and central Asia; the largest nation (3.7 million square miles) in Asia and the world's most populous (1.178 billion in 1993).

China was declared the People's Republic of China on October 1, 1949, at Beijing, the capital city. The history of the PRC may be divided into four periods: establishment and consolidation (1949-1957), the Great Leap Forward and its aftermath (1958-1966), the Cultural Revolution (1966-1976), and modernization (since 1977). In 1949, MAO ZEDONG was chairman and Liu Shaoqui vice chairman. ZHOU ENLAI was the premier and headed all government departments and ministries. The year 1949 marked the beginning of a major transformation affecting one of the oldest existing civilizations.

Establishment and Consolidation. According to its constitution, the PRC is a socialist state under the "people's democratic dictatorship." The three most important political institutions are the Chinese Communist Party (CCP), the government, and the military. The party formulates political, economic, and social policies, which the executive branch carries out. The military provides national defense and performs functions parallel with those of the government. The party dominates every aspect of the national organizations. Most of the leaders in the government and the army also hold high party positions.

The National People's Congress that meets in Beijing is the highest government organization. Members of this congress are elected for five-year terms by provincial people's congresses. The congress has legislative duties and various other responsibilities. The electoral laws, established in 1953 and modified in 1979, set up a system of allegedly representative government. The people elect representatives, who, in turn, elect the members from the list of candidates recommended by the CCP. The Congress started to

Chinese Communist troops enter Nanjing in April, 1949. Following a victorious military campaign that ousts the Chinese Nationalists, the Communists proclaim the founding of the People's Republic of China in October. (AP/Wide World Photos)

meet annually after 1978. The state council, headed by a premier, directs the administration of the government. The congresses elect the president of the republic and appoint the premier of the state council. The CCP defines this system as "democracy under the leadership of centralism" and ensures that all congressional candidates follow the party line. CCP members are integrated throughout all the governmental organizations and extend their influence through mass organizations. The armed forces have their own unified military commanders, as established in the 1982 constitution. The chairman and vice chairmen are selected by the National People's Congress and are responsible to that body. The Supreme People's Court is the highest judicial body in China. There are twenty-two provinces, five autonomous regions, and three municipalities.

Mao Zedong directed political, economic, and cultural developments in the PRC from 1949 to 1976. The Marriage Law was promulgated in 1950. The traditional authority of the elders in the family system became illegal, and the clan was destroyed as a political force at the local level. The original revolutionary goal of gender equality, however, was not achieved. China is still a patrilineal and patrilocal society. Land reform laws resulted in the redistribution of about 56 percent of China's farmland to between 60 and 70 percent of farmers' households. Two campaigns, the "Three-Anti" and the "Five-Anti," were waged against corruption, waste, and bureaucracy in 1951 and 1952. Mao welcomed technical and economic assistance from the Soviet Union to design the first five-year plan in 1953. After a few years, however, he rejected Soviet assistance and renounced the Sino-Soviet Treaty of Friendship, Alliance, and Mutual Assistance (1950). During the first five-year plan (1953-1957), the overall rate of growth averaged about 7 percent a year, with agricultural output increased to an annual rate of 3 percent and industrial growth to about 9 percent.

The Central Committee held a conference to discuss the question of the intellectuals: Guidelines were determined for work in education, science, and culture that led to a campaign based on the slogan "Let a hundred flowers blossom and a hundred schools of thought contend." In the spirit of this slogan, some intellectuals made suggestions critical of the party. As a result, they were denounced and regarded as enemies of the nation for deviating from the party line. Later, party leaders stated that the scope of this crackdown had been exceeded and that a great number of intellectuals had been unjustly labeled as "rightist elements."

Chinese Communist Party Chairman Mao Zedong. (AP/ Wide World Photos)

The Great Leap Forward. The Great Leap Forward, the People's Communes, and the Great Line movement were projects by which the party intended to use China's rural workers to expand rapidly agricultural and small-scale industrial productivity. Instead, these projects generated economic dislocation. The break with the Soviet Union and bad weather added to the deteriorating situation and drove the country into a dangerous economic crisis in 1958. In 1962 some party leaders criticized Mao for the excesses of the Great Leap Forward. Many people considered the subsequent depression to be the worst one since 1949. Mao was so frustrated that he accused his critics of striving to restore capitalism.

The Cultural Revolution. In May, 1966, Mao launched the Cultural Revolution, designed to replace the party-government-military power elite with more revolutionary elements. His purge of the national and local leadership and his terrorization of the intellectual strata led to violence as Red Guards—students who vowed to carry out Mao's initiative—engaged in factional struggles and power seizures across the country. So serious was the ensuing chaos that Mao was obliged to call the People's Liberation Army to suppress conflicts among rival Red Guard factions and to discipline the unruly radicals. The Cultural Revolution caused widespread death and destruction. The humili-

ating tactics used against the elite and the older generation and the overall chaos that resulted traumatized the
country. The Cultural Revolution was later criticized
by Premier Zhao Ziyang and party leaders Hu Yaobang
and Deng Xiaoping as a "total disaster."

Modernization. After the restoration of the party's
control over the military and Mao's virtual retirement,
Premier Zhou Enlai emerged as the guiding force in
politics. He started a series of developments in foreign
relations, including China's admission to the United
Nations in 1971. To rebuild the state, Zhou rehabili-
tated many party leaders who had been "purged," including former party general secretary Deng Xiaoping.
Both Zhou and Mao died in 1976. Subsequently, Jiang
Qing, Mao's widow, and three allies (the "Gang of
Four") were accused of plotting to have her named
party chair. Within one month, moderate party and
government leaders moved to arrest the Gang of Four
on charges of conspiracy and attempting to modify or
abandon Mao's policy.

Under Deng, China sought closer ties with the
United States, which was considered a source of aid in
modernizing the economy. The two nations reestab-
lished diplomatic relations in 1979. The CCP passed a
resolution for socialist modernization—the "Four
Modernizations" of agriculture, industry, science and
technology, and the military—designed to enable
China to become a major industrial and military power
by the year 2000. The programs involved the decen-
tralization of the economy, the restoration of material
incentives (including limited private enterprise), and
the strengthening of democracy and the "rule of law."

China's population rose from about 540 million in
1949 to 1.178 billion in 1993. Because of this enormous growth, the government instituted a "one child
per family policy." The age-old preference for boys
has led to a renewal of female infanticide, as the unbalanced ratio of males to females indicates.

While overpopulation continues to be a concern,
China's economy has experienced enormous growth.
Exports have skyrocketed, and a rising standard of
living has created a surging market for consumer
goods. At the same time, China is playing an increasingly active role in economic affairs throughout Asia.

Silk factory laborer in Guangdong Province, China. (Gerald Lim, Unicorn Stock Photos)

Economic liberalization has been combined with ongoing political repression. The brutal suppression of the student-led prodemocracy movement in the TIANANMEN SQUARE INCIDENT (June, 1989) drew worldwide attention to China's repressive internal policies. Despite the outcry, and inconsistent pressure from abroad (chiefly in the form of periodic threats from the United States not to renew China's most-favored-nation trading status), there is little evidence of improvement in China's human rights record. The response of the Chinese government to such criticism has for the most part been uncompromising, essentially telling other nations to mind their own business.—*Carol C. Fan*

SUGGESTED READINGS: • Cheng, Chu-yuan. *Behind the Tiananmen Massacre: Social, Political, and Economic Ferment in Modern China.* Boulder, Colo.: Westview, 1990. • Dreyer, June Teufel. *China's Political System: Modernization and Tradition.* New York: Paragon House, 1993. • Hsu, Immanuel. *China Without Mao: The Search for a New Order.* New York: Oxford University Press, 1983. • Meisner, Maurice. *Mao's China and After: A History of the People's Republic.* New York: Free Press, 1986. • Rodzinski, Witold. *The People's Republic of China.* New York: Free Press, 1988. • Spence, Jonathan D. *The Search for Modern China.* New York: W. W. Norton, 1990. • Whyte, Martin K., and William Parish. *Urban Life in Contemporary China.* Chicago: University of Chicago Press, 1984.

China, People's Republic of—recognition (1979): On January 1, 1979, the United States extended formal diplomatic recognition to the People's Republic of CHINA. Simultaneously the United States abrogated its mutual-defense treaty with the Republic of China on TAIWAN.

On December 15, 1978, following about seven years of negotiations, President Jimmy Carter had severed diplomatic relations with Taiwan, announcing the intention of the United States to recognize the Communist government in Beijing "as the sole legal government of China." Ever since the October 1, 1949, proclamation of the People's Republic of China (PRC) by MAO ZEDONG, the United States had chosen to recognize the Taiwan government as the legitimate government of China (notwithstanding the fact that it controlled only Taiwan and some small adjacent islands), out of political opposition to the Communist Beijing regime. In 1971, however, the Chinese and American governments had begun to indicate a mutual

desire to improve relations. The United States invited the Chinese Ping-Pong team to visit the country, and later U.S. National Security Adviser Henry A. Kissinger paid a secret visit to Beijing to negotiate a public visit by President Richard M. Nixon in 1972. The U.S. government agreed to end its opposition to the PRC taking the China seat at the United Nations. After 1972 the United States maintained the Special Envoy's office in Beijing but did not yet formally recognize the Communist government there.

After Carter's election in 1976, negotiations for formal recognition resumed, culminating in the events described above. Some congressional leaders challenged Carter's abrogation of the 1954 mutual-defense treaty, but the Supreme Court upheld the president.

Following the "normalization of relations" with China, Carter signed into law the Taiwan Relations Act of 1979 in order to continue unofficial relations with the Chinese Nationalist government of Taiwan. (See AMERICAN INSTITUTE IN TAIWAN.)

China, Republic of: Founded by SUN YAT-SEN in 1912, it was established following the overthrow of the Qing Dynasty (1644-1911), the last of the imperial Chinese dynasties. The Republican era (1912-1949) spans the years between the CHINESE REVOLUTION OF 1911 and the founding of the People's Republic of China.

Although Sun briefly led the new republic, he was pressured to resign in favor of Yuan Shikai, an ambitious military leader who gradually sought to increase his power. In 1915 Yuan went so far as to proclaim himself emperor. The civil unrest that resulted—still turbulent after Yuan's death in 1916—ushered in a period of instability during which China lacked an effective central government and was dominated by rival warlords.

Against this backdrop Sun's GUOMINDANG (Nationalist Party) began to gain members. The party was further strengthened when, in 1923, Sun agreed to cooperate with the recently established Chinese Communist Party. After Sun's death in 1925, CHIANG KAI-SHEK assumed control of the Nationalist Party and soon brought an end to this united front. In 1927 Chiang established a Nationalist government in Nanjing.

The next two decades in China were marked by civil war between the Nationalists and the Communists, interrupted by the Sino-Japanese War (1937-1945); the invasion by the Japanese in 1937 forced China's contending parties to work together, to a degree, against a

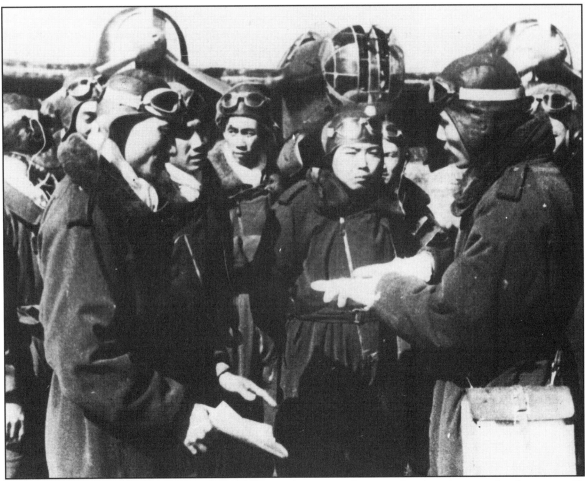

Assisted by U.S. military forces based in China, Chinese airmen were better equipped against superior Japanese odds during World War II. Here an air crew receives instructions before taking off. (AP/Wide World Photos)

common enemy. The Nationalists were ultimately defeated by the Communists in 1949. Led by Mao Zedong, the victorious Communists proclaimed the founding of the People's Republic of China on October 1, 1949. The defeated Nationalists—including about 800,000 troops and some two million civilians—fled to Taiwan.

Chiang and his followers on Taiwan regarded themselves as China's legitimate government, prepared someday to reclaim the mainland. Even in the early 1990's, the official name of the government of Taiwan remains the Republic of China.

China-Aid Society. *See* **Korean National Revolutionary Party of Los Angeles**

China Books and Periodicals: Bookstore specializing in the sale of English-language books, magazines, and audio materials from the People's Republic of China, founded in 1960. The store opened in Chicago, under the leadership of Henry Noyes, the son of Presbyterian missionaries working in China. He imported and distributed books from China, including a million copies of *Quotations from Chairman Mao Tse-tung* (1966), and in the process played an instrumental role in reopening ties between the United States and China.

The U.S. government had, through its Trading with the Enemy Act (1951), imposed severe restrictions on commercial ties between China and the United States. The act banned all trade with, and forbade the export of money to, China. Despite widespread social and official disapproval of establishing any relationship with a Communist country, Noyes persevered in his efforts to set up an import business. The bookstore finally obtained the only exemption from the general ban: It received a U.S. Treasury Department license that authorized the import of publications from China but mandated that payments be held in escrow in a blocked account at a U.S. bank. This restricted license was finally terminated in 1971, and U.S. funds could be transmitted directly to China from the book business.

In 1964 the bookstore moved its operations to San Francisco and became a gathering place for those who had a personal or academic interest in China, including overseas Chinese, students and teachers, government officials, businesspersons, and others who favored opening trade channels between the two countries.

The business reached its zenith shortly after the U.S. government began normalization of ties with China in the early 1970's. In addition to the San Francisco store, Noyes and his associates opened a location in New York in 1971, and a few months later they reopened a center in Chicago.

As the main distributor of English-language books and magazines in the United States, the bookstore has worked most closely with the China International Book Trading Corporation (formerly Guoji Shudian), a Beijing-based import firm.

The enterprise sells its products through wholesale accounts, field representatives, and exhibits at gatherings of the American Booksellers Association, American Library Association, Association for Asian Studies, and U.S.-China People's Friendship Association.

China Camp (also, Chinese Camp): A town in the Sierra Nevada foothills of California (about ninety miles east of San Francisco on the road to Yosemite National Park), which was the site of the first outbreak of anti-Chinese violence in the United States. Currently Chinese Camp has only a handful of residents, but in 1849 it was a flourishing mining camp. These mining camps scattered throughout the Sierra Nevada mountains often took names from the nationality of residents, as names such as "French Camp" are also found in the area.

In the early gold rush days, there were not yet state and county laws barring Chinese from the mining occupations, and the Chinese were still encouraged to come to the United States to work on the railroads. Even as early as 1849, however, opposition to the Chinese as miners had developed in the mining area. During these early days the miners were subjected to vigilante trials before local popular tribunals and to mob violence. The town of China Camp was the sight of the first major uprising against a mere sixty Chinese who were attempting to mine small amounts of gold from depleted mines that had already been deserted as useless by white miners. The fact that these mining

locations had been abandoned did not seem to deter those who attacked the Chinese.

These vigilante efforts were not backed by official legal channels but were often mere resolutions from groups of citizens in the towns. Unlike the later state laws that imposed a monthly or quarterly per capita tax on any Chinese person who wished to be a miner, these early resolutions flatly barred the Chinese from working in the mines or staking a claim in the area.

China Daily News (*Huaqiao Ribao*): Chinese-language daily newspaper founded in New York City in 1940. Principal shareholders were members of the CHINESE HAND LAUNDRY ALLIANCE and progressive Chinese. During World War II the paper developed a nationwide readership. Generally recognized as the voice of the Chinese Marxist left, the paper supported the Chinese Communist revolution and was highly critical of Nationalist misrule, especially during the period of the civil war in China after World War II. Amid the anti-Communist hysteria in the United States during the 1950's, the newspaper and its staff as well as supporters and subscribers were persecuted and hounded by federal authorities. Circulation dropped precipitously and the paper had to go to semiweekly publication in 1963. After the tension between the United States and the People's Republic of China (PRC) relaxed in the 1970's, the paper resumed daily publication in 1977 with major financial support from offshore sources friendly to the PRC. However, in 1989 the paper supported the Democracy Movement demonstrations in Beijing's Tiananmen Square. Soon after the PRC government's bloody crackdown on the Beijing demonstrators on June 4, the paper's major backers withheld further financial support, forcing the paper's management to declare suspension of publication on July 28. Its successor publication is the pro-PRC *The China Press*, which began publication in 1990.

China Fire Engine Company: Organization formed in Honolulu in 1878 for the purpose of securing a steam fire engine for use in the city. Before that time, fires had destroyed much property owned by Chinese merchants in Chinatown. The merchants, determined to protect their lives and property and unwilling to rely any longer on the white fire engine companies, set out to find their own steam engine.

China Institute in America (CI): Founded in 1926 to assist students and scholars from China, Taiwan, and Hong Kong to adjust to life in the United States while studying in U.S. universities and institutions. The institute offers classes and lectures on art history, Chinese language, folklore, geography, history, religion, and Sino-American relations. Studio courses include calligraphy, cooking, music, painting, and *tai chi chuan*. Publications include a newsletter that features book reviews and upcoming institute events.

China lobby: American political pressure group. "China lobby" is a somewhat pejorative term referring to a loose-knit group of individuals and organizations that, from the late 1940's to the mid-1960's, lobbied the U.S. Congress and the American voting public on behalf of the Chinese Nationalist regime of Chiang Kai-shek and against Mao Zedong and the Communists. (See GUOMINDANG.)

The China lobby was a product of the Cold War. It first emerged in the late 1940's as the civil war between the Nationalists and the Communists resumed in China. The China lobby then pressured President Harry S Truman not to curtail American assistance to Chiang even as his forces were being routed by the Communists. Fortuitously, the outbreak of the Korean War in June, 1950, prevented the Communists from completing the "liberation" of China by taking the Nationalists' last stronghold on Taiwan. Thereafter, the China lobby labored, successfully, to maintain and strengthen American diplomatic and military ties to Chiang's refugee regime on Taiwan, to forestall American recognition of the mainland government, and to bar the Communists from taking over China's seat at the United Nations. The China lobby also popularized the theory that China had been "lost" to the Communists because of the misguided, perhaps disloyal, actions of a few highly placed State Department employees and influential academics. The Foreign Service officers were purged, the academics, intimidated.

Members of the China lobby came mostly, but not exclusively, from the extreme right wing of American politics during the Cold War era. Its most active member was Alfred Kohlberg, a wealthy retired San Francisco importer. Other prominent individuals included congressional leaders, notably Representative Walter H. Judd of Minnesota, Senator Joseph R. McCarthy of Wisconsin, and Senator William F. Knowland of California, as well as the publisher Henry R. Luce and the journalist George E. Sokolsky. A few Chinese Americans (the journalist and political lobbyist Anna C. CHENNAULT, for example) were also members. The China lobby did its work through various organi-

zations, the foremost of which, though not founded until 1953, was the Committee of One Million Against the Admission of Communist China to the United Nations. The committee had support from not only conservative Republicans but also liberal Democrats, all of whom were opposed to international communism.

The China lobby began to lose influence when the supposed monolith of international communism broke apart in the early 1960's with the Sino-Soviet split. Also, American popular protests against U.S. involvement in the Vietnam War in the late 1960's eroded the instinctive anticommunism of the previous decade. The lack of organized opposition to President Richard M. Nixon's initiative in 1971 to normalize relations with the People's Republic of China was clear evidence of the demise of the lobby.

China politics in the Chinese American community: During the hundred years between the formation of the first Chinese political parties in North America, in the 1890's, and the first high-level meeting between representatives of the People's Republic of CHINA (PRC) and TAIWAN, in 1993, the Chinese in America bore the burden of having to respond to political changes in their motherland. During the twentieth century, China witnessed the fall of an imperial dynasty, the turmoil of the warlordism of the 1920's, the Japanese invasion of the 1930's, the triumph of the CHINESE COMMUNIST PARTY (CCP) over the GUOMINDANG (GMD), or Nationalists, in the late 1940's, the Cold War and the uneasy coexistence of the two Chinas, and the bloody Tiananmen Square massacre of June, 1989. (See TIANANMEN SQUARE INCIDENT.) As a consequence, the Chinese community in America became politically fragmented, and America's CHINATOWNS provided a battleground in which various political groups jockeyed for power and influence. In the meantime, the United States' hazy and inconsistent policy toward China often added to the allegiance problem for the Chinese who lived in America.

Near the end of the nineteenth century, the two major political movements vying for support of the Chinese in America were the reformist BAOHUANGHUI (Chinese Empire Reform Association) and the revolutionary TONGMENGHUI (Chinese United League). The reformers wanted to use Western techniques to supplement Chinese tradition and proposed a program whereby the modernization of China could be accomplished within the framework of the imperial administration. Their most influential spokesmen were KANG YOUWEI and Liang Qichao, both natives of Guang-

Chinese pro-democracy demonstrators erect the head of the thirty-three-foot-tall "Goddess of Democracy," an adaptation of the Statue of Liberty, in Tiananmen Square in 1989. (AP/Wide World Photos)

dong Province, as were the vast majority of the Chinese immigrants in the United States. The revolutionaries, by contrast, were antidynastic rule and anti-Manchu and wanted more drastic changes for China. SUN YAT-SEN, who was also Cantonese and who had turned against the dynasty as early as 1885, emerged as one of their dynamic leaders.

The rivalry between the reformers and the revolutionaries in China in the 1890's soon spilled over into North America after repeated visits by Kang, Liang, and Sun to America's Chinatowns. The very presence of these prominent Cantonese in America brought China's political problems even closer to their countrymen. Once open conflict between the reformers and Sun broke out, however, the Chinese community was hopelessly divided. At the outset the reform movement received enthusiastic support from the more affluent Chinese immigrants, whereas Sun found his supporters in the secret society CHEE KUNG TONG. In the long run, because Kang and Liang could not directly communicate with the immigrants at large, they remained intellectually remote and politically ineffective. Even though Sun Yat-sen had to wage an uphill and protracted battle against Kang and Liang's faction, he ultimately held sway over the Chinese in America.

Both groups raised hundreds of thousands of dollars from the Chinese immigrants who believed that they were the hope of the future of China. Kang and Liang, in fact, used their surrogates to set up various commercial enterprises in America, ranging from banking and book publishing to restaurants and real estate. Profits from these enterprises were channeled to such political programs as military training, education, and newspaper propaganda. The Chinese Empire Reform Association (later the Constitutionalist Party), for example, established twenty-two paramilitary schools throughout the United States—Kang Youwei personally wrote the school songs of these schools—and retired American army officers were employed to drill the Chinese youths. The party also sponsored a number of Chinatown newspapers. (See CHINESE WORLD and CHINESE AMERICAN PRESS.)

Sun Yat-sen, by contrast, joined the Triad secret society to recruit members for his revolutionary movement. By the spring of 1904 he had become a close ally of Wong Sam Ark (Huang Sande), the chief of America's Chee Kung Tong. Also among the young recruits was Lee See Nam (Li Gongxia), a U.S.-born Chinese who in 1907 joined the Tongmenghui in Hong Kong and two years later founded the YOUNG CHINA ASSOCIATION in San Francisco to serve as a front for Sun's

revolutionary organization. The association's organ, the *Young China*, stepped up the republican revolutionary propaganda, and in 1911 Sun established the Triad Subscription Bureau and was able to channel substantial amounts of money from America to various revolutionary groups in Hong Kong and China until the Manchu Dynasty was finally overthrown.

The Chinese in America greeted the successful revolution of 1911 as the dawning of a new era. During the early years of the Republic, the Chinese American community was both significantly involved in the development of the new China and profoundly affected by its creation and existence. A great number of Chinese returned to China, introducing into their motherland American concepts of technology, management, and government, while those who remained in the United States contributed large sums of money for the construction of roads, public buildings, schools, and hospitals, especially in the province of Guangdong. The brief history of the Republic inspired the Chinese in America, but it also disappointed them, because a strong and prosperous China did not emerge as the overseas Chinese had expected. On the contrary, China was plagued by the turmoil of warlordism and the continued exploitations of imperialism.

The Chinese in America were again at a loss as to how to react to the constant political chaos in their motherland. The Chee Kung Tong members who were waiting for rewards that the newly established Republic could not deliver were naturally disappointed. Triad chief Wong Sam Ark, in particular, was bitter about the way the new government treated his organization. In fact Wong began to criticize Sun Yat-sen and later allied himself with Sun's political enemies, such as Yuan Shikai and Cen Chunxuan. From the 1920's onward, however, the Chee Kung Tong declined in political influence among the Chinese in America, while Sun's revamped political organization, the GMD, was able to absorb most of the young people and reassert its role as a major force in Chinatown politics. Yet before CHIANG KAI-SHEK emerged to become the paramount GMD leader in 1928, several Chinatown groups also flirted with such prominent GMD figures as Wang Jingwei and Hu Hanmin. A small group of Chinese immigrants even openly supported the "Christian warlord" Feng Yuxiang.

Following the Japanese invasion of Manchuria in September, 1931, and their subsequent assault on Shanghai in early 1932, the Chinese community in America demanded resistance and revenge. In defiance of an appeasing government headed by Chiang

Pro-China marchers in America urge the U.S. government to support the Chinese war effort against Japan during World War II. (Asian American Studies Library, University of California at Berkeley)

Kai-shek in Nanjing, the Chinese 19th Route Army, commanded by General Cai Tingkai, held the Japanese at bay for thirty-four days. Even though Cai was afterwards dismissed by Chiang on charges of insubordination, he brought the pressing problems of China closer to the Chinese in America when he visited the United States in 1934. Cai's gallant resistance against the Japanese invaders and his valor made him the most popular hero in the Chinese community throughout the United States. Chinese Americans adored him because, in a weakening China, where defeat, retreat, and concessions to imperialism had become commonplace, Cai's exceptional performance in Shanghai was, to the Chinese in America, refreshing and encouraging. Many American Chinese hoped he would take up the mantle of Sun Yat-sen, but that did not happen, as Cai never had a chance to command his own army during World War II. His warm reception in the United States was, nevertheless, symbolic of the growing Chinese American support for national reform in China.

When full-scale war between China and Japan finally broke out in July, 1937, the Chinese community in America immediately made financial and other contributions to help Chaing Kai-shek's government, which was soon forced to move to the mountainous city of Chongqing. In spite of the fact that the GMD and the CCP continued to wage an on-again, off-again civil war, politics in America's Chinese community had, for the first time in several decades, become rather uncomplicated. During the wartime period, the Chinese community spoke with one voice and held high their one clear goal, which was to help Chiang Kai-shek's Nationalist government defeat the Japanese. Under the prodding of the Chinese consulate-general in San Francisco, the CHINESE CONSOLIDATED BENEVOLENT ASSOCIATIONS, known also as the Six Companies, called an emergency meeting on August 21, 1931, to which ninety-one Chinese organizations throughout America sent representatives. The meeting resulted in the founding of the CHINA WAR RELIEF

ASSOCIATION of America, which included forty-seven chapters in the Western Hemisphere. The Chinese began their boycott against Japanese merchants, organized anti-Japanese parades in major U.S. cities, and picketed the shipyards of Los Angeles; Everett, Washington; and Astoria, Oregon, in early 1939 so as to stop Japanese ships from carrying scrap iron and other forms of raw materials out of American harbors. The Chinese also bought large quantities of wartime bonds issued directly by the Central Bank of China. In addition they gave approximately 25 million dollars in cash to Chiang Kai-shek's government in Chongqing.

The unprecedented unity among the various groups of the Chinese community in America ironically came to an end when the Japanese surrendered in 1945. The ensuing civil war (1946-1949) in China and the politics of the Cold War ultimately cast a pall over the Chinese community as the rising power of the Communists and the crumbling of the Nationalists created powerful repercussions in America's Chinatowns. Chinese Americans, with a population of about 150,000 in 1950, and the approximately five thousand so-called stranded students—Chinese who had been admitted to the United States for the pursuit of specific education and training during World War II—once again faced the question of loyalty and allegiance. Some of them, represented mainly by the more conservative Six Companies, shared traditional values taught through generations and tended to identify themselves with the GMD government, which was, in 1949, driven to the island of Taiwan. Others, alienated by GMD politics and heartened by dreams of a powerful China under socialist government, voiced support for the newly established Beijing regime of the PRC.

Criticism of the GMD in the Chinese American community came from conservative as well as left-wing factions. A strong critical voice was the newspaper *Chinese World* of San Francisco, an organ of the Constitutionalist Party. In 1945, when Dai Ming Lee became the paper's editor in chief, he unleashed a series of vitriolic attacks on the GMD. In a short span, the paper's circulation increased to more than four thousand, and for several years it had the largest circulation of any Chinese-language daily in the United States. On several occasions, however, pro-GMD elements disrupted Lee's office and even threatened to kill him. China's politics certainly had once again spilled over into the Chinese community in America.

Chinatown's left-wing organizations included the New York CHINESE HAND LAUNDRY ALLIANCE (CHLA), founded in 1933, and the CHINESE WORK-

ERS' MUTUAL AID ASSOCIATION (CWMAA), founded in San Francisco in 1937. Both of these organizations were suspected by the Six Companies of supporting Mao Zedong's Communist revolution, and many of their members were frightened at the outbreak of the Korean War, when Washington regarded the PRC as a Soviet subsidiary and a new instrument in the monolithic Communist plan of world conquest. The CWMAA was disbanded in 1959, but some of its members persevered and continued their antiestablishment activities. Another anti-GMD organization was the Chinese Youth League on the West Coast, locally known as the MIN QING in San Francisco. Beginning in 1956, the U.S. Federal Bureau of Investigation (FBI) started a technical surveillance of the MIN QING and consequently caused several members to drop out of the organization. Finally, the warlord Feng Yuxiang also founded his own anti-GMD organization when he visited the United States in 1946-1947. Called the Overseas Chinese League for Peace and Democracy, the membership of this organization rarely exceeded two hundred, and its dissident voice against Chiang Kai-shek and the Chinatown establishment had little or no impact on the Chinese community.

There were, however, many casualties during the internecine Chinatown warfare of the 1950's. One of the victims was New York's *CHINA DAILY NEWS*, which became the organ of the Chinese left wing but also the target of the McCarthyites. Early in 1952, Eugene Moy, editor and president of the paper, and a number of his staff were indicted by a New York City grand jury for violating the Trading with the Enemy Act of 1950. They were all found guilty by a New York federal court: Moy was sentenced to a one-year jail term, and his paper was fined $25,000. Another victim of Cold War politics was Qian Xueshen, a renowned expert in aeronautical engineering and jet propulsion and a professor at the California Institute of Technology. In August, 1950, Qian tried to return to mainland China but was stopped in Honolulu, and truckloads of his books and research notes were seized by U.S. authorities. Qian remained under security surveillance until September, 1955, when he and seventy-five other Chinese intellectuals and scientists were allowed to leave for China following negotiations between Washington and Beijing representatives at Geneva.

Encouraged by the GMD and eager to express their loyalty to the United States, a number of anticommunist organizations suddenly appeared in the 1950's, the most notable one being the All-American Overseas Chinese Anticommunist League, with branches in every major Chinatown. Ironically, it was these anti-communist organizations that had successfully headed off mass deportation of Chinese who had entered the United States illegally. Through a so-called Confession Program, the national Chinese Welfare Council, a subsidiary of the Six Companies, was able to help nearly all the illegal Chinese aliens to stay in America. Only a small group of disaffected leftists who had pronounced affinities for the PRC were rounded up, denaturalized, and deported. It seems safe to conclude that in the 1950's and 1960's, the pro-communist groups served only as a pale shadow in the Chinese community, with Chinatowns totally dominated by the Guomindang and its surrogates, who generally ran the Six Companies.

An increasing feeling of entrapment and powerlessness among the poorer and younger Chinese in America was translated into action when a small handful of young radicals in 1968 formed the Chinatown Red Guards to protest a long-smoldering list of social grievances. Undoubtedly these young radicals were inspired by the anti-Vietnam War sentiment and also were responding to the call for a Great Proletarian Cultural Revolution from Chairman Mao. The Red Guards in San Francisco attacked the blatant discrimination and racist attitudes of the dominant white society. They addressed such issues as the social ills of Chinatowns and the neglect of the Chinese elderly. In February, 1970, a bilingual paper, GETTING TOGETHER, was founded by the I WOR KUEN in New York City. In Philadelphia a group of young Chinese founded the Yellow Seeds and published irregularly a bilingual newspaper of the same name. Both papers challenged the authority of the older establishment and called for a new leadership to solve the new problems of the Chinese community. Because of a lack of funds and also partially because of their radicalism, however, neither *Getting Together* nor *Yellow Seeds* could generate broad community support. The traditional Old Guard of the Chinatowns, who were generally wealthy and influential citizens, viewed such political activism as alien, disreputable, and a threat to the social tranquillity of the Chinese community. Most residents of Chinatowns, frightened by associations with the coun-

Memorial gathering in an American city in honor of overseas Chinese killed in Communist-occupied regions of Asia. (International Daily News)

At the Chinese embassy in San Francisco, California, Asian students rally to protest the Communist government's killing of student revolutionaries during the Tiananmen Square incident. (International Daily News)

terculture, also reacted unfavorably toward the Red Guards.

Nevertheless, the New Left ideology of the 1960's, which rejected white America's traditional middle-class values and suggested a need for violence, did stir a great number of young Chinese to protest. Chinese students took part in demonstrations, sit-ins, marches, burnings, riots, and other violent protests during the late 1960's and early 1970's throughout major U.S. universities. The leaders of student radicalism were mostly American-born Chinese youths who were un-happy with persistent racism and who called for active involvement in both Chinatown and campus politics. The foreign-born Chinese students, by contrast, were concerned mainly with the future of China and Taiwan and faced the difficult decision of whether to remain loyal to the Nationalist government on Taiwan or switch allegiance to the PRC.

In the early 1970's, a movement led by foreign-born Chinese students and professors sponsored demonstra-tions not against American social injustices but against the GMD's handling of a territorial dispute with Japan over a potentially oil-rich deposit in the Ryukyu archi-pelago. Called the Diaoyutai Islands (the fisherman's terrace) by the Chinese and the Sengaku Islands by the Japanese, the islands were part of the Okinawa chain then administered by the United States. When the Nixon Administration announced its intent to return the islands to Japan in 1972, Chinese students across the United States voiced their opposition and began the emotionally charged Protecting Diaoyutai move-ment. It started in September, 1971, when several hun-dred Chinese students and scholars met at Ann Arbor, Michigan, to discuss "urgent national issues." The manifesto they issued denounced the manner in which the GMD government had handled the Diaoyutai is-sue. Soon after the meeting, some 523 Chinese profes-sors from major U.S. universities and colleges signed a petition to Taiwan President Chiang Kai-shek, request-ing that he concede not one inch of territory to the Japanese. The Protecting Diaoyutai movement gradu-ally turned into a campaign for a peaceful unification between the two Chinas. In the early 1970's, Chinese intellectuals held a series of seminars, conferences, and workshops in Berkeley, New York, Chicago, and Washington, D.C., to discuss urgent Chinese matters.

Major U.S. campuses were enlivened by a flowering of Chinese student organizations of various political shades. Publications discussing the future of the two Chinas poured from mimeograph and photocopy machines. Popular topics included the new socialist motherland, China's nuclear weapons and international status, and Taiwan society.

The Protecting Diaoyutai movement and the unification campaign worked effectively to embarrass the GMD government, but the overtures of the Chinese American intellectuals to Beijing were not altogether appreciated. Following the establishment of diplomatic ties between Beijing and Washington in 1979, many Chinese Americans, for the first time, had opportunities to visit mainland China. To their dismay, they saw the misery and poverty of the Chinese people under Communist rule. They also learned that during the Cultural Revolution, hundreds of thousands of Chinese intellectuals had been sent to labor camps, and that millions of Chinese people had been executed, imprisoned, or starved to death. Instead of seeing a happy, smiling, prosperous utopian society, they were appalled that living standards were still terribly low, that party leaders had become a privileged elite, and that corruption had become a way of life. Many believed that they had been misled by Communist propaganda, and indeed, most of the Protecting Diaoyutai movement leaders, having learned a bitter political lesson, renounced all unification activities. Several of them actually came out to denounce the Communist leadership after the Tiananmen Square massacre had become the target of worldwide condemnation. In the meantime, the GMD government refurbished its policy toward the Chinese in America, devising a series of programs to attract and hold their allegiance. It even took effective measures to deal with yet another complicated political issue, the Taiwan independence movement, which enjoys considerable support among Taiwanese Americans. Yet the most effective means of improving Taiwan's image in the Chinese American community has been Taiwan's remarkable economic and educational achievements.

On the opposition between Beijing and Taipei, there is no consensus. So long as there are two Chinas, the unification issue will continue to divide the Chinese American community.—*Shih-shan Henry Tsai*

SUGGESTED READINGS:

• Huang, Jerry S. "Mass Media Use and the Image of the People's Republic of China Among Chinese Students in the Twin Cities Area." Ph.D. diss., University of Minnesota, 1976. This unpublished work provides a good case study of China's politics and the Chinese student community in a liberal American metropolitan city.

• Kwong, Peter. *Chinatown, New York: Labor and Politics, 1930-1950*. New York: Monthly Review Press, 1979. A writer and community activist, Kwong provides insight into the struggle and aspirations of thousands of Chinese laborers living in a semisegregated environment.

• Liu Boji. *Meiguo huaqiao shi* (a history of the Chinese in the United States). 2 vols. Taipei: Liming Publishing, 1976 and 1981. A pro-GMD writer and Chinatown leader, Liu used invaluable Six Companies documents to account for the rise of the Chinese community in America.

• Ma, L. Eve Armentrout. *Revolutionaries, Monarchists, and Chinatowns*. Honolulu: University of Hawaii Press, 1990. A specialist in Asian American Studies, Ma made a thorough analysis of Chinese politics in the Americas and the Chinese Revolution of 1911, in particular the rivalry between the Kang-Liang reform party and Sun Yat-sen's revolutionary group.

• Tsai, Shih-shan H. *China and the Overseas Chinese in the United States, 1868-1911*. Fayetteville: University of Arkansas Press, 1983. The book examines the active roles of the Chinese community in America in the development of the diplomatic relationship between China and the United States, 1868-1911.

• Wong Sam Ark. *Hongmen geming shi* (the revolutionary history of the Hong League). 1936. Wong Sam Ark was probably the most powerful Triad chief in America's Chinatowns in the early twentieth century. This is a firsthand account of his own life and the involvement of the Chee Kung Tong in China politics.

China trade: Most often refers to the trade under the so-called Canton system before the OPIUM WARS (1839-1842, 1856-1860). The Qing government restricted European trade, which was dominated by the BRITISH EAST INDIA COMPANY, to Canton and gave a corresponding monopoly to designated Chinese merchant houses, the Thirteen Hongs.

Historians see the China trade as part of a thousand-year-old network stretching from Japan to Africa. In the thirteenth century, the Mongol Empire had briefly made overland commerce safe, tempting Europeans with Asian luxuries. Mongol disintegration forced Portuguese, Dutch, and Spaniards to sail around the Horn of Africa, creating the multicultural trade in which the British East India Company became engaged. Its legacy is reflected in words such as "mandarin" (from Malay through Portuguese), "coolie" (originally Hindi), rice "paddy" (also Malay), and "junk" (Javanese). North American silver and new plants (corn, peanuts, tobacco, sweet potatoes, and chili peppers) flowed through this network, enriching, transforming, and challenging the cultures that they touched. The Canton system created in the 1750's was thus the Qing attempt to control disruptive growth in an old system.

For Americans, whose first ship after independence, the *Empress of China*, sailed in 1784, the trade evoked romantic images of fast-sailing Yankee clippers bringing Chinese manufactures such as blue willow Canton ware, silks, and the tea dumped in Boston harbor in 1775. In return, Americans offered raw materials such as ginseng root for Chinese herbal medicine, Oregon furs, and Hawaiian sandalwood.

Since China did not buy enough to balance trade, Westerners turned to less romantic opium smuggling and eventually the barbarous COOLIE TRADE. The commerce was immensely lucrative. A leading Canton *hong* merchant, known as Howqua, was reputedly the richest man in the world even after paying substantial fees and bribes to government officials. American profits financed railroads and Western land development. The Canton system, however, also prevented direct contact or negotiation. Westerners became frustrated in their developing desire to sell factory goods in China on a free trade, nation-to-nation basis. The Opium War both doomed and emerged from the early modern Canton trade.

China War Relief Association: An association organized in 1937 to allow the Chinese American community to help China in her war with Japan. Founded in San Francisco after Japan's all-out attack on China, the association channeled aid to China at a time when the United States maintained official neutrality. When the United States entered the war in 1941, the association largely ceased to exist.

Japan's aims in China seemed to be limited to control of China's northern provinces, until the summer of 1937, when this policy changed to that of the conquest of all of China. After major battles near Beijing and Shanghai, San Francisco's Chinese Six Companies set up the China War Relief Association to help the Nationalist government of the Republic of China led by CHIANG KAI-SHEK.

Most San Francisco Chinatown organizations joined the association, including the regional and "family" (surname) associations, the churches, the

tongs, and of course the Chinese Nationalist Party (GUOMINDANG). The China War Relief Association raised tens of thousands of dollars within the first six months of its existence, including large contributions from wealthy businessmen such as Joe SHOONG. The money went primarily to the Chinese government, its ruling Chinese Nationalist Party, and the local government in Guangdong Province.

As the war dragged on, other Chinese American organizations began to raise money, but they donated their funds to the International Red Cross for use in China. These organizations acted as independent branches of the China War Relief Association and were located outside San Francisco. There was one in Oakland, for example, composed principally of church-affiliated groups and organizations whose members were native-born Americans of Chinese ancestry. Their fund-raising efforts included benefit dances and sales of paper flowers in addition to appeals for money.

In 1938 a Chinese American member of the Institute of Pacific Relations (Pardee LOWE) organized a third type of fund-raising effort loosely associated with the China War Relief Association. This one enlisted the sponsorship of prominent Americans such as Theodore Roosevelt, Jr., for a series of benefits called "Bowl of Rice" dinners in various cities. These dinners raised more than $64,000 in California alone.

Also associated with the China War Relief Association were an airplane pilot and mechanics' school for Chinese Americans hoping to volunteer for the Chinese air force and an organization called "Boycott Against Japan." The former got most of its support from the CHEE KUNG TONG. The latter included as members the International Longshoremen's and Warehousemen's Union (ILWU), several American Federation of Labor-Congress of Industrial Organizations (AFL-CIO) unions, and the Guomindang. Boycott Against Japan tried to persuade Bay Area businesses to boycott Japanese goods and organized a picket line in 1939 to prevent a ship's being loaded with scrap iron for Japan. The ship eventually sailed with its cargo, but the picket line inspired publicity and sympathy for China.

Chinaman's chance: Derogatory term implying that one has as little chance as a person from China or a Chinese immigrant. It provided an appropriate characterization of the situation of Chinese immigrants, who, during the nineteenth century, faced numerous discriminatory laws and ordinances that rendered their life in the United States more difficult. Chinese during the nineteenth century were often the targets of hostility and violence on American soil and frequently labored under arduous and sometimes dangerous conditions.

Chinatown History Museum: Community research institution in New York City that collects, stores, and interprets the history of the Chinese in the New York area and throughout the Chinese diaspora. It was founded in 1980 as the New York Chinatown History Project (NYCHP) by John Kuo Wei TCHEN and Charlie Lai, who had met at the BASEMENT WORKSHOP. Its first special exhibit, "Eight Pound Livelihood: History of Chinese Laundry Workers in the U.S.," opened in December, 1984. The museum assumed its present name in 1991, signaling a broader focus. In addition to its collection of exhibits, the museum provides educational and community programs such as lectures, readings, films, and book fairs as well as research facilities.

Chinatowns: Chinese workers came to the United States in the mid-nineteenth century to work in the gold mines and on the railroads. These laborers formed camps there to help one another. Later, as they moved into cities, they clustered into neighborhoods. They maintained the customs from the homeland and started businesses that served their community and, to a lesser extent, tourists and other outsiders. By the 1950's Chinatowns were in decline as the established Chinese American community migrated to the suburbs, but the post-1965 influx of new immigration has revived existing Chinatowns and created new ones.

Why Chinatowns Formed. In the mid-nineteenth century, many Chinese came to the United States. Because few of the immigrants spoke English, they lived in separate communities or neighborhoods.

The immigrants started small stores to meet their basic needs. During the gold rush period, many Chinese lived near the mines, and they formed China camps. During the railroad days, they also formed

"The Street of the Gamblers"—an early photograph of Ross Alley in San Francisco's Chinatown by Arnold Genthe, circa 1900. (Library of Congress)

China camps. In many cities, they formed China alleys or Chinatowns. The camps disappeared with the end of the mining and the completion of the railroads, and the Chinatowns grew as the workers moved to the cities.

All major cities in the United States have Chinatowns. Among the largest are those in San Francisco, Los Angeles, Seattle, Portland, Houston, Chicago, Boston, New York, Philadelphia, and Washington, D.C. In some cases, new Chinatowns have sprung up in the suburbs. If a city has four hundred or five hundred Chinese people, it often has a Chinatown. It usually has a Chinese Consolidated Benevolent Association (CCBA) that acts like a small municipal government and conducts many affairs for the members of the association. (See CHINESE CONSOLIDATED BENEVOLENT ASSOCIATIONS.)

In the late nineteenth century, Chinatowns contained both homes and businesses. A century later many Chinese families had moved to other areas, and many Chinatowns became largely commercial areas. As the Chinese Americans moved to the suburbs, stores serving them began to appear there, too.

Later Years. At the start of the twentieth century, Chinatowns had three major functions. First, they served as supply stations for the immigrants. The stores sold such Chinese products as food, tools, clothes, and medicine to the workers, who ate Chinese food and lived much as they had back home in China. Some stores served as wholesalers, supplying other stores.

Second, the Chinatown became a social center. On weekdays the Chinese worked hard. On weekends they went to Chinatown to meet their friends, shop, and entertain themselves. Some Chinatowns had Buddhist temples and practitioners of traditional medicine. Many Chinatowns had benevolent associations that helped members find work and solve various kinds of problems. Chinatowns have long been centers of commercial and social life for many Chinese.

Third, Chinatowns drew tourists from other ethnic groups. Many Chinatowns contained buildings built in traditional Chinese style, Chinese products, and, perhaps most important, restaurants. Tourists came to see the signs written in Chinese and the people wearing clothing from China and speaking Chinese. Even today Chinatowns are major tourist attractions.

The Development of Chinatowns in the United States. Chinatown growth depended on the flow of immigrants. There were four major periods. The first, from 1850 to 1882, began the building of Chinatowns. Then from 1882 to 1943 laws severely limiting immigration from China, along with the return of Chinese laborers to their homeland, diminished the Chinatown populations. The third period was from 1943 to 1965. In 1943, with China an ally in World War II, the U.S. government permitted limited immigration. Finally, from 1965 onward, Chinatowns have flourished, with approximately twenty thousand Chinese entering the United States each year. One reason for the influx was the revision of immigration law to permit entire families to enter the United States. Not all moved into Chinatowns, but most maintained a close relationship with Chinatowns. CCBA activities have attracted both old and new immigrants. Chinatowns have been full of vitality.

Problems. During the nineteenth century most of the Chinese who came to America were poor laborers, so most lived in low-rent areas on the edge of cities. This is where Chinatowns developed. As the Chinese moved up the economic ladder, the Chinatowns remained. Poor living conditions were a major problem. In San Francisco's Chinatown at the end of the nineteenth century, three-fourths of the Chinese living units had no heat. Many had no private kitchen or bath. Such conditions prompted people to move out later, for remodeling was difficult in the old buildings set in narrow streets.

Security also was a major problem. The Chinese distrusted banks, so they kept their cash in their homes. Chinese businesses generally were open until late at night. Homes and businesses both were vulnerable to robbery. This pattern continued until late in the twentieth century.

Ten Largest Chinatowns in the U.S., 1940	
Location	Chinese Population
San Francisco, California	17,782
New York, New York	11,051
Los Angeles, California	4,736
Oakland, California	3,201
Chicago, Illinois	2,013
Seattle, Washington	1,781
Portland, Oregon	1,569
Sacramento, California	1,508
Boston, Massachusetts	1,383
Brooklyn, New York	1,251

Source: Shih-Shan Henry Tsai, *The Chinese Experience in America.* Bloomington: Indiana University Press, 1986.

The gateway to Los Angeles' Chinatown. (David Fowler)

Disappearing Chinatowns. As Chinese Americans have moved into all parts of their communities, some Chinatowns have disappeared. For example, the Wild West town of Deadwood, South Dakota, had more than six hundred Chinese residents in 1875. They built a Chinatown on the main street. Later, because of economic decline, the Chinese left, most moving to San Francisco or Denver. No sign of Deadwood's Chinatown remains. The trend continues as Chinese Americans continue to become part of the American economic mainstream.

Chinatowns Around the World. The United States is not the only country that has Chinatowns. Some of the largest Chinatowns outside the United States are in Canada, Japan, the United Kingdom, Germany, and France. Their development and functions resemble those of American Chinatowns.—*George C. Y. Wang*

SUGGESTED READINGS: • Beck, Louis. *New York's Chinatown*. New York: Bohemia Publishing Company, 1898. • Colman, Elizabeth. *Chinatowns U.S.A.* New York: Asia Press in association with John Day Company, 1946. • Kinkead, Gwen. *Chinatown: A Portrait of a Closed Society*. New York: HarperCollins, 1992. • Kwong, Peter. *The New Chinatown*. New York: Hill and Wang, 1987. • Wong, Bernard P. *Chinatown: Economic Adaptation and Ethnic Identity of the Chinese*. New York: Holt, Rinehart and Winston, 1982. • Zhou, Min. *Chinatown: The Socioeconomic Potential of an Urban Enclave*. Philadelphia: Temple University Press, 1992.

Chinda Sutemi (1856, Hirosaki, Japan—1929): Japanese ambassador to the United States. Chinda served as ambassador from 1912 until 1916, during the administration of President Woodrow Wilson. Pre-

viously, Chinda was Japanese consul in San Francisco, beginning in 1890. As consul he was especially alarmed at reports of Japanese prostitution in the Western states. Convinced that such unrestricted immigration of these and other "lower class Japanese" to the United States would someday trigger the same anti-foreign exclusionist activity directed at the earlier Chinese, he urged his government to tighten the immigrant selection process. On behalf of Japan, in 1906 he protested the segregation of Japanese students in San Francisco public schools. This effort led to the GENTLEMEN'S AGREEMENT of 1907, which limited the number of Japanese immigrant laborers to the United States. In 1913 Chinda asked Wilson to exert pressure to block passage of California's proposed antialien land bill, but to no avail.

Chinese almanac: Reference book or table containing the Chinese lunar calendar, weather forecasts, the zodiac, horoscope, and other miscellaneous information. Such an item is commonly used by farmers in China to predict seasonal changes.

Chinese American Bank: Independent local banking institution. Started in 1916, the bank served the needs of Chinese businesspersons who believed that banks owned by white persons were discriminatory. Because of competition with other established banks, the bank temporarily closed in 1932; it reopened in 1936 as American Security Bank.

Chinese American businesses: Chinese immigrants early established businesses in the United States, from very small, one-person operations to huge concerns with branches all over the world. Even in the nineteenth century, some of the businesses were very large. The types of businesses changed greatly over the years, influenced by economic events, by American reception of Chinese (Chinese exclusion and the like), and by world events.

The Early Period, 1850's to the 1890's. Many Chinese entered business upon their first arrival in the United States. Early businesses ranged from peddling goods to operating large import-export firms doing hundreds of thousands of dollars worth of business a year (when a laborer's daily wage was $1.00 a day or less). During the 1850-1890 period, import-export (centered in San Francisco) was the main big business in the Chinese community. At first, this meant leasing ships to transport Chinese immigrants to the United States, but by the mid-1850's, businessmen were also

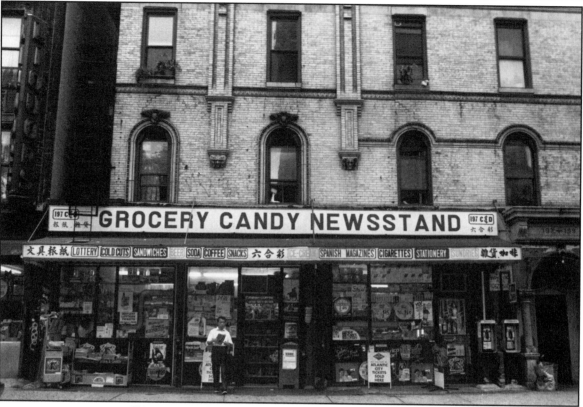

Chinese-operated grocery store in New York. (Frances M. Roberts)

importing large quantities of rice, tea, and silver. In terms of value, the rice that they handled was the largest single item of import into San Francisco from China between the mid-1850's and the mid-1860's—and China was San Francisco's third largest trading partner.

For the return trip, the Chinese merchants sent gold, wheat flour, ginseng, mercury, and dried seafood back to China. Gold was the single largest item of export between San Francisco and China, but the Chinese merchants probably handled less than a quarter of it. (Much of the rest was later reshipped to other countries.)

Chinese also engaged in a variety of medium to small businesses. One was commercial fishing and its corollary, the drying of fish, squid, and other seafood for shipment to China or for sale to inland communities in the Western states. Peddling of fresh seafood in cities and towns along the Western coast was another business, as was peddling of many other sorts: fresh fruit and vegetables, pots and pans, dry goods, and the like. Other Chinese went into business as truck farmers, enjoying a reputation for being very skillful. Still others started medium to small manufacturing con-

cerns in the garment industry, in cigar making, in shoe-making, and in other industries. Chinese gambling establishments were another flourishing form of business, with patrons drawn from the white as well as the Chinese communities.

There were also retailers for goods exchanged within the Chinese community and wholesalers who sold to the larger community—up until the 1880's, San Francisco's Chinese wholesalers of fresh fruit and vegetables were especially prominent. Furthermore Chinese ran some of the best rooming houses in San Francisco in the 1850's (patronized by people of all races), and Chinese early went into the restaurant and laundry businesses.

Diversifying, 1890's to the Depression of the 1930's. By the 1880's and 1890's, the anti-Chinese movement and Chinese exclusion laws had squeezed many Chinese out of their businesses. Most small manufacturing concerns had to shut down, the Chinese import-export firms were hard hit, and the ability of Chinese to engage in commercial fishing and truck farming was greatly restricted. (In the San Francisco area, some truck farms were replaced by commercial flower growing). In spite of this climate, however, businessmen in the community continued to find opportunities. Several entrepreneurs (such as Thomas Foon Chew and Lew Hing) established large canning operations that included not only the canneries themselves but also farmland, especially in the Sacramento-San Joaquin delta. Other Chinese also operated large farms in the delta and in the Monterey area. These businessmen were particularly important for California's potato and asparagus industries, but they also canned and grew fresh fruit and vegetables generally, and canned fish and other seafood.

Around the beginning of the twentieth century, there was even more diversification. Look Poong Shan and a few others started the Canton Bank in 1907 with headquarters in San Francisco. Between 1899 and 1908 the BAOHUANGHUI (Chinese Empire Reform Association) established a series of interlocking businesses, including a hotel and restaurant in Chicago, a newspaper in San Francisco, two banks (of which one had a branch in New York City), real estate operations in Mexico and Panama, and a rice brokerage in Singapore. Called the Commercial Corporation, these interlocking businesses were managed out of Canada and the United States. In 1915 Look Tin Eli founded San Francisco's China Mail Steamship Company, which ran ships from the United States to China until 1923, when it ceased operation.

Medium and small businesses included Chinese-language newspapers, such as the Reverend NG POON CHEW's *Chung Sai Yat Po*, published in San Francisco. Restaurants and laundries flourished, as did retail shops catering to the Chinese community. Peddling of fresh fruit and vegetables was still a viable business, especially in Western coastal cities; the peddlers turned first to horse and wagon, then to trucks in the years prior to the Depression. Finally, gambling concerns and the like remained profitable.

Marketing, 1930's to the End of the Vietnam War. The Depression ruined what remained of Chinese big businesses and worked great hardship on the medium to small ones. During World War II, however, with the end of Chinese exclusion, diminishing anti-Chinese

Chinese American Businesses in the U.S. by Type and Receipts, 1987

Total Chinese American businesses owned: 89,717

Total receipts: $9,609,000,000

Rank order among Asian Americans: 1st in businesses owned, 1st in receipts

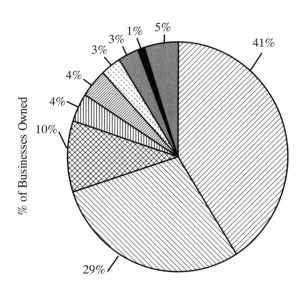

% of Businesses Owned

41%
29%
10%
4%
4%
3%
3%
1%
5%

Services: $2,186,744,000

Retail trade: $4,268,139,000

Finance, insurance, and real estate: $429,065,000

Wholesale trade: $1,429,316,000

Construction: $333,144,000

Manufacturing: $494,044,000

Transportation and public utilities: $175,923,000

Agricultural services, forestry, fishing, and mining: $40,304,000

Other industries: $252,013,000

Source: Susan B. Gall and Timothy L. Gall, eds., *Statistical Record of Asian Americans.* Detroit: Gale Research, Inc., 1993.

sentiment, and the great need for goods and services, more of the now-Chinese American community (naturalization had become possible) entered the mainstream of the American economy. The largest business that operated at this time was Joe SHOONG's NATIONAL DOLLAR STORES, a dry goods chain. Founded in the 1920's as an outgrowth of an earlier store, it reached its height after the end of World War II, operating more than fifty stores in the Western states.

As for medium to small businesses, most earlier ones continued on, although most of the peddlers disappeared, to be partially replaced by neighborhood markets and even supermarkets. Chinese Americans opened filling stations, restaurants that now catered as much to non-Chinese as to Chinese, small clothing manufacturers (sewing shops), and other types of businesses. Hand laundries declined, however, hard hit by competition from large, very modern establishments.

New Influx of Capital, Post-Vietnam War Period. The post-Vietnam War period saw greatly renewed Chinese immigration (including ethnic Chinese refugees from Southeast Asia) as well as a major infusion of capital from Hong Kong and Taiwan. This led to a new period of diversification. In terms of big business, import-export firms once again flourished, especially in the computer industry. Many banks and savings and loan associations were started either with Chinese American capital or with Chinese capital from overseas. Another favorite, real estate development, included some very large projects. Chinese Americans

also established some big manufacturing concerns, especially in computers. In terms of medium to small businesses, thousands of new shops opened in the now-revived CHINATOWNS. There were also businesses directed toward Chinese-language speakers, such as television stations broadcasting in Mandarin and Cantonese. Yet for the most part, by the 1980's Chinese American businesses could hardly be distinguished in terms of type and operation from businesses owned by any other sector of the American community.—*L. Eve Armentrout Ma*

SUGGESTED READINGS: • Chinn, Thomas W., H. Mark Lai, and Philip P. Choy, eds. *A History of the Chinese in California: A Syllabus*. San Francisco: Chinese Historical Society of America, 1969. • Lydon, Sandy. *Chinese Gold*, Chapter 14. Capitola, Calif. Capitola Book Company, 1985. • Ma, L. Eve Armentrout. "The Big Business Ventures of Chinese in North America, 1850-1930." In *The Chinese American Experience*, edited by Genny Lim. San Francisco: Chinese Historical Society of American, 1984.

Chinese American Citizens Alliance (CACA): Organization established in 1895 to advance the concerns of Chinese Americans by means of political participation.

Early Years. On May 4, 1895, Chun Dick and a group of native-born Chinese Americans established the United Parlor of the NATIVE SONS OF THE GOLDEN STATE in an effort to represent the approximately 4,760 native-born Chinese Americans in San Francisco. Because of pressure from Chinese Americans outside of California who wanted to affiliate, and antagonism from the politically influential anti-Asian Grand Parlor of the NATIVE SONS OF THE GOLDEN WEST, the Grand Lodge decided to change its name and in 1915 adopted the name Chinese American Citizens Alliance for all lodges outside California. In 1929 the name officially was adopted for the entire organization, with the Grand Lodge in San Francisco and subordinate lodges in San Francisco, Oakland, Los Angeles, Fresno, San Diego, Portland, Chicago, Pittsburgh, Detroit and Boston. Between 1950 and 1961 lodges were established in Salinas, Houston, San Antonio, and Albuquerque. A minimum of twenty-five male, native-born members were required for the establishment of a subordinate lodge. Although New York organized a Chinese American Citizens Alliance, founded in 1923, it was not affiliated with this national organization.

With the new name came revisions of the original 1895, 1904, and 1912 purposes: "[T]o unite citizens of

Top 10 Types of Chinese Businesses in New York City, 1988	
Type of Business	Number
Restaurants	781
Garment factories	437
Insurance, real estate, and stockbrokers	320
Medical doctors	300
Grocery stores	187
Lawyers	186
Importers and exporters	164
Travel agencies	115
Barber shops and beauty salons	111
Accountants	107

Source: Min Zhou, *Chinatown: The Socioeconomic Potential of an Urban Enclave*. Philadelphia, Pa.: Temple University Press, 1992.

A branch meeting of the Chinese American Citizens Alliance. (Asian American Studies Library, University of California at Berkeley)

the United States of Chinese descent into closer bonds, elevate the moral standard among its members, disseminate among them true ideas of personal and public morality as well as principles of political rights and liberties, promote the general welfare and happiness of its members and the Chinese communities in America . . ." and so forth. Membership was considered an honor and a recognition of one's accomplishments in the community. From its inception to 1976 only men who were age twenty-one or older and American citizens could be members. In the 1940's women could participate as auxiliary members if their husbands were members. In 1976, however, Mrs. Noel Lim was the first woman admitted to membership. In 1991 Virginia Gee was made the first woman president of the San Francisco Lodge of the CACA, followed in 1992 by Joyce Chen as the first woman president of the Oakland Lodge.

Political Involvement. The CACA has a long history of involvement in national and local politics. In 1913 the CACA successfully blocked a California state senator's efforts to disenfranchise Chinese Americans. In 1924 the group successfully fought against Sections 4 and 13 of the National Origins Quota Act of 1924 and consistently agitated for the rights of Chinese males to bring their wives to the United States. In 1925 it successfully worked toward the defeat of the "Cinch Bill" of 1925, which was concerned with the regulation of the manufacture, sale, and use of herbs, roots, and other natural products used in the treatment of diseases. The CACA sent representatives and lobbyists to Washington, D.C., to testify during hearings of the MCCARRAN-WALTER ACT of 1952 and its subsequent revisions as well as later proposed laws. In addition to immigration issues, the CACA focused its attention upon the legal rights of Chinese Americans and their descendants, removal of discriminatory laws and policies, registration of voters, and endorsement of candidates.

The Grand Lodge of the Chinese American Citizens Alliance was in San Francisco. (Asian American Studies Library, University of California at Berkeley)

The organization worked toward fostering a more positive image of the Chinese in the United States. When Charles R. Shepherd's *The Ways of Ah Sin* was published in 1923, the leaders took a stand against this type of sensational anti-Chinese literature because of the prejudice and negative images it conveyed and unsuccessfully called for a suppression of the book. Members continually watched for derogatory literature and spoke out against such material. The CACA hoped to promote and enhance "the study of Americanism and patriotism" through oratorical and essay-writing contests while at the same time promoting the study of conversational Chinese by pioneering new teaching methods that stemmed from Western methodology instead of traditional practices.

Social and community service also were a major part of CACA activities. Socials included the New Year's dances, Valentine's Day dances, Western nights, Halloween costume parties, golf tournaments, baseball games, and numerous dinners and picnics. The CACA

supported numerous community organizations, such as Cameron House, Self-Help for the Elderly, and the Chinese Historical Society of America (CHSA) as part of the effort "to promote and strengthen the general welfare and happiness of the Chinese community." In the late 1940's in Los Angeles, the Mandarins, a junior affiliate, sponsored a softball league, basketball team, and other youth activities.

Other Ventures. In 1921 the members proposed the creation of the United Publishing Company, which later became the Chinese Times Publishing Company. After a shaky beginning, they established the first successful daily newspaper, the *Chinese Times*, that was owned, edited, and published by Chinese Americans. The paper made its debut on July 5, 1924, and quickly had the largest circulation among Chinese newspapers published in San Francisco between 1929 and 1980. The newspaper was written and published in Chinese because the leaders lacked capital and staff to support an English-only or bilingual publication. Shortly after its move to larger quarters on Sacramento Street in 1977, the newspaper became an independent body in the 1980's.

The CACA, a majority of whose members had attended or graduated from college after the 1930's, also was active in promoting equal educational opportunities and educational endeavors. The members fought for a change in name of the former Oriental School, which in 1924 became Commodore Stockton, that served San Francisco's Chinatown. Under the leadership of attorney Kenneth Fung, the CACA fought for desegregation in San Francisco in the 1920's and early 1930's. Fundraising for scholarships and supporting internship programs so that Chinese Americans could have "hands-on" experience are also part of CACA programs.

The CACA has made many contributions to the improvement of Chinese communities in the United States, raised the political consciousness of Chinese Americans, and provided a springboard for greater assimilation while retaining some aspects of Chinese cultural heritage.—*Sue Fawn Chung*

Suggested Readings: • Chung, Sue Fawn. "The Chinese American Citizens Alliance: An Effort in Assimilation." Unpublished bachelor's honors thesis in history, University of California, Los Angeles, 1965. • Chung, Sue Fawn. "The Chinese American Citizens Alliance: An Effort in Assimilation, 1895-1965." *Chinese America: History and Perspectives*, (1988): 30-57. • Daniels, Roger. *Asian America: Chinese and Japanese in the United States Since 1850*. Seattle:

University of Washington Press, 1988. • Tsai, Shih-shan Henry. *The Chinese Experience in America.* Bloomington: Indiana University Press, 1986.

Chinese American Democratic Club: Membership-supported nonprofit political organization incorporated in 1958 in San Francisco, California. The group seeks to encourage Chinese Americans to run for political office; to develop meaningful political awareness within the community; to foster active participation in the democratic process by all citizens; and to study, develop, and support issues relevant to the empowerment and civil rights of Chinese Americans.

Chinese American Democratic Youth League. *See* **Min Qing**

Chinese-American Librarians Association (CALA): Professional association founded in 1973 to serve the interests of Chinese American librarians in the United States. Activities are focused in the following areas: library services to the community, publishing trends, cultural preservation and development, Chinese libraries and librarians internationally, and equal employment opportunity.

The CALA started in two places independently: in 1973 in Illinois as the Mid-West Chinese American Librarians Association and in 1974 in Northern California as the Chinese Librarians Association. They merged into the present CALA in 1983.

The CALA annually awards a library school scholarship and a Distinguished Service Award for lifetime achievement. The association publishes a newsletter and a professional journal, and it maintains affiliate status with the American Library Association (ALA).

Chinese American literature: The definition of Chinese American literature is controversial. Does it include all works by writers of Chinese American ethnicity, or only those works with distinctively "Chinese American" themes? And how broadly is "Chinese American" to be defined? Kai-yu Hsu and Helen Palubinskas, in selecting works for their pioneering anthology *Asian-American Authors* (1972), understandably gave priority to writers who had lived in the United States for a considerable time. In the 1990's, however, given the rapid growth of what University of California, Berkeley Chancellor Chang-lin Tien calls "America's global population," it seems that Chinese American literature should be defined as inclusively as possible, to encompass all works by writers of Chinese descent

who have decided to reside in America permanently.

History. The development of Chinese American literature can be divided roughly into two periods. The first period lasted for about a century. It started with the publication of some bilingual pamphlets and phrase books, such as Wong Sam's *An English-Chinese Phrase Book* (1875), and culminated in Maxine Hong KINGSTON's autobiographical novels *The Woman Warrior* (1976) and *China Men* (1980). This period was marked by Chinese American writers' interest in using an autobiographical approach to identify their relationship with mainstream American culture, reflecting a sharpened sensitivity built on their increased awareness of their own cultural heritage.

Pardee LOWE's *Father and Glorious Descendant* (1943) and Jade Snow WONG's *Fifth Chinese Daughter* (1945) use the genre of autobiography to describe the writers' struggle with not only intercultural but also intracultural conflict. Virginia LEE's *The House That Tai Ming Built* (1963), Chuang Hua's *Crossings* (1968), Kingston's *The Woman Warrior* and *China Men*, and Shawn WONG's *Homebase* (1979) are fictionalized memoirs that can be read as semiautobiographies. *The Woman Warrior* and *China Men* were among the first works that brought mainstream America's attention to the literary and artistic achievement of Chinese Americans.

In the same period there were also Chinese American writers who experimented with other literary forms and approaches. Louis CHU's novel *Eat a Bowl of Tea* (1961), for example, presents a satirical but accurate depiction of Chinatown's bachelor society. It is one of the few works in Chinese American literature that deal with the struggle of lower-middle-class Asian Americans.

Frank CHIN's *The Year of the Dragon* (pr. 1974) and *The Chickencoop Chinaman* (pr. 1972) were pioneering works in dramatizing what Kai-yu Hsu calls "the Chinatown culture." *The Year of the Dragon* was the first Asian American play on national television, and *The Chickencoop Chinaman* was produced by the American Place Theater of New York. Like Kingston, Chin is an important figure in Chinese American literature. He participated in founding the ASIAN-AMERICAN THEATRE COMPANY in San Francisco. As a member of the COMBINED ASIAN-AMERICAN RESOURCES PROJECT, he has been instrumental in promoting the study of Asian American history and culture. Like Kingston, he has been influential not only among Chinese American writers but among Asian American writers in general.

A sampling of titles by contemporary Chinese American authors that reflect the diversity of the Chinese experience in America.

Chinese American Renaissance. The second period of Chinese American literature, fulfilling the promise of anthologies such as Hsu's *Asian-American Authors, Aiiieeeee! An Anthology of Asian-American Writers* (1974), edited by Chin with Jeffery Paul CHAN, Lawson Fusao INADA, and Shawn WONG, and Joseph Bruchac's *Breaking Silence: An Anthology of Contemporary Asian American Poets* (1983), gathered momentum in the late 1980's and early 1990's. In this second period, autobiography is no longer the predominant form of expression in Chinese American literature but rather one form among many. Chinese American writers in this period are interested in searching for forms and styles that reflect their experience more accurately.

This diversity is evident in the enormously varied landscape of contemporary Chinese American poetry. Diana CHANG, Li-Young LEE, Nellie WONG, and John YAU, to name only a few, are highly distinctive poets, each quite different from the others yet all reflective of the Chinese American experience.

This renaissance includes works from established figures and from new voices. Kingston's novel *Tripmaster Monkey: His Fake Book* (1987), like her first two books, uses stories from traditional Chinese literature and mythology, but the form is new, breaking out of the conventions of autobiography. Chin's collection of short stories, *The Chinaman Pacific and Frisco R. R. Co. (1988), and his novel, Donald Duk (1991), are characteristically powerful and vitriolic.*

In 1988, David Henry HWANG's M. Butterfly opened in Washington, D.C., at the National Theater. The play dramatizes the pernicious effect of illusions built on stereotypes and false assumptions. It won the Tony for best play, the Outer Critics Circle Award for best Broadway play, the John Gassner Award for best play, and the Drama Desk Award for best new play. Hwang's success marks the maturity of the Asian American theater.

Among the anthologies published in this period, two have pointed in a new direction: Making Waves: An Anthology of Writings By and About Asian American Women (1989), edited by Asian Women United of California, and Shirley Geok-Lin LIM's *The Forbidden Stitch: An Asian American Women's Anthology* (1989), as the titles indicate, take feminist approaches to the treatment of the Asian American experience. Both included previously unpublished works by Asian American women, from the early 1970's onward.

The publication of Amy TAN's novel *The Joy Luck Club* (1989), a critically acclaimed bestseller, was an important cultural event—a breakthrough book for Chinese American literature. Just two years later, in 1991, there were major publications by five Chinese American writers. Tan's novel *The Kitchen God's Wife* was another success. Gish JEN's first novel, *Typical American*, received rave reviews from both *People* magazine and *The New York Times Book Review*. David Wong LOUIE's short-story collection, *Pangs of Love*, explores themes of universal significance, themes such as intercultural and intergenerational conflict. Gus LEE, a lawyer from California, published a popular autobiographical novel, *China Boy*. And Chin's novel *Donald Duk*, mentioned above, appeared as well.

At the same time, a body of scholarly literature is growing in response to the explosion of new writing and the rediscovery of earlier works, and increasingly, Chinese American writers are represented on high school and college reading lists. A door has been opened.—*Qun Wang*

SUGGESTED READINGS: • Chin, Frank, et al., eds. *The Big Aiiieeeee! An Anthology of Chinese American and Japanese American Literature.* New York: Meridian Books, 1991. • Hsu, Kai-yu, and Helen Palubinskas, eds. *Asian-American Authors.* Boston: Houghton Mifflin, 1972. • Kim, Elaine H. *Asian American Literature: An Introduction to the Writings and Their Social Context.* Philadelphia: Temple University Press, 1982. • Ling, Amy. *Between Worlds: Women Writers of Chinese Ancestry.* Elmsford, N.Y.: Pergamon Press, 1990.

Chinese American magazines: Creative writings and writings on literary and cultural subjects have existed among the Chinese in America since the mid-nineteenth century. For the most part such works were published in the *fukan* (literary supplement) of newspapers. Sometimes editors even allowed groups to use the *fukan* as their literary magazine section. Literary magazines were also published separately. Most were short-lived.

An early San Francisco magazine was the biweekly *Chinese Outlook* (founded in 1914), devoted to the promotion of education. Later there was CHINESE YOUTH MAGAZINE (1917-1924), issued at ten-day intervals. In 1918 there was *Qiao Sheng Xiaoshuo Yuebao* (voice of overseas Chinese fiction monthly). A number of short-lived magazines also were published in Honolulu during this period. An early magazine in New York was *Huaqiao Zazhi* (overseas Chinese magazine; founded in 1931).

During World War II a number of magazines featuring news as well as cultural and literary essays and writings were published in New York. Some examples were CHINESE AMERICAN WEEKLY (1942-1970), *China Post* weekly (1942-1964), *China Life* semimonthly (founded in 1952), and *Chinese American Digest* biweekly (founded in 1956). Although there were fewer such magazines in the West, a publication that did last for awhile was the bilingual *Pan American Chinese Weekly* (1958-1964) in Los Angeles.

Magazines with creative writings and literary essays also appeared during this period, such as New York's *Huaqiao Wen Zhen* (overseas Chinese literary array; 1942-1946), published by the Huaqiao Wenhua She (overseas Chinese cultural society), and San Francisco's *Zhandou* (battle; 1943-1945), published by the Chinese Youth League. After the war some writers connected with Huaqiao Wenhua She came out with *Xin Miao Yuekan* (the bud monthly; founded in 1947). Geared more for leisure reading was *Tienfeng Monthly* (1952-1953); founded by Lin Yutang).

1970's and After. With the increase in the Chinese population beginning in the 1970's more magazines appeared. Some, such as *Hsintu* monthly (new soil; founded in 1978) and *East West Forum* bimonthly (founded in 1991), were targeted at intellectuals. Others, such as *People and Events* monthly (founded in 1983) and *Chinese Journal*, were aimed more at the popular taste. There were also literary periodicals such a *Women* bimonthly (founded in 1986 by Chinese writers from Vietnam, Cambodia, and Laos) and *Wenhua Guangchang* quarterly (public square for culture; founded in 1990 to publish the writings of mainland China émigrés).

Slanted more toward diversion rather than stimulation of the intellect are the widely distributed weekly television guides, the rise of which were spurred by the rapidly expanding Chinese television industry in major population centers since the early 1970's. Besides program listings these guides usually included popular reading materials such as news, anecdotes, and gossip about the community and the entertainment industry.

English-Language Magazines. English-language magazines appeared during the early twentieth century with the widely circulated CHINESE STUDENTS' MONTHLY (1905-1931), published by the Chinese Students' Alliance of America in New York. In 1935 came CHINESE DIGEST, which started as a newsweekly but became a monthly magazine from 1937 to 1940 with news items and feature articles. After World War II American-born Chinese founded *East Wind* quarterly (1945-1948) in Cleveland, Ohio. It was followed by *San Francisco Chinese News* biweekly (1953-1958). After that there were few ventures until the 1970's, when publishers sought to broaden their markets by targeting Asian Americans. Some magazines founded by Chinese Americans, such as the bimonthly BRIDGE magazine (1971-1985) and the irregularly published *East Wind* (founded in 1982), were activist in tone. Others, such as *Jade* (1974-1984), a quarterly, and *Rice* (1987-1989), a monthly, appealed to the middle class. By contrast, *Chinese American Forum*, a quarterly founded in 1986, publishes articles on Chinese American society and culture. Creative writings are also included in the scholarly publication AMERASIA JOURNAL.

Other Magazines. Periodicals of a partisan political nature were numerous over the years. An early one was Honolulu's *Da Sheng Bao* (loud voice report; founded in 1908), an organ of the Revolutionary Party. In San Francisco one of the earliest was *People's Tongue* (1914-1916), a Guomindang political monthly. In 1920 the Stockton branch of the Guomindang also published *Kuang Shi Yuebao* (rectify the times), a monthly. From the 1920's into the 1930's numerous periodicals were published by political groups such as the Guomindang, the Chinese Constitutionalist Party, the anarchists, and the communists to propagate their political viewpoints. During the Sino-Japanese War (1937-1945) propaganda magazines were published to exhort support for the war effort. After the war various movements to support the Taiwan government, to defend the Diaoyutai Islands, to support Taiwan independence, to promote friendship with China, to push for more democracy in China, and so forth have resulted in numerous strongly partisan, and mostly ephemeral, periodicals.

In the 1980's magazines specializing in such topics as real estate, automobiles, philately, and numismatics also began to appear.—*Him Mark Lai*

SUGGESTED READINGS: • Lai, Him Mark. "The Chinese American Press." In *The Ethnic Press in the United States: A Historical Analysis and Handbook*, edited by Sally M. Miller. New York: Greenwood Press, 1987. • Lai, Him Mark. "The Chinese Press in the United States and Canada Since World War II: A Diversity of Voices." In *Chinese America: History and Perspectives, 1990*, edited by the Publication Committee. San Francisco: Chinese Historical Society of America, 1990. • Lai, Him Mark. "The Ups and Downs of the Chinese Press in the U.S." *East/West*, Nov. 20, 1986. • Liu, Pei Chi. *A History of the Chinese in the United States of America, II*, pp. 399-404. In

Chinese. Taipei: Liming Wenhua Shiye Youxian Gongsi, 1982.

Chinese American nightclubs: Chinatown has always been San Francisco's number-one tourist attraction. By 1938 the city was being visited every year by one million tourists who would spend about $5 million annually on Chinatown alone. Tourists basically went to the restaurants, and sometimes to a Cantonese opera, but most of the time, they would be shopping among the curio shops that sold Japanese-made souvenirs. Other than this, there was not much in the form of nightlife entertainment in Chinatown.

A New Business. With the end of the Prohibition era in 1933, nightclubs grew nationwide in popularity. In San Francisco, several Chinese American entrepreneurs took advantage of the booming nightclub business. They began with bars and cocktail lounges in Chinatown. The Chinese Village was the first bar to open, on November 12, 1936. Others that followed included the Chinese Pagoda, the Jade Palace, Ricksha, and Twin Dragons. The success of the Chinese Village led to the entry of Chinese Americans into the nightclub business. On December 31, 1937, Chinatown's first nightclub was opened—Andy Wong's Chinese Penthouse—located in the Grandview Hotel on

Charlie Low, owner of the Forbidden City nightclub, circa 1941. (Asian Week)

the corner of Pine and Grant (it later changed its name to the more familiar Chinese Sky Room). This was followed successfully by other Chinese American nightclubs such as the Club Shanghai, Dragon's Lair, Kubla Khan, Lion's Den, and Charlie Low's world-renowned FORBIDDEN CITY Nightclub. More establishments began to sprout across the nation, such as the Shanghai Terrace Bowl in Oakland, Eddie Wan's South Seas in Honolulu, and the China Doll in New York City. Every one of them had one thing in common: They advertised an all-Chinese revue, using mainly an all-Chinese American cast of performers (of which some were actually of another Asian ethnicity) and a mainly white band of musicians.

The Chinese American nightclubs basically marketed themselves to white audiences. Using the existing exotic stereotypes and images of the Chinese (and especially of Chinese women), the nightclubs printed posters and programs with Chinese dressed in silk robes or holding fans. Owners promoted their revues with titles such as "Chinese Follies," "Chinatown Fantasie," "Chinese Capers," "Celestial Scandals," and "Sing Song Scandals." In order to lure the white audience, the performers would be labeled as "Chinese Frank Sinatra," "Chinese Fred Astaire and Ginger Rogers," "Chinese Sophie Tucker," "Chinese Sally Rand," and so forth even though the Chinese performers were not always imitating their namesakes.

Combating Stereotypes. Chinese Americans were discriminated against in the American entertainment world. They were considered to have no creative ability to sing or dance; it was said that they had two left feet and no rhythm. It was also not easy within the community to be an aspiring Chinese American entertainer. Men were not encouraged to sing or dance but to become engineers and businessmen. Women were ostracized by the Chinese community for performing in public, especially since they had to bare their shoulders and legs before an audience of men.

When Chinese American nightclubs opened in the late 1930's, they provided the opportunity for many Chinese Americans to realize their dream of performing in an otherwise hostile and unsympathetic world. The performers broke many stereotypes when they finally showed that they could sing and dance. Yet this was ignored and trivialized. Their community did not always appreciate their rebelliousness. Mainstream American newspapers seldom reviewed their acts according to their individual ability or talent. Some were unfairly criticized for lack of talent and were judged more on their level of "cuteness." The attraction and popularity of the Chinese American nightclubs were based simply on the exotic novelty of ethnic Chinese performing American song-and-dance routines.

The press played another major role in accepting Chinese American nightclubs and putting them in the spotlight. National magazines such as *Life* and columnists such as Herb Caen, Lee Mortimer, Ivan Paul, and Walter Winchell described the novel acts but more importantly wrote about the many celebrities, politicians, and high-society people patronizing these nightclubs. The Chinese American community too began to go to these nightclubs. The media helped immensely to boost attendance and profits.

The War Years. Besides being novel, Chinese American nightclubs also became very popular during the 1940's because of World War II. An estimated 1.5 million military personnel and more than twenty-three million tons of war supplies passed through San Francisco alone during this period. Soldiers who had never seen Chinese people and who grew up only with Hollywood stereotypes of the Chinese went to the nightclubs to watch the Chinese bubble or fan dancer and to sit and drink with exotic "China dolls." Few went to enjoy seriously the talent offered in the shows. Most went to satisfy their curiosity.

When the war was over, Chinese American nightclubs continued to survive for a brief time period. Yet the novelty of an all-Chinese revue was beginning to wither. The acts were becoming repetitive and their quality deteriorated. Reduced patronage, rising operation costs, and unionization further contributed to the eventual demise of these nightclubs. By the 1950's, the Bohemian, or Beatnik, generation created a new source of entertainment. Bohemian-type shops, galleries, restaurants, and coffeehouses pulled customers away from the nightclubs. Then came the discotheques and topless bars in the 1960's and 1970's that replaced the cabarets and nightclubs as key evening entertainment spots. Chinese American nightclubs could not escape from being a casualty of all these factors. Their heyday had disappeared by the 1950's.—*Lorraine Dong*

SUGGESTED READINGS: • Dong, Lorraine. "The Forbidden City Legacy and Its Chinese American Women." *Chinese America: History and Perspectives* (1992): 125-148. • *Forbidden City, U.S.A.* Video. DeepFocus Productions, 1989.

Chinese American Planning Council: Publicly funded social-service organization for the Chinese community in New York City, founded in 1983.

Chinese American press: Chinese newspapers have been published since the early years of the Chinese community in the 1850's. The first Chinese newspaper in the United States was the weekly *Golden Hills' News* (founded in 1854). Its place was taken by the weekly *Oriental* (*Tung-ngai San-luk*; founded in 1855 by William Speer) with a Chinese section for Chinese readers and an English section for the non-Chinese. In 1856 Ze Too Yune in Sacramento launched the first daily, *Chinese Daily News*. Both efforts had failed by 1857.

As the community grew, however, there were renewed efforts to establish newspapers. The 1870's through the 1890's saw the appearance of more than half a dozen Chinese newspapers in San Francisco. Most were weeklies, although there was a short-lived *San Francisco Chinese Daily Evening News* (1884). One paper, *The Oriental* (*Wah Kee*), was published from 1875 until the early 1900's.

By the 1880's Honolulu had become another center of Chinese journalism with the founding of the weekly *Hawaiian Chinese News* (1883-1907) by C. Winam. Until the early twentieth century, however, efforts east of the Mississippi failed to survive.

Nineteenth century Chinese American newspapers generally had lithographed handwritten texts on four tabloid-sized pages. Into the twentieth century newspapers grew to six or eight large pages similar in size to mainstream newspapers. The text was set with lead type. Early newspapers included only news items and advertisements, but by the twentieth century most newspapers also published regular editorials as well as a *fukan*, or literary supplement. There was also a greater focus on China politics.

China Politics. The Chinese Empire Reform Association (later the Chinese Constitutionalist Party; see BAOHUANGHUI), followed by the CHEE KUNG TONG and the TONGMENGHUI—and their successor, the GUOMINDANG (GMD)—established news organs in major communities. After the founding of the Republic of China each group supported different political factions in China. Organs of the Constitutionalist Party and the Chee Kung Tong declined, however, after the GMD gained ascendancy in China in 1927. Meanwhile a power struggle within the GMD beginning in the late 1920's led to separate party organs supporting each faction in major communities. The Marxist Left also began publishing the weekly *Chinese Vanguard* (1930-1933) in New York. It was succeeded by the weekly *China Salvation Times* (1938-1939) and then by the *China Daily News* (1940-1989).

Pressroom of the Chinese Times. (Asian American Studies Library, University of California at Berkeley)

Independent newspapers also coexisted with the party organs. The earliest was San Francisco's *Chung Sai Yat Po* (1900-1951), founded by NG POON CHEW. Walter U. Lum and other members of the CHINESE AMERICAN CITIZENS ALLIANCE (CACA) established the *CHINESE TIMES* (founded in 1924), also in San Francisco. Thomas P. Chan founded the *Chinese Journal of Commerce* (1928-1944) in New York.

National Newspapers. After World War II the circulation of Chinese newspapers decreased as older immigrants departed and the younger generation became less fluent in Chinese. Many newspapers had ceased publication by the 1960's. With the large influx of immigrants after 1965, however, the decline in circulation reversed. At this time publishers abroad also entered for a share of this growing market. By 1970 Sally Aw Sian's *Sing Tao Jih Pao* of Hong Kong was publishing separate editions in San Francisco and New York; in 1976 Taiwan's *United Daily News* group founded *World Journal*, with New York and San Fran-

cisco editions; immigrants Tao Chen and Chao-chu Fu began publishing the *International Daily News* (founded in 1981) in Los Angeles and *CENTRE DAILY NEWS* (1982-1989) in New York and San Francisco, respectively; Yu Chi-zhong's *China Times* of Taiwan began a U.S. edition in 1982. All were nationally distributed. During this period other new newspapers also emerged in the community, grabbing for a share of the market. Los Angeles, with its rapidly increasing Chinese population, became another major center of Chinese journalism, replacing Honolulu, where the Chinese press had become moribund.

Nationally distributed dailies used the latest technology and introduced a higher, more professional standard of journalism. They greatly increased the number of pages and published separate editions with local news tailored for Chinese communities in different locations. Some included a magazine section in the weekend editions. These were features that locally owned papers with their limited capital could not match. After a period in the 1970's, during which many newspapers competed for readers in the Chinese market, financially marginal operations had begun to fail by the 1980's. By the 1990's only a few locally owned dailies, such as San Francisco's *Chinese Times*, New York's *United Journal*, and Houston's *Southern Chinese Daily News* (founded in 1983 by Wea Lee) were still publishing. The nationally distributed papers for a time were also reduced to *Sing Tao Jih Pao* and *World Journal*, with the *International Daily News* a distant third. They were joined by New York's *China Press* (founded in 1990 by pro-communist Chinese interests as the successor to the *China Daily News*, which closed in 1989). The *China Press* became national in 1992 when it started a San Francisco edition.

Community Newspapers. The postwar era saw the rise of monthlies, biweeklies, weeklies, and semi-weeklies, usually tabloid size, emphasizing community news. An early one was San Francisco's liberal *Chinese Pacific Weekly* (1946-1986), edited by Gilbert Woo. By the late 1960's technological advances making possible lower production costs encouraged the rise of an increasing number of such publications, especially in smaller Chinese communities such as those in Houston, Boston, Washington, D.C., Miami, Chicago, Denver, Seattle, and Phoenix. There are also newspapers established by ethnic Chinese from Vietnam, Cambodia, and Laos who resettled in North America beginning in the late 1970's. The earliest of these was Los Angeles' *Vietnam-Chinese Newspaper*, founded in 1981. Other similar weeklies are published in San Francisco, New York, Philadelphia, San Diego, Seattle, and other cities.

English-Language Newspapers. English-language community newspapers were targeted at the English-reading Chinese. The earliest was Honolulu's bilingual weekly *Hawaii Chinese News* (1926-1931), edited by Ruddy F. Tongg, followed by the short-lived *Oriental Tribune* (founded in 1926 by Charles Ling Fu), one of the earliest Asian American newspapers. Subsequently there were the *Hawaii-Chinese Journal* (1937-1957), edited by William Lee, and the *Hawaiian Chinese Weekly* (1958-1959).

The first English newspaper for Chinese in the con-

Newspapers serving the various segments of the Asian American community deliver news from overseas as well as more localized items and announcements of interest. (James L. Shaffer)

tiguous United States was San Francisco's *CHINESE DIGEST* (1935-1940), founded by Thomas CHINN, followed by the *Chinese News* (1940-1952), founded by Charles LEONG and William Hoy. Out of the fight for equal opportunities came the bilingual weekly *East/West* (1967-1989), founded by Gordon Lew, followed by the weekly *SAN FRANCISCO JOURNAL* (1976-1980), founded by Maurice Chuck. A rival aimed at the Asian American market, *ASIAN WEEK*, founded in 1979 by John FANG, had reached a circulation of thirty thousand by 1993. In New York there were the *Chinese American Times* (1954-early 1970's), edited by William Chang, and the *Asian-American Times* (1987-1989).

Chinese-language newspapers have experimented with publishing English supplements, but the only sustained effort was by the *CHINESE WORLD*, which published an English section from 1949 to 1969.—*Him Mark Lai*

SUGGESTED READINGS: • Lai, Him Mark. "The Chinese American Press." In *The Ethnic Press in the United States: A Historical Analysis and Handbook.* edited by Sally M. Miller, pp. 27-43. New York: Greenwood Press, 1987. • Lai, Him Mark. "The Chinese Press in the United States and Canada Since World War II: A Diversity of Voices." *Chinese America: History and Perspectives* (1990): 107-155. • Lai, Him Mark. "The Ups and Downs of the Chinese Press in the U.S." *East/West*, Nov. 20, 1986. • Lo, Karl. "Kim Shan Jit San Luk: The First Chinese Newspaper Published in America." *Chinese Historical Society of America Bulletin* 6 (October, 1971): 1-4. • Stellmam, Louis J. "Yellow Journals: San Francisco's Oriental Newspapers." *Sunset* 24 (February, 1910): 197-201.

Chinese American radio and television programs: Radio and television programs have been a part of the Chinese American community cultural life since the 1930's.

Before World War II. The first Chinese radio show, a weekly hour-long Cantonese program, went on the air on April 30, 1933, sponsored by Chinese Broadcast Bureau of Honolulu. It was taken over by Chinese Broadcast Service in October and continued until the eve of World War II. A rival program, *Hawaii Chinese Radio News*, began broadcasting on May 1, 1933. It was taken over by New World Broadcast Service in 1935 but ceased broadcasting after a few weeks.

In the continental United States, Thomas Tong put Golden Star Radio Hour on the air in April, 1939, to advertise his radio repair and refrigerator store. The

program, which continued for thirty-nine years until April, 1978, featured Cantonese operatic and musical recordings and current events read in Cantonese. For a number of years, it also broadcast a weekly news commentary by Gilbert Woo, *CHINESE TIMES* editor.

Post-World War II Commercial Radio. In 1957 Frank Lee in collaboration with the San Francisco newspaper *Young China* began nightly hour-long broadcasts of the *Voice of Chinatown*. In 1959 the program moved to FM and expanded its airtime to three hours. In November, 1960, the program also began to be aired in Southern California. The program continued on the air until 1974. From 1957 to spring, 1959, the *Chinese Times* also was sponsor of a weekly program.

In 1951 New York record-shop owner Louis Chu started a weekly (later five days per week) Cantonese and English program, *Chinese Festival*, on FM featuring Chinese records. The program continued for about a decade. In Los Angeles, however, early attempts were not too successful. In 1955 Dan Yee started the weekly hourly program *Chinese Bell* in Los Angeles and went off the air in less than a year. Two other attempts in 1963 and 1967 also lasted only one or two years.

Chinese pay radio began in New York in 1964 when Chung Hwa Broadcasting Company piped Cantonese programs fourteen hours per day via telephone lines to subscribers. Round-the-clock broadcasting came in 1976, when Arthur Liu's Sino Radio Broadcasting Corporation broadcast Cantonese programs in New York City that could be heard only on special receivers. In the 1980's the corporation became Global Communications Enterprises Corporation, broadcasting programs to subscribers in U.S. and Canadian Chinese communities via communication satellite. Other competing local subscription radio programs also appeared. Some of these were San Francisco's *Sinocast* (1977; Cantonese programs), Los Angeles' *Chinese Radio* (1984; Mandarin programs), New York's *Chinese American Voice* (1986; Mandarin and Taiwanese programs), and, again in California, Sunnyvale's *All Star Chinese Radio Station* (1992; Mandarin programs).

Commercial Television. In 1972 Taiwan immigrant Fu-chuan Ma and his wife established Chinese Overseas Broadcasting Corporation to pioneer the airing of Chinese television programs. These consisted of Taiwan-produced videotapes augmented with locally produced newscasts and interviews. In New York, Overseas Television also began broadcasting daily programs on

China TV News, a public-access channel, providing coverage of Chinese New Year's festivities in New York City. (Ed Bridges)

cable around 1973, while in San Francisco Leo Chen founded Amasia TV productions to begin airing weekly programs in 1974. These programs found a receptive audience in the Chinese community, and Chinese television rapidly expanded. For example, in 1986 there were eight Chinese television weekly or daily programs airing in the San Francisco Bay Area.

At the beginning practically all programs were produced in Taiwan. As the competition became intense, some broadcasters tried to attract the large Cantonese audience by airing more costly Hong Kong programs. In 1980 broadcasts of Mandarin programs from the People's Republic of China (PRC) also began when New York' Hong Sheng Broadcasting Company started broadcasting on cable. Hua Sheng Television and Dunhuang Television broadcast similar programs in San Francisco and Los Angeles, respectively, starting in 1982 and 1984. By the late 1980's other stations were also selectively airing PRC programs, although

the bulk of broadcasts remained programs produced in Taiwan or Hong Kong. Most programs are in Mandarin or Cantonese, but through the early 1990's some programs from Taiwan are in Taiwanese.

Most Chinese American television broadcasters leased time to air their programs. In 1986 Channel 66 in the San Francisco Bay Area became the first Chinese American-owned station. The same year Leo Chen became board chairman of Channel 38, which aired English and Asian language programs. One of the first non-Chinese producers of Chinese programming was Channel 26 in San Francisco, which began airing news in Cantonese in 1989 and in Mandarin in 1991.

The popularity of Chinese television and availability of video players/recorders stimulated rapid expansion of sales and rental of videocassettes. Videotapes were also dubbed into other Asian languages such as Vietnamese. In order to control better the distribution of program broadcasting rights and videocassette sales, Taiwan's Taiwan Television, China Television, and Chinese Television established International Audiovisual Communications in the United States in 1980. Its subsidiary, United Chinese TV, also began broadcasting programs in the three major Chinese communities as well as smaller communities such as Honolulu, Washington, D.C., Chicago-Milwaukee, and Houston.

In 1985 Hong Kong's TVB, whose highly popular videocassettes had been distributed by Hong Kong TV in the United States since the early 1980's with many of its programs broadcast by other stations in American cities, established Los Angeles' Jade cable channel to broadcast its own programs as well as Mandarin programs produced in Taiwan. In 1992 it expanded to San Francisco. Programs produced by TVB's Hong Kong rival Asian TV were being broadcast and its videotapes distributed by others. Through early 1993 TVB had not set up production and broadcasting facilities in the United States.

Because of the high costs, intense competition in a limited market, and uncertain revenues, there are frequent changes in the ranks of broadcasters. Yet the expanding market continued to attract investors. A big technological step forward was taken in 1989, when North America Telecommunication Corporation of Rosemead, California, began broadcasting via satellite to North American audiences. Reception requires special installations by subscribers. By 1991 North America Telecommunication was broadcasting six hours daily, and in some areas it was also on cable.

Non-Commercial Radio and Television. Community pressure in the 1970's led to airing of Chinese media programs in a number of cities, mostly on noncommercial stations. (See CHINESE MEDIA COMMITTEE COMMUNITY RADIO PROGRAMS.) One of the earliest was *Hon Sing Chinese Community Hour*, a weekly Cantonese radio program of news, community issues, and music sponsored by Chinese for Affirmative Action (CAA). It broadcast from 1971 to the mid-1980's. During the 1970's CAA also sponsored a Mandarin program, *Chinese Youth Voice*, and an English program, *Dupont Guy*. In 1972 CAA also began Cantonese simulcasts of English-language television news, and it broadcast a *Learning Mandarin* series in 1973. CAA also produced and aired *Sut Yung Ying Yee*, which received a 1971 Emmy Award, to teach English to immigrants. In 1974 CAA sponsored production of the children's program *Yut Yee Sahm, Here We Come*. In New York there is the nonprofit ASIAN CINEVISION (ACV), whose Chinese Television began to produce

and air programs on community issues. With tighter budgets and a conservative political climate during the 1980's, however, television stations became much less cooperative in producing and broadcasting Chinese community-oriented programs.—*Him Mark Lai*

SUGGESTED READINGS: • Edmondson, Brad. "Radio's Tower of Babel." *American Demographics* 9 (March, 1987): 23-24. • Fong-Torres, Ben. "And Now, the News in Mandarin: Ethnic Broadcasts Serve Thousands." *San Francisco Chronicle*, September 16, 1991. • Hamilton, Mildred. "Ethnic TV, the Multi-Lingual Tube." *San Francisco Examiner & Chronicle,* Scene/Arts section, October 8, 1978. • Lai, H. M. "Chinese-Language TV Flourishes in Bay Area: 36 Hours Weekly in Cantonese and Mandarin." *East/ West*, July 10, 1986. • Leung, James. "Big Business in Videotapes: Hong Kong Soaps Are U.S. Hits." *San Francisco Chronicle*, January 2, 1989. • Marlane, Judith. "The World of Chinese Television." *Television Quarterly* 26, no. 2 (1992): 25.

Chinese American Weekly (*Zhong-Mei Zhoubao*): Chinese-language weekly magazine founded in New York City in 1941 by Ching Foo Wu, who had just been ousted as chief editor at the Nationalist organ *Mun Hey Daily* (also published in New York) in an intra-party power struggle. Although the magazine often was critical of the Nationalist government, it was basically anti-Communist. The publication, which included current events and commentaries as well as photographs, feature articles, literary works, and letters to the editor, quickly became a success and was distributed widely in North American Chinese communities during the war years. The profit was sufficient for its management to purchase a headquarters building to house its facilities and staff. In 1952 Wu also founded the daily *United Journal*, which at one point during the 1970's led all Chinese newspapers in the East in circulation. *Chinese American Weekly* ceased publication in 1970.

Chinese American women: Since their arrival in the United States in 1834, Chinese women have faced many obstacles in finding equality in American society. Immigration laws and cultural inhibitions barred many from coming until 1965. Those who immigrated despite the CHINESE EXCLUSION ACT OF 1882 found life in the United States alienating and hard. Until World War II, immigrant women and their American-born daughters suffered discrimination on the basis of race and sex in their efforts to gain access to profitable

Chinese American mother and daughter. (Jim Whitmer)

employment, decent housing, higher education, and social acceptance in mainstream society. Since the Civil Rights movement in the 1960's, Chinese American women have taken advantage of greater opportunities for education, employment, and social integration. Yet the contributions of Chinese American women to their families, to their communities, and to American society have yet to be acknowledged.

Pioneering Women, 1834-1882. War and poverty in China led many Chinese to emigrate to the United States during the California gold rush. Discouraged from traveling abroad by cultural mores, limited economic resources, and anti-Chinese sentiment and violence, few women were among these early immigrants. In 1860 there were eighteen Chinese men for every Chinese woman in the United States.

Afong Moy, Marie Seise, and Ah Toy were the earliest known women to immigrate from China to the United States. Moy was brought to New York in 1834 as an exotic showpiece to satisfy the curiosity of the American public. Seise arrived in San Francisco in 1848 as a servant in the household of trader Charles V. Gillespie. Toy immigrated alone a year later, becoming

a successful courtesan and well-known personality in the courtroom, where she sued clients who tried to pay her with brass filings instead of gold. While little is known of Moy and Seise, newspaper accounts report that Toy lived in the San Francisco Bay Area until her death at the age of ninety-nine.

Because of the sex imbalance and laws that forbade interracial marriage, the majority of Chinese women in nineteenth century America were prostitutes who had been kidnapped, lured, or purchased from poor parents in China and sold to Americans for high profits. Treated as chattel and abused physically and mentally, the average prostitute did not outlive her contract term of four to five years. The fortunate ones were redeemed by wealthy clients or sought refuge at Protestant mission homes. Not until the early twentieth century did organized prostitution decline because of the enforcement of antiprostitution legislation and the successful rescue raids led by Protestant missionaries such as Donaldina CAMERON.

Life Under Exclusion, 1882-1943. After the Chinese Exclusion Act and subsequent discriminatory legislation, women could only immigrate as wives or daughters of merchants and U.S. citizens. The IMMIGRATION ACT OF 1924 further barred the immigration of wives of U.S. citizens. It was not until 1943, when China and the United States were allies in World War II, that the Exclusion Act was repealed and the Chinese were allowed to immigrate at the quota rate of 105 per year. As increased numbers of wives had come before 1924 to join their husbands and as they gave birth to daughters, the population of Chinese females in the United States slowly increased from 4,522 in 1900 to 20,115 in 1940.

Immigrant wives lived either in urban CHINATOWNS or in remote rural areas where their husbands could find work. Until the 1920's Chinatown wives seldom left their homes, where in addition to housework, caring for their children, and maintaining cultural traditions, they often worked for low wages sewing, washing, rolling cigars, shelling shrimp, and making slippers and brooms. In rural areas women also tended livestock and vegetable gardens, hauled in the catch and dried seafood for export, or took in boarders to help with the family income. As Chinese men, driven out of the better-paying jobs in the labor market, became concentrated in opening laundries, grocery stores, and small restaurants throughout the country, women helped out in these businesses while raising families on the premises.

In the 1920's, as women's emancipation took hold

in China and in the United States, Chinese immigrant women began working outside the home in the garment and food-processing industries. Those who were more educated and Westernized began to play a more active role in the community, participating in church functions and women's clubs organized to promote education, charitable work, and Chinese nationalist causes. During the 1930's their public roles expanded as they helped their families and communities weather the Depression and provide support for China during the Sino-Japanese War (1937-1945). It was also at this time that Chinese women participated in their first strike against conditions in Chinatown sweatshops. In 1938 Chinese garment workers in San Francisco picketed the NATIONAL DOLLAR STORES for thirteen weeks and won a union agreement for higher wages and improved benefits.

Second-generation Chinese American women came of age in the 1920's. Like other children of immigrant parents, they experienced cultural conflicts and identity crises in attempting to follow both Chinese and American values and customs. In addition their sex and race often proved to be liabilities, both within and outside their ethnic communities. Despite their ability to speak English, their high educational attainment, and their Western outlook, American-born Chinese

women had difficulty finding employment in their chosen fields as well as acceptance in the larger American society. Many ended up providing local color as elevator girls in white business establishments, taking up menial jobs as domestic or garment workers, or doing clerical and sales work in Chinatowns. Like other American girls, they engaged in sports, club activities, dating, and civic affairs, albeit in a segregated setting because of racial discrimination. Some, such as movie actress Anna May WONG, writer and ceramist Jade Snow WONG, and physician Bessie Jeong, challenged traditional gender roles by seeking higher education, careers, and marriage partners of their own choosing. In essence second-generation women resisted socioeconomic restraints by accommodation, carving a new bicultural identity and lifestyle for themselves.

Post-World War II Years. World War II was a turning point for Chinese Americans. Having proven their loyalty and worth by serving in the armed forces, volunteering at the home front, and working in the war industries, Chinese Americans were rewarded with improved educational and employment opportunities and the repeal of laws that had limited their civil rights and social interactions. The easing of immigration restrictions—particularly the WAR BRIDES ACT OF 1945 and

As immigrant Chinese women in America gradually became more assimilated, their preferences in clothing became more Westernized. (Library of Congress)

the IMMIGRATION AND NATIONALITY ACT OF 1965—
led to a large influx of Chinese women from different
socioeconomic backgrounds into the United States.
Their population grew from 40,621 in 1950 to 204,850
in 1970 and 398,496 in 1980.

Following the war an expanding technological
economy and a more favorable racial climate led to
improved conditions for Chinese American women,
advanced further by the civil rights and women's
movements. While many immigrant women still found
themselves trapped in Chinatown garment factories,
increased numbers of Chinese American women began moving into the technical, sales, and professional
fields. Because of discrimination, however, their earning power was often not commensurate with their level
of education. Moreover stereotypes of them as subser-
vient, exotic China dolls impeded their advancement
up the managerial ladder. Nevertheless women such as
physicist WU CHIEN-HSIUNG, California Secretary of
State March Fong EU, author Maxine Hong KING-
STON, news anchor Connie CHUNG, and architect
Maya Ying LIN made history for Chinese American
women through their outstanding contributions in the
public arena.

In the 1990's economic survival and parity remain a
major concern of Chinese American women even as
they work to improve conditions for their families,
communities, and country. As wager earners, wives,
and mothers they have been able to maintain a tenuous
balance between these roles—a balance that is easily
upset if husbands choose not to cooperate or if social
changes gained through the civil rights and women's
movements are reversed. In the spirit of multiculturalism Chinese American women also continue to work
toward assimilation into American society while maintaining a strong sense of their ethnic heritage.—*Judy
Yung*

SUGGESTED READINGS: • Chan, Sucheng. "The Exclusion of Chinese Women." In *Entry Denied: Exclusion and the Chinese Community in America, 1882-
1943*, edited by Sucheng Chan. Philadelphia: Temple
University Press, 1991. • Hirata, Lucie Cheng. "Chinese Immigrant Women in Nineteenth-Century California." In *Women of America*, edited by Carol Ruth
Berkin and Mary Beth Norton. Boston: Houghton Mif-
flin, 1979. • Kingston, Maxine Hong. *The Woman
Warrior: Memoirs of a Girlhood Among Ghosts*. New
York: Alfred A. Knopf, 1976. • *Linking Our Lives:
Chinese American Women of Los Angeles*. Los Ange-
les: Chinese Historical Society of Southern California,
1984. • McCunn, Ruthanne Lum. *Thousand Pieces of
Gold*. Boston: Beacon Press, 1988. • Wong, Jade
Snow. *Fifth Chinese Daughter*. 1945. New ed. Seattle:
University of Washington Press, 1989. • Yung, Judy.
Chinese Women of America: A Pictorial History. Seat-
tle: University of Washington Press, 1986.

Chinese Americans: The Chinese American community is one of the oldest established Asian American
communities. With a population of 1,648,696 in the
1990 census in the continental United States and Hawaii, it is also one of the largest. The course of development of this community over the years had been
shaped both by American immigration policies and by
domestic policies toward Asians.

Early Arrivals: 1785-1848. The Chinese first appeared in North America through the medium of the
Manila-Acapulco trade. The China trade then brought
them to the United States and Canada. In 1785, two
years after Great Britain recognized the independence
of the United States of America, the *Pallas*, a China
trade vessel sailing from Canton, docked at Baltimore.
The crew, including three Chinese, were stranded at
the port when the ship made no plans for a return
voyage. This was the first recorded instance of Chinese in the United States.

During the next half century, Chinese crewmen continued to touch the east and west coasts of North
America. Others entered the United States as students,
merchants, servants, circus performers, and in various
other occupations. Up to the mid-nineteenth century,
however, the number of Chinese immigrants entering
the country was minuscule, and the total number in the
United States by early 1849 was estimated to be only
fifty-four.

Top 5 Occupations of Chinese Women in California in Rank Order, 1860-1880		
1860	1870	1880
Prostitute	Prostitute	Keeping house
Wife or possible wife	Keeping house	Prostitute
Laundress	Servant	Seamstress
Miner	Laundress	Servant
Servant	Seamstress	Laundress

Source: Lucie Cheng Hirata. "Chinese Immigrant Women in Nineteenth Century California," in *Asian and Pacific American Experiences: Women's Prespectives*, edited by Nobuya Tsuchida. Minneapolis: Asian/Pacific American Learning Resource Center, University of Minnesota, 1982.

Educational Attainment, Labor Status, and Occupation of Chinese American Women, 1990

Education of Women 25 Years or Older	
	Percent
High school graduate	16%
Some college or associate degree	19%
College graduate	22%
Advanced or professional degree	13%
Total high school graduate or more	70%

Women 16 Years or Older	
	Percent
In labor force	59%
(Unemployed	5%)
Not in labor force	41%

Employed Civilian Women 16 Years or Older

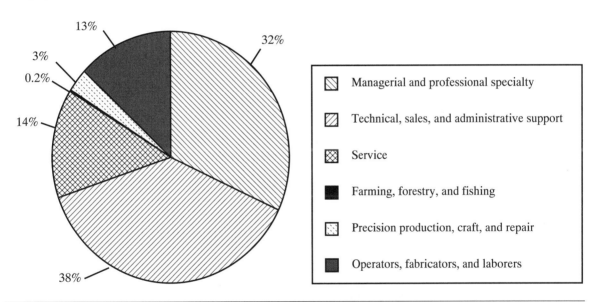

Managerial and professional specialty

Technical, sales, and administrative support

Service

Farming, forestry, and fishing

Precision production, craft, and repair

Operators, fabricators, and laborers

Source: U.S. Bureau of the Census, *1990 Census of Population: Asians and Pacific Islanders in the United States,* 1993.

As early as 1788 the China trade also brought the first Chinese to Hawaii. Many were merchants. Early in the nineteenth century enterprising Chinese also installed small sugar cane mills to begin the sugar industry in the islands. By 1828 there were thirty to forty Chinese living in Honolulu, and by mid-century the population had increased to about 350.

Unrestricted Immigration: 1848-1882. Large numbers of Chinese began arriving in California with the Gold Rush of 1849. By 1852, the Chinese population had jumped from approximately 359 in 1849 to more than 25,000, with many in the gold-mining regions. Subsequently Chinese also migrated successively to Nevada, southwest Oregon, across the international border to British Columbia as well as the upper Columbia River in Washington Territory, southwest Idaho and northeastern Oregon, Montana, Colorado, South Dakota, and Arizona as new gold strikes occurred.

As the gold fever subsided, California turned to development of her nonmining economy. Chinese immigrant labor became an essential part of the work force. Since almost all were able-bodied males, Chinese constituted up to 25 percent of the laborers, although they were only approximately a tenth of California's population. As other regions of the West developed, the use of Chinese workers became wide-

Chinese Immigration to the U.S. by Decade, 1850's-1980's

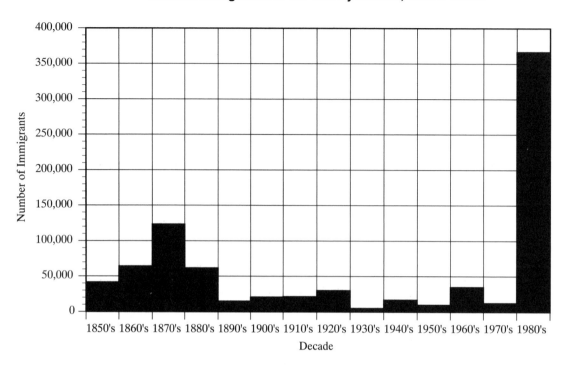

Source: Susan B. Gall and Timothy L. Gall, eds., *Statistical Record of Asian Americans.* Detroit: Gale Research, Inc., 1993.
Note: Chinese immigration totals include Taiwan from 1957-1982.

spread, although not to the extent found in California. By 1880 the Chinese population exceeded 100,000 in the continental United States, with 99 percent concentrated in the West and 71 percent in California.

In California, Chinese laborers reclaimed tule swamps in the Sacramento-San Joaquin River delta and constructed roads, rock walls, flumes, and reservoirs in Northern and central California. They worked borax deposits in California, Oregon, and Nevada, while in California they also mined quicksilver. In Wyoming and Washington they were hired as coal miners.

Chinese were a major factor in developing California agriculture. Many were harvest workers; others became skilled fruit packers. Their horticultural skills facilitated the success of sugar beets and celery as commercial crops. In Sebastopol and in Watsonville they bought apple crops for drying. Others became tenant farmers and truck gardeners. Wineries in Napa County used Chinese to work vineyards and also to excavate limestone caves for wine storage. Some even became winetasters. In Fresno County, Chinese harvested grapes for the raisin industry. Some Western

ranchers used Chinese as shepherds; a few Chinese even became cowhands.

Chinese developed the shrimp fishery in the San Francisco Bay Area and expanded operations to Louisiana. Their California-built oceangoing junks ranged along the Pacific Coast from Northern California to Baja California to harvest abalone. They made up the bulk of the labor force in salmon canneries in the Pacific Northwest and later Alaska. In the San Francisco Bay Area they made up the majority of workers in light industries such as woolen mills, and factories manufacturing shoes and boots, slippers, cigars, and garments. Chinese also started factories in the labor-intensive shoe-and-boot, slipper, cigar, and garment industries. Other Chinese became domestic servants, cooks, or laundrymen, occupations that later became the stereotyped trades of Chinese on the American mainland.

Chinese constituted the bulk of the laborers building the Central Pacific, Southern Pacific, and Northern Pacific sections of the transcontinental railroad, and were instrumental in the completion of a railroad network in the West. After completion of construction, many discharged laborers settled in towns along the routes; some took the trains to settle in the Midwest and on the eastern seaboard. Thus by 1890 Chinese were counted in every state and territory in the Union.

Chinese communities, commonly called Chinatowns and often segregated with a predominantly bachelor population consisting primarily of laborers, sprang up in many towns during the nineteenth century. Merchants and labor contractors provided the leadership role in organizing a network of *huiguan* and clan associations for social control and mutual help.

In the continental United States, San Francisco became the economic, political, and cultural hub of the Chinese in America. *Huiguans* making their headquarters there formed the CHINESE CONSOLIDATED BENEVOLENT ASSOCIATIONS (Chinese Six Companies) to act on behalf of the Chinese community in America

and to deal with the larger community. Their rivals in the community were the secret societies—the Triads and fighting *tongs* derived from the Triads, who controlled activities such as prostitution, gambling, and opium dens that flourished in the bachelor society. During the late nineteenth and early twentieth centuries these secret societies posed a serious threat to law and order and the leadership of the merchants. Their violent disputes gained notoriety as "TONG WARS."

Most early Chinese immigrants to the continental United States were Cantonese villagers from the Pearl River Delta area in Guangdong on the southeast China coast. The majority were from Siyi (Sze Yup), but sizable minorities came from Xiangshan (Heungshan; now Zhongshan [Chungshan]), and Sanyi (Sam Yup). A small number were from areas in Guangdong where the Hakka dialect and variations of the Min (Fujian)

Early Chinese immigrants in North Adams, Massachusetts, learn the craft of shoemaking inside a factory. This sketch is dated July, 1870. (Culver Pictures)

Top 5 States of Chinese Residence, 1870 and 1880

State	1870	1880
California	49,277	75,132
Idaho	4,274	3,379
Oregon	3,330	9,510
Nevada	3,152	5,416
Montana	1,949	1,765

Source: Elmer Clarence Sandmeyer, *The Anti-Chinese Movement in California*. Urbana: University of Illinois Press, 1973.

dialect were spoken.

Chinese immigration to Hawaii also increased during the last half of the nineteenth century as the island's economy developed. White sugar plantation owners imported large numbers of Chinese laborers to work in the cane fields. Others worked on Chinese rice plantations or became vegetable and fruit growers. Many became shopkeepers and skilled craftsmen as part of Hawaii's growing middle class. By the 1880's the Chinese population in Hawaii was more than 18,000, about 23 percent of Hawaii's total population. In contrast to the makeup of the Chinese community on the mainland, about three-quarters of the Chinese population of Hawaii were Cantonese speakers from Xiangshan while one-quarter came from Hakka-speaking areas. Chinese society in Hawaii was also basically a bachelor society; however, many Chinese married native women to form Chinese Hawaiian families. The Chinese in Hawaii formed organizations similar to those on the mainland; however, in Hawaii, in contrast to the mainland, Triad societies did not evolve into highbinder *tongs*. The organization corresponding to the Chinese Six Companies for the Chinese community in Hawaii is the UNITED CHINESE SOCIETY of Honolulu. (Honolulu played a role for the Chinese in Hawaii similar to that played by San Francisco in the continental United States.)

White America was not slow in expressing nativistic, anti-foreign sentiments against the Chinese. During the Gold Rush period, white miners pressured the California legislature to levy a tax on foreign miners, namely the Chinese. However, such anti-Chinese actions were limited in scope and organization until the 1870's, when an economic depression hit the West and thousands became unemployed. Agitators began blaming Chinese for taking jobs away from white workers. An anti-Chinese movement spearheaded by labor unions developed in California and spread all over the West. This created political pressures, to which Congress responded by passing the CHINESE EXCLUSION ACT OF 1882. This law, which prohibited the entry of Chinese laborers for ten years and barred Chinese from naturalization as American citizens, represented a basic change from a policy of free unrestricted immigration to one discriminating on the basis of ethnicity and social class. In subsequent years the Chinese Exclusion Act was amended and extended. The ban on Chinese labor was extended indefinitely in 1904.

Exclusion: 1882-1943. Chinese immigration greatly declined during the exclusion era of sixty-one years. The Chinese American population declined to a low of 23,507 in Hawaii in 1910 and 61,639 on the mainland in 1920. Due to the exclusion of laborers, institutions associated with the bachelor society slowly declined; "*tong* wars" decreased in frequency during the first half of the twentieth century. Immigration regulations allowing entry of exempt classes while banning the entry of laborers led to a relative increase in the percentage of families in the population. This in addition to natural increase resulted in the Chinese American population in the contiguous United States climbing slowly to 77,504 by 1940, while the ratio of males to females gradually decreased from a high of twenty-seven to one in 1890 to 2.9 in 1940. In Hawaii the population increased to 28,774 in 1940, while the male-female ratio dropped from 3.8 in 1910 to about 1.3 in 1940. Both on the mainland and in Hawaii, Chinese migrated from rural areas to concentrate in urban areas.

During the exclusion period, the Chinese in America, particularly in California, were socially isolated from mainstream society. They were banned from many public facilities; they could not purchase property in many locations; they were forbidden to marry Caucasians, and in San Francisco their children had to attend segregated schools. They were also excluded from many occupations, and in order to survive, a disproportionate number became domestic servants and cooks or laundrymen. Others entered the restaurant business; chop suey became a well-known Chinese American dish. In California and in the Southeast and Southwest, Chinese operated small businesses such as butcher shops and groceries. A selected few became professionals or clerical workers. Two rare successes in mainstream society were cinematographer James Wong HOWE and actress Anna May WONG, who both found careers in the motion picture industry.

Around the turn of the century Chinese entrepreneurs began to invest in capital-intensive enterprises such as canneries and also founded their own financial institutions. In 1915, Chinese merchants in San Francisco pooled capital to establish the China Mail Steamship Company to sail the Pacific. Most of their major enterprises failed due to the isolation of Chinese in American society, their lack of capital to compete effectively with existing large corporations in America, and their lack of managerial experience. The only major Chinese businesses to survive and prosper were Joe Shoong's NATIONAL DOLLAR STORES, a chain of department stores in the West, and K. C. Li's WAH CHANG TRADING COMPANY in New York, which imported tungsten and antimony from China.

In Hawaii, where there was a relatively small *haole* (white) population and a native Hawaiian middle class was practically nonexistent, the Chinese were needed in many sectors of the developing economy in spite of the prejudice against them. By the twentieth century, Chinese entrepreneurs had established two Chinese-owned banks and operated a number of successful businesses. Particularly successful were the C. Q. Yee

Hop interests (see CHUN QUON), which by the 1930's included a meat market and grocery, a cattle ranch, a hardwood company, a brewery, and a realty company.

During the exclusion era, local-born Chinese in Hawaii were also increasing in number. Many began to enter the professions beginning at the turn of the century. By the 1920's American citizens had become the majority in the community. They became increasingly active in civic affairs and electoral politics. In 1925 they formed the Hawaiian Chinese Civic Association to strive for their civil rights and to help elect Chinese Americans to local offices.

In the meantime, the American-born Chinese on the mainland were becoming increasingly westernized, influenced primarily by the public schools and the Christian church; however, they were still rejected by mainstream society. As early as 1895 they formed the NATIVE SONS OF THE GOLDEN STATE to fight for equal rights. In 1915 it became the CHINESE AMERICAN CITIZENS ALLIANCE, a national organization. There was very limited Chinese American participation in mainstream politics, however, until the late 1930's. This

Chinese American Population by Census Year, 1860-1990

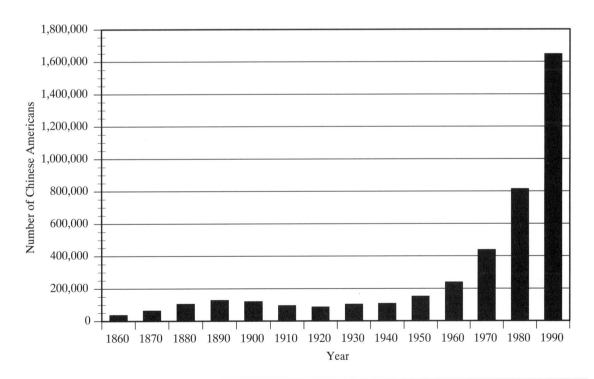

Sources: Roger Daniels, *Prisoners Without Trial: Japanese Americans in World War II.* New York: Hill and Wang, 1993. Susan B. Gall and Timothy L. Gall, eds., *Statistical Record of Asian Americans.* Detroit: Gale Research, Inc., 1993.

was when American citizens became a majority among mainland Chinese, and Chinese American political activities increased correspondingly.

Many Chinese Americans, however, were frustrated at the apparent lack of a future in the United States for them and their children, and placed their hopes on building a strong, modernized China that could improve their status abroad. Around the turn of the century they supported the Reform movement to establish a constitutional monarchy (see BAOHUANGHUI), and the revolutionary movement to establish a republic (see SUN YAT-SEN). These expressions of nationalism also stimulated the founding of many Chinese newspapers and Chinese schools.

After establishment of the republic many Chinese continued to support the republic and the Chinese Nationalist Party (GUOMINDANG). Some went to China to seek careers. Still others invested in business enterprises in China and Hong Kong. They also donated money for public projects, such as schools, libraries, hospitals, and roads, efforts which contributed to the modernization of the Pearl River Delta.

Nowhere was the Chinese Americans' deep interest in developments in their ancestral land better expressed than in their support for China's fight against Japanese aggression. Some went to China to join the armed forces, particularly the air force, but most of the support was in the form of financial contributions.

In spite of the exclusion laws, Chinese still sought to enter the United States in quest of economic opportunities. Some stowed away on transpacific steamers or served as seamen and jumped ship upon arrival at a seaport. Others were smuggled across the international borders or waters from Canada, Mexico, or the West Indies. Many more entered with assumed identities as alleged members of exempt classes—diplomats, students, teachers, merchants, tourists.

The Chinese also won numerous court cases to better define their legal rights of entry. By the twentieth century an increasing number were seeking entry claiming American birth or derived citizenship as the offspring of citizens.

Immigration officials were aware of the widespread use of assumed identities. They detained Chinese applicants at entry ports, the principal ones of which were Honolulu and San Francisco (and, later, San Pedro and Seattle), for interrogation to determine the validity of their claims. At San Francisco, where most Chinese disembarked, immigration authorities maintained a detention facility on Angel Island from 1910 to 1940 to process Chinese arrivals to determine the validity of their claim to right of entry. (See ANGEL ISLAND IMMIGRATION STATION.)

Restricted Immigration: 1943-1965. World War II was a turning point for the Chinese in America. Many served in the armed forces or in the merchant marine. At the same time, the wartime labor shortage opened opportunities for minorities in skilled and technical occupations.

By this time the Chinese were only a small minority and no longer were a major target for racists. China's heroic resistance to Japanese aggression had also created a favorable image. In a move designed to counter the propaganda of the Axis powers and to encourage China to continue to fight Japan, Congress repealed Chinese exclusion in 1943. (See IMMIGRATION ACT OF 1943.) In order to ensure passage with minimal opposition, the law assigned a token annual immigration quota of 105 for Chinese; more significant, they were given the right of naturalization.

Postwar legislation allowed the wives of servicemen, including Chinese, to immigrate, and between 1946 and 1950 almost eight thousand Chinese females arrived, constituting nine-tenths of Chinese immigrants entering the country during this period. By 1950 the male to female ratio on the mainland dropped to 1.9 and in Hawaii to 1.1.

In the meantime, in China the Communists were winning a civil war against a Nationalist government beset with inflation and corruption. After the Communists established the People's Republic of China (PRC) in 1949, approximately five thousand Chinese students, mostly non-Cantonese, chose to remain in the United States. Subsequently, refugee professionals, entrepreneurs, intellectuals, and ex-government officials from Nationalist China joined their ranks. Beginning in the late 1950's an increasing number of students from Taiwan and Hong Kong also arrived to study. More than 90 percent stayed after completing their education. These represented the beginnings of a greater presence of Chinese from other regions of China.

The unstable political situation in China continued to spur an exodus. Many sought to enter the United States. In order to circumvent still restrictive American immigration laws, the use of assumed identities for entry continued to flourish. By the late 1940's, the U.S. government had begun investigating and prosecuting violations. Hostilities between the United States and China on the Korean Peninsula and the anti-Communist hysteria in the United States during the 1950's intensified concern over this problem.

Numerous markets owned and operated by Chinese American families have sprung up in cities across America. Here a Chinese family poses in front of its grocery. (Smithsonian Institution)

In 1955, Everett F. Drumright, American consul in Hong Kong, issued a report charging the Chinese with wholesale immigration fraud and raising the specter of Communist infiltration. However, the use of assumed identities among Chinese immigrants was so pervasive that the government faced the unacceptable prospect of tying up the courts for decades if it were to prosecute all violators. Thus immigration authorities worked out with Chinese American community leaders a program under which Chinese confessed their true identities to immigration authorities and adjusted their status. Some twenty thousand Chinese went through this CONFESSION PROGRAM.

At the same time that the Chinese were accused of immigration fraud, discriminatory barriers against the Chinese and other minorities were being lowered in American society. Chinese began to find greater employment opportunities in mainstream occupations, especially in the professional and clerical sectors. Many

became outstanding in their fields. In 1957 Chen Ning YANG and Tsung-Dao LEE received the Nobel Prize in Physics. Another well-known professional was I. M. PEI, the architect.

Many Chinese remained small entrepreneurs. The laundry business, traditionally connected with the mainland Chinese, had begun to decline by the end of the 1950's as home washing machines became more available; however, the restaurant business expanded as increasing numbers in mainstream America learned to appreciate Chinese food. On the Pacific Coast and in the Southwest, Chinese expanded meat markets and small grocery stores into supermarkets and shopping centers.

As the social and economic status of Chinese Americans improved, many moved to live among the general population. In the meantime the embargo imposed by the United States on the PRC had led to the severance of many cultural and economic ties with the

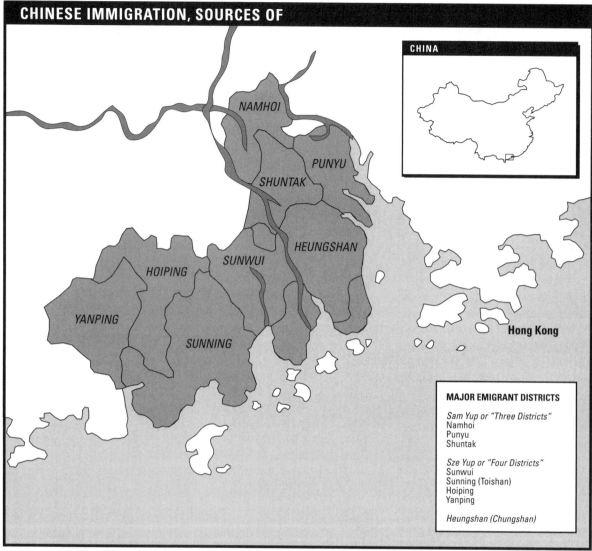

CHINESE IMMIGRATION, SOURCES OF

CHINA

NAMHOI

PUNYU

SHUNTAK

HEUNGSHAN

HOIPING

SUNWUI

YANPING

SUNNING

Hong Kong

MAJOR EMIGRANT DISTRICTS

Sam Yup or "Three Districts"
Namhoi
Punyu
Shuntak

Sze Yup or "Four Districts"
Sunwui
Sunning (Toishan)
Hoiping
Yanping

Heungshan (Chungshan)

Source: Franklin Ng, *Chinese Americans Struggle for Equality.* Vero Beach, Fla.: Rourke, 1992.

ancestral land. Chinese-language schools and newspapers declined. The Americanization process accelerated as the younger generation lost familiarity with the Chinese language and Chinese customs. This process was particularly rapid among the Chinese in Hawaii and those living in suburbs and in small towns on the mainland.

Following the lead of Chinese in Hawaii, Chinese on the mainland also began to venture into mainstream politics. By the end of the 1940's, some Chinese had been appointed to minor city commissions in San Francisco. In 1956, Warren Chan in Seattle became the first Chinese American on the mainland to be appointed municipal judge. In electoral politics Wing ONG of Phoenix, Arizona, was elected state assembly-man in 1946, becoming the first Chinese American elected to office on the mainland. The first Chinese American elected to office at the national level was Hiram Fong, who became U.S. Senator from Hawaii in 1959 and served four terms before retirement.

Immigration on an Equal Basis: 1965-   . In the 1950's, there was increasing pressure in Congress to reform immigration policy. The decisive change was finally made with the Immigration and Nationality Act of 1965, which established a new system in place of the national-origins quota system that had governed immigration to the United States since the 1920's. Restrictions on Asian immigration had been in place even longer. While the old law strongly favored immigration from Northern and Western Europe, the 1965 law was much more even-handed.

Many Taiwan and Hong Kong students adjusted their status under the new law to obtain permanent residency and citizenship status. Moreover, after the law went into effect, Chinese immigration from Hong Kong and Taiwan increased dramatically. Other troubled parts of the world during the 1960's and 1970's, such as Cuba, Burma (now Myanmar), and the Philippines, added to the influx. Normalization of U.S. relations with the PRC and the relaxation of the PRC's emigration policy in the late 1970's also led to a great increase in Chinese immigrants from the mainland.

Many Chinese newcomers settled in the East, and the Chinese population in New York increased to equal that in the San Francisco Bay Area. The Chinese population on the mainland grew to 382,795 in 1970 and almost doubled again to 749,246 in 1980. The growth in Hawaii was much slower, to 52,039 in 1970 and 56,260 in 1980.

In 1982 a separate quota of 20,000 was given to Taiwan, and in 1987 the Hong Kong quota was raised to 5,000. Starting in the late 1970's, as a result of the Vietnam War and political persecution in its aftermath, there was also a mass exodus from Vietnam, Cambodia, and Laos. By the 1990's more than one million Indochinese refugees had arrived in the United States, with a high percentage of these being ethnic Chinese. Many were non-Cantonese, and the influx has resulted in the increased diversification of the Chinese American population. In 1980, a sizable majority of the Chinese in the United States were foreign-born; in Hawaii, which attracted far fewer immigrants than the mainland, only about 25 percent of the Chinese were born abroad.

CHINATOWNS, which had been declining as Chinese moved to better housing, once again became busy and crowded places. Los Angeles became a third major center of Chinese in America, rivaling San Francisco and New York, and new concentrations of Chinese

The traditional Chinese Dragon Dance is perhaps the highlight of the Chinese New Year celebration as well as a loud and colorful tourist attraction. (Asian American Studies Library, University of California at Berkeley)

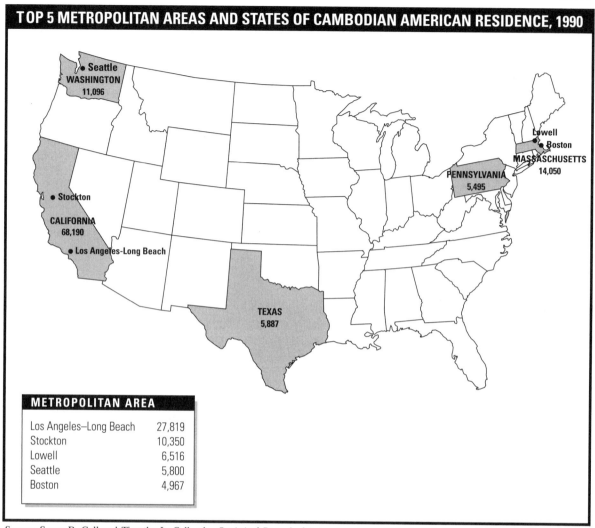

TOP 5 METROPOLITAN AREAS AND STATES OF CAMBODIAN AMERICAN RESIDENCE, 1990

Seattle
WASHINGTON
11,096

Lowell
Boston
MASSACHUSETTS
14,050

PENNSYLVANIA
5,495

Stockton

CALIFORNIA
68,190

Los Angeles-Long Beach

TEXAS
5,887

METROPOLITAN AREA

Los Angeles–Long Beach	27,819
Stockton	10,350
Lowell	6,516
Seattle	5,800
Boston	4,967

Source: Susan B. Gall and Timothy L. Gall, eds., *Statistical Record of Asian Americans.* Detroit: Gale Research, 1993.

arose in such places as Monterey Park, Westminster, San Jose, and San Diego, California; Flushing, on Long Island; and Houston. Chinese banks were established to handle Chinese capital flowing in from Hong Kong, Taiwan, and Southeast Asia. Much of this money went into real estate, and property values in some areas skyrocketed.

Besides the still popular restaurant business, Chinese entered many new fields of endeavor. Taiwanese operated numerous hotels and motels in Southern California. Chinese from Vietnam, Cambodia, and Laos opened many groceries and supermarkets. Other Chinese were active in the high technology sectors, and during the 1970's Wang Laboratories was a leading firm in the computer field.

In the community there was a resurgence in Chinese language and culture. Chinese schools and bookstores increased in number; Chinese newspapers again flourished. In the 1970's Chinese television also began to appear to exploit the potential of this expanding population.

The large and rapid influx, however, also led to the aggravation of social problems in metropolitan areas. Chief among those were unemployment and under-employment, a shortage of affordable housing, and youth-gang-connected crime and violence. Many newcomers lacked English skills and found themselves in low-paying, menial jobs. They constituted a large part of the Chinese in service occupations, which in 1990 employed one-sixth of all Chinese workers.

At the same time, however, many Chinese Americans—about 54 percent in 1990—have had some higher education. They constitute a large part of the more than one-third of the Chinese in managerial and professional specialty occupations, and the slightly less than one-third in technical, sales, and administrative support occupations. Beginning in the late 1960's, these middle-class Chinese became involved in the struggle of ethnic minorities for equal opportunities and affirmative action; associated with this struggle was a heightening of ethnic consciousness, resulting in greater interest in their historical experience and in defining a Chinese American culture.

As a result of the Civil Rights movement, the job horizon of Chinese Americans broadened as they entered fields formerly closed to them. Chinese Americans such as television newscaster Connie CHUNG, novelist Maxine Hong KINGSTON, playwright David Henry HWANG, and filmmaker Wayne WANG became well known in mainstream America. Accompanying these developments was a demand for greater participation in the decision-making process. Chinese worked with other Asian Americans in order to have greater political strength to attain common goals. The activism of the 1960's led to increased political participation, and more Chinese filled appointed and electoral offices.

By the 1990's Chinese were found throughout the United States, but four out of ten still lived in California. They were concentrated in metropolitan areas, with New York City, San Francisco, and Los Angeles being the centers with the largest populations. Due to increased immigration since 1965, seven out of ten were foreign-born.

The contemporary Chinese American community can roughly be classified into categories as follows:

One group consists of those who are closely associated with Chinatowns; they may or may not live in a Chinatown, but many of their activities are centered on Chinatown. They are overwhelmingly Cantonese-speaking immigrants or their descendants. Those admitted before the 1960's originated from rural areas. In

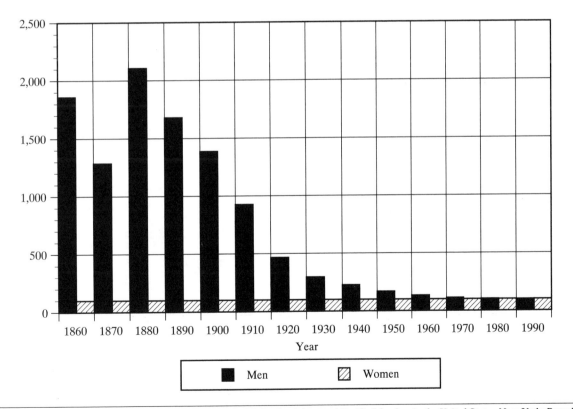

Male-to-Female Ratio of Chinese American Population, 1860-1990

Source: Herbert Barringer, Robert W. Gardner, and Michael J. Levin, *Asians and Pacific Islanders in the United States.* New York: Russell Sage Foundation, 1993.
Note: Data show number of Chinese American males per 100 Chinese American females.

Chinese American Statistical Profile, 1990

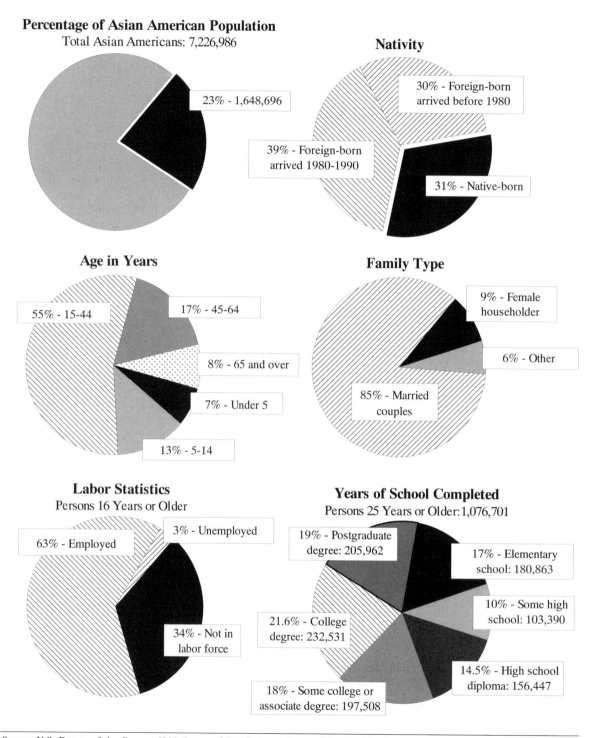

Percentage of Asian American Population
Total Asian Americans: 7,226,986

23% - 1,648,696

Nativity

30% - Foreign-born arrived before 1980

39% - Foreign-born arrived 1980-1990

31% - Native-born

Age in Years

55% - 15-44

17% - 45-64

8% - 65 and over

7% - Under 5

13% - 5-14

Family Type

9% - Female householder

6% - Other

85% - Married couples

Labor Statistics
Persons 16 Years or Older

63% - Employed

3% - Unemployed

34% - Not in labor force

Years of School Completed
Persons 25 Years or Older: 1,076,701

19% - Postgraduate degree: 205,962

17% - Elementary school: 180,863

10% - Some high school: 103,390

21.6% - College degree: 232,531

14.5% - High school diploma: 156,447

18% - Some college or associate degree: 197,508

Source: U.S. Bureau of the Census, *1990 Census of Population: Asians and Pacific Islanders in the United States,* 1993.

recent decades, however, an increasing number had lived for years in urban surroundings. Many who have arrived since the late 1970's came from the PRC and thus had lived for decades in a socialist society. There are other dialect groups with smaller populations such as Hakka, Hinanese, Fujianese, and Shanghaiese who are also associated with the Chinatowns.

Another large segment consists of ethnic Chinese refugees and immigrants from all over the world, but particularly from Vietnam, Cambodia, and Laos. The Chinese speak a diversity of dialects, but many also speak Cantonese, and they blend well into the existing Chinatowns. These newcomers have also formed new business concentrations in areas such as Westminster, Long Beach, San Diego, and San Jose.

Chinese having little association with existing Chi-

Occupation

Employed Persons 16 Years or Older	Percentage
Managerial and professional specialty	36%
Technical, sales, and administrative support	31%
Service	16%
Farming, forestry, and fishing	0.4%
Precision production, craft, and repair	6%
Operators, fabricators, and laborers	11%

Income, 1989

Median household income	$36,259
Per capita	$14,877
Percent of families in poverty	11%

Household Size

Number of People	Percentage
1	17.6%
2	23.9%
3	19.1%
4	20.0%
5	10.7%
6	4.9%
7 or more	3.8%

Source: U.S. Bureau of the Census, *1990 Census of Population: Asians and Pacific Islanders in the United States,* 1993.

natowns are a diverse group. Before immigration many were urban dwellers from different parts of mainland China, Taiwan, and Hong Kong. Earlier postwar immigrants tend to have a higher education level and economic status than the existing Chinatown population, with many being academics and professionals or businessmen in mainstream society. Many live in the suburbs or in university towns mixed with the general population. Many are Mandarin speakers, but there has been an increasing influx also of upper-middle-class and more affluent Cantonese speakers from Hong Kong with the colony's pending change of political status in 1997. Since the 1970's an increasing number have also been Taiwanese-speaking, and business concentrations somewhat resembling the older Cantonese-dominated Chinatowns have sprung up in cities such as Monterey Park, Flushing, and Houston.

Chinese using English as their primary medium of communication are another major group. Many exhibit a high degree of acculturation and integration into the American mainstream. In the 1990's the overwhelming majority in this group are American-born descended from earlier Cantonese immigrants; however, the situation is changing as the second and third generations of the other groups take their places in American society.

Each of the above groups has its own associated institutions and activities. But as such, each is also a component making up the diverse entity known collectively as the Chinese American community.—*Him Mark Lai*

SUGGESTED READINGS:
• Barth, Gunther. *Bitter Strength: A History of the Chinese in the United States, 1850-1870.* Cambridge, Mass.: Harvard University Press, 1964. Analyzes the development of the early Chinese American community. The author's main thesis is that contrasts between Chinese values and Western values led to conflict.
• Chen, Jack. *The Chinese of America: From the Beginnings to the Present.* New York: Harper and Row/San Francisco, 1980. Jack Chen is an artist and journalist known for his writings on China. This work, his first on Chinese American history, is written for a general audience. The principal emphasis is on the role of Chinese labor in the western United States during the nineteenth century and on the anti-Chinese movement.
• Chinn, Thomas W., Him Mark Lai, and Philip P. Choy, eds. *A History of the Chinese in California: A Syllabus.* San Francisco: Chinese Historical Society of America, 1969. A sourcebook giving the essentials of

the history of the Chinese in California, focusing on the role of the Chinese during the nineteenth century.

• Chiu, Ping. *Chinese Labor in California, 1850-1880: An Economic Study*. Madison, Wis.: State Historical Society of Wisconsin, 1963. A groundbreaking study using documentary sources and census data to analyze the role of Chinese labor in various sectors of the California economy during the nineteenth century.

• Coolidge, Mary R. *Chinese Immigration*. New York: Henry Holt, 1909. A classic work written by a Stanford University professor to refute the arguments of the anti-Chinese movement. Coolidge discusses in detail the contributions of the Chinese in California as well as events of the anti-Chinese movement up to the early 1900's. Dated, but still of real value.

• Glick, Clarence E. *Sojourners and Settlers: Chinese Migrants in Hawaii*. Honolulu: University Press of Hawaii, 1980. A sociological work analyzing the evolution of the Chinese community in Hawaii beginning in the eighteenth century. Much of the research was done by the author for his Ph.D. dissertation, completed in 1938.

• Kung, S. W. *Chinese in American Life: Some Aspects of Their History, Status, Problems, and Contributions*. Seattle: University of Washington Press, 1962. A well-researched book analyzing the Chinese American community of the 1960's. The analysis of immigration laws is particularly detailed.

• Lee, Rose Hum. *The Chinese in the United States of America*. Hong Kong: Hong Kong University Press, 1960. The first scholarly work using modern sociological methods to analyze the Chinese American community of the 1950's. The author contends that assimilation is the ultimate fate of the Chinese community.

• Lum, Arlene, ed. *Sailing for the Sun: The Chinese in Hawaii 1789-1989*. Honolulu: Three Heroes, 1989. Collection of articles covering different aspects of the history of the Chinese in Hawaii, published to commemorate the bicentennial of the Chinese arrival in Hawaii. Profusely illustrated with historical photographs.

• Mark, Diane M. L., and Ginger Chih. *A Place Called Chinese America*. Washington, D.C.: Organization of Chinese Americans, 1982. Work covering the history of the Chinese community both on the mainland and in Hawaii. Based on documentary research and oral history interviews, and written at the middle school level, the book is especially strong on the modern American-born community.

• Nee, Victor, and Brett Nee. *Longtime Californ': A Documentary Study of An American Chinatown*. New York: Pantheon Books, 1973. A work using oral history to narrate the story of the Chinese in San Francisco through the personal experiences of individuals. Also includes background materials based on the authors' documentary research.

• Sung, Betty Lee. *A Survey of Chinese American Manpower and Employment*. New York: Praeger Publishers, 1976. Before retirement, the author was a faculty member of the Asian Studies department at City University of New York. This work gives a detailed picture of the Chinese American community based on 1970 census data.

• Sung, Betty Lee. *Mountain of Gold: The Story of the Chinese in America*. New York: Macmillan, 1967. The first postwar nonacademic work on the Chinese in America written from a Chinese American perspective. The object was to help mainstream readers to better understand the Chinese American community as a part of American society.

• Tsai, Henry Shih-shan. *The Chinese Experience in America*. Bloomington: Indiana University Press, 1986. The author is professor of history and chairman of the Asian Studies program at the University of Arkansas. The work examines the experiences of different subgroups in the Chinese community; it is especially strong when dealing with the student and Mandarin-speaking communities from which the author originated. The author also draws on his expertise in Asian Studies in his analysis of the influence of international issues on Chinese in the United States.

Chinese Americans in the military: Chinese Americans have served in the American armed forces for nearly as long as Chinese have lived in the United States. There are accounts of a handful of Chinese serving with both the Union and Confederate armies during the American Civil War (1861-1865). Later, a number of Chinese nationals and Chinese Americans served in the U.S. Navy during the American campaign in the Philippine Islands during the Spanish-American War of 1898, and in the American suppression of the Filipino resistance that followed the war between the United States and Spain.

World War II. While a small number of Chinese Americans served during World War I, it was during World War II that Chinese Americans gained recognition for their military service. As often noted, the war was a watershed event in American social history; this was particularly true for the Chinese American community. Jobs opened up in industry, technical fields,

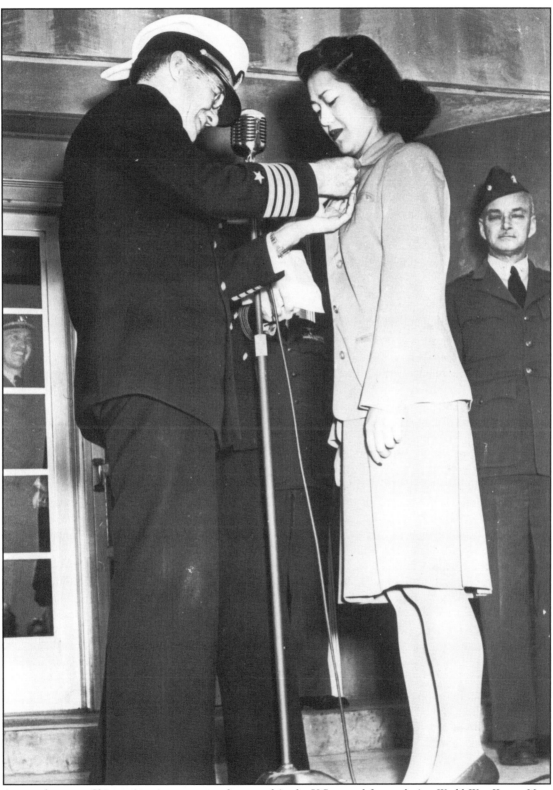

Among the many Chinese American women who served in the U.S. armed forces during World War II was Mary May Lee. Here she is being decorated for her outstanding contribution to war production. (Asian American Studies Library, University of California at Berkeley)

and other occupations that previously had been closed to Chinese American men and women. The wartime relationship between the United States and China also led to a softening in American attitudes toward China, and the Chinese Exclusion acts were finally repealed in 1943, allowing for a small quota (105 a year) of Chinese immigrants to enter the United States and, most significantly, giving Chinese immigrants the right to apply for American citizenship.

The year 1943 was also an important year for Chinese Americans who entered the military. More than 20 percent (fifteen to twenty thousand) of the adult Chinese American male population served in the armed forces during the war, in both the European and the Pacific theaters. They served in greatest number in the Army, followed by the Army Air Corps, and then the Navy, Marines, and Coast Guard. A smaller number of Chinese American women also served in the Women's Army Corps (WAC), Women's Auxiliary Volunteer Emergency Services (WAVES), and the Women's Airforce Service Pilots (WASP). In addition to their military service, Chinese American women found employment in defense-related industries and contributed substantially to war-relief efforts in their communities, thus entering the American public sphere in unprecedented numbers.

Military Units. One of the most significant developments during the war was the formation of predominantly Chinese American units, usually headed by Caucasian commanding officers. These units were created in 1943 with the understanding that they would serve in the China-Burma-India (CBI) theater and facilitate better relationships between American and Chinese troops stationed there. The majority of these units were under the umbrella of the 14th Air Service Group, which in turn was affiliated with the 14th Air Force, which became known collectively as the Flying Tigers.

The 14th Air Service Group was made up of a number of outfits that were primarily support units for the 14th Air Force and other larger contingents. These units consisted of the 407th Air Service Squadron, 555th Air Service Squadron, 1077th Quartermaster Company, 1157th Signal Company, 1544th Ordnance Company, 1545th Ordnance Company, 2121st Quartermaster Trucking Company, 2122nd Quartermaster Trucking Company, and the Headquarters Squadron. In addition, there was another all-Chinese American unit, the 987th Signal Communications Battalion, which was affiliated with the Office of Strategic Services (OSS). The units in the 14th Air Service Group

served in all the air bases in north and southwestern China and in many of the airfields in India under American command.

Postwar period. At the end of the war, a number of these troops stayed in China for a short period of time. During this time some managed to visit with family members, and a number took advantage of the WAR BRIDES ACT OF 1945 and got married, returning to the United States with wives. This heralded the beginning of the first major influx of Chinese immigrant women to enter the country since the imposition of exclusion legislation. The majority of Chinese American veterans used the GI Bill to help purchase homes or continue their education, marking their advancement into the American middle class.

Chinese Americans continued to serve in the military, seeing action in the Korean and Vietnam wars. While fewer Chinese Americans choose careers in the military than do other Asian American groups, they still serve their country with distinction and honor in the American armed forces.—*K. Scott Wong*

SUGGESTED READINGS: • Lim, Christina, and Sheldon Lim. *In the Shadow of the Tiger*. San Mateo, Calif.: Japanese American Curriculum Project, 1993. • Phan, Peter. "Familiar Strangers: The Fourteenth Air Service Group, Case Study of Chinese American Identity During WWII." In *Chinese America: History and Perspectives*, *1993*. San Francisco: Chinese Historical Society of America, 1993. • Strobridge, William. "Chinese in the Spanish-American War and Beyond." In *The Chinese American Experience: Papers from the Second National Conference on Chinese American Studies*, edited by Genny Lim. San Francisco: Chinese Historical Society of America, 1984.

Chinese banks: Chinese-owned banks first appeared in American cities around the beginning of the twentieth century and have served the Chinese communities since then. Since the 1970's the growing Chinese population and economic activity in the Pacific basin has stimulated a proliferation of banking institutions. The capital may be domestic or foreign, or a combination of both.

Early Banks. Chinese banks first appeared on both coasts at about the same time. Hong Kong's Huayi Bank, an enterprise of the Chinese Constitutionalist Party, established an agency in New York around 1906-1907. It was dissolved around 1908. San Francisco's Canton Bank, founded in 1907 by Look Poong Shan (Lee Eli), I. P. Allen, and Chinatown merchants, was more successful. Handling business transactions, remittances, and deposits of Chinese throughout the West and Mexico, the bank operated profitably until the end of World War I. Ownership control passed into the hands of the Dongfang Bank of Hong Kong in 1924. When the Hong Kong bank failed in 1926, the California state superintendent of banks closed Canton Bank.

Canton Bank financial transactions in the Far East were handled by the Bank of Canton in Hong Kong, established by Look Poong Shan in 1912. This bank had established an office on Wall Street in New York by 1922 and a branch in San Francisco by 1924. The Bank of Canton failed in 1935, but the San Francisco branch reopened in 1937 as the Bank of Canton of California after infusion of capital by T. V. Soong and other investors.

Chinese banks also appeared in Honolulu during the early twentieth century. In 1916 the CHINESE AMERICAN BANK, founded by Chung Kun Ai and others, opened for business, followed in 1922 by the LIBERTY BANK, founded by Lum Yip Kee and others. The Chinese American Bank was closed by the territorial government in 1933 over insufficient assets to cover liabilities; it opened as the American Security Bank in 1935 after reorganization.

The 1950's and 1960's. After World War II the growing financial strength of the Chinese American community was shown in the appearance of more Chinese banking institutions. In Seattle, Robert Chinn and others founded the United Savings and Loan Association in 1952. This was followed by the Bank of Trade of San Francisco (founded in 1961 by Paul H. Louie and others) and the Cathay Bank of Los Angeles (founded in 1962 by George T. M. Ching and others). The first Chinese American-owned bank in New York appeared in 1967, when Robert O. P. Yu and Raymond S. D. Yoh led the reorganization of the New York agency (established during the early years of the Sino-Japanese War) of the Bank of China into the Chinese American Bank. In Hawaii, Chinese and other investors founded the Hawaii National Bank, which opened its doors in 1962.

The 1970's and Afterward. More Chinese-owned banks appeared in the major Chinese American communities as the Chinese population in the continental United States grew rapidly after the Immigration and Nationality Act of 1965. There was also an increased influx of Chinese capital from Taiwan, Hong Kong, and Southeast Asia. San Francisco, Los Angeles, and New York especially became important centers of Chinese banking activity. New institutions such as the

BANK OF THE ORIENT (founded in 1971 by Ernest Go, member of a Chinese banking family in the Philippines), the American Asian Bank (founded in 1974 by Tung financial group of Hong Kong and Southeast Asian interests), the Sincere Savings and Loan Association (founded in 1979 by Thomas Leung and others; name changed to the Sincere Savings Bank in 1983), and the Golden Coin Savings and Loan Association (founded in 1979 by Hiram Woo and others) appeared in the San Francisco Bay Area. In Los Angeles and Orange counties new institutions appeared, such as the East-West Federal Savings and Loan Association (founded in 1972 by F. Chow Chan and others; name changed to East-West Federal Bank in 1983); the Far East National Bank (founded in 1974 by Henry Hwang and others); the General Bank (founded in 1980 by Li-Pi Wu and a Taiwan financial group), the Monterey Park National Bank (founded in 1980 by Frederic Hsieh and others, including other minorities; changed to Omni Bank in 1982); the United National Bank (founded in 1983 by Robert C. T. Chang and others); and the United American Bank (founded in 1983 by Vietnamese Chinese Phil Trinh Chen and Caucasian investors). In New York City there were new institutions such as the United Orient Bank (founded in 1981), the Chinatown Federal Savings Bank (founded in 1984), the Eastbank (founded in 1984 by local and Southeast Asian investors), the Abacus Federal Savings Bank (founded in 1984), the Great Eastern Bank (founded in 1986), and the Amerasia Bank (founded in 1988). By the 1990's Chinese banking institutions had appeared also in Houston, Chicago, Philadelphia, Washington, D.C., and other communities. Chinese banks from Taiwan, Hong Kong, the People's Republic of China, and Southeast Asia have also established agencies in larger Chinese communities in America. By 1989 there were about fifty Chinese American banks in the United States, but this figure continued to grow through the early 1990's.

Changes in Ownership. During the 1970's and 1980's some Chinese banking institutions ran into financial difficulties and ownership changed hands. In 1985 federal banking authorities closed New York's Golden Pacific Bank (founded in 1977 by Joseph Chuang) for having insufficient assets to cover liabilities, charging bank management with irregularities. In 1986 the United Savings Bank (founded by Ben Hom and others as United Savings and Loan Association in 1979; changed to a bank in 1983), after suffering heavy loan losses, was forced by the Federal Savings and Loan Insurance Corporation (FSLIC) to be sold to

Hibernia Bancshares. The latter was owned by Indonesian Chinese Sudono Salim's (Liem Sioe Liong) First Pacific group, which had purchased the non-Chinese-owned Hibernia Bank of San Francisco in 1982. In 1980 the Lippo group of Indonesian Chinese James T. Riady bought the Bank of Trade of San Francisco (name changed to Lippobank in 1990).

The Lippobank was founded originally in 1961 as the Bank of Trade, one of the oldest Chinese-owned state-chartered banks in the United States. It is associated with the Lippo Group, among the largest financial groups in Southeast Asia. (LIPPOBANK)

Other Chinese capital bought into non-Chinese-owned institutions. In 1979 Hong Kong entrepreneur Linton S. K. Chu, representing Hong Kong banker Oen Yin Choy, bought the Hispanic-owned Pan American National Bank of Monterey Park, California, and changed it to the Trans American National Bank. In 1982 Ming Yu Tsai from Japan bought the Los Angeles National Bank; in 1984 Harold Chuang and others acquired controlling interest in the American International Bank in Los Angeles.

Expansion. Most Chinese banks operate in only one city or metropolitan area. Some institutions, however, have begun to expand outside their local areas. In 1976 San Francisco's Amerasia Bank opened a branch in Beverly Hills, California. The United Savings Bank, before its change of ownership, was one of the largest minority-owned banks in the nation, with twenty-six branches in California. The Trans American National Bank and the Far East Bank of Los Angeles established branches in San Francisco in 1984 and 1987, respectively. In turn San Francisco's Lippobank expanded to Los Angeles in 1986.

Association. In 1987 Chinese-owned banks formed the National Association of Chinese American Banks. Twenty-six banks belonged to the group in 1989.— *Him Mark Lai*

SUGGESTED READINGS: • Liu, Pei Chi. *A History of Chinese in the United States of America, II*. In Chinese. Taipei: Liming Wenhua Shiye Youxian Gongsi, 1982. • Luke, William K. "The First Chinese Bank in the United States." *Chinatown News* 3 (July, 1974): 10. • Ma, L. Eve Armentrout. "The Big Business Ventures of Chinese in North America, 1850-1930." In *The Chinese American Experience: Papers from the Second National Conference on Chinese American Studies*, edited by Genny Lim. San Francisco; Chinese Historical Society of America and Chinese Culture Foundation of San Francisco, 1982. • Mai Liqian (Him Mark Lai). *Cong Huaqiao dao Huaren: Ershi Shiji Meiguo Huaren Shehui Fazhan Shi* (from overseas Chinese to Chinese American: the development of Chinese American society during the twentieth century). Hong Kong: Joint Publishing, 1992.

Chinese boycott of 1905: Chinese reaction to American exclusion laws, and also a sign of rising Chinese nationalism. Prior to 1905 the U.S. government had passed numerous laws and acts such as the Chinese Exclusion Acts of 1882 and 1884 and the Geary Act (1892), which prohibited Chinese laborers from coming to the United States. There were also countless outrages committed by white Americans against the Chinese, mostly in the Western states of the Union. In the spring of 1902, the U.S. Congress again passed, and President Theodore Roosevelt signed, a bill to prohibit the entry and to regulate the residence of Chinese in Hawaii and the Philippines. The Chinese boycott of American goods, officially begun in May of 1905, was therefore an attempt on the part of the Chinese to put pressure on their own government not to renew the so-called GRESHAM-YANG TREATY, which had been signed on March 17, 1894, between Secretary of State Walter Q. Gresham and the Chinese Minister to Washington, D.C., Yang Ru. The treaty stipulated that Chinese laborers be prohibited from coming to the United States for a period of ten years. It also stated that if six months before the expiration of the treaty neither government gave notice of its final termination to the other, the treaty would remain in full force for another ten years.

Chen Jiyan of Hawaii, who was also the editor of a Chinese newspaper, the *Xin Zhongguo ribao* (*new China daily*), was believed to be the first person to suggest a boycott against American goods. Chinese merchants in the United States, through their ongoing exchanges with the Chinese bourgeois class in China, made it clear that American injustices could best be countered by economic pressure. As a consequence, in Shanghai those sympathetic to the merchants openly declared on May 10, 1905, that when the government proves itself unable to act, then the people must rise up to do so. In less than a month, this first antiforeign boycott spread throughout China, and it continued into 1906. The Chinese government, under the pressure of such an emotional outburst, refused to renew the Gresham-Yang Treaty. The United States, however, unilaterally extended and reenacted all the anti-Chinese exclusion legislation, dictating the course of Chinese immigration until the repeal of these laws in December, 1943, China having become an ally of the United States during World War II.

Chinese Buddhism: Buddhism, a religion founded by Siddhartha Gautama in South Asia, advocates the quitting of all desires in order to end the painful cycle of rebirth and achieve the ultimate status of enlightenment, Nirvana. While conflicting with some of the most fundamental concepts of traditional China, it has had greater impact on China than any other foreign religion or philosophy. From its entry into China in the first century C.E. until the mid-ninth century, Buddhism offered a great attraction to Chinese scholars through its sophisticated metaphysical reasoning. Its promise of a better future world was appealing to rich and poor alike at a time when China was often split and plagued by war and famine and when its chief rival, Confucianism, was in relative decline.

The Spread of Buddhism. Before Buddhism entered China, it had already been divided into two major schools: Theravada, or Hinayana (the lesser vehicle), and Mahayana (the greater vehicle). Theravada spread southward to Sri Lanka, Burma, Thailand, and Cambodia, while Mahayana came to be accepted in China, Korea, Japan, and Vietnam.

Buddhism appeared in China proper as early as the mid-first century C.E. during the Latter Han Dynasty (23-220). Unsatisfied with the often contradictory Buddhist teachings in China, devoted Chinese monks made long journeys under treacherous and grueling conditions to India in search of original Buddhist sutras. Best known among these Buddhist pilgrims were Faxian and Xuanzang. Faxian went to India via Central Asia in 399 and came back by sea in 414 at a time when China was politically split into the Northern and Southern dynasties. Xuanzang made his trip to and from India by land between 629 and 645 during the Tang Dynasty (618-907). Both of them brought back valuable Buddhist scriptures for translation, which greatly stimulated the growth of Chinese Buddhism. They also kept precious records about the areas through which they traveled, which have since become indispensable sources on the history and customs of India and Central Asia.

Buddhism made its fastest progress during the Period of Division (220-589 C.E.), especially in the North, where the non-Han rulers were often less biased against foreign religions. Under the Northern Wei Dynasty (386-534), founded by the seminomadic Xianbei people, Buddhism became the de facto state religion. By the sixth century it had conquered the South as well.

The economic and intellectual flourishing of Buddhism continued under the Sui (581-618) and the early part of the Tang dynasties. Active support by Empress Wu gave a tremendous boost to Buddhism in the late seventh century. After centuries of Sinification, however, Chinese Buddhism was transformed into doctrines and sects that were far different from original Buddhism.

Doctrinal and Sectarian Characteristics. Buddhism came to China mainly in the form of the Mahayana (greater vehicle) school. It was so named because in comparison with the original school of Theravada, the followers of Mahayana believed that the boat in which they carried the salvaged human beings toward enlightenment was much bigger. The Mahayanists referred to Theravada, not without contempt, as Hinayana (the lesser vehicle). While Theravada insisted on the existence of only one historic Buddha, Chinese Buddhism, which was based on Mahayana, believed that the Buddha existed in various forms of reincarnation in the past, the present, and the future. One of the traits of the Buddha, known as *bodhisattva*, came to be deified as a god, one who had achieved the enlighten-

Worshippers leaving an offering at a Buddhist shrine. (Ed Bridges)

ment of a Buddha but who chose to stay behind in the world in order to help save others. Previously Buddhism had stressed enlightenment though one's own efforts. With the concept of *bodhisattvas*, the emphasis was shifted to salvation through the strength of others. Consequently *bodhisattvas* became popular gods, objects of worship. Nirvana, the ultimate stage of enlightenment, came to mean afterlife in paradise.

In their efforts to assimilate Buddhist doctrines, Chinese Buddhists organized different, sometimes contradictory, philosophical ideas of Buddhism into sects. One of these was Tiantai, which was founded by Zhiyit and was named after its mountain headquarters in Zhejiang. Zhiyi reorganized Buddhist teachings into several levels. The highest doctrine was represented by the Lotus Sutra. Later in the eighth and ninth centuries, the Tiantai sect was to become the dominant Buddhist sect.

The most popular Buddhist sect was that of PURE LAND, or Jingtu. Pure Land was the name for the Western Paradise, ruled by one of the many Mahayana Buddhas, Amitabha. Followers of this sect believed that the simple act of invoking Amitabha's help by calling out his name was able to bring about salvation. By the end of the fifth century, these ideas had become firmly entrenched in China, and Pure Land later became the strongest Buddhist sect in East Asia. (See AMIDISM, JODO SHINSHU, and PURE LAND SECTS.)

The last important sect was Chan, the meditation sect. Although Bodhidarma, a Buddhist saint from India who came to China in the sixth century, was often credited with its creation, Chan Buddhism began to take concrete shape only in Tang times, and it did not become prominent until the ninth century. It owed a debt to Taoism in its emphasis on nature, simplicity, and spontaneity. In contrast to the complex philosophical tradition of Buddhist metaphysics, it sought to capture the moment of enlightenment through meditation and intuitive insight.

Decline. In premodern China, Buddhism went through four major periods of persecution. One of them took place in 845 under Wuzong, a Tang emperor, and did irreparable harm to Chinese Buddhism, which was never able to regain its previous level of prosperity. Meanwhile greater odds were stacked against Buddhism. With its steady decline in India, inspiring ideas needed to revive Chinese Buddhism were no longer forthcoming. In China, Neo-Confucianism, with its concept of metaphysics and its hold on the government, was on the rise and attracted the literati away from Buddhism. Only two major sects remained: Pure land and Chan, which eventually became less distinguishable from each other. Gradually Buddhism was reduced to a grass-roots religion.—*Victor Cunrui Xiong*

SUGGESTED READINGS: • Chen, Kenneth. *Buddhism in China: A Historical Survey*. Princeton, N.J.: Princeton University Press, 1964. • Weinstein, Stanley. *Buddhism Under the Tang*. Cambridge, England: Cambridge University Press, 1987. • Wright, Arthur. *Buddhism in Chinese History*. Stanford, Calif.: Stanford University Press, 1988. • Zürcher, Erich. *Buddhist Conquest of China: The Spread and Adaptation of Buddhism in Early Medieval China*. Leiden, The Netherlands: E. J. Brill, 1959.

Chinese calendar: Ancient Chinese dating system initially developed as early as the twenty-seventh century B.C.E. The longest unbroken sequence of time measurement in history, the Chinese calendar is used concurrently with the Gregorian calendar in the People's Republic of China, Taiwan, overseas Chinese communities, and some other Asian countries such as Japan and Korea.

Officially named *nongli* (agrarian calendar) and commonly called *yinli* (lunar calendar), the Chinese calendar is lunisolar with *shichen* (time of the day), day, month, *jiegi* (joints and breadths of the year), and year as its basic unit.

In the Chinese system a day is divided into twelve two-hour periods (*shichen*). These periods are named after the Earthly Branches (*dizhi*) of the Chinese zodiac. The first period, which begins at 11:00 P.M., is called the time of *zi*, or the time of the Rat.

The months alternate between twenty-nine and thirty days, and a year may consist of twelve or thirteen months. A twelve-month year is called *pingnian* (ordinary year) while a year with an intercalary month is known as *runnian* (complete year). Intercalation occurs seven times at stated intervals every nineteen years to harmonize the calendar year with the solar year.

A Chinese year is also apportioned into twenty-four periods (*jiegi*) of approximately fifteen days each. Based on the positions of the sun on the ecliptic, these periods predict atmospheric and climatic changes. The first period, *lichuan*, forecasts the beginning of spring.

The Chinese years are not numbered; they are grouped into chronological cycles of sixty years each

and are named according to one of two systems. The first system joins a Heavenly Stem (*tiangan*) to an Earthly Branch to form the name of a certain year. The second system combines one of the five "elements"—Wood, Fire, Earth, Metal, and Water—with an Earthly Branch.

For purposes other than official record-keeping, the years are often named after the animals in the Chinese zodiac: Rat, Ox, Tiger, Rabbit, Dragon, Snake, Horse, Sheep, Monkey, Rooster, Dog, and Pig. This naming system is beginning to arouse interest outside the Chinese-speaking world; for example, the U.S. Postal Service issued a commemorative stamp in 1993 to mark the Year of the Rooster.

Chinese Christians: The spread of the Christian faith among the early Chinese immigrants was slow and arduous. Given their early experience of discrimination and violence during the California gold rush, this cautious response is understandable. Yet receptivity by the Chinese did improve as the Chinese church experienced four significant development stages in its life.

Beginnings: 1852-1900. While Chinese laborers were crossing the Pacific en route to the gold rush, missionaries were seeking conversions and adherents to the faith in China. The missionary effort had entered China under the privileges granted by the First Opium War (1839-1842) and dictated by the Treaty of Nanjing (1842) along with the Treaty of Wangxia (1844). Much resistance was experienced by the Americans, as the missionary movement was perceived by the Chinese as a component of Western imperialism. Many missionaries therefore decided to return to the United States to fix their concerns upon the growing numbers of Chinese arriving in San Francisco.

The Presbyterian Board of Foreign Missions dispatched William Speer and his wife in 1852 to open a mission in the port city. Having served as medical missionaries in China, they were well-versed in Cantonese. A church was established in 1853 with four Chinese immigrants from Hong Kong. A Sunday school for Chinese children was begun in 1859. That same year J. L. Shuck began the first Southern Baptist mission in Sacramento, and in 1870 Otis Gibson initiated the first Methodist mission. These and other former missionaries to China modeled in California what they did in China, providing medical care, educational instruction, and social services. they also spoke out against the rising tide of anti-Chinese sentiment.

By 1890 there were seven established congregations divided among the cities of San Francisco, Oakland,

and Los Angeles, with a total of about four hundred members. Many Chinese availed themselves of the services of the churches, but few of them accepted the Christian way. Growing discrimination and popular uprisings against them made evangelism difficult. The Chinese Exclusion Act of 1882, barring all Chinese from entering the United States, led to the attrition of membership.

Deepenings: 1900-1943. Although membership levels were on hold, if not in decline, Chinese indigenous leadership that would lead eventually to receptivity and growth was coming to the fore. This leadership came from the maturing converts along with mature believers from Hong Kong prior to 1882. Such indigenousness led to a deepening of faith and commitment, with increased attraction to outsiders seeking both a faith and socialization with their cultural kin.

With the completion of the transcontinental railway system on May 10, 1869, and with the gold fields in decline, many Chinese Christians had chosen to travel East in search of new fortunes. This led to the expansion of the Chinese Christian presence and the multiplication of churches. Meanwhile many other railroad lines were planned and built. By 1923 J. S. Tow could report forty-one missions scattered among the states of California, Arizona, Washington, Illinois, Pennsylvania, New York, and Massachusetts. Chinese branches of the Young Men's Christian Association (YMCA) existed in the cities of San Francisco, Seattle, New York, and Boston. Young Women's Christian Associations (YWCAs) of Chinese ethnicity were located in Oakland, Sacramento, and New York. A Chinese Students Christian Association (CSCA) was also in force uniting believers to grow in character and to do aggressive Christian work. By 1931 there were sixty-four established Chinese churches in the United States and Canada. In spite of racial antagonism the Chinese church had survived and had grown in depth and breadth.

Invigoration: 1943-1965. The Immigration Act of 1943 effectively rescinded the discriminatory laws that had severely limited Chinese immigration, including the Chinese Exclusion Act of 1882. This moved the climate of public opinion from antagonism to at least toleration. It was somewhat forced, in that China was now a political ally of the United States, having sided with the Americans against the Japanese in World War II (1939-1945).

A yearly quota of 105 Chinese were now allowed entry into the country. This provided an impetus to church growth in that wives and children could now enter and family restoration and formation could en-

Missionary teachers and their students at the Chinese Mission School of Monterey, California. (Asian American Studies Library, University of California at Berkeley)

sue. Taught in American public schools and acculturating quickly alongside the native-born, many Chinese were responsive to numerical presence and force. With relaxed immigration many Christian leaders came from Hong Kong to strengthen the leadership level.

In 1962 there were sixty-two bilingual, bicultural Chinese congregations in the United States alone and another four in Hawaii. Forty-seven were divided up among eleven different denominations, including five interdenominational bodies. The remaining groups were independent churches. Average attendance was 155, with a total of 7,000 students in Sunday school. Most churches were self-supporting.

The native-born Chinese were youthful and not the main focus of the church. This encouraged the formation of joint youth and young adult Bible conferences for the purpose of relevant nurture and growth in leadership. The Eastern Chinese Bible Conference (ECBC) was established in 1950, founded by Christians in New York and Philadelphia. In turn, the conference motif was adopted by Chicago believers, and the Midwest Chinese Bible Conference (MCBC) began in 1956. In a short span of time a Bible conference for American-born Chinese was established on the West Coast. Out of the conferences, if not the local church, came candidates for missionary and pastoral commitment and service, many of whom would serve the church for two decades and more. Beyond the confines of the local church, in 1957 a Chinese students conference of about a hundred persons convened at Harvey Cedars, New Jersey. A student movement under Ambassadors for Christ (AFC) was soon formed and blossomed into an active group. At the same time the Chinese Christian Mission (CCM) was formed, initially to perform a Christian literature ministry, later to become a formal mission board. These entities marked the beginning of so-called parachurch efforts serving the Chinese and led by Chinese.

Sustained Development: 1965-1990. The IMMIGRATION AND NATIONALITY ACT OF 1965, coming after the Civil Rights Act of 1964, opened immigration privileges to all the peoples and nations of the world. Each sovereign world state was allowed a yearly quota of 20,000 entries, with the Eastern Hemisphere alloted a total sum of 170,000 each year, all on a first-come, first-served basis. This led to a massive Asian influx, including the Chinese from Taiwan. Boosted by transfer growth and some conversion, by 1984 there were more than five hundred Chinese congregations in the United States with a total of about sixty-nine thousand attendees. The churches were scattered over thirty-one

Taiwanese family attending church. (Don Franklin)

states, with 50 percent in the Pacific region.

The North American Congress of Chinese Evangelicals (NACOCE) was formed in 1972 to promote unity, cooperation, and mission among the growing number of churches. In 1979 the Fellowship of American Chinese Evangelicals (FACE) was established as a voice and support group for English-speaking Chinese believers. Along another cultural track the Evangelical Formosan Church of Los Angeles founded a church-planting movement to evangelize the Taiwanese. Literature, radio, and television proselytization efforts were started, along with formal and informal training schools for the laity and Chinese seminaries for potential pastors.—*Hoover Wong*

SUGGESTED READINGS: • Cayton, Horace R., and Anne Q. Lively. *The Chinese in the United States and the Chinese Christian Church.* New York: National Council of Churches, 1955. • Ling, Samuel. "Three Short Pieces: The Metamorphosis of Chinese Church Growth in North America, 1943-1983." *Chinese Around the World,* October, 1983. • Mark, Diane Mei Lin, and Ginger Chih. *A Place Called Chinese America.* Dubuque, Iowa: Kendall-Hunt, 1982. • Pang, Wing Ning. *Build Up the Kingdom: A Study of the*

North American Chinese Church. Pasadena: North American Congress of Chinese Evangelicals, 1980. • Pang, Wing Ning. *The Chinese and the Chinese Church in America*. Houston: National Convocation on Evangelizing Ethnic America, 1985. • Tow, J. S. *The Real Chinese in America*. New York: Academic Press, 1923.

Chinese Communist Party (Kungchantang): Political organization created in July, 1921, at the Po-wen Middle School for Girls in the French Concession of Shanghai. Delegates to this First Congress inaugurated a movement that overcame myriad domestic and foreign opponents to establish the People's Republic of CHINA (PRC) on October 1, 1949. Under the leadership of MAO ZEDONG, the Chinese Communist Party (CCP) unified the country after decades of division and launched ambitious, disruptive, and ruthless campaigns to consolidate its rule and modernize the nation. The TIANANMEN SQUARE INCIDENT of June, 1989, probably signaled the party's loss of legitimacy, the principal questions thereafter being when the party would lose its monopoly of power and to whom.

Formative Years. Founded in response to the collapse of the dynastic system (1911), the onset of warlordism (1916), and the persistence of imperialism, the CCP was one of two major parties (the other being the GUOMINDANG, or Nationalist Party) to forge a plan to unite China and deal with the imperial powers. These fledgling parties formed the First United Front (1924-1927) under Soviet Russian direction, which provided SUN YAT-SEN's Guomindang (GMD) both funding and Leninist organizational techniques and gave the CCP a more moderate image. The United Front collapsed after the death of Sun (1925) and the ascendancy of CHIANG KAI-SHEK, who turned against the CCP in 1927, nearly destroyed it, and began to consolidate GMD control over China. Communist remnants scattered to the countryside, where party leaders commenced futile campaigns to retake the cities, the home of China's small proletariat. The urban strategy a failure, a new party leadership emerged to forge a rural blueprint based on peasant support and guerrilla warfare, which nevertheless could not withstand the encirclement campaigns of Chiang Kai-shek and his German advisers. The Long March (1934-1935) followed, taking the bulk of the party from its main base in Jiangxi Province in the southeast some sixty-six hundred miles to Shaanxi Province in the northwest and witnessing the ascent of Mao Zedong to CCP leadership. Meanwhile Japan's encroachment on China

forced Chiang Kai-shek to suspend operations against the CCP and join forces with the CCP against Japan. This Second United Front (1937-1945) roughly coincided with World War II, which gave the CCP an opportunity to expand from its Yenan base by organizing peasant resistance to Japan. At war's end the CCP had grown stronger while the GMD, removed from its modern urban base along the east coast to Chongqing in the southwest, became much weaker. The ensuing Chinese Civil War (1945-1949) produced a clear CCP victory; the vanquished GMD fled to Taiwan.

The People's Republic. Under CCP direction China "leaned" toward the Soviet model of economic development and tended to follow Moscow in foreign policy. After mobilizing the peasants to liquidate the landlords and redistribute land, Mao concluded that individual peasant plots would have to be consolidated, first into agricultural producers' cooperatives and finally in the late 1950's into communes. This Chinese road to socialism, known as the Great Leap Forward (1958-1960), caused a famine in which millions of people died. The economy was further disrupted when Soviet economic advisers departed. Mao's plans were discredited, and he was forced into semiretirement. It was to avoid political eclipse that he launched the Cultural Revolution in 1966 to eliminate his political rivals, chiefly Liu Shaoqi. By 1969 the violence and turmoil as well as the Sino-Soviet border crisis forced Mao to reestablish order, and the reconstituted CCP, shorn of Mao's rivals, now comprised a military-laden leadership. Nor did this eliminate political trauma, as Mao's chosen successor, Lin Biao, was implicated in an attempted coup and killed. As Mao's health waned, his hopes for the continuation of the revolution were pinned on the "Gang of Four," headed by his wife, Jiang Qing. His death in September, 1976, quickly led to the gang's demise and to the attenuation of the Maoist vision under his successor as party chairman, Hua Guofeng.

After Mao. Deng Xiaoping had reemerged after several purges to lead the party and set China on a more orthodox road to modernization. By then the party faced ongoing problems that had to be addressed, all of which touched directly on the party's legitimacy. After decades of absolute rule, the economy remained backward, the annual per capita income in 1991 being only $360 (compared to $7,900 in Taiwan). Corruption associated with monopolistic power gave forty million party members (up from three million in 1949) prior claim to jobs and perquisites, a situation exacerbated by modernization efforts. No system has emerged to

Chinese Communist Party chairman Mao Zedong announcing the founding of the People's Republic of China. (AP/Wide World Photos)

ensure a stable transfer of power, resulting in anointed heirs apparent being purged or killed (Liu Shaoqi, Lin Biao, the Gang of Four, Hu Yaobang, and Zhao Ziyang). Finally, many party campaigns testify to the ongoing opposition to CCP rule (or at the very least its policies), from the anti-Rightist campaign against intellectuals in the 1950's to the campaigns against spiritual pollution and bourgeois liberalization in the 1980's, culminating in the crushing of protesters in June, 1989.—*Thomas D. Reins*

SUGGESTED READINGS: • Guillermaz, Jacquez. Translated by Anne Oesteray. *A History of the Chinese Communist Party.* New York: Random House, 1972. • Ladany, Laszlo. *The Communist Party of China and Marxism, 1921-1985: A Self Portrait.* Stanford, Calif.: Hoover Institution Press, 1988. • Meisner, Maurice J. *Mao's China and After: A History of the People's Republic.* New York: Free Press, 1986. • Schwartz, Benjamin I. *Chinese Communism and the Rise of Mao.* Cambridge, Mass.: Harvard University Press, 1951. • Uhalley, Stephen. *A History of the Chinese Communist Party.* Stanford, Calif.: Hoover Institution Press, 1988.

Chinese Consolidated Benevolent Associations (CCBAs): Bodies formed by Chinese American community leaders to deliberate and make decisions on affairs of concern to the entire community. The concept was established in San Francisco during the early 1850's and spread to other communities. CCBAs still play leadership roles in many modern Chinese communities, although their power and influence have changed greatly over the years.

Origins. When Chinese first established *huiguan* (district associations, or companies) in San Francisco, the *huiguan* presidents and leading Chinese merchants took upon themselves the prerogative of making collective decisions on public affairs involving the Chinese community. By 1862 the *huiguan* had formalized this coalition into a loose federation that by consensus made decisions on matters affecting the general interest of the Chinese on the Pacific Coast. It dealt with such matters as settling disputes between people of different companies, consulting on the best means to contest or seek relief from anti-Chinese laws, devising means to bar the import of Chinese prostitutes, entertaining public figures, and so forth. Since at the time there were six associations, or companies (Ning Yung, Hop Wo, Kong Chow, Young Wo, Sam Yup, and Yan Wo), this federation became known to non-Chinese as the Chinese Six Companies (CCBA-SF).

The Chinese Six Companies became seven when the Sue Hing Company was founded in the mid-1870's and later was admitted to the CCBA-SF. The membership became eight with the emergence of the Yen Hoy Company. It became seven again when the Sue Hing and Yen Hoy companies merged in 1909. No new *huiguan* members had been added to the organization since that time. Non-Chinese had, however, continued to use the name Chinese Six Companies throughout these and subsequent changes. This name is applicable only to the CCBA-SF.

In 1882 San Francisco Chinese Consul-General Huang Zunxian promoted the formation of a Chinese Consolidated Benevolent Association (CCBA-SF) to succeed the earlier group in order to provide more effective leadership in the fight against anti-Chinese actions. This organization incorporated under the laws of the state of California in 1901.

After the founding of the CCBA-SF, Chinese diplomatic officials encouraged the formation of CCBAs in other major Chinese American communities and even across international boundaries to Honolulu (1884), Victoria, British Columbia (1884), and Lima, Peru (1885). During the first half of the twentieth century, many smaller Chinese communities in the United States also established CCBAs, and by the 1960's such organizations existed in some twenty-six Chinese American communities.

Powers. The CCBA-SF established the office of president in 1880. This office was held in rotation by one of six *huiguan* presidents. (The Yan Wo Association was excluded from this position until 1989.) Until the late 1920's these individuals were all titled scholars from China.

During the first half of the twentieth century the CCBA-SF was the acknowledged leader of the Chinese community. It led fights against measures deemed inimical to the community's well-being. It supported founding of a community dispensary in 1900 and was one of the founding organizations of the CHINESE HOSPITAL in the early 1920's. In 1905 it established a school to teach Chinese language and culture to Chinese children. Before the advent of the Chinese Chamber of Commerce, the CCBA-SF witnessed changes of ownership and property sales. To protect Chinatown against nocturnal crimes, the CCBA-SF hired night watchmen to make the rounds. It also acted as a clearinghouse for fund-raising efforts, and before World War II its approval of fund-raising projects opened many Chinese doors for donations. CCBAs in other communities had similar powers.

Gathering of leaders of San Francisco's Chinese American community at the city's Chinese Consolidated Benevolent Association. (International Daily News)

Chinese all over the country also looked to the CCBA-SF for leadership in certain areas of common concern such as fighting anti-Chinese actions. These expectations extended even to Chinese in Latin American countries, many of which were then without Chinese diplomatic representation. The association retained a lawyer on an annual basis to facilitate the handling of such legal affairs.

Structure. Organizational structures of CCBAs vary widely. The CCBA-SF, the oldest, adheres to a hierarchical structure that evolved during the nineteenth century. Membership is limited to the seven *huiguan* existing during the 1900's. Below them are the *shantang* and *zongqinhui* (family or clan associations) associated with each *huiguan*.

In CCBAs outside San Francisco the hierarchical relationships are not observed as rigidly. Being products of a more modern era, most CCBAs admit onto their board of directors on an equal basis a diverse number of community organizations, including HUIGUAN, locality associations (*tongxianghui*), clan associations (*zongqinhui*), SECRET SOCIETIES (*tongs*),

Chinese political parties, even Western-type organizations such as churches and civic and fraternal organizations. In a few communities, such as Honolulu, membership is on an individual basis.

Before World War II the CCBA-SF regarded all other CCBAs in the continental United States as subordinate to it, and it was the only organization entitled to speak for all the Chinese living there. As other Chinese communities increased in population and affluence over the years, however, some CCBAs, such as that in New York, have grown to rival the CCBA-SF in influence and stature.

After World War II. After World War II, as American society gradually lowered many social and economic barriers to nonwhite minorities, numerous Chinese Americans became a part of the American mainstream. Participation in Chinatown affairs declined, and CCBAs lost much of their influence. The rise during the 1960's and 1970's of social agencies and Chinese American civic and political organizations with connections to American mainstream organizations further chipped away at CCBAs' authority. Also, newcomers from China and other troubled areas of the world who have been coming to America since the late 1960's, particularly the non-Cantonese, have established their own institutional networks outside the CCBA system to fill their need for mutual aid and socialization. Nevertheless, because of the close relationship that evolved over many decades between the CCBA and established Chinatown merchant elites, the CCBA remains a force to be reckoned with in the Chinatowns.

Federation. The need for interorganizational contacts among CCBAs led to the formation of a Federation of Chinese Organizations of America in 1977. By 1980 the organization had expanded to include CCBAs in the Americas with a membership of fifty-seven organizations. Representatives of these organizations meet periodically to discuss problems and issues of common concern.—*Him Mark Lai*

SUGGESTED READINGS: • Hoy, William. *The Chinese Six Companies.* San Francisco: Chinese Consolidated Benevolent Association, 1942. • Lai, Him Mark. "Historical Development of the Chinese Consolidated Benevolent Association/*Huiguan* System." In *Chinese America: History and Perspectives, 1987*, edited by the Publication Committee, pp. 13-51. San Francisco: Chinese Historical Society of America, 1987. • Lee, James T. "The Chinese Consolidated Benevolent Association: An Assessment." *Bridge: The Magazine of Asians in America* 1 (July/Aug., 1972): 15-16, 41, 43, 46-47. • Lee, James T. "The Story of the New York Chinese Consolidated Benevolent Association." *Bridge: The Magazine of Asians in America* 1 (May/June, 1972): 15-18. • Lyman, Stanford M. "Forerunners of Overseas Chinese Community Organizations" and "Chinese Community Organization in the United States." In *Chinese Americans.* New York: Random House, 1974. • Nee, Victor G., and Brett de Bary. "The Establishment." In *Longtime Californ': A Documentary Study of an American Chinatown.* New York: Pantheon Books, 1973.

Chinese contract labor: Primary means through which Chinese immigrants financed their passage from China to the United States. During the 1852-1882 period most of the Chinese men who left their villages for American soil did so to escape poverty. They did not possess the capital resources necessary to finance the trip. Therefore the most common method used to pay for their passage was the labor contract, or credit ticket. (See CREDIT-TICKET SYSTEM.) Under this system a local recruiter, prospective employer, or steam-

Chinese laborer at an iron and lead smelting factory. (Asian American Studies Library, University of California at Berkeley)

ship company agreed to absorb the cost of transportation in exchange for a laborer's commitment to stay on the job until his debt, plus interest, was repaid. Creditors deducted installments from monthly wages on a percentage basis. After fulfilling this contract the worker was then free to pursue other employment opportunities or enter business for himself. Sometimes the immigrants made individual commitments, but often men from the same village entered into a group contract—an arrangement most common in railroad construction and agriculture. Plantation owners in Hawaii recruited both women and men as contract laborers, but on the American mainland the system was almost exclusively confined to males.

Contract immigration, though voluntary, suffered from an incorrect association with its antecedent, the quasi-slave COOLIE TRADE. Used in the Caribbean, Central America, and South America, this method of securing workers relied on kidnapping or deception. Individuals unfortunate enough to find themselves ensnared by traders were condemned to indefinite servitude, and most died before obtaining their freedom. Although anti-Chinese leaders in the United States frequently used the coolie label to argue for the exclusion of Chinese immigrants, contract laborers came by choice. They often endured dishonest employers and unsafe working conditions, but they faced such adversities even as free people.

Constituting most of the immigrant population before 1882, Chinese contract laborers played a major role in developing the American West. They provided the chief labor supply for the construction of both the Western railroad and agricultural industries. Their ingenuity, effort, and courage carved tunnels through the mountains, turned swamps into fertile fields, harvested the resources of the Pacific Coast, and, even more important, laid the foundation for a Chinese American society.

Chinese contributions to the English language: The disparity between Chinese (Sino-Tibetan) and English (Indo-European) in every aspect of language precludes systematic mutual influence and borrowing. Unlike Arabic or Sanskrit, China's language and script obstructed the spread of its unique contributions to world civilization in its original terminology. The philosophical systems of Confucianism, Taoism, and Zen Buddhism lent their names, but few precepts, in Chinese. At best, English has absorbed random items of vocabulary picked up by missionaries, China coast traders, and military and diplomatic personnel. Pidgin, supposedly a Chinese approximation of "business" English, was the *lingua franca* of commercial regions in China during the nineteenth century, but this was more a reduction of English to simple forms, such as "Confucius say," and "long time no see," than accommodation of Chinese.

Typically, Chinese words were adopted for commodities for which no English term existed. The most prominent trade goods were silk, porcelain, and tea. "Silk" is the Chinese word *si*, known to the early Greeks, who named the Chinese *Seres* (silk people). Household pottery simply assumed the generic name "china." The Chinese word *cha*, for "tea," provides the common British slang "char," as in "a nice cuppa char."

Chinese cuisine provides other untranslatable terms, such as *dim sum*, commonly translated as "point of heart." (Actually, *dim* means "ignite," hence "fire the heart," or "tempt.") "Chow mein" (*chao* meaning "fried," *mian* meaning "noodles"), "litchi" (*lizhi*), and "wok" (*guo*, cooking pot) fall within this category.

Systematic phonology apparently occurs in "chop suey," "chopsticks," "chop-chop" (hurry), and "chop" (seal, stamp), but the Chinese characters for *chop* are different, respectively being, *zasui* (odds and ends), *jizi, jiji,* and *zha*. Conversely, *ty* in both "tycoon" and "typhoon" means "great." In Chinese, *taijun* for example, means "great lord," and *taifeng* means "great wind." *Taipan* (grand manager) and *taichi* (shadow boxing) incorporate the same element.

Other Chinese words, such as "coolie," "kung fu," "rickshaw," and "sampan," remain in currency. Such words, however, are rare and do not represent systematic linguistic or cultural interchange.

Chinese Cultural Center of Visalia: Nonprofit, nonpartisan cultural center established in 1990 in Visalia, California, to promote Chinese and Chinese American history and culture. Built to resemble a Confucian temple, the center hosts art exhibitions and weekly cultural events; displays art antiques dating back to 500 B.C.E., and offers classes on Chinese American history. More than forty thousand guests visited the center during its first two years of operation.

Chinese Culture Foundation of San Francisco (CCFSF): Nonprofit cultural corporation established in 1965 to provide support for the Chinese Culture Center, which seeks to facilitate the understanding and promotion of Chinese and Chinese American culture. The center offers myriad cultural and educational programs, including lectures, workshops, painting classes, art and history exhibitions, community concerts, youth research internships, and other social activities.

San Francisco's Chinese Culture Center offers art exhibits and many other aspects of Chinese culture. (Chinese Culture Center)

Chinese Daily News: Chinese-language newspaper founded in Monterey Park, California, in 1981. Designed to serve the fast-growing Chinese immigrant readership of Los Angeles County, it was competing directly with at least four other Chinese-language dailies by 1993. The paper is considered to have the largest circulation of any Chinese-language publication in Southern California and is a subsidiary of the Taiwan-based *United Daily News*. Prepared by a staff of some 170 workers at its Monterey Park headquarters, the *Chinese Daily News* covers a broad range of local, national, and international news considered to be of particular interest to the Chinese American community.

Chinese dance. *See* **Chinese music and dance**

The Chinese Diaspora: A substantial number of Chinese nationals and people of Chinese descent live permanently outside the borders of China. They are found in varying numbers and in varying degrees of assimilation in most countries of the world. While estimates of their total number vary, there are probably between 30 and 40 million Chinese living outside China. The area of their greatest concentration is in Southeast Asia, which the Chinese call Nanyang, particularly in the countries of Thailand, Malaysia, Singapore, the Philippines, and Indonesia. Numerically but a small minority (Singapore and Malaysia excepted), they traditionally dominate important sectors of the local economy in these countries.

Terms. In both popular and scholarly discussions, many Chinese terms are used to refer to the overseas Chinese. No one term is universally accepted or appropriate in every context. One widely used term is *huaqiao*. Some scholars use this term generically to refer to all overseas Chinese. Others, however, prefer to stick to its narrower meaning, "sojourners," applying the term *huaqiao* only to those in the diaspora who still retain Chinese citizenship. Those with citizenship of the host country are *waji huaren*. Another inclusive term for overseas Chinese is *haiwai huaren*, referring to all of Chinese descent regardless of citizenship status.

The Creation of the Chinese Diaspora: First Phase. Chinese people have been migrating abroad for more than five hundred years. Mostly this migration is migration overseas rather than overland. This pattern of migration derives from sociological, political, and geographical factors. In the interior of China, the excess population was often channeled to those parts of the country of lesser population density where arable land was still available. It was the policy of the Chinese imperial government to actively sponsor interregional migration and internal colonization. Toward the end of the nineteenth century, when the population density everywhere in China proper approached the saturation point, vast tracts of prairieland in Manchuria and Inner Mongolia were conveniently made available by the government, becoming a new frontier for the land-hungry peasants to settle.

Residents of the provinces of Guangdong and Fujian, backed up by the mountain ranges that run along the entire Southeast China coast, were oriented toward the sea. From an early date they became fishermen and mariners and established trading relations with the Nanyang countries. Thus when they ran out of land in their hilly homeland and when opportunities in Nanyang beckoned, the more adventurous of them would relocate over there to trade, and eventually settle down.

Internal migration to Guangdong and Fujian also played a role. During the Qing Dynasty there was much movement of the Hakkas from the mountainous areas into the central and southern part of Guangdong. Their settlements in the Siyi (Sze Yup) region led to friction with the local Cantonese which eventually took the form of armed conflicts. This was one of the factors causing an exodus abroad from Taishan in the mid-nineteenth century. Political factors contributed to out-migration as well, as was the case when the fall of the Ming Dynasty prompted migration to Vietnam.

Chinese immigration into Nanyang predated the coming of Europeans and continued unabated under the European colonial regimes. Colonial regimes generally welcomed Chinese immigrants because in most Nanyang countries they were indispensable to the prosperity of the local economy, as they handled the export and import business from China, plied the retail trade, and mined gold or tin where feasible.

Second Phase. The Chinese Diaspora entered into a new era around 1850 with the gaining of access to Hawaii, Australia, California, Cuba, Peru and other

Chinese Diaspora, 1990		
Location	Number of People in Millions	Percentage of Total
Hong Kong	1.8	4.6%
Indonesia	7.2	18.5%
Malaysia	5.2	13.3%
Philippines	1.0	2.6%
Singapore	2.0	5.1%
Taiwan	1.8	4.6%
Thailand	6.0	15.4%
United States	13.2	33.8%
Vietnam	0.8	2.1%

Source: The Christian Science Monitor, March 23, 1994.

Custom House Business Astoria Oregon, July 28-1891

Descriptive list of Chinese Merchant furnished to the
following Chinese Merchant, Departing temporarilly from the
United States, to be presented to the Customs Officers on his
return to the United States.

Discription

Name-Go Chow, Age-28 Years, Occupation-Merchant, of the firm of
Tai wo Long & Co doing business at No 557- 3 d Street Astoria
Oregon, Height 5 feet 2 & 1/2 Inches Complexion-Dark, Eyes-Dark
Physical Marks-One Small Scar on Right Temple, One Small Scar
on Left Eyebrow,

This is to certify that the above described
Chinese Merchant presented himself before me at Astoria Oregon
before departing from the United States, and is given as Prima
Facie evedence of his right to return, Photograph hereto
attached is a true likeness at time of departure
Given under my hand and Seal the date above written

Notary Public for State of Oregn

We the undersigned, hereby certify
that we know the above described
Go Chow, and that he is a Chinese
Merchant doing business as
above described

Under U.S. laws that were once in force, immigrant alien Chinese who had left the United States
would be readmitted upon return only after presenting a federal certificate of reentry, such as this
one dated 1891. (National Archives)

Chinese coolies bound for the New World. (Asian American Studies Library, University of California at Berkeley)

localities in the New World. From the outset, migration into the New World followed a different pattern. Most of the immigration to Nanyang was voluntary, with the prospective immigrant fully apprized of overseas opportunities by plugging into preexisting networks of kinship and other connections. There was also, however, export of indentured labor based on the credit-ticket system. Often deception was used to induce the laborer to sign on, and there was much abuse in applying the system. Immigration into the New World involved this element of coercion to a significantly greater degree, although there was substantial voluntary migration to the New World as well.

Keen on developing their economies, many New World countries sought to import laborers to toil in their plantations, mines, and construction projects. The traditional source of labor, African slaves, was drying up as Britain stepped up efforts to suppress the slave trade. These countries were therefore interested in an alternative source of labor (contract or indenture) and

in the country that could supply it, China.

Thus arose the infamous "COOLIE TRADE." Operators would set up in a port city on the South China coast and send their agents to collect the coolies. With a full load of human cargo onboard, the ship would set sail, and upon arrival at its destination would dispose of the coolies by public auction. In theory, the coolies were free men capable of entering into contractual obligations voluntarily. In reality, their situation was little better than that of the African slave. Enticed by the labor agent's false promises, they were coerced into signing away their freedom under conditions not fully disclosed to them. Not infrequently, they were kidnapped. Overcrowding on coolie ships and their shocking treatment at the hands of captains and crew took a heavy toll of human life during the long trans-Pacific passage. In the New World, their employers sometimes treated them worse than slaves, branding them with a hot iron, like cattle, to prevent their running away. The horrors of the trade eventually provoked a popular outcry, and under international pressure, the coolie operations were shut down. Many coolies who served out their obligations were repatriated back to China, but many others decided to stay. These Chinese pioneers in the New World permitted their compatriots to join them under less harrowing circumstances.

The Chinese population in the New World would have been much higher but for various forms of discrimination. The United States provides a good case in point. Chinese miners were prominent in the mining camps all along the West Coast in the 1850's. When mining operations wound down, another source of employment opened up for the Chinese: construction work on the railroad. Indeed, the completion of the transcontinental railroad was made possible by the contributions of Chinese workers. Often they constituted the entire labor force on stretches of the roadway. Then came the severe economic downturn of the

1870's. With hard times threatening the livelihood of thousands, Caucasian Americans took out their frustration on the hapless Chinese, accusing them of moral perversion, lynching them, and driving them out of town. Demagogues exploited the situation, proposing discriminatory legislation. Finally, the CHINESE EXCLUSION ACT OF 1882 was passed by the U.S. Congress, prohibiting the entry of Chinese laborers for a ten-year period. Subsequent legislation extended and broadened the restrictions on Chinese immigration and declared alien Chinese—those who were not already citizens—ineligible for naturalization. Exclusion was never complete. As a result of these restrictions, however, and the discouraging climate they created, the Chinese population in the United States declined steadily between 1890 and 1920. The exclusion acts remained in effect until 1943.

Third Phase. The end of World War II and the fall of

Immigrant Chinese laborers landing in the New World ended up as far north as Deadwood, South Dakota. Here the only two known Chinese "hose" teams (firefighters) in the United States compete in a race through the center of town in 1888. (Library of Congress)

mainland China to the Communists inaugurated the third stage in the creation of the Chinese diaspora. Previously, by the operation of the principle of *jus soli*, Chinese born in British Malaya, French Indochina, or the Dutch East Indies automatically acquired European citizenship or were permitted to acquire European citizenship after meeting some additional requirements, such as education. Nevertheless few Chinese with European citizenship thought it desirable to relocate to Europe. At the end of World War II, a process of decolonization set in for all European colonies in Asia. Facing the uncertainties of new regimes, many Chinese decided to pull up stakes and start over again. Chinese who left Indonesia after independence, for example, contributed to the growth of the Chinese community in the Netherlands.

The Communist victory in the Chinese civil war and the establishment of the People's Republic of China (PRC) in 1949 sent shock waves to the overseas Chi-

nese communities, the effects of which are still being felt nearly half a century later. The character of Chinese emigration changed. Previously, for the most part, the Chinese elites had stayed at home, but under the radical program of the Communist leadership to restructure Chinese society, the tables were turned on the erstwhile elites. An exodus was in fact underway before 1949, for many among China's educated, professional, and monied classes, anticipating the ultimate Communist victory, managed to flee to Hong Kong, Macao, or Taiwan. Most Chinese immigration from the 1950's to the 1970's came from this group, as the PRC's emigration policy became increasingly restrictive. Some settled permanently in the above named places, while for others these were simply way stations en route to their ultimate destination in Nanyang, the Americas, or Europe.

Simultaneous with changes in the character of Chinese emigration, a new pattern in the countries receiv-

Communist posters adorn a city wall following the invasion of Beijing by the Chinese Communist army. (National Archives)

Proprietors of the Nankin Cafe (1920-1935) in Old Chinatown, Olympia, Washington. (Wing Luke Museum)

ing Chinese immigrants emerged. Countries in Nanyang which hitherto received the bulk of Chinese immigrants were becoming less hospitable. With decolonization completed and nationalism a dominant ideology, they already had their hands full coping with their large and as yet unassimilated population of overseas Chinese. For this reason, other than for allowing the reunification of families or to bring in individuals possessing desired skills, new immigration was generally banned.

The preferred region for the vast reservoir of potential emigrants from Taiwan and Hong Kong was North America, and particularly the United States. The appeal of the United States was universal. In the decade immediately following the end of World War II, the United States with its fabulous standard of living was indeed the land of opportunity, and as such beckoned to Chinese of all walks of life. With rising affluence and increased disposable income among the vast middle class, there was money to be made for adult Chinese going into retail trade and the service industries (e.g., restaurants, laundries), hitherto the mainstay of Chinese employment in America. With world class universities positioned at the cutting edge of scientific

research, America acted as a magnet for Chinese college graduates who would top off their own education in Taiwan or Hong Kong by pursuing an advanced degree at American universities. Armed with appropriate educational credentials, they found suitable employment in America, thus making the transition from temporary visitors to permanent residents en route to citizen status. Institutional barriers against Chinese employment were dropping. Enjoying sustained economic expansion in the postwar years, the United States actually offered inducements for highly trained Chinese personnel to immigrate to fill job vacancies in academic, defense, and other related fields.

The liberalization of U.S. immigration policy under the IMMIGRATION AND NATIONALITY ACT OF 1965 permitted non-elite Chinese to obtain immigrant visas. Illegal immigration, which had waxed and waned since the passage of the first exclusion acts in the 1880's, also went on at a brisk pace. The rapid increase of the Chinese population in the United States, due to immigration and natural increase, could not be accommodated within the traditional urban ghettoes (the picturesque CHINATOWNS). A majority of American Chinese now live in the suburbs, blending into the

Canada has been something of a magnet for immigrants from Hong Kong. Here individuals of varying ethnicities celebrate multiculturalism during a festival in Edmonton, Alberta, Canada, on Heritage Day, 1992. (Photo Search Ltd., Murty)

mainstream of American society.

In the 1980's and 1990's, the pressure for residents of Taiwan to emigrate has diminished. With the Communist leadership in the post-Mao era softpedalling Marxist ideology and pushing for economic reform, the threat of a military invasion and takeover of the island has faded. In contrast, the pressure for Hong Kong residents to emigrate has intensified. The Sino-British Agreement of 1984 stipulates the termination of British rule and the resumption of Chinese sovereignty by July of 1997. While the agreement is accompanied by a Chinese commitment to maintain the current (pre-1977) socioeconomic system of the territory unchanged for the next fifty years, many are inclined not to take the word of China at face value. The TIANANMEN SQUARE INCIDENT (June 4, 1989) further undermined credibility of the Communist leadership, convincing many in Hong Kong of the wisdom of relocating before the 1997 deadline. While the situation has stabilized since 1991, and the local economy continues to boom, an undercurrent of fear persists.

Beyond doubt a sizable proportion of the people

emigrating from Taiwan and Hong Kong have ended up in the United States. The Chinese population in the United States increased by 80 percent during the 1980's, reaching between 1.6 and 1.7 million in the 1990 census.

Rivaling the United States as a destination for prospective emigrants from Hong Kong is Canada. Immigrants from Hong Kong have been flooding into Canada since the 1970's, when immigration requirements were changed to make them easier for Hong Kong residents to meet. Although the total Chinese population in Canada is smaller than its counterpart in the United States, it is more concentrated. In Vancouver, for instance, the rise of the Chinese immigrant population from Hong Kong in the 1980's has been so spectacular and their impact on the culture and economy of the city so dramatic that a cynic has suggested changing the name of the city to "Hongcouver."

While the United States and Canada are the first choices of many Chinese immigrants, they are by no means the only countries where there is significant Chinese immigration. Australia and Brazil, for example, have both experienced significantly increased Chinese immigration.

The Perpetuation of the Overseas Chinese Communities. King Rama IV of Thailand (reigned 1851-1868) characterized the overseas Chinese as the Jews of Asia. This was an apt analogy. Just as the Jews dispersed in the gentile world had preserved their own identity for countless generations, so to a lesser extent had the overseas Chinese. The Jews were reputed to be shrewd businessmen and ruthless competitors; so were the overseas Chinese. As a conspicuous minority without a country of their own, the Jews everywhere were vulnerable to persecution. The overseas Chinese were not exactly a people without a country. Nevertheless, they were equally vulnerable insofar as the imperial government of China until the end of the nineteenth century showed little interest in them and assumed no responsibility for their protection.

Despite the similarity of outcome, the historical circumstances producing the outcome were very different. The Jewish diaspora was accompanied by the virtual destruction of the Jewish homeland in Palestine, so that each Jewish community in the diaspora was likely to be a microcosm of the Jewish nation, complete with rabbis and other essential personnel to guarantee the perpetuation of the community physically and culturally. Encapsulated by culture, as a chrysalis by its cocoon, the Jews in the diaspora survive into the present day.

In contrast, throughout the first and second stages in the evolution of the Chinese diaspora, the overseas Chinese communities were drawn disproportionately (both geographically and in terms of social class) from certain segments of China's population. Those who emigrated were also predominantly male; it was not until the lifting of the Qing government's general ban against emigration in 1893 that respectable women began to travel overseas, and then only as married women accompanied by or on the way to join their husbands in Nanyang. Single, unmarried girls almost never ventured overseas alone.

The Transient Character of Chinese Communities. In general, immigrant societies comprising males only and without elite participation are defenseless against the assimilative forces of the host societies. The resilience of the overseas Chinese society is due to special circumstances. First, such communities had a pronounced transient character. Most members exhibited a sojourner mentality: Their greatest aspiration was to make their fortunes quickly and return to China to retire. Those who died in Nanyang often expressed a dying wish to have their remains interred in the old country. Meanwhile the place of those who returned home or died would be taken by a fresh crop of new immigrants. It was the constant influx of immigrants that sustained the Chinese character of these communities.

Despite the sojourner mentality, many would marry local women and put down roots. In due course, a new breed of Chinese born and raised abroad would materialize. Partaking of the heritage of both parents, fluent in the local language, and capable of moving with equal ease among both Chinese and indigenous society, they were usually a transitional type. With each passing generation, their Chinese heritage would be progressively deemphasized so that before long they would identify with the indigenous society completely.

Local-born Chinese Community in Nanyang. This was the scenario that unfolded in Thailand. Of the same racial stock as the Chinese, the Thai religion (Hinayana Buddhism), diet, and general habits were also compatible with the immigrant Chinese. Thus there were no insurmountable barriers to total assimilation, and assimilated (Thai-ified) Chinese moved easily among the Thai ruling elite and took service as royal ministers and provincial governors.

The assimilation of the Chinese community in Thailand, however, was slowed not only by the continued influx of immigrants at fairly high levels but also by an institutional barrier rooted in the fiscal administration of the country. Until the reform of King Chulalongkorn (1868-1910) the vast majority of the Thai populace had a semi-servile character: they were required to be registered as clients of noble families. People who identified themselves as Chinese by wearing the queue and by paying a poll tax were exempt from this requirement. This situation forced the offspring of Chinese-Thai unions to opt for a definite status, either Thai or Chinese. For those who aspired to follow in the footsteps of their fathers as businessmen, the Chinese status conferred upon them definite advantages, including freedom of movement throughout the Thai kingdom.

In Vietnam, Burma (now Myanmar), and to a lesser extent in the Philippines, the situation resembled that of Thailand with regard to barriers against total assimilation. Assimilation, however, took place at a slower rate because under colonial rule there was a noticeable trend toward pluralism. Since the political elite was composed of European administrators and since membership in this group was denied Chinese, assimilation to the host society as a prerequisite for upward mobility did not happen. Moreover, colonial policy generally sought to preserve the separateness of the Chinese communities, in the spirit of divide and rule.

In Malaya and the Dutch East Indies, where Islam predominated, the situation was entirely different. Since Islamic law prohibits Islamic women from marrying non-Islamic men, the only way for immigrant Chinese to marry local women was to convert to Islam. Conversion, however, necessitated a drastic break with the Chinese way of life, so that for most people it was not a realistic option. Without intermarriage, the forces of assimilation were held in check.

Despite the scarcity of Chinese women and despite the barriers to intermarriage, a local-born Chinese community did materialize, known as Baba in Malaya and Peranakan in Java. Their emergence was made possible by the fact that during the initial phase in the Islamicization of Malayan and Javanese societies (prior to the eighteenth century), the natives were more tolerant of deviations from the Islamic norms, so that intermarriage between Chinese men and local women did take place. The offspring of these marriages readily took to native habits of dress, diet, and table manners and were generally more fluent in the speech of their native mothers than of their Chinese fathers. In the case of the Babas of the Straits Settlement in Malaya, they dispensed with the use of Chinese speech altogether. The process of their assimilation into the host society, however, was arrested in midstream by the religious barrier. In their religious practice, in self-identification, they were Chinese, and were treated as such by the colonial authorities.

The immigration of Chinese women brought a salutary influence to the rough and tumble world of the hitherto predominantly male immigrant society, making it possible for Chinese culture in its entirety to be duplicated in Nanyang. Meanwhile significant events transpired strengthening the attachment of the overseas communities to the home country.

Involvement of the Government in China. As part of the reform movement which the Qing government undertook to recoup lost prestige after the fiasco of the BOXER REBELLION of 1900, efforts were stepped up to offer protection to Chinese nationals abroad. More legations and consulates were set up to provide assistance on the spot. To be more effective when intervening on behalf of Chinese citizens abroad, a nationality law was promulgated in 1909, the first enactment of its kind, defining in precise terms the legal status of the overseas Chinese. The operative principle was *jus sanguinis*, asserting that all individuals born of Chinese parents, regardless of the place of birth, were Chinese citizens. While this law removed the ambiguity concerning the legal status of the locally born Chinese, it gave rise to a new source of ambiguity. Previously, the Dutch colonial government, in response to pressures for democratization, had decided to confer Dutch citizenship on the upper strata of the Peranakan Chinese. The question may be raised: Were those Peranakan Chinese who formally assumed Dutch citizenship still considered Chinese citizens in the eyes of the Chinese government and thus still subject to its jurisdiction? The ambiguity was only partially resolved after protracted negotiations. The upshot was to treat the Peranakan Chinese as people of dual nationality. Accepted as Dutch citizens as long as they stayed in the East Indies, their Chinese citizenship would be activated when they journeyed back to China. They would be treated as Dutch citizens in China only if they went through the formal procedure of renouncing their Chinese citizenship. This nationality law apparently remained in effect during the Republican era, and the issue of dual nationality was one that plagued Chinese relations with the Nanyang countries for a long time.

Long used to being relegated to the margins of Chinese society, the overseas Chinese were afforded an opportunity in the 1900's to participate in a movement that would shape the destiny of their homeland for years to come, namely the antimonarchical revolutionary movement. And they responded with alacrity. SUN YAT-SEN, the revolutionary leader par excellence, spent many years during his adolescence in Honolulu, Hawaii, to which his family had partially immigrated. Many of his earliest followers and some of his trusted lieutenants were overseas Chinese, including Liao Chung-kai from the United States and Eugene Chen from Trinidad. While most overseas supporters of the revolutionary cause did not go as far as Liao or Chen, namely pulling up their stakes and joining Sun's retinue, they were generous in providing a crucial support, money. Without the financial backing of the overseas Chinese communities, the revolutionary cause might have fizzled out. In acknowledgment of their invaluable contribution, overseas Chinese have been eulogized as "the mother of the Revolution."

Recognizing the sizable population of the overseas Chinese as a valuable resource, the Nationalist government of the GUOMINDANG set up a high level agency, the Commission of Overseas Chinese Affairs, to manage it. The Commission strove to stimulate the patriotism of the people and mobilize them in support of government policy. To this end it vigorously promoted

Chinese language education in the belief that attending Chinese schools, following a curriculum prescribed by the ministry of education, the foreign-born Chinese student would shed his parochial outlook, develop a keen sense of his Chinese heritage, and commit irrevocably to the cause of China. To mobilize support for government policies, the commission published newspapers and cultivated the goodwill of the leaders of the Chinese communities.

With the end of World War II and the wave of decolonization that followed, the overseas Chinese population of Nanyang faced unprecedented challenges. Busily engaged in making a living, with their politics oriented to China rather than to their host countries, many were not involved in the movements that culminated in the creation of the postcolonial independent states of Vietnam, Burma, Malaysia and Indonesia. There was always a significant minority, however, which identified with the host country and participated in the struggle for independence. Whatever their stance, in the postindependence period the Chinese were frequently regarded as an alien element, an obstacle to the integration of the newly independent nation-state. To solve this problem, most Nanyang countries pursued a strategy to speed up assimilation of the Chinese. Generally this took the form of discriminatory regulation rather than policies designed to encourage identification with and participation in the

host society. Chinese-language education was restricted, if not entirely prohibited, and vital areas of the economy were reserved for citizens only. In many localities, anti-Chinese sentiments, fanned by official propaganda, flared up into mob violence.

As long as the law of 1909 remained in effect and the overseas Chinese continued to look to China for succor, the government of China was theoretically responsible for their protection, although realistically it could do little to ameliorate their plight. To extricate itself from this untenable situation, the PRC government, starting in 1957, gradually abandoned the traditional approach and adopted a new policy line toward the overseas Chinese. The principle of *jus sanguinis*, the basis of the 1909 law, was quietly dropped, and those eligible to apply for local citizenship were encouraged to do so. Those who opted for local citizenship were urged to learn the local language and contribute to the well-being of their country of adoption. Thus China bowed to reality and assented to the principle that the solution of the overseas Chinese problem was assimilation. The obstacles to total assimilation, however, remain formidable, especially in the Islamic countries of Indonesia and Malaysia.

The Contemporary Scene. The overseas Chinese population, distributed over the entire world, is characterized by extreme diversity. The situation varies in each country with regard to the proportion of the over-

Illegal Chinese immigrants are detained by U.S. authorities after being captured near the Golden Gate Bridge in San Francisco in May, 1993. (AP/Wide World Photos)

seas Chinese to the total population, the ratio of new immigrants to the locally born, the degree of assimilation or acculturation to the host country, and the occupational profile. Juxtaposed to the universal sources of diversity is one peculiar to the overseas Chinese communities, linguistic diversity. The mother tongue of individual overseas Chinese may be Hokkien, Teochiu, Hakka, Cantonese, or others. The differences between these so-called Chinese dialects are more than dialectical, constituting real obstacles to mutual intelligibility. Following the usage of G. William Skinner, we will refer to the speakers of these dialects as speech-groups.

Inter-speech-group communication is rendered easier by the phenomenon of immigrants of the same speech-groups settling in the same place, so that in many localities a certain speech-group enjoys a clear numerical superiority over other speech-groups. When this is the case, for instance, with the Teochiu in Thailand and the Sze-yap speech-group in the United States (before World War II), the speech of the dominant groups (or a gentrified version of the speech; e.g., Cantonese rather than Sze-yap in the United States) serves as the *lingua franca* in inter-speech-group gatherings. With the popularization of Chinese language education, the use of Mandarin (*putonghua*) has made substantial progress.

While Chinese-language education and the use of Mandarin are definitely homogenizing influences in overseas Chinese communities, they have not eroded the deep cleavages along the lines of the speech-groups. Reliance on formal organization based on the speech-groups was in fact part of the strategy for survival of the pioneer Chinese immigrants. During the first two stages in the creation of the Chinese diaspora, while the governments in the host countries tolerated the existence of the Chinese community, they felt no obligation to extend to them the benefits of citizenship. Nor could the overseas Chinese look to China for protection. They had to fend for themselves, and thus they organized. In organizing, they built upon the bases of affinity close at hand, namely kinship, district of origin, and speech-group. These organizations flourished because they were also vested with functions of self-government. They adjudicated disputes among members, provided relief to the poor, and arranged for the burial of the indigent dead. Whereas these organizations generally operated in the open, sometimes the interests of the Chinese community could be served better by an organization operating underground, using surreptitious means. This rationale explains the existence of secret societies (e.g., Triads) among the overseas Chinese. The latter, however, were, and still are to some extent, involved in unsavory activities such as gambling, prostitution, and drugs.

Today, overseas Chinese continue to participate avidly in voluntary associations of all descriptions to advance their interests. According to statistics released by the Taiwan government's Commission of Overseas Chinese Affairs, as of June, 1991, there were a total of 9,081 overseas Chinese organizations.

People of Chinese descent have done well in most places, distinguishing themselves especially in the business world, the professions, and in academia. Individually some of them have won the highest honors available to members of their field. While they do not necessarily profess allegiance to the governments of China, there is no question that to the well-being of China they constitute a valuable asset. Just as in former times overseas Chinese sent remittances to their relatives at home and were generous in endowing schools and hospitals in their home communities, so today (since the start of the economic reform in the late 1970's) they have been the principal source of investment capital for financing the rapid economic development of mainland China.—*Winston W. Lo*

SUGGESTED READINGS:

• Chen, Ta. *Emigrant Communities in South China.* Edited by Bruno Lasker. New York: Institute of Pacific Relations, 1940. This is a detailed study of three coastal localities in Guangdong and Fujian with strong ties to the Nanyang Chinese communities. Very useful for understanding the motives of emigration and the nature of the ties that bound the emigrants to their home communities.

• Chew, Sock Foon. *Ethnicity and Nationality in Singapore.* Athens: Ohio University Center for International Studies, 1987. A solid contribution to our understanding of the current orientation of the Singaporean Chinese.

• Fitzgerald, Stephen. *China and the Overseas Chinese.* Cambridge: Cambridge University Press, 1972. This is a competent treatment of the new policy of the PRC government toward the overseas Chinese which evolved in the years 1957-1961.

• Mackie, J. A. C., ed. *The Chinese in Indonesia.* Honolulu: University Press of Hawaii, 1976. A collection of five essays exploring the post-World War II situation of the Indonesian Chinese.

• MacNair, H. F. *The Chinese Abroad, Their Position and Protection.* Shanghai, China: Commercial Press, 1924. This is a comprehensive survey of the situation of the overseas Chinese communities all over the world prior to the 1920's. The efforts made by the Chinese government for their protection also receive in-depth treatment.

• Skinner, G. W. *Chinese Society in Thailand: An Analytical History*. Ithaca, N.Y.: Cornell University Press, 1957. Treating the evolution of Chinese society in Thailand historically, this book set a standard for Southeast Asian studies at the time of publication. It remains to this day a classic in the literature of the overseas Chinese.

• Wang Gungwu. "The Status of Overseas Chinese Studies." *Chinese America: History and Perspectives* (1994): 1-18. The keynote address for the Luo Di-Sheng Gen Conference: The Legal, Political, and Economic Status of Chinese in Diaspora, held in San Francisco, November 27-29, 1992.

• Wickberg, Edgar. *The Chinese in Philippine Life, 1850-1898*. New Haven, Conn.: Yale University Press, 1965. The best of the historical literature on the subject.

• Winzeler, Robert. *Ethnic Relations in Kelantan*. Singapore: Oxford University Press, 1985. A very informative study of the Chinese and Thai as ethnic minorities in a Malay state. Illuminates the derivation and the complexity of the Chinese populations.

• Yen, Ching-Hwang. *Coolies and Mandarins: China's Protection of Overseas Chinese During the Late Ch'ing Period (1851-1911)*. Singapore: Singapore University Press, 1985. A scholarly treatment of the subject.

Chinese Digest: First major English-language news publication in the continental United States for and by second-generation Chinese Americans, founded in 1935. (The bilingual *Hawaii Chinese News*, the first paper to offer substantial English-language coverage for the Chinese community in Hawaii, preceded it by a decade.) At the time the *Chinese Digest* began publication, the only other major newspaper written for and by second-generation Chinese Americans was the evening daily CHINESE TIMES (San Francisco), a Chinese-language publication founded in 1924 as the official organ of the CHINESE AMERICAN CITIZENS ALLIANCE (CACA).

The *Chinese Digest* began publication in San Francisco in November, 1935, and was the brainchild of Thomas W. CHINN. Chinn persuaded Chingwah Lee to join in the venture. *The Digest* began as a weekly under the editorship of Chinn from 1935 to 1937. It then became a monthly under local historian William Hoy from 1937 to 1939. Finally, in January, 1940, it

became the irregularly published journal of Lee's newly formed organization, the China Culture Society of America, with its last issue dated July, 1940.

From the very beginning, the *Chinese Digest* was understaffed and underfinanced. The original staff was composed of Chinn, Lee, Hoy, Fred George (Chuey) Woo (sports), Clara Chan (fashions), Ethel Lum (community welfare), Robert G. Poon (circulation), and George Chow, with Daisy (Mrs. Thomas) Chinn unofficially helping with the final copy. Only Chinn, Lee, and Hoy had previous journalism experience. Later the staff included such notables as Patrick Sun, the Chinese vice-consul in San Francisco, who used the pseudonym "Tsu Pan"; Lim P. LEE, a social worker for the Public Welfare Office and Juvenile Court and later, in 1967, postmaster of San Francisco; Helen Fong; and photographer Wallace H. Fong.

The *Chinese Digest* originally had five main goals: to correct some of the misleading stereotypical impressions of Chinese Americans; to report truthfully events in Asia, especially after the Japanese invasion and takeover of Manchuria and the events that led to the Sino-Japanese War of 1937-1945; to stir up interest in Chinese language and culture as a means of enriching American life; to establish communications among Chinese Americans; and to encourage the employment of Chinese in corporations and firms by publicizing those that hired Chinese.

The significance of the *Chinese Digest* was that it reflected the concerns of the American-born Chinese who saw the United States as their permanent home but who were unwilling to forget the aspects of their Chinese cultural heritage that made them distinctive. Readers were urged to vote, to fight against discrimination, to be concerned about the moral training of the younger generation, especially during the aftermath of the Depression, and to support war relief efforts during the Sino-Japanese War. Concerns about social and health welfare, the development of San Francisco's Chinatown, the rise and fall of Chinatowns elsewhere, labor issues, employment, discrimination, events in China, and other timely issues were addressed. The activities of prominent people and organizations were reported. Consequently the *Chinese Digest* is an excellent source of information about Chinese Americans in the period 1935 to 1940.

Chinese Educational Mission. *See* **Chinese students**

Chinese Empire Reform Association. *See* **Baohuanghui**

Chinese Exclusion Act of 1882: Law passed by the U.S. Congress in May, 1882, that made it illegal, effective for a period of ten years, for Chinese laborers to come to or stay in the United States. Never before had a group been denied entry to the United States on the basis of race, ethnicity, or national origin. The 1882 act established a precedent for a series of discriminatory acts against the Chinese in particular and Asian Americans in general. It marked the end of open immigration and the rise of nativism, culminating in the restrictive and racially discriminatory IMMIGRATION ACT OF 1924.

The 1882 act, which came after years of agitation by the anti-Chinese movement, reversed U.S. policy established in the BURLINGAME TREATY (1868). Chinese labor had been welcome in the United States up to the 1870's, especially to work on the railroads. With an economic downturn, the situation changed; cheap Chinese labor was seen as a threat to the native American workforce. From the beginning, even in boom times, Chinese immigrants had been subjected to racist violence and discriminatory legislation, which they con-

tested in the courts. Economic insecurity fueled existing anti-Chinese sentiment.

While the 1882 act was limited in scope, subsequent legislation, such as the Amendment of 1884, the SCOTT ACT OF 1888, and the GEARY ACT OF 1892, extended and broadened the restrictions on Chinese immigration. As a result, the Chinese American population declined steadily between 1890 and 1920. Not until passage of the IMMIGRATION ACT OF 1943 were these restrictions lifted.

Chinese for Affirmative Action (CAA): Nonprofit, membership-supported civil rights organization in San Francisco, California, established in 1969 and dedicated to providing equal access to economic, employment, and educational opportunities for all persons. The group provides assistance to victims of racial discrimination; offers job referrals and job counseling to non-English speakers; promotes the accurate portrayal of Asian Americans in the media; and conducts research on issues that affect the Asian American community.

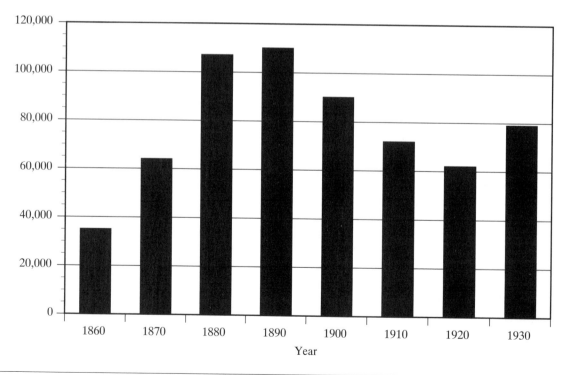

Chinese Population in the Contiguous U.S., 1860-1930

Source: John Wilson, *Chinese Americans.* American Voices series. Vero Beach, Fla.: Rourke Corp., 1991.

Members of the Young Lions performing arts troupe, composed of young Chinese who emigrated from Vietnam to new homes in America. (Ben Klaffke)

Chinese from Southeast Asia: The first Chinese immigrants to the United States arrived during the early nineteenth century. Sustained Chinese immigration to America, however, did not start until after the discovery of gold in California in 1848. After 1849 large numbers of Chinese came to California in search of gold. Substantial immigration of Chinese from Southeast Asia did not begin until more than a century later, but in the 1990's this group is a significant presence in the Chinese American community.

Impact of Legislation. Racial discrimination, the CHINESE EXCLUSION ACT OF 1882, and subsequent restrictive legislation curtailed Chinese immigration to America. The Chinese population in the continental United States declined from a peak of about 106,000 in 1880 to a low of 62,000 in 1920. Between 1931 and 1940, only about 5,000 Chinese immigrated to the United States. Even after the repeal of the Chinese Exclusion Act in 1943, Chinese immigration remained low. About 17,000 Chinese immigrated to the United States between 1941 and 1950. The majority of the Chinese in the United States at that time could trace their ancestry to Guangdong Province in South China.

Before the late 1950's, only a small number of Chinese came to the United States from Southeast Asia, mainly because parts of Southeast Asia were under the control of Western powers as colonies. Thus immigration to the United States was limited by both the American quota system and the policy of the colonial authorities. Even after independence the number of immigrants coming to the United States from these countries was small because of the American quota system. For example, from 1961 to 1970, only 4,600 Vietnamese entered the United States as immigrants. Furthermore, very few Chinese residing in Southeast Asian countries were citizens of these countries. Before the quota system was repealed, when they applied for immigration to the United States they were still included in the small quota allocated for China.

This situation changed gradually for two reasons. One was the liberalization of nationality laws of some Southeast Asian countries, such as Thailand, to allow Chinese in their countries to become citizens. The second reason was the repeal of the U.S. quota system in 1965. Yet even with these changes, Chinese immigration from Southeast Asia was still low. For example, only 4,401 immigrants came to the United States from Singapore from 1978 to 1988.

The Tide of Refugees. The breakthrough for Chinese immigration from Southeast Asia to the United States came after the end of the Vietnam War in 1975. The United States felt a moral responsibility to help the postwar refugees from Indochina resettle in the United States. Between 1975 and 1990, more than one million immigrants from Vietnam, Cambodia, and Laos were admitted into the United States, more than 90 percent of whom were classified as refugees. It is estimated that at least 35 percent of these refugees were ethnic Chinese. It was reported that among the "boat people" from Vietnam in the late 1970's and early 1980's, about 70 percent were ethnic Chinese.

Large numbers of Chinese left Vietnam for two main reasons. First, after the occupation of South Vietnam, the new regime launched a discriminatory campaign to persecute the Chinese living there. Second, many of the Chinese in South Vietnam were businesspeople and professionals who did not want to live under Communism. They attempted to seek a better life in the United States for themselves and their children.

The states that had admitted the largest number of Indochinese refugees by 1985 were California (290,000), Texas (52,500), Washington (33,300), New York (25,500), Pennsylvania (24,300), Illinois (24,000), Minnesota (23,000), Virginia (21,400), Massachusetts (20,100), Mississippi (17,700), Oregon (17,400), and Louisiana (13,800). This pattern of settlement coincided roughly with the pattern of settlement of Chinese refugees from Indochina.

It is difficult if not impossible to calculate precisely the number of ethnic Chinese among the Indochinese

refugees. Many ethnic Chinese were citizens of Vietnam, Cambodia, or Laos and were simply classified in U.S. immigration statistics as immigrants from those countries without any indication of their ethnic background. Ethnic Chinese from some other Southeast Asian countries, such as Thailand and Indonesia, are also difficult to identify partly because of their adoption of local names.

Still, it is fairly safe to say that of the 1.645 million Chinese residing in the United States as of 1990, a large minority came to the United States from Southeast Asia. The majority of Southeast Asian Chinese immigrants are on the West Coast, California in particular. The Chinese from Southeast Asia prefer to settle in California because of its mild climate, welfare system, school system, and large Chinese population. With continued admission of new immigrants from Southeast Asia and internal migration from other states, California's population of Chinese from Southeast Asia will continue to increase.

Life in America. The Chinese refugees from Indochina suffered great losses in terms of the separation of their family members and loss of property. When the refugees first arrived in the United States, most of them did not speak good English. It was difficult for them to survive on their own in the new country. Fortunately, the U.S. government refugee relief programs provided them with their basic requirements during the initial period of resettlement in the United States. Gradually they began to support themselves.

Most of them began by working at menial jobs. Slowly they branched out to better jobs. Many set up their own small businesses, such as grocery stores and restaurants. Some began by working in factories. They saved as much money as possible to bring their families to the United States from Southeast Asia. The refugees also saved money for their children's education. A very high percentage of their children go to college. As a result, many of the younger generation of Chinese from Southeast Asia have degrees from colleges and universities. They have found professional jobs and become members of the middle class. A small number of them have become wealthy entrepreneurs.

Socially Chinese from Southeast Asia tend to stay together. They are somewhat separated from the Chinese from mainland China or Taiwan. They are also separated from the Vietnamese from Vietnam, although many of the Chinese are former citizens of Vietnam and some still speak the Vietnamese language. Some of the organizations of Chinese refugees from Indochina even applied for government grants

Chinese immigrants from Cambodia, now transplanted to the United States. Refugees from Southeast Asia often work very long hours to support themselves and their families. (Ben Klaffke)

separately from other Indochinese refugee organizations.

In cities with large numbers of Chinese from Southeast Asia, the refugees have established their own social organizations according to regions, such the Association of Chinese from Indochina. It is reported that more than fourteen states in the United States have such organizations.

Some Chinese from Southeast Asia have also participated in the activities of organizations of mainstream Chinese American communities—communities of Chinese from mainland China or Taiwan, for example. This is particularly true in the case of small Chinese communities. In smaller cities, Chinese from Southeast Asia have often become integrated socially into the larger Chinese community and have received help from better-established Chinese. Most of the refugees speak the Cantonese dialect and can more easily socialize with the Cantonese-speaking Chinese from China.

The social organizations of Chinese from Southeast Asia serve as mutual aid societies. They hold meetings on special occasions, such as celebrating Chinese New Year. They also provide job opportunities, educational programs, religious services, recreational facilities, and information about government welfare programs. They also secure funds from the federal, state, and local governments for the benefit of their members, such as for computer training and health care.

The Overseas Chinese Affairs Commission of the government of Taiwan has made special efforts to take care of Chinese from Indochina. It has sponsored conferences of the Association of Overseas Chinese from Vietnam, Cambodia, and Laos. This government organization on Taiwan is responsible for overseeing the welfare of ethnic Chinese living outside China, including Chinese in the United States from Southeast Asia. It provides them with some financial assistance and supplies Chinese-language and cultural instruction materials for educational purposes.

The Next Generation. As the second generation of Chinese from Southeast Asia grows up in the United States, a serious generational gap between parents and children has developed. As the young people become Americanized through schools and peer groups, they are moving away from the traditional values of their parents. The latter try to educate them in such a way as to retain Chinese traditions. Children are sent to study Chinese in CHINESE-LANGUAGE SCHOOLS after regular school or on weekends. Yet when the children are older, many of them resist taking Chinese language

lessons or speaking Chinese.

In most families of Chinese refugees from Southeast Asia, financial necessity dictates that both parents work long hours. The absence of close parental control and supervision has weakened the traditional family ties and exacerbated cultural and intergenerational conflicts. In part as a result of these conditions, crime and gang activities are on the rise among juveniles. (See CHINESE GANGS and SOUTHEAST ASIAN GANGS.)

The Chinese from Southeast Asia are still struggling to improve their economic and social conditions in the United States. Although some of them are fairly successful, the majority of them have not yet realized the "American dream." At present, their main interest is their economic well-being and the education of their children. They are not seriously interested in assimilation or political participation. The Chinese from Southeast Asia are a subgroup among the Chinese in America. In many respects, the former are more isolated than Chinese from mainland China or Taiwan because they have no strong moral support from another country. With the gradual reduction of government support of Indochinese refugees, the Chinese from Southeast Asia must rely on self-help to establish themselves in America.—*George P. Jan*

SUGGESTED READINGS: • Chan, Sucheng. *Asian Americans: An Interpretive History.* Boston: Twayne, 1991. • Chen, Jack. *The Chinese in America.* San Francisco: Harper & Row, 1980. • Daniels, Roger. *Asian America: Chinese and Japanese in the United States Since 1850.* Seattle: University of Washington Press, 1988. • Overseas Chinese Affairs Commission, the Republic of China. *We Always Stay Together: A Report on Overseas Chinese Affairs.* Taipei, Taiwan: Overseas Chinese Affairs Commission, 1991. • Takaki, Ronald. *Strangers from a Different Shore: A History of Asian Americans.* Boston: Little, Brown, 1989.

Chinese gangs: Chinese gangs in the United States began to appear in the late 1950's and early 1960's, principally in areas with large Chinese populations such as San Francisco and New York City. In these early years, Chinese youth groups were divided largely according to immigrant or native-born status. Over the years, however, origin has been less important. While self-protection was and continues to be one of the most significant reasons for young Chinese males to band together, family conflict, cultural differences, alienation, social bonding, and economic support are also reasons for participating in gangs. Gang members have been involved in a variety of legal and illegal activities. While some Chinese gangs have a relatively defined leadership structure, others are very loosely organized.

Emergence. Prior to the latter part of the 1950's, reports of juvenile delinquency in CHINATOWNS were relatively absent. Popular conceptions indicated that this absence was traceable to the strong family and community values and practices of the Chinese. This notion of cultural distinctness, however, only partially explains the low incidence of delinquency in the Chinese community. Immigration restrictions dating back to the 1880's resulted in an extremely unbalanced gender ratio that persisted into the 1930's. There were few Chinese women and, hence, few Chinese youngsters in the United States. Among those families in the United States, their "alien" status also contributed to the families' close supervision of Chinese youngsters. Moreover, Chinese families and the local community devised a number of social control mechanisms to deal with the troublesome behavior of Chinese children.

By the end of the 1950's, family development had become more of an issue for the Chinese population in the United States. The number of American-born Chinese adolescents rose, and some of the males in San Francisco's Chinatown started to join such groups as the Raiders, the Bugs, and the 880s. Their activities involved largely rebellious activities, harassment of new immigrant youth, burglaries, and minor delinquency. American-born Chinese youth in New York formed the Continentals, also engaging in some delinquent activities and defending themselves against other ethnic youths.

The United States rescinded discriminatory immigration restrictions with the passage of the IMMIGRATION AND NATIONALITY ACT OF 1965. Chinese families immigrated collectively, moving primarily to established Chinatowns on the West and East coasts. Young immigrant males were immediately confronted with crowded living conditions, limited job and recreational opportunities, cultural and language differences, and scorn by American-born Chinese adolescents. Many young immigrants united to provide protection for one another from American-born Chinese youth and other ethnic groups.

The Wah Ching (Chinese Youth), the first immigrant youth group in San Francisco, initially tried to develop a youth movement to obtain improvements and alternatives for youth in Chinatown. Their efforts were unsuccessful, and by the late 1960's, the Wah Ching had fragmented. Many former members began working as lookouts and debt collectors for the *tongs'* gam-

bling operations. As members split away from the original group, a gang war emerged and continued through the 1970's. In 1977, gang warfare took the lives of five innocent people in the GOLDEN DRAGON RESTAURANT MASSACRE in San Francisco's Chinatown.

The White Eagles were among the first immigrant groups in New York. They were originally called the On Leong Youth Club, founded by one of the principals of the On Leong Tong. In these early years, members were involved primarily in the martial arts and protection of the community from outsiders. Toward the end of the 1960's, some of the White Eagles split off from the group and created the Black Eagles. The rivalry between these two groups led to violent conflict in New York's Chinatown.

Reasons for Joining. Participation in Chinese gangs can be attributed to several factors. Many Chinese males, especially newcomers, have been victimized by other Chinese youth and other ethnic adolescents. The gang readily offers protection.

There are, however, other reasons. Many newcomers and native-born Chinese youth are confronted with family conflict. The conflict is often two-pronged. First, family economic constraints and considerations frequently result in both parents working prolonged hours. There is little time to provide supervision. Second, there is increasing cultural and generational distance between the youth and the parents. The gang as a social group provides a sense of belonging and acts as a family bonding mechanism. Members typically indicate that they are brothers, and that the group is like a family. Alienation from American culture and social institutions also influences participation in these groups. Economic incentives sometimes contribute to gang involvement.

Activities. Gang activity includes interracial and intraethnic fighting, extortion of Chinatown businesses and restaurants, burglaries, robberies, drug sales, and auto boosting. Gang activities are not, however, exclusively of an illegal nature. Gang members report that hanging out, especially in coffee shops, restaurants, recreational centers, and parks, accounts for much of their time. Moreover, while many gang members are involved in illegal activities, not all are.

Organizational Structure. Since the emergence of Chinese gangs in San Francisco and New York during the 1960's, other groups have formed in these areas and in Los Angeles. There is great variability in the social organization of the gang. Some groups are loose collections of individuals with no clear organizational structure. Other gangs identify a leadership structure. Some are short-lived; others are institutionalized in the community.

In the 1980's and 1990's, authorities have concluded that some Chinese gangs are connected to criminally influenced *tongs* and Triads. These gangs are allegedly well organized and, with the *tongs* and Triads, are involved in organized crime activities such as heroin trafficking and gambling operations. While several gangs in San Francisco and New York previously were tied to *tongs*, in-depth studies are needed to explore this issue in the 1990's.—*Karen A. Joe*

SUGGESTED READINGS: • Chin, Ko-lin. *Chinese Subculture and Criminality.* New York: Greenwood Press, 1990. Dannen, Fredric. "Revenge of the Green Dragons." *The New Yorker* 68 (November 16, 1992): 76-99. • Joe, Karen. "Chinese Gangs and Tongs: An Exploratory Look at the Connection on the West Coast." Paper presented at the 44th Annual Meeting of the American Society of Criminology, New Orleans, Louisiana, November, 1992. • Kelly, Robert J., Ko-lin Chin, and Jeffrey A. Fagan. "The Dragon Breathes Fire: Chinese Organized Crime in New York City." *Crime, Law and Social Change* 19 (April, 1993): 245-269. • Kifner, John. "New Immigrant Wave from Asia Gives the Underworld New Faces." *The New York Times*, January 6, 1991, p. 1. • Liu, Melinda. "The New Slave Trade: Chinese Gangs Are Smuggling Illegal Immigrants by the Thousands into America Often Forcing Them into a Life of Servitude." *Newsweek* 121 (June 21, 1993). • Toy, Calvin. "Coming Out to Play: Reasons to Join and Participate in Asian Gangs." *The Gang Journal* 1, no. 1 (1992): 13-29.

Chinese garment workers: Following the tradition of other immigrant workers in the American garment industry, there is a large concentration of Chinese immigrants in the industry. Approximately 10 percent of the 220,000 members of the International Ladies Garment Workers Union (ILGWU) are Chinese. Most of the Chinese garment workers in the ILGWU are members of Local 23-25 in New York City. Other sizable numbers of unionized Chinese garment workers live in San Francisco, Boston, Vancouver, and Toronto.

In February of 1938, three hundred Chinese garment workers began a strike against the NATIONAL DOLLAR STORE owned by Joe SOONG, located at 720 Washington Street in San Francisco's Chinatown. Soong owned twenty National Dollar Stores throughout California and forty-two such stores across the country. At the time, the labor force in San Francisco

was entirely Chinese, mainly alien immigrants. The women worked as dressmakers, the men as cutters and clerks. They earned an average of thirty dollars a week working fourteen to sixteen hours a day.

The strikers demanded better working conditions and increased wages from Soong. The strike lasted for 105 days and received the support of Local 1100 of the Retail Clerks Union. During the course of the strike, Chinese garment workers formed the Chinese Ladies Garment Workers Union Local 341, the first of such Chinese locals within the ILGWU. Subsequently, Soong closed the factory and ended the strike. Local 341 lasted for more than a year, and the Chinese members joined other locals of the ILGWU.

In 1982, twenty thousand Chinese garment workers in New York's Local 23-25 rallied in support of the ILGWU in opposition to the city's Chinese garment contractors. The demonstrators assembled in Chinatown and marched through the Chinatown streets demanding that the contractors sign union agreements guaranteeing decent working conditions. This show of

Garment Factories in New York City, Selected Statistics, 1965-1980

Number of Chinese-owned Garment Factories in Chinatown

Year	Number
1965	34
1974	209
1980	430

Chinese Persons Employed, 1980

Women	16,000
Men	4,000

Characteristics of Chinese Immigrant Women Garment Workers, 1980

Median age	45
Mean earnings, 1979	$5,321

Characteristic	Percent
Arrived after 1965	86%
U.S. citizen	41%
Have some high school education	35%
Speak English well	14%
Operators or laborers	95%

Source: Min Xhou, *Chinatown: The Socioeconomic Potential of an Urban Enclave.* Philadelphia, Pa.: Temple University Press, 1992.

The garment industries of New York and San Francisco Chinatowns, with their low wages, continue to be one of the largest industries that immigrant Chinese enter. (Asian American Studies Library, University of California at Berkeley)

unity on the part of the Chinese workers surprised many who suspected that intraethnic cohesion would supersede labor solidarity. All of the contractors who disputed the strength of the union signed agreements within twenty-four hours of the demonstrations.

Chinese Hand Laundry Alliance (CHLA): Laundry-men's labor union founded in New York City in 1933 to combat the efforts of white laundrymen to drive out the city's Chinese operators. The alliance consisted of more than 250 Chinese hand laundries and was born in response to a crisis caused by a new city ordinance that would require all laundrymen to pay an annual licensing fee of $25 and a security bond of $1,000. In addi-

tion it required all public laundry operators to have American citizenship. If passed the bill would have driven all Chinese laundrymen out of business. The newly founded CHLA mobilized all of its resources to oppose the ordinance. As a result the eventually passed law was greatly modified—it exempted "Orientals" from the citizenship requirement and reduced the annual licensing fee to $10 and the security bond to $100. The CHLA emerged from this success as a credible grass-roots organization and soon became the largest organization of Chinese laundrymen on the East Coast, with a membership of more than three thousand.

In the 1930's and 1940's the CHLA was actively involved in the campaign to support China's war of

Headquarters of the Chinese Hand Laundry Alliance, New York City. (Asian American Studies Library, University of California at Berkeley)

resistance against Japan's invasion as well as in the fight for equal treatment of Chinese Americans in the United States. In 1940 it founded the *CHINA DAILY NEWS*, a Chinese-language newspaper, to allow Chinese Americans to discuss various issues and express their opinions. The paper encouraged its readers to participate in American politics and to foster a democratic transformation in Chinatown. To free the laundrymen from the exploitation of the Chinese power laundries that did "wet-wash" for them, the CHLA established its own Wah Kiu Wet-Wash Factory in 1947.

In the 1940's the CHLA consistently criticized the Nationalist regime in China, and in 1949 it publicly celebrated the founding of the People's Republic of CHINA by the CHINESE COMMUNIST PARTY. From 1950 to the 1970's it was under U.S. Federal Bureau of Investigation (FBI) surveillance, and its members were harassed and persecuted. As a result the CHLA's membership declined. In the mid-1950's some three hundred core members remained. In the 1960's and 1970's the CHLA supported the Civil Rights movement and called for the normalization of U.S.-China relations. By the early 1990's, as the Chinese hand laundries as a whole permanently declined, the CHLA had about a hundred members.

Chinese Historical Society of America (CHSA): Organization founded in 1963 to study, preserve, and promote the history of Chinese Americans as an integral part of American life and history. The CHSA was established by Chingwah Lee, H. K. Wong, Thomas Wu, and C. H. Kwock in San Francisco during the Civil Rights movement, when ethnic consciousness was heightened.

In 1966 the CHSA established its offices and the first museum of Chinese American history in San Francisco through a donation from the Shoong Foundation. The museum featured an exhibit of photographs and artifacts, giving an overview history of Chinese Americans from their first arrival in the United States in the mid-nineteenth century until the present.

Also in 1966 the CHSA began issuing a monthly bulletin to its dues-paying members with news of the society and articles of historical interest. In 1987 the society began publishing *Chinese America: History and Perspectives*, an annual journal of scholarly essays, oral histories, and translations from Chinese. Other significant CHSA publications include *A History of the Chinese in California: A Syllabus* (1969),

The Life, Influence, and the Role of the Chinese in the United States, 1776-1960 (1976), and *The Chinese American Experience* (1983).

To promote public interest in Chinese American history, the CHSA has sponsored monthly lectures, field trips to historical sites, traveling exhibits, and two national conferences. Its efforts to inform mainstream society of Chinese American contributions in the development of the United States have led to the preservation of historic landmarks such as the ANGEL ISLAND IMMIGRATION STATION, CHINA CAMP, the town of LOCKE, and Hanford's Chinese temple. The CHSA's accomplishments have also inspired the establishment of the Hawaii Chinese History Center (1971), the Chinese Historical Society of Southern California (1975), the New York Chinatown History Project (1980; now called the CHINATOWN HISTORY MUSEUM), and the CHINESE HISTORICAL SOCIETY OF THE PACIFIC NORTHWEST (1980).

Chinese Historical Society of the Pacific Northwest: Formed in 1980 in Seattle, Washington. The group joined the Alliance for Chinese American Historical Societies, establishing a working relationship with similar organizations in San Francisco, Los Angeles, Honolulu, and New York City. In 1984, with the Center for East Asian Studies and Western Washington University, the group published an annual publication, *The Annals of the Chinese Historical Society of the Pacific Northwest*.

Chinese Hospital: Chinese community-supported hospital founded in 1925. Chinese in San Francisco from the 1840's to 1900 were not provided with public health facilities by the city. During the early years, most Chinese district associations had facilities to provide only minimal medical care for the ill among their constituents. Attempts by the community to establish a Chinese hospital during the 1880's and 1890's were unsuccessful.

In 1900 the Chinese Consolidated Benevolent Association (CCBA) sponsored establishment of Tung Wah Dispensary, where patients had the choice of using Chinese or Western medicine. When the facility became inadequate for the needs of the growing community, a meeting was held among representatives from the CCBA, the seven district associations, the CHINESE AMERICAN CITIZENS ALLIANCE (CACA), the Chinese Chamber of Commerce, the Chinese Nationalist Party, the Chinese Constitutionalist Party, the CHEE KUNG TONG, the Chinese Christian Union, and the Young Men's Christian Association (YMCA). At this time Chinese patients were restricted to receiving care at the county hospital, where they could not communicate with hospital personnel, where they were segregated from Caucasian patients, and where their cultural and dietary needs were disregarded. Thus the gathering decided in 1922 to build a hospital instead. The Reverend Lok Sang Chan headed the building committee, which raised $200,000. To get around the ALIEN LAND LAWS, three Chinese American citizens (T. J. Gintjee, M. S. Jung, and Yituan Tan) acquired the land and the construction permit under their names and then transferred title to the hospital. After the objections of Caucasians living in the neighborhood had been overcome, a fifty-five-bed Chinese Hospital was constructed and opened on April 18, 1925.

At first the hospital offered both Chinese and Western medicine. Later Chinese medicine was dropped, and for half a century this facility was the only Western hospital operated by the Chinese community in America. In 1976 city, state, and federal authorities demanded that the hospital be replaced to meet current hospital standards. In 1977 a Comprehensive Health Care Center was completed on an adjoining parcel of land with $5.5 million raised from the Chinese community and federal grants. The upper floors were then converted into a fully equipped 59-bed inpatient hospital, which was opened on September 29, 1979.

Chinese immigration to the United States. *See* **Chinese Americans; Chinese diaspora; Chinese from Southeast Asia; Chinese students**

Chinese in agriculture: Chinese involvement in California's agriculture development was crucial in the late nineteenth and early twentieth centuries. The Chinese first arrived to work at the gold mines in 1849, and between 1860 and 1869 many Chinese were directly recruited from China to work on the Central Pacific link of the transcontinental railroad in the Sacramento-Sierra region. After the completion of the railroad in 1869, thousands of Chinese dispersed throughout California and became farm laborers, farm cooks, gardeners, tenant farmers, and labor contractors. Because Chinese farmers contributed their expertise to the infant fruit and vegetable agribusiness, they saved California from economic disasters that hit the rest of the nation in the 1870's and 1890's. By 1890 the Chinese constituted 75 percent of the total agricultural labor force in California. The Chinese were concentrated in regions such as the San Joaquin and Sacramento valleys, Santa Clara and Fresno counties, and Southern California. Their accomplishments in agriculture can be summarized below:

Reclamation of Swamp Land for Farming. In the Sacramento-San Joaquin delta region, the intensive construction of levees by the Chinese beginning in 1870 enabled the fertile land to be reclaimed for farming. From 1860 to 1870 the work was done manually by Chinese laborers. Levee construction was hard work. In an effort to maximize the effects of labor, innovations had to be developed. The Chinese were the first to devise the tule shoe, an oversized horseshoe, which distributed the horse's weight over a large area and prevented it from sinking into marshland. From 1860 to 1880 Chinese manual laborers reclaimed eighty-eight thousand acres of rich delta land. Once the land became fit for agriculture, the Chinese remained in the area to plant, harvest, and preserve the crops. Thousands of them worked as laborers and tenant farmers.

Main Labor Force in Agriculture. The Chinese engaged in farming at a time during which all the work had to be done by manual labor rather than by machinery. Many Chinese worked as farmhands. They were hired as fruit pickers harvesting cherries, pears, apples, and oranges. The Chinese laborers were poorly paid but were in demand everywhere in California's farms and orchards. Labor contractors would recruit and manage a group of Chinese workers for landlords or tenant farmers. The landlords and tenant farmers dealt only with the labor contractors, not with individual laborers. Laborers were not required year-round; their wages were often determined by the job instead of the hours worked. Contractors, landowners, and tenant farmers could relinquish their obligations to their workers when the job was over. This labor system greatly lowered production costs in the nineteenth century, which contributed to the economic success of California agriculture.

In the 1860's CHINATOWNS were already in existence in the two largest cities of Southern California—Los Angeles and San Diego. Gradually Chinese laborers spread out along the coast and moved inland to the interior valleys. In the 1880's, Chinese became the principal labor force throughout much of Southern California, and thousands of Chinese were transported south from San Francisco, Fresno, and other northern points to work in the grape and citrus harvests in Southern California. By the end of the 1880's Chinatowns had arisen and were flourishing in most of the citrus-growing towns of Southern California. There

The contributions of Chinese Americans have helped to ensure the success of the California agricultural industry. (Asian American Studies Library, University of California at Berkeley)

were Chinese settlements in Riverside, Redlands, San Bernardino, Pomona, Pasadena, San Gabriel, Anaheim, Santa Ana, Orange, Cucamonga, and many other citrus communities.

Established California System of Farm Tenancy. Because of the ineligibility of Chinese to own land in the United States and a lack of capital, many Chinese had to form partnerships to lease land for farming. These tenant farmers paid a fixed amount plus a percentage of the gross profits to the landlords. The landlords usually provided shelter, tools, equipment, and chemicals; they could also determine what kinds of crops would be grown and marketing and pricing policies. Chinese tenant farmers were in charge of all production and harvesting. This system provided a means for some Chinese laborers to improve their economic status. Under this system the landlords could avoid many unnecessary expenses, and tenant farmers could stay year-round to care for the farms.

Introduction of New Varieties of Crops. A variety of crops were planted in the reclaimed lands of the delta region. Chinese tenant farmers leased large tracts from landowners or corporations. In 1860-1879, 25 percent

of the farms operated by Chinese farmers produced fruit and 23 percent produced vegetables. The most important crops were fruit (especially Bartlett pears), asparagus, and potatoes.

California owes much of its agricultural diversity to the early Chinese farmers, who introduced such crops as strawberries, sugar beets, celery, and asparagus and who, by 1877, were producing nearly two-thirds of all vegetables in California. By the 1870's strawberries had become one of the most important crops grown by Chinese farmers in Santa Clara County. By the spring of 1886 three hundred Chinese were working in strawberry fields around Watsonville. Chinese farm laborers also made the sugar beet industry vital in both the Salinas and Pajaro valleys.

Ah BING was a Chinese horticulturist who succeeded in crossbreeding a new cherry variety. In 1899 the American Pomological Society placed this variety on its approved list. Subsequently the "Bing cherry" became well known. Another Chinese horticulturist, LUE GIM GONG, worked in an orchard in Delano, Florida. Besides developing many special varieties of fruits, he crossbred a new variety of orange named for himself that could stay on the tree for one year without spoiling. He was given the Wilder Silver Medal for this variety of orange by the American Pomological Society in 1911.

Wherever Chinese farmers and laborers went throughout California from 1860 to 1910, they left behind an agricultural legacy in the towns and communities where they worked. Their lives were characterized by long hours of backbreaking labor. With their diligence and practical skill, they set California on a course of agricultural prosperity for decades to come.—*Peter C. Y. Leung*

SUGGESTED READINGS: • Chan, Sucheng. *This Bittersweet Soil: The Chinese in California Agriculture, 1860-1910.* Berkeley: University of California Press, 1986. • Leung, Peter C. Y. *One Day, One Dollar: Locke, California, and the Chinese Farming Experience in the Sacramento Delta.* Edited by L. Eve Armentrout Ma. El Cerrito, Calif.: Chinese/Chinese American History Project, 1984. • Lydon, Sandy. *Chinese Gold: The Chinese in the Monterey Bay Region.* Capitola, Calif.: Capitola Book Company, 1985. • McCunn, Ruthanne Lum. *An Illustrated History of the Chinese in America.* San Francisco: Design Enterprises of San Francisco, 1979.

Chinese in Canada: The history of the Chinese in Canada is broadly comparable to the Chinese experience in the United States. Gold-mining activities and the construction of the transcontinental railroad provided the first impetus for thousands of Chinese to come to Canada in the second half of the nineteenth century. Initially in the West and spreading slowly to the East, their presence aroused considerable anti-Chinese sentiments that were manifested in popular prejudice and discriminatory laws. Overt racism against the Chinese receded only after World War II (1939-1945). In other ways as well, important changes in the postwar years had ushered in a new era.

Early Immigration and Settlement. Chinese began to come to Canada in the wake of the gold rush in the Fraser River Valley, British Columbia, in 1858. They first arrived from California and other Western states, where Chinese had taken part in similar gold-mining ventures a decade earlier. Those who sailed directly from South China quickly followed. By the early 1860's the Chinese population in British Columbia had reached an estimated six thousand. Their number apparently declined as the gold rush subsided. It was, however, replenished by another influx during the building of the Canadian Pacific Railway (CPR) from

Edmonton Chinese Community Parade, Edmonton, Alberta, Canada. (Photo Search Ltd.)

1881 to 1885. In this later period more than seventeen thousand Chinese entered Canada. Many of them were recruited by the construction company as railroad builders from the United States and Hong Kong; others were engaged in the provisioning and servicing of this Chinese labor force.

Before the completion of the CPR, virtually all the Chinese in Canada were in British Columbia. A small number journeyed eastward thereafter, forming small communities in the Prairies, Ontario, Quebec, and other cities in eastern Canada. Still, more than half of the Chinese population in the country resided in British Columbia up until World War II.

Chinese were widely dispersed in mining camps and construction sites in the earliest phase of their settlement. Later on they tended to concentrate in the urban areas and within each city in an ethnic neighborhood. The first Canadian Chinatown dated back to 1858 in Victoria. The one in Vancouver emerged later in the 1880's, but it soon grew into the largest Chinatown in Canada after the beginning of the twentieth century.

Until the 1950's the Chinese communities consisted predominantly of adult males. Most of these men, except the merchants, had to endure prolonged separation from their families in China. The lives of the Chinese revolved almost entirely around their Chinatown, which provided them with all the convenience of employment, affordable accommodation, shopping for daily necessities and social life. Chinatown was a cultural shelter where its inhabitants re-created fragments of native Chinese culture and society. The ethnic enclave was also a product of involuntary segregation. In the late nineteenth and early twentieth century, Chinese were treated in the larger society as an inferior people, not assimilable, and a threat to public morality. It was extremely difficult for them to find a job in a Canadian firm (other than those that catered to a Chinese clientele) or to move out of Chinatown into other residential neighborhoods.

Encounter with Canadian Racism. Racial prejudice against the Chinese was commonplace before World War II. There were occasions of mob violence such as the riots in Vancouver in 1887 and 1907, when Chinese suffered physical assault and property damage. Fed-

eral, provincial, and municipal legislation endorsed racial discrimination by imposing different kinds and degrees of disabilities on the Chinese. The best-known examples are probably the head tax and the exclusion act.

Beginning in 1885, Ottawa collected a head tax of $50 from Chinese individuals entering the country. The sum was raised to $100 in 1901 and to $500 two years later. The objective of deterring their immigration, however, was not met because Chinese continued to leave their poverty-stricken country for a better livelihood overseas. In the first quarter of the twentieth century, the number of Chinese in Canada increased from about eighteen thousand to more than forty thousand. Eventually, in 1923, the Canadian parliament passed an immigration act that gave full vent to the Canadian exclusionist impulse against the Chinese. Except for a few carefully specified categories, such as diplomatic personnel, foreign students, and merchants of sizable fortune, Chinese were totally barred from admission into Canada.

Chinese Canadian Population, 1880-1991

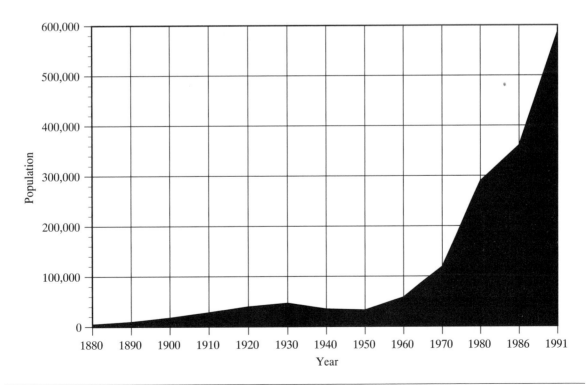

Sources: Roger Daniels, "Chinese and Japanese in North America." *Canadian Review of American Studies* 17:2 (Summer, 1986). Susan B. Gall and Timothy L. Gall, eds., *Statistical Record of Asian Americans.* Detroit: Gale Research, Inc., 1993.

In British Columbia, where anti-Chinese sentiments were the strongest, Chinese were denied franchise at all levels of government elections as early as the 1870's. This entailed certain economic disadvantages as well, as Chinese were then barred from practicing licensed professions, even if they had the qualifications and the language competence. Before the 1940's, some citizenship judges in the province were also known habitually to reject Chinese applications for naturalization.

A New Era After World War II. Beginning in the late 1940's, the Chinese in Canada benefited from the steady eradication of racist elements in government legislation. The exclusion act was repealed in 1947, and Chinese in British Columbia were fully enfranchised by 1949. The establishment of a communist regime in China was another landmark of 1949. For many immigrant Chinese the "loss" of the native country was agonizing, for they could no longer realize the ultimate dream of returning to the home village at the end of a fortune-making sojourn.

The traumatic events in China coincided with the increasing tolerance of Canadian society toward its Chinese minority. The younger Chinese, particularly the Canadian-born generations, took advantage of the breakdown of racial barriers to move into a large range of previously inaccessible occupations and professions. This vertical mobility was accompanied by a horizontal one as former Chinatown residents relocated and many postwar immigrants chose not to settle in the ethnic enclave. Gradually, Chinatown lost its once all-encompassing characteristics, though for many Chinese and non-Chinese it remained as the core of a minority society with its high density of ethnic institutions and businesses.

Finally, renewed Chinese immigration—under a few limited categories after 1947 and an indiscrimi-nate scheme since 1967—unleashed changes in many important ways. It contributed significantly to the expansion of the Chinese population that reached more than 400,000 by the mid-1980's. A formerly aging population was rejuvenated, the structural imbalance in sex ratio was redressed, and intact conjugal families became the norm. The unprecedented diversity in the territorial origins of post-1960's Chinese immigrants—from mainland China, Taiwan, Southeast Asia, Latin America, South Africa, and particularly Hong Kong—added an interesting dimension to the internal differentiation among the Chinese population in Canada toward the end of the twentieth century.—*Wing Chung Ng*

SUGGESTED READINGS: • Anderson, Kay J. *Vancouver's Chinatown: Racial Discourse in Canada, 1875-1980.* Montreal: McGill-Queen's University Press, 1991. • Lai, Chuenyan David. *Chinatowns: Towns Within Cities in Canada.* Vancouver: University of British Columbia Press, 1988. • Li, Peter S. *The Chinese in Canada.* Toronto: Oxford University Press, 1988. • Ward, W. Peter. *White Canada Forever: Popular Attitudes and Public Policy Toward Orientals in British Columbia.* 2d ed. Montreal: McGill-Queen's University Press, 1990. • Wickberg, Edgar, ed. *From China to Canada: A History of the Chinese Communities in Canada.* Toronto: McClelland and Stewart, 1982.

Chinese in fishing: Chinese started the commercial saltwater fishing industry on the United States' West Coast. Starting in the 1850's Chinese fishermen located many of the fishing grounds, introduced numerous fishing techniques, and developed much of the market. Anti-Chinese sentiment and changes in the availability of fish and related seafood had eliminated the Chinese presence in the industry by the end of World War II.

In 1850 or 1851 Chinese fishermen built fishing villages on San Francisco and Monterey bays and started the commercial saltwater fishing industry on the Pacific Coast. By 1870 they also had established medium to large fishing centers in San Diego, along the San Joaquin-Sacramento River, in Oregon, and in Canada's British Columbia. There were smaller ones near Los Angeles, at Bolinas Bay, on the Santa Barbara Islands, and in Washington State. With the exception of the San Joaquin-Sacramento River, Chinese were virtually the only ones to fish in these areas until the 1880's. At the height of their involvement, there were probably between two thousand and three thousand

Top 5 Provinces of Chinese Canadian Residence, 1991	
Total Chinese Canadian population: 586,645	
Province	Population
Ontario	273,870
British Columbia	181,185
Alberta	71,635
Quebec	36,815
New Brunswick	1,255
Source: Statistics Canada, "The Daily," February 23, 1993.	

Chinese fisherman outside his seaside tent. (Asian American Studies Library, University of California at Berkeley)

Chinese fishermen in California alone. Even after the 1880's Chinese dominated most of these fisheries until shortly after the beginning of the twentieth century, when the accumulation of anti-Chinese legislation and policies made it too difficult for them. (These laws included discriminatory taxes, limitations on Chinese using ocean-going junks, a prohibition against using a favored net, and a ban against exporting dried shrimp.)

The Chinese fishermen built their own villages and fishing craft. Fishing villages varied. Some were dedicated to the pursuit of ocean fish, some to bay fishing or, in the case of the San Joaquin-Sacramento fishery, river fishing. Bay fishermen were further divided into those who fished from boats (sampans or smaller junks) and those who fished from the shore (staking out an area and anchoring nets to the bottom). According to the village and location, the fishermen pursued a variety of catch: sturgeon, smelt, rock lobsters, rock cod, shrimp, squid, abalone, and barracuda. They generally did not fish for salmon: A nineteenth century chronicler stated that because of anti-Chinese feeling, the Chinese would probably have been killed if they had tried since salmon brought in so much money.

In the 1870's and 1880's these fishermen produced an annual product worth several hundreds of thousands of dollars. Only about 20 percent of what they caught was sold fresh (because of limited refrigeration). The rest was dried. They exported most of the dried product to China.

After the virtual exclusion of Chinese from commercial fishing in the early 1900's, the development of a new kind of net to replace one earlier made illegal allowed the large-scale revival of the San Francisco Bay shrimp fishery in the 1920's and 1930's. The Chinese fishing villages revived, and the industry helped many families in the Chinese American community survive the Depression. The shrimp fishery ceased operation in the 1940's in part because of a tremendous decline in the number of shrimp.—*L. Eve Armentrout Ma*

Chinese in mining: On January 24, 1848, shortly before California was ceded to the United States by Mexico, gold was discovered thirty-five miles northeast of

The discovery of gold in California triggered an influx of Chinese migration to America. The prospect of finding gold became the best reason to come to America—which the Chinese called "Gam San," or "Gold Mountain." Here a Chinese miner uses placer, or cradle, mining to search for the precious metal. (Asian American Studies Library, University of California at Berkeley)

Sacramento. The Chinese of southeastern China took note as the news resonated around the world. Beset with floods, famine, and epidemic diseases, engaged in civil war with the Hakka interlopers from the north, the men of Guangdong and Fujian provinces began looking to the sea as a way of escape. Passage was cheap to San Francisco, and indentured labor could be secured. Mining merely $300 worth of gold dust would guarantee the average Chinese miner a most congenial life for himself and his family back home. The Chinese dimension of the California gold rush ensued.

In the Mine Fields. In the spring of 1848, twenty-five Chinese joined the first contingent of miners in Sacramento. About 323 more Chinese arrived in the fields in 1849, with about 450 more in 1850. Over the next thirty years approximately 300,000 would migrate from China to San Francisco, most of them to work as miners, others to labor in support services. During this same period almost half of them would return to Guangdong and Fujian, some with wealth and a sense of accomplishment.

The Chinese miners confined themselves largely to placer or cradle mining. It included drawing from the stream with a pan, allowing water to wash away the debris, then removing the rest by hand—and, if fortunate, to find grains or nuggets of gold on the bottom. Such ease of mining continued to 1860, after which more sophisticated means were employed. Some would divert whole streams in order to get at the bedrock. Others would dig deep vertical shafts in the ground or horizontal shafts as long as two hundred feet in the hillside. Later, hydraulic mining and powerful jet streams were employed.

By intimidation the whites preempted the lucrative gold claims on the Sierra slopes. The Chinese reconciled themselves to lesser claims, including surface mines abandoned because of declining yields. As the California mines declined in overall yield, silver and other minerals became evident in Utah, Montana, Nevada, Colorado, and Wyoming. Both white and Chinese miners worked these sites. In 1860 there were 83,000 miners in the fields, 24,000 of them Chinese. In 1870 the total was 30,000 in the fields with 17,000 being Chinese.

Backbreaking toil, improper shelter and care, and other hardships led to a lonely life. Cold winters and hot summers often resulted in dysentery, fevers, and rheumatism. Some Chinese became cooks, storekeepers, and peddlers in order to support and assist other Chinese miners. Chinese food was brought in from San Francisco, and money packets and letters were carried back for mailing to Hong Kong and eventually to the villages in southeastern China. Auxiliary services included the shipment of a deceased persons' bones back to China for burial in his ancestral village.

Manifest Destiny and Violence. From 1848 to 1882 the Chinese miners and support corps faced a host of incompatibilities and difficulties, beginning in the mining camps and fields. It was a time of popular uprisings and discriminatory acts by public laws. Previously vilified by diplomats, traders, and even missionaries in China, the migrant sojourners were stereotyped as unregenerate beings without souls, as people of corrupt ethics, and as foreigners carrying loathsome diseases. They were seen as highly adverse to assimilation, white supremacy, and conformity. In that they sent their diggings and riches home to China, they were seen as unpatriotic, depriving the United States of indigenous wealth. Antagonism grew as the Chinese vied with the whites in the fields. Governed by a sense of "manifest destiny," that God by divine providence had ordained California (and its wealth) for the white race, the white populace excused its acts of intimidation and violence on the basis of putting others in their place. Having earlier dealt with the American Indians, Chileans, Peruvians, Mexicans, French, and blacks, they now turned full force upon the growing numbers of Chinese.

Such violence occurred first at a Chinese mining camp in Tuolumne County in the autumn of 1849, as sixty-six miners were driven out. Such an act sparked other similar efforts throughout California. In May, 1852, the community of Columbia near the Sacramento mother lode drew up a resolution expelling all "Asiatics" from the mines and established a vigilance committee to enforce its decision. As a public spectacle, at times with marching bands, the Chinese were driven out of North Forks, Horseshoe Bar, Coyote Flat, Rock Creek, and Buckeye. Later, when the Chinese worked the mine fields in British Columbia and as far as Alaska, they were again resisted, harassed, and violated by nativistic movements. As late as 1906 fifteen thousand Canadians destroyed the Chinese quarter in Vancouver with dynamite.

Along with force and violence, discrimination was made legal by public laws. A miner's tax for foreigners was levied at $4.00 a month. This law was but the forerunner of a multitude of unjust laws at the local, state, and federal levels. The CHINESE EXCLUSION ACT OF 1882 and subsequent discriminatory legislation severely limited Chinese immigration to the United

Miners at a mill in Searchlight, Nevada, circa 1907. (Asian American Studies Library, University of California at Berkeley)

States until the mid-twentieth century.

Chinese Contribution. As intended, the Chinese did manage to send huge sums of money back to their families, with $11 million sent as of 1876. Such monies fed their families and assisted them in the payment of their taxes and indemnities as required by the First Opium War (1839-1842) and the Treaty of Nanjing (1842). The new monies also served to modernize the provinces of Guangdong and Fujian. The returned sojourners and visitors became the sources for nationalistic, democratic, and revolutionary ideas for a new China.

For the United States itself, the Chinese contributed significantly to the country's transformation. The Foreign Miner's Tax payments averaged as much as $1 million a year, funds that largely supported local and state governments. Claim fees amounted to almost $1.4 million a year in 1862 alone, while water costs came to more than $2.2 million. In all the Chinese paid $14 million in fees of every kind in 1862. In terms of mining, prior to 1848 $8,000 worth of gold had been extracted in California. Between 1848 and 1857, $400,000 was extracted. From 1861 to 1866, even with the fields in decline, $150 million was produced.

In the following fifty years the United States became the richest and most powerful nation in the world. The mineral wealth was the basis for a new infrastructure, the opening up of harbor facilities, the laying of railways across the land, and irrigation and land reclamation projects, all of them leading to heightened commercial activity and national wealth. With the decline of the mining industry and the advent of a dream—the transcontinental railway—the Chinese that remained in the United States next turned their efforts to the consolidation of the nation, the joining of East and West with bands of steel.—*Hoover Wong*

SUGGESTED READINGS: • Axon, Gordon. *The California Gold Rush.* New York: Mason/Charter, 1976. • Chinn, Thomas. *A History of the Chinese in America.* San Francisco: Chinese Historical Society 1973. • Greever, William. *The Bonanza West: The Story of the Western Mining Rushes, 1848-1900.* Norman: University of Oklahoma Press, 1963. • Seward, George. *Chinese Immigrants: Its Social and Economic Aspects.* New York: Arno Press, 1970.